Humane Interfaces

Questions of method and practice in
Cognitive Technology

HUMAN FACTORS IN INFORMATION TECHNOLOGY *13*

Series Editors:

Hans-Jörg Bullinger

FhG-IAO
Stuttgart
Germany

Peter G. Polson

Institute of Cognitive Science
University of Colorado
Boulder, Colorado, USA

Assistant Series Editors:

Klaus-Peter Fähnrich

Jürgen Ziegler

FhG-IAO, Stuttgart, Germany

ELSEVIER

AMSTERDAM · LAUSANNE · NEW YORK · OXFORD · SHANNON · SINGAPORE · TOKYO

Humane Interfaces

Questions of method and practice in Cognitive Technology

Edited by

JONATHON P. MARSH

Centre for the Advancement of University Teaching
The University of Hong Kong
Hong Kong Special Administrative Region
China

BARBARA GORAYSKA

Department of Computer Science
City University of Hong Kong
Hong Kong Special Administrative Region
China

JACOB L. MEY

Institute of Language and Communication
Odense University
Odense
Denmark

1999

ELSEVIER

AMSTERDAM · LAUSANNE · NEW YORK · OXFORD · SHANNON · SINGAPORE · TOKYO

ELSEVIER SCIENCE B.V.
Sara Burgerhartstraat 25
P.O. Box 211, 1000 AE Amsterdam, The Netherlands

First edition 1999

Library of Congress Cataloging in Publication Data

```
Humane interfaces : questions of method and practice in cognitive
   technology / edited by Jonathon P. Marsh, Barbara Gorayska, Jacob L.
   Mey.
       p.   cm. -- (Human factors in information technology ; 13)
   Includes bibliographical references and index.
   ISBN 0-444-82874-5 (alk. paper)
   1. Human-computer interaction. 2. User interfaces (Computer
systems)   I. Marsh, Jonathon P.  II. Gorayska, Barbara.  III. Mey,
Jacob L.   IV. Series.
QA76.9.H85H86533 1999
004'.01'9--dc21                                     99-19385
                                                        CIP
```

ISBN: 0-444-82874-5

FOREWORD

'BEEING ORDINARY'

And some people, as a matter of kicks, could say: 'Let's do "being ordinary" tonight.
We'll watch TV, eat popcorn' etc. (Sacks 1984)

Tonight, let's turn on the computer
Watch the screen, bite our nails
(No popcorn here)
The machine-god waits for its dues
The human sits powerlessly
Waits for the idol to speak —
Or crash divinely out of sight

'Doing Being' (a nerd?)

The bees are dancing
Their hi-tech flight
Coding information
Mapping out territory
Guiding their tribe to the honey place

'Doing Bee-ing' (a bee)

I have a dream
Gods being human
Humans being like gods
Intercoursing freely with computers
('No hands, Ma!')
The screen comes thick with pleasure
Forms itself unto our touch
The programs enter our bloodstream
But we stay on top:
"Neuro from the paths — the silver paths"
Of screen to mind, of mind to screen
And mind to mind

"Romancer-Neuromancer?"
Who knows?

'Doing Beeing CT'

Jacob Mey, Austin, Tex., June, 1998

Ever since the first successful International Cognitive Technology (CT) Conference in Hong Kong in August 1995, a growing concern about the dehumanising potential of machines, and the machining potential of the human mind, has pervaded the organisers' thinking. When setting up the agenda for the Second International CT Conference in Aizu, Japan, in August of 1997, they were aware that a number of new approaches had seen the light, but that the need to integrate them within a human framework had become more urgent than ever, due to the accelerating pace of technological and commercialised developments in the computer related fields of industry and research.

What the present book tries to do is to reemphasise the importance of the 'human factor' — not as something that we should 'also' take into account, when doing technology, but as the primary driving force and supreme aim of our technological endeavours. Machining the human should not happen, but humanising the machine should. *La Humacha* should replace the *Hemachine* in our thinking about these matters.

Let me use a time-honoured analogy. When Marx commented (in his *Capital*) on the bee as the master engineer of hive construction, he also pointed out that bees, for all their technological skills, are not aware of what they are doing, nor why they are doing it. This observation is usually interpreted as a negative feature affecting the bees' intelligence, their evolutionary stage and hopes for progress, and so on. But one could turn the tables and point to the immense advantage that bee-like ventures offer. No time is lost in unnecessary discussions, no constructional blind alleys have to be followed up and labour disputes are unthinkable. Bees are good at what they do, precisely because they are 'doing bee-ing' (to paraphrase an expression due to the late ethnomethodologist Harvey Sacks in a seminal article; 1984). This quality of 'automatic affordances' the bees exhibit (to paraphrase another Gibson, 1984:289) is one that we want to exploit in CT. We wish to ensure that human technological effort will work towards ensuring humane technology outputs, just as 'apified' technology operates to perform its hive construction in bee-like ways.

To do this is not to abrogate the human privilege of control and checking. On the contrary: humans will be relieved of the everyday business of 'running the show', since their technological helpers will do it for them, and in their spirit. And in fact, many of today's human ventures would be impossible, even outright dangerous, without the help of technology. An aircraft approaching a carrier deck can only make a safe landing if its movements are guided by a computer, making and executing the necessary decisions: implementing them manually, in human reaction time, would simply be too slow. The key question, of course, is where we want to stop — the classic example is the decision to 'press or not to press that button', familiar from the Cold War period. And this is precisely the question that the papers in the present volume address, each in its own way. A question that could be formulated, as we have done it in our introduction (p. 6), as follows:

"How can we define, predict, and recognise the threshold at which technological enhancement of human ability or performance becomes technological constraint?"

Not to forget the other, all-important question:

How can we guarantee that this constraint does not 'proliferate', constraining our human capabilities beyond another threshold, that of 'Humane Interfaces'?

REFERENCES

Gibson J. J., 1977. *The ecological approach to visual perception.* Boston: Houghton Mifflin.

Gibson, W., 1984. *Neuromancer.* London: HarperCollins.

Sacks, H., 1984. 'On doing "being ordinary"'. In: Max Atkinson and John Heritage, eds. *Structures of social action.* Cambridge: Cambridge University Press. p. 415.

Jacob L. Mey
Institute of Language and Communication
Odense University

ACKNOWLEDGEMENTS

In bringing the work on this book to an end, it behoves the Editors to reflect on their efforts and test them against their own proclaimed standards and goals of humanising the technology. That means, as well as implies, that we should include, in our reflections, the humans who have been material in our battle with technology.

Doutzen Abma of Elsevier Science deserves an out and out honourable mention for her unfailing support all the way through, even at times when the whole enterprise was about to founder in the mishaps of human factors and technological snags, single or combined. Not only did she graciously accept a first delay, but she even did not utter a single (audible) groan when told that we wanted an additional six months to deliver our product. Showing this flexibility, while at the same time cheerfully and constantly keeping us to the grindstone, Doutzen has been a major source of support and inspiration in our endeavours, thus continuing the tradition established by her predecessor, Kees Michielsen, about whom we said similar things on the occasion of publishing our first CT volume at Elsevier. Thanks also to Titia Kraaij for responding constructively and supportively when Doutzen was away from the fire.

Christopher Legault has, with his usual adaptability, shown us how to cheerfully cope with something the editors of the previous volume (i.e. Barbara and Jacob) swore never to touch again: the technology of desktop publishing and camera-ready copy-making. That the present volume sees the light of day, even though belatedly, has been made possible due to Christopher's willingness to labour under duress; the delays are ours, not his.

As every editor knows, the chief players in a game such as this are the individual authors of the articles composing the volume. Without their efforts and dedication, all our work would have come to naught. We want to acknowledge, and thank them for, their input, as well as for their gracious acceptance of our repeated suggestions for change, and for sticking with the project until the very end, even in the face of many personal and professional problems and difficulties.

Finally, each of us wants to thank the other two, colleagues-cum-collaborators in the editing process: for their patience, understanding, and perseverance in the face of unthought odds. We hope we did not overstay the boundaries of what is humanly acceptable in making the technologically possible happen.

Hong Kong & Odense, 28 June 1998
Jonathon P. Marsh
Barbara Gorayska
Jacob L. Mey

CONTENTS

INTRODUCTION

THEORETICAL PERSPECTIVES

MIND CHANGE OR CHANGED MINDS?

AUGMENTATION, MEDIATION, INTEGRATION?

APPLIED METHODS

HOW DO WE CONVERT PRINCIPLES INTO VALID AND VALIDATED APPLIED METHODS?

Humane Interfaces: Questions of method and
practice in Cognitive Technology
J.P. Marsh, B. Gorayska and J.L. Mey (Editors)

Introduction

METHODS AND PRACTICE IN COGNITIVE TECHNOLOGY
A question of questions

Barbara Gorayska
City University of Hong Kong

Jonathon Marsh
The University of Hong Kong

Jacob L. Mey
Odense University

The search for some characteristic features of a *humane* interface in human/technology interaction was the central theme of the first collection of contributions to the newly emerging scholarly discipline of Cognitive Technology (henceforth referred to as CT) (Gorayska and Mey, 1996a). That first volume was primarily intended as an initial investigation into possible ways of exploring various aspects of human cognition via the technologies the mind produces. This exploration took as its point of departure the question: 'What happens when humans produce new technologies?' From that seemingly simple question two interdependent (and somewhat more complicated) perspectives were derived from which the study of such production could be approached:

HOW and WHY constructs that have their origins in human mental life are embodied in physical environments when people fabricate their habitat, even to the point of those constructs becoming that very habitat;

and

HOW and WHY these fabricated habitats affect, and feed back into, human mental activity and development.

That volume called for reflection on what constitutes a tool, drawing strong parallels between CT and environmentalism. Both were seen as trends originating in the need to understand how we manipulate our natural habitat by means of the tools we have created. This habitat consists, on the one hand, of the cognitive environment, which generates thought and determines action, and on the other, of the physical environment in which thought and action are realised. Both trends endeavour to protect the human habitat from the unwanted or uncontrolled impact of technology, and are ultimately concerned with the ethics and aesthetics of tool design and tool use.

CLARIFICATION OF THE PROPER INTERESTS OF CT

Collaborative intellectual effort to date has been directed primarily at properly defining CT as a field of inquiry. By way of summary, the following points may help to clarify the interests of CT outlined thus far:

- CT represents a departure from the conventional approaches practised within HCI.
- CT proposes to study the processes related to cognitive wholeness. It aims to humanely develop the cognitive eco-systems generated from the interaction between mind and machine. It is mainly concerned with the adaptation of mind which occurs as a consequence of that interaction. Hence, CT abandons the concept of a 'man-machine interface' and, instead, promotes the design of humane tools especially with respect to our interaction with computer technology.
- While the HCI approach is characterised by a trend towards anthropomorphizing machine outputs to promote "naturalness" in human-machine exchanges, CT is conversely interested in the fundamental issue of what happens to humans when they augment themselves, either physically or cognitively, by technologically amplifying their natural capabilities.
- It is assumed that an understanding of the processes involved should serve to inform design decisions and reduce from the outset any undesirable side-effects of technological development on human adaptation.
- CT is a process: an approach to design, not a product of such a design. Tools can be designed according to CT principles; they are not in themselves instances of CT.

It is the point of CT to evaluate the impact of proposed technological solutions to problems on the mindset of the *humans* who apply them, and accordingly take a *humane* approach to devising the necessary tools which incorporate these solutions. Consequently, the focus is on *human* inputs to technologically mediated interaction and not on the technological outputs related to that interaction.

TOWARDS A METHOD OF INQUIRY

One of the most significant hypotheses in CT, is the conjecture that human cognition can be "technologised", that is to say, it can dialectically adapt itself, both unconsciously and by conscious induction, to the relatively simplistic but strongly deterministic dynamism of the technological environments (Gorayska and Marsh, 1996, Gorayska and Mey, 1996b). This hypothesis has given rise to two distinct directions for further CT investigations: *cognitive prosthetics,* on the one hand, and *cognitive regression,* on the other[1].

Cognitive prosthetics encompasses studies of the positive impacts of tool use on human cognition. It focusses on how and why technology is able to aid people in performing tasks which normally would have fallen outside their cognitive resources. Here belong such areas of investigation as: overcoming cognitive impairment, effective interactive learning, technology as a cognitive microscope, and technology as an instrument for the scientific study of the mind.

Cognitive regression, by contrast, is concerned with the negative impacts of technological environments on humans, especially with respect to their cognitive capabilities. It is primarily concerned with what happens to people as a consequence of extensive exposure to a wide variety of mental prosthetic devices. In particular, we believe that greater effort needs to go into properly understanding the cognitive effects of large scale, widely significant socio-technological phenomena. These include issues such as 1) the global displacement and local isolation of individuals interacting and communicating electronically, 2) information overload, and 3) the inability amongst technology users to relate effectively to the complex but weakly deterministic dynamisms of natural environments as a result of prolonged interaction with and through mechanised communication tools.

While current practices within HCI have benefited from the steadily evolving methodologies for designing user friendly applications, CT, with its new emphasis on technological cognition as a major source of information for bringing humane practices to bear on such designs, has so far concentrated largely on informal observation. This has led to an awareness of, and a need for, the analytical observation of larger bodies of human-machine related phenomena from a CT perspective. As a result of this preliminary work, three further needs have been identified:

1. the need for a unified understanding of what CT is,
2. the need for systematic collection of basic data about the cognitive prosthetics and the cognitive regression phenomena, which can provide the empirical basis for further theoretical development, and
3. the need for a method of enquiry which properly reflects the interests of CT.

---

1 See further the contributions to Gorayska and Mey, 1996c.

While clear-cut solutions are still some way off, many of the issues involved in responding to these needs are spoken to in this collection of papers.

In accordance with its title, this book falls broadly into two main parts. The first part is concerned primarily with theoretical and methodological issues (chapters 1 through 12), while the second part (chapters 13 through 20) deals with more practical and applied aspects of CT. However, regardless of the specific interest of any one contribution, as a whole this volume is concerned with asking questions about the way we think about human-machine interactions. More importantly, it is concerned with asking ourselves questions about whether or not the questions we are and have been asking so far are the right sorts of questions to ask.

In his recent contribution to the Cognitive Technology agenda, Frank Biocca (1998:12-13, reprinted in this volume), echoing Marshall McLuhan, observed that "...the most important part of science is not theory, methods, or instrumentation, but asking the right question...accompanied by "probes", a kind of intellectual shot into the darkness." Ask the right question for your time, place, tools, and abilities and "... the answers it engenders can be more than a flare. It can be explosive, lighting the horizon as it casts long shadow on the intellectual terrain." In keeping with this spirit, we can say that:

> *Each newly emergent scholarly discipline is best defined by the questions it formulates.*

In the domain of human technology interactions, many areas of study have been differentiated according to the central questions they address. For example, the issue of how users communicate with application systems has driven research in the broad field of user-centred Human Computer Interaction (HCI). Great efforts have been, and are still, expended in order to achieve a better users' understanding of what the system can do for them and what they, as users, can do with the system. Consequently, HCI design methodologies strive for correct marketing metaphors, graphical interfaces (GUI) for direct screen object manipulation, and recently, tangible interfaces (TUI) (Ishii and Ullmer, 1997) which involve direct interaction with real physical world objects, coupled with digital information. The main objective has been to arrive at an appropriate cognitive fit (Vessey and Galletta, 1991; Day, 1995) at the level of perceived representation.

A separate branch of HCI, known as *Cognitive Ergonomics* (Card, Moran, and Newell, 1983), at its outset asked a related but different question: Are the physiological needs of human perceptual processing, especially those related to the spatio-temporal correlates of habitual eye and body movements, met by the working environment? In search for an answer, the main focus of this research has been on hardware interface components, as seen in relation to the user, as well as on the interaction objects figuring on screen displays. Given this focus, it is not a coincidence that, with respect to those aspects of design which deal with human decision making processes based on goals, operations, methods and strategies, Cognitive Ergonomics methods are in practice employed to test the temporal aspects of user-system performance and are limited to expert users.

Cognitive Engineering (Norman, 1986; Rassmussen, 1988; Woods and Ross, 1988), by contrast, came about when the need arose to integrate system functions within the user's tasks, so as to achieve optimal user control and system flexibility. The main issue here has been whether a global problem that the user and the system will be jointly solving has been properly analysed and its parts appropriately distributed between both user and system. Central here is the notion of an 'internal model': both a conceptual model that the user must have of the system and a user model that the system must have of the user (see also Norman and Draper, 1986). The need to build correct models of this interaction called for research into *Human Factors*, where the key question has been: Are the limits of human performance fully accommodated and the advantages of the human operator fully exploited? The usual way of deciding this question has been to compare alternative designs for a piece of equipment.

In a related area, *Engineering Psychology* (Wickens, 1992) has taken on the role of determining human performance limits. Its aims and objectives are to provide technology designers with psychological profiles of users, so that designers may better understand and eliminate design flaws. Hence, the main question addressed here is: Are the capabilities and limitations of the human well understood and accounted for in ways that afford a straightforward choice for optimal design?

What the above cognitive approaches within HCI have in common is that all of them aim at improving overall system performance by optimising the effectiveness and efficiency of the human agents involved. The view taken is that this efficiency is heightened by minimising stress and fatigue and maximising comfort, safety and job satisfaction. They further believe that the way to achieve both these objectives is to investigate dichotomous interactions between human mental processes and technological outputs. In so doing, the current cognitive approaches use methods and practices which make technology adapt to the demands of people. However, in spite of their rhetoric to the contrary, such methods remain predominantly system-centred, their application serving primarily the interests of computing technology and business, or the academic pursuits of cognitive science. In Mey's words (1994), the methods described centre on adaptivity, not adaptability.

This covert system orientation leads to a vital omission of many pressing and important questions that to us are paramount in the tug-of-war which has been going on between humanity and technology ever since humans started to use tools. Common belief has it that current advances in telecommunication and computerisation have transformed the world into the much acclaimed and long awaited 'global village', where information flows freely between physically and geographically displaced but nonetheless interconnected members of the population. However, in this there has also been a price to pay, especially with respect to our identity, our community and culture, the way we construct our knowledge, the speeds with which we process incoming data, the way we interact with others, and the way we integrate with our environment. The crucial issue here is reconciliation. For example, while remaining "connected" across the globe, we have to come to terms with the possibility that the lack of immediate physical presence among communicating agents has disrupted the traditional pragmatic norms governing feedback-and-consequence driven behaviour. In extreme cases this may lead to serious media addiction and personality disorder (Turkle, 1995 & 1996; Janney, this volume), dysfunctional education (Stoll, 1995), or local isolation and alienation (Slouka, 1995). We have to reconcile our increased reaction time due to extensive use of certain entertainment software with the decreased reaction time in textual interchanges by e-mail (Harnad, 1996). We have to accommodate an increase in visual stimulation with a decrease of tactile contact with other human beings. We have to learn to function in and integrate with, interchangeably, two different kinds of environments: the relatively simplistic, but strongly deterministic dynamism of computerised media, and the highly complex, but weakly deterministic dynamism of the natural world. The trade-off between a strengthening of the "global collective" through on-line communication and the weakening of local community interaction contribute to what we refer to as the (perhaps epiphenomenal) process of epistemic disruption associated with "virtual" existence (Gorayska and Marsh, 1996). The real question, however, is not how people reconcile these opposing traits (of the Net), as this would be like asking how we can reconcile the immense pleasure of heroin use with the health threats inherent in its use. Rather, the question ought to be how we can establish first and foremost whether or not the opposing traits can be reconciled.

In our view, such a reconciliation is hardly possible without changing the nature of the interaction of people with environments; either through a fundamental adaptation of the user or by changing the characteristics of the engaging environment. Hence, it is no longer enough to know how technology can adapt to the demands of people. We also need to know how *people* adapt to the demands of technology. The key CT question is thus:

How can we define, predict and recognise the threshold at which technological enhancement of human ability or performance becomes technological constraint?

In asking this key question, CT seeks to support and inform other cognitive approaches to tool design, not to replace them.

The observed body of phenomena which fall within the CT scope of interest have not yet been subjected to a coherent, analytical investigation. The reason for this is twofold. First, the methods and practice in the traditional cognitive approaches to tool design have not been applied, or are inappropriate, to conduct the analytical investigations in question. Second, CT as a scholarly discipline is still at the stage of the emerging awareness that these phenomena, observed informally, are indeed susceptible to such investigations. In particular, the following questions have largely been left unanswered:

1. *What are the possible approaches to conducting research in CT?*
2. *What kind of rationalisation and evidence is required?*
3. *How can accurate data be collected?*
4. *How can data from various sources be combined coherently?*

It is the attempt to respond to these questions which forms the *raison d'être* of this book.

REFERENCES

Biocca, F., 1998. Cyborg's Dilemma: Progressive Embodiment in Virtual Environments. *Proceedings of the Second International Cognitive Technology Conference,* August 25-28, 1997, Aizu, Japan, Los Alamitos: IEEE Computer Society Press, pp. 12- 13. (Reprinted in this volume).

Card, S. K., T. P. Moran, and A. Newell, 1983. *The Psychology of Human-Computer Interaction.* Hillsdale, N. J.: Lawrence Erlbaum Associates.

Day, D. L., 1995. Adaptive Discovery and Least Commitment: An extension of cognitive fit. In. H. Hasan and C. Nicastri, eds, *HCI: A Light into the Future,.Proceedings of the 4th conference of the Computer Human Interaction Special Interest Group of the Ergonomics Society of Australia. (OZCHI'95),* November 270-30, Wollongong, NSW, Australia., pp. 256-261

Gorayska, B. and J. Marsh, 1996. Epistemic Technology and Relevance Analysis: Rethinking Cognitive Technology. In: B. Gorayska and J. L. Mey, eds, *Cognitive Technology: In Search of a Humane Interface,* Advances in Psychology, 113. Amsterdam: North Holland. pp. 27-39.

Gorayska, B., J. Marsh, and J. L. Mey, 1998. Putting the Horse Before the Cart. *Proceedings of the Second International Cognitive Technology Conference,* August 25-28, 1997, Aizu, Japan, Los Alamitos: IEEE Computer Society Press, pp. 1-9.

Gorayska, B. and J. L. Mey, eds, 1996a. *Cognitive Technology: In Search of a Humane Interface.* Advances in Psychology, 113. Amsterdam: North Holland.

Gorayska, B. and J. L. Mey, 1996b. Of Minds and Men. In: B. Gorayska and J. L.

Mey, eds, *Cognitive Technology: In Search of a Humane Interface*, Advances in Psychology, 113 Amsterdam: North Holland, pp. 1-24.

Gorayska, B. and J. L. Mey, eds, 1996c. *AI & Society, 10*. Special Issue on Cognitive Technology.

Harnad, S., 1996. Interactive Cognition: Exploring the Potential of Electronic Quote/Commenting. In: B. Gorayska and J. L. Mey, eds, *Cognitive Technology: In Search of a Humane Interface*, Advances in Psychology, 113. Amsterdam: North Holland, pp. 397-414.

Ishii, H., and B. Ullmer, 1997. Tangible Bits: Towards Seamless Interface between People, Bits, and Atoms. *Proceedings of CHI'97 Conference*, Reading, MA: Addison Wesley, pp. 234-241.

Mey, J. L., 1994. Adaptability. In: R. Asher, ed., *The encyclopedia of language and linguistics, Vol. 1*. Oxford: Pergamon Press, pp. 25-27

Norman, D. A., 1986. Cognitive Engineering. In D. A. Norman and S. A. Draper, eds, *User Centred System Design*, Hillsdale, N.J.: Erlbaum, pp. 31-63.

Norman, D. A., and S. A. Draper, 1986. *User Centred System Design*. Hillsdale, N.J.: Erlbaum.

Rasmussen, J., 1988. *Information Processing and Human-Machine Interaction: An Approach to Cognitive Engineering*. Amsterdam & New York: North Holland/Elsevier.

Slouka, M., 1995. *War of the Worlds: the assault on reality*. London: Abacus.

Stoll, C., 1996. *Silicon Snake Oil: second thoughts on the information highway*. New York: Anchor Books.

Turkle, S., 1985. *The Second Self: computers and the human spirit*. New York: Simon and Schuster.

Turkle, S., 1996. *Life on the Screen: identity in the age of the Internet*. London: Weindenfeld & Nicolson.

Vessey, I., and D. Galletta, 1991. Cognitive Fit: an empirical study of information acquisition. *Information Systems Research,* 2(1), pp. 63-84.

Wickens, C., 1992. *Engineering Psychology and Human Performance*. 2nd edition. New York: Harper Collins.

Woods, D. D., and E. M. Ross, 1988. Cognitive Engineering: Human Problem Solving with Tools. *Human Factors,* 30(4), pp. 415-430.

THEORETICAL PERSPECTIVES

Humane Interfaces: Questions of method and practice in Cognitive Technology
J.P. Marsh, B. Gorayska and J.L. Mey (Editors)
© 1999 Elsevier Science B.V. All rights reserved.

MIND CHANGE OR CHANGED MINDS?

Barbara Gorayska
Jonathon P. Marsh
Jacob L. Mey

COMMENTARY

Cognitive Technology, as a separate discipline, began with the Fabricated World Hypothesis of Gorayska and Lindsay (1989). They postulated that the ways in which people structure their habitats have a major influence on the degree to which various cognitive mechanisms are able to function inside of those habitats. If structured habitats are externalisations of human memory (which facilitate simple but sufficient algorithms for dealing with the complexities of the material world and, at the same time, act as reminders for intention directed behaviour), then the organisation of the human mind and the external world must be interrelated in intricate and inseparable ways. It also follows that the structure given to the human fabricated environment must have a profound reflective influence on the organisation of the mind. This thesis has since become one of the major areas for explorations in Cognitive Technology (Gorayska and Mey, 1996)

When it comes to a discussion of the effect cognitive tool use has on the mind of the user, it may be fruitful to distinguish between long term effects (with an interesting extension to effects that last for the life of the user) and effects which are of a shorter duration and more easily measured in experimental terms. In one attempt to study and expose possible long term effects, Olson (1994) has tried to demonstrate how writing systems function as tools which externalise and record human thought. Based on the diachronic analyses he brought to bear on this demonstration, he conjectured that such externalisations, over centuries, may have contributed to the evolution of human metacognition due to a process of conscious reflection on the outcomes of the unconscious mental processes involved (cf: Ong, 1992; Gorayska, 1993). The related issue here is whether or not new technologies do more to our minds than simply force us to superficially adapt to relatively simple constraints within the fabricated environment.

How we may go about studying and effectively coming to understand the depth of such accommodation, and the degree of reversibility in the changes it invokes, requires some hard thinking. Several perspective related questions emerge:

1.   *What do we mean when we talk about minds, and how do different understandings of the mind generate different methods for studying mental processes?*

2. *What is it we are referring to when we talk about mind change and what kinds of phenomena provide reliable evidence for such change?*
3. *What constitutes the fabricated environment as opposed to the natural one?*
4. *What possible perspectives can be usefully brought to bear on the concerns of CT?*
5. *Can a variety of perspectives be integrated to form an effective unified theoretical framework?*
6. *How can existing methodology be repurposed to address the concerns of CT?*

The thoughts and work of the authors in this section explore some aspects of these questions.

CHAPTER SUMMARIES

Chapter 1
Barbara Gorayska and Jonathon Marsh
Investigations in Cognitive Technology: Questioning perspective

Barbara Gorayska and Jonathon Marsh consider the requirements that a holistic outlook on the tool mediated integration of humans with the environment imposes on possible methods of CT inquiry. They rethink the way in which designers tend to ask questions related to this integration. They explore the implications of answering these questions with respect to developing both a) our ongoing understanding of how tool use affects the human mind, and subsequently b) how this understanding can be brought to bear on the design processes we employ when developing technology. The nature of current investigations into human cognition within diverse disciplines of cognitive science is frequently subjectively biased due to the relationship of relevance which holds between the investigator's research goals, the subject of his or her investigation, and the research tools at his or her disposal. The authors argue that reversing perspectives in design by continually critiquing the way we ask relevant questions may be one way of ensuring new insights and preventing designers from looking at things with a locked mind. They see the reversing process itself as the core principle of the self-reflective nature of a CT methodology. The methodological self-reflection, they hold, is governed by, and governs in its turn, the cognitive processes of relevance ascription and activation of action affordances. Since the very act of analysing the affordance activation problem is an act of CT, the authors conclude that CT in itself is a tool of design construction.

Chapter 2
Roger Lindsay
Can We Change Our Minds? The Impact of Computer Technology on
Human Cognition

If one is genuinely interested in usefully defining a novel field of enquiry it is never a good idea to present only those ideas which are supportive of one's own position. In the interest of trying to create as broad an understanding as possible and to avoid possible pitfalls one must take on board the notion that perhaps one's ideas are fundamentally ungrounded or at least must be reshaped to better accommodate the issues. To that end, Roger Lindsay critically examines the belief that externalised technologies, i.e. tools, can change the human mind in much more profound ways than what is commonly understood as adaptation through learning. Limiting his analysis to computer based technologies, he considers the senses in which minds can be changed and argues that there is no direct evidence of the occurrence of any nontrivial, qualitative, substantial, generalised, and/or irreversible effects of computers on human cognition. He points out the methodological difficulty in assigning a clear interpretation to the idea of evolutionary mind-change which is both of empirical interest and free from contradiction. He argues that we must first be clear on what we understand 'mind' to be, as different theories of mind will result in different things being brought to bear as evidence of change. Second, we must clarify which level of the mind we are talking about and within which we expect to see permanent change occurring. Is it the 'wetware' commonly called the brain, with its biochemistry and cognitive architecture? Or, is it the fuzzier level of memory and the ways in which we generate internal representations of the external world? While in some of these aspects mind changes can be shown to occur, such changes can hardly be considered abnormal and, therefore, should not give rise to undue concern. A further difficulty emerges from the fact that new technologies are designed by people. Hence at least some members within a given community must have shifted their mind states prior to and irrespective of any novel tool use. A diachronic analysis of mind changes, such as witnessed by developments in literacy, reveals that there is no unequivocal evidence of drastic, sudden switches in cognitive states or of irreversible, long term effects leading to incompatibilities in understanding across millennia. It is suggested that at least some of the features of mind change can be accommodated if the change is conceptualised as a shift in the representational format commonly used by a group of cognitive agents. An attempt is made to establish a methodology capable of evaluating this claim.

Chapter 3
Richard Janney
Computers and Psychosis

In order to validate the need for CT type investigations, it is necessary first to demonstrate, both through logical argument and through practical observation, that significant mental adaptation does in fact occur as a result of tool use. To further that end, in his contribution, Richard Janney addresses some issues emerging from the psycho-pragmatics of the human-computer interface. He explores how prolonged, heavy use of computer based tools may force users to engage in a psychotic-like communication process. He likens the pattern to the function and effects of other types of prosthetic human organ replacement. Being more specialised and less complex than the parts of the body they replace, prosthetic devices have a tendency to monopolise one particular function of the original organ, thereby reducing its other functions. Hence, an artificial hand may be able to grasp objects with enormous strength but it does not feel or sense warmth. When it comes to communicating, the computer as a partner lacks intentionality and empathy, and is therefore incapable of producing felicitous speech acts. This severely disrupts the existential conditions for the 'I-Thou' relationship between interlocutors in that it destroys the pragmatic basis of human communication. As a result, people resort to communication strategies reminiscent of those used by schizophrenics. Technology users who engage in this type of discourse for any length of time are likely to adopt communicative strategies adapted to users who express themselves in arcane, 'machine' type ways, finally becoming responsive to only those utterances of others which "compute" for them.

Chapter 4
Hartmut Haberland
Natural Language and Artificial Technology: It ain't necessarily so

The question of what is artificial and what is natural is at the heart of Hartmut Haberland's contribution. The author examines the parallels between the linguistic discipline of Pragmatics and the concepts of CT. Of particular interest to him is the CT claim that tools are externalisations of the human mind. The argument centres on the difference in constraint imposed by "natural" language on human to human communication as compared to those imposed by "artificial" machines on human-machine communication. To the extent that natural linguistic manifestations are a product of the human mind, and must therefore be at least in part a result of conscious planning, the non-artificial nature of human language can be called into question. At the opposite end of the spectrum, the degree to which machine driven dialogues can be considered non-natural is reduced as the constraints governing such interactions come more and more to resemble those which govern interactions between people. With respect to human/machine dialogue, it therefore becomes increasingly more important to address questions such as: Who has access to information? Who controls turn taking? Who monitors interruptions and overlap during discourse? The challenge for Cognitive Technology is to seek out such questions and attempt to answer them.

Chapter 5

Alonso Vera
Understanding Users: The Knowledge-Level of Analysis

In his contribution, Alonso Vera speculates critically on the difficulty of defining a distinctive CT methodology. He argues that, although the theoretical foundations for the design of human-machine interactions might need to be modified in light of the aims and goals of CT, traditional HCI methodologies, if properly adhered to, are not at odds with these aims and goals and may be sufficient. He claims that a central reason why current technology often seems poorly suited for common human use is not that the methodologies of HCI have failed, but that they have seldom been properly used. When carefully applied, they have resulted in notable success stories. Gain saying Karpatschof, but in agreement with Lindsay (this volume), Vera rejects the view that social change translates formatively into a genuine cognitive make-up of technology users. He endorses the position that to ensure a high quality interface, we need to focus on learnability and usability. These particular aspects of human behaviour, being governed by motivation, dedication, leadership, and analytical skills, among others, are not the study domain of neuroscience, but of the behavioural sciences: cognitive science, psychology, sociology, anthropology and economics. What HCI methodologies can offer, in particular those that employ analyses based on goals, operators, methods and selection rules (GOMS), is a greater understanding of how systems will perform in relation to their users. These methodologies are also important inasmuch as they allow us to effectively test systems before they are released for use by the target user population. Hence they help avoid integration problems before they arise. This benefit notwithstanding, it appears necessary to combine HCI methodology with techniques which have to do with practical applications (such as visual screen displays) in order to achieve a happy usability equilibrium.

REFERENCES

Gorayska, B., 1993. Reflections: A commentary on Philosophical Implications of Cognitive Semantics. *Cognitive Linguistics*, 4(1), pp. 47-53.

Gorayska, B. and R. Lindsay, 1989. *On Relevance: Goal Dependent Expressions and the Control of Planning Processes.* Technical Report # 16. School of Computing and Mathematical Sciences, Oxford-Brookes University, UK.

Gorayska, B. and J. L. Mey, 1996. Cognitive Technology. In K. S. Gill, ed., Information Society: *New media, ethics, and Postmodernism*, London and

New York: Springer Verlag, pp. 287-294. (First presented at the International Conference on New Visions of Post-Industrial Society. Brighton UK, 9 July 1994)

Olson, D. R., 1994. *The World on Paper: The conceptual and cognitive implications of writing and reading.* Cambridge: University Press, Cambridge.

Ong, W.J. 1992. The Linguistics of Literacy. In P. Downing, S. D. Lima, and M. Noonan, eds, *The Linguistics of Literacy*, Amsterdam: John Benjamins, pp. 294-319.

Humane Interfaces: Questions of method and practice in Cognitive Technology
J.P. Marsh, B. Gorayska and J.L. Mey (Editors)
© *1999 Elsevier Science B.V. All rights reserved.*

Chapter 1

INVESTIGATIONS IN COGNITIVE TECHNOLOGY
Questioning perspective

Barbara Gorayska

Department of Computer Science
City University of Hong Kong
Hong Kong Special Administrative Region
China

Jonathon P. Marsh

Centre for the Advancement of University Teaching
The University of Hong Kong
Hong Kong Special Administrative Region
China

"To a man with a nail
everything looks like a hammer."

INTRODUCTION

The above reversal of the well known aphorism "To a man with a hammer everything looks like a nail" reflects what we feel to be the central purpose of this book: the need not only to ask pertinent questions but, in the manner of Argyris (1974), to rethink the way in which we go about asking them. Consequently, this chapter considers a number of questions and tries to explore the implications of answering them with respect to developing both our ongoing understanding of how tool use affects the human mind, and subsequently how this understanding can be brought to bear on the design processes we employ when developing technology.

Background

To date, the effort spent to define Cognitive Technology (CT) as a distinct field of inquiry, has emphasised the need to pragmatically understand the dialectic relationship between the use of augmenting artefacts and the process of cognitive adaptation resulting from exposure to fabricated environments[1]. The central position has been defined as the need to study human cognitive inputs to the integration between people and tools and in so doing produce greater a priori insight into the socio-cognitive impact of technological innovation. We need to do this in order to directly benefit people rather than simply facilitate and speed up technological progress. If we do not, the value to the user of the ensuing form of "user centred" tool design may remain essentially a matter of rhetoric.

It has been further proposed that, in order to achieve this objective, cognitive technology studies must first be grounded in a coherent theory of adaptation, with defining principles of human-artefact integration through interaction which can be brought to bear on the process of designing technology. What has emerged from these considerations is a number of critical issues that need to be addressed by anyone interested in investigating the co-evolution of tools and the minds that create them. Of particular interest are the issues embodied within two key CT questions:

> *How can we define, predict, and recognise the threshold at which technological enhancement of human ability/performance becomes a constraint on that very ability/performance?*

and/or

> *How do we design humane user-tool interfaces?*

However it is not sufficient to simply ask these questions. We need also to consider how and to what end they have been formulated? Are they properly situated within an appropriate conceptual framework? To what degree does the language they are framed in condition the kind of answers we look for?

Reversal of perspective

It is reasonably safe to assume that, upon hearing either form of the aphorism mentioned earlier, most people would agree almost uniformly on the relative

---

[1] Cognitive Technology as a distinct field of inquiry was first introduced at the International Conference on New Visions of Post Industrial Society, 9 July 1994, Brighton, UK, now available in print as Gorayska and Mey (1996d). For the multidisciplinary contributions that followed see Cox, Anderson, and Marsh (1995), Gorayska and Mey (1996a,c), and Marsh, Nehaniv, and Gorayska (1998). Our own position is discussed in Gorayska and Marsh (1996) and Marsh and Gorayska (1997).

meaning and common sense truth of what is expressed in either. However, taking time to consider the ways in which the two differ may serve to provide a meaningful example of how we can gain insight by consciously altering our questioning perspective. One indication that this reflection may be timely is the observation of Meurig Beynon (1997) that a field as young as Cognitive Technology necessarily suffers from an extreme eclecticism of perspective and understanding. Hence, an elaboration on how we might consciously alter our questioning perspective might serve (especially in the case of this particular example) to expose something deeper in terms of what we believe the Cognitive Technology perspective to be. At least in so far as we have thus far conceived it.

The unfolding of various metaphors entailed in the *person-hammer-nail* aphorism emerged gradually during discussions at the CT'97 conference in Aizu, Japan. Kari Kuutti first introduced it (figure 1) to focus attention on the mutual dependence between technological progress and the culture in which it occurs. Kuutti was arguing against an earlier conception of tools as augmenting devices (Engelbart, 1963; Biocca, 1996) in favour of the conception of tools as devices for mediating, and being mediated by, socially accumulated experience. Using an iconic example, he explained that hammers could only have been conceived within cultural communities that employed a particular geometry in constructing habitats, and had the raw materials required to successfully build related constructions. Kuutti's position, which favours closely scrutinising cultural mediation in the processes of technological invention, has much in common, *mutatis mutandis*, with other methodologies such as Activity Theory (Leontiev, 1978; Nardi, 1996), Situated Cognition (Suchman, 1987; Greeno, 1994; Lueg and Pfeifer, 1998) and its refined variant Ecological Psychology (Wicker, 1984). All of them stress the vital role of the environment in shaping and guiding activity related cognitive outputs.

Figure 1. A mutual dependence between culture and technological progress.

By slightly modifying the language and hence the questioning perspective, Dick Janney derived a different metaphor from the same aphorism (figure 2). His perspective focused on what actually happens at the user-tool interface. There is now a long tradition in interface design which aims at developing ergonomically sound systems that naturally extend human physical and cognitive characteristics. However, as Janney pointed out (see also this volume), no matter how ergonomically well designed a tool is, in some sense, by virtue of it being a tool, it is always a form of prosthesis. Because they are prostheses, their prolonged use necessarily affects the user. To Janney this is mainly due to a mismatch between the functional complexity of the processes inherent in the tools and those inherent in the users which engage one another at the interface. The consequent adjustments may become irreversible for specific individuals within certain contexts. The issue here is one of *thresholds*. Coping with physiological blisters (as in figure 2) over time leads to calluses as a matter of course (see also Biocca 1996). However what Janney is inviting us to explore in a much more systematic way than we have in the past, are not matters of physiology but the processes by which our minds cope, in an equally matter-of-course manner, with technologically induced "cognitive blisters". In other words, we need to understand how and why minds become technologised as a result of exposure to technological environments.

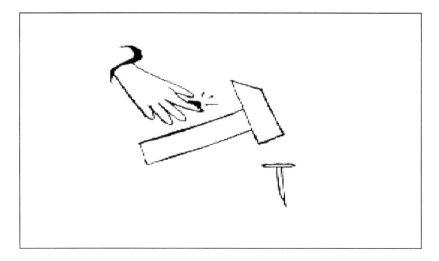

Figure 2. Human maladaptation to tools

Our set of variations in perspective would not be complete if we failed to consider cases where either hammer or nail are missing. Interestingly, people who possess hammers but not nails and people who possess nails but not hammers inhabit two related but nonetheless different worlds. A hammer is primarily an instrument for amplifying a manual force and is, therefore, action oriented. A nail is primarily a device for holding two separate items together and, for this reason, it is closely associated with some state in the world which signals an achievement. It is true to say that both hammers and nails afford hitting (in the Gibsonian sense, 1979). It is also true that, when they are not available while in demand, both hammers and nails cause people to inappropriately load values on external objects and internal goal structures. However, the absence of either one carries different cognitive implications and can lead to different sets of final outcomes. That is, hammers and nails affect people and consequently the world in different ways.

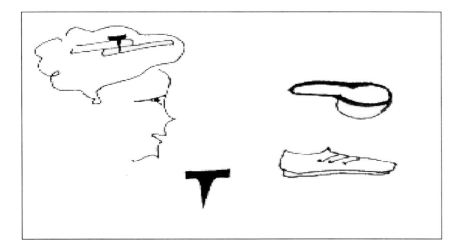

Figure 3. Tool mediated perception of the external and internal environment

It is important to note that hammers and nails differ with respect to the measure of their prosthetic effect (i.e. how closely they relate to and extend our bodies). In relation to people nails are once removed, in the sense that to be functional they require another tool (figure 3). Hammers, on the other hand, directly extend the human arm and hand, which activates the usefulness of hammers as tools more immediately. If the situation arises which requires two things to be nailed together, it leads to the formulation of a problem from the mindset of a person with a nail. If the situation exists whereby a person is holding a hammer, it leads to the formulation of a problem from the mindset of a person with a hammer. Because the perception of the hitting affordance is different in these two situations, one as the need for a hitting object and the other as the need for an object to hit, two different design processes will result with respect to building a solution. What this discrepancy shows is how different tools tap in differently into both the divergent and convergent cognitive processes involved in generating intentional actions. In terms of the hitting outcome there is no meaningful end game. By contrast, because nails are often conceived of as parts of goal structures, upon perception they generate cognitive effects which tend to converge on a single outcome. The satisfaction conditions for the same act of effective hitting are quite diverse depending on which tool or combination of tools is present despite the availability of prior knowledge about the functionality of either tool.

In his discussion of the origin and function of goals Roger Lindsay (Lindsay and Gorayska, 1994) has proposed a functional distinction between cognitive and terminal goals. Goals are cognitive if they are parts of complex goal chains and their achievement contributes to the construction or execution of a higher order plan. Terminal goals are the top goals in such goal chains. The satisfaction conditions (i.e. the state of the problem environment upon goal achievement) for terminal goals are not dictated by the execution requirements of higher order plans. Instead, they are dictated by the desirability of the state brought into existence upon their achievement. Thus, terminal goals directly relate cognition with motivation. Lindsay's distinction may be helpful in further elaborating upon our example of the differential impact of hammers and nails on human cognition. Hammers have a strong primitive affordance value which shows little specificity with respect to a terminal goal. Consequently, multiple possible applications and variable cognitive goals emerge from this direct and relatively simple functional extension of the human arm. By contrast, nails, being further removed from immediate body extension, have a high degree of relevance to a somewhat more specific desired goal, that of fastening two objects together. In other words, they have higher terminal goal value.

The distinction between cognitive and terminal goals can be applied effectively to a wide variety of tools. We conjecture that the further removed a tool is from direct body extension, the higher its terminal goal value. Conversely, the more direct a tool's prosthetic capability is in extending natural human functionality, the higher its primitive affordance value and the lower its specificity with respect to motivational relevance.

We have so far looked at three different iterations of the hammer-person-nail metaphor and each has yielded a different set of insights into the nature of the relationship between people and the tools they create and use. We think the multiple processes inherent to tool mediated cognition, illuminated by the distinct questioning perspective generated by each iteration, are equally valuable and actually integrated with one another. This integration constitutes a set of feedback effects involving each participating source component: the mind, the body, and the world. In the past such feedback effects were more noticed with regard to the overt development of culture or technological progress, and less so with regard to the covert, internal mechanics of the mind. Recently, scholarly interest in cognition has undergone a noticeable shift. For example, the archaeologist Steven Mithen[2] has put forward the view that human consciousness owns its reason d'être to the evolution of its capacity to make artefacts and other externalisation processes, such as the various forms of artistic expression, which engaged thought in creative problem solving. Olson (1994) argues that the development of metacognition is the direct product of interactions between cognition and writing systems in literate

---

[2] Reported in the Times Higher Education Supplement, 1 May 1998, p. 9.

communities. Similar effects are noted and addressed by Winograd and Flores (1986) with respect to hermeneutics. The co-evolution of the human mind and the tools it generates has been noted in (Gorayska and Mey, 1996a), while the need to consider how and why the brain, body, and world have to come together has been framed philosophically by Clark (1997). We suspect that many more similar arguments will follow because any methodology for tool design which is derived from, and subsequently advocates, accounts of user-tool interaction and cognition-tool integration from a single questioning perspective, to the exclusion of other related perspectives, is likely to distort the holism of the picture.

Changing or reversing our questioning perspective (e.g., from exploring interaction to exploring integration, or from exploring the cognitive processes of dealing with the outside world to exploring the processes of dealing with the impact of the external world on internal representations and metacognition) is one means by which we might rethink what it is we are studying when we explore the human factors involved in technological advance. For example, we often use abstract models of the things we study in order to facilitate scrutiny. We may construct an image of human mental processes as mechanistic and highly predictable which interact with the outside world in formally determinable ways (such as those that underlie the current research and development of Rodney Brooks' humanoid robot (Brooks, 1998; Beynon, 1997)). Such a model may go a long way to explain a great deal about how humans think and subsequently externalise their thoughts. However a simple rethinking of the model to reflect a less precisely predictable and more fluid set of heuristically determined interactions between volatile sets of data opens up a whole new set of possibilities for understanding and improved practice, without negating the value of the previous model. Our position is that the process of interactively changing the questioning perspective to facilitate the building of better models of tool mediated, situated cognition is critical to the work of CT.

QUESTIONS THAT STEM FROM A REVERSAL OF PERSPECTIVE

Any explanatory account of integrating users with tools, situations, and cultures must take into consideration the phenomenon of *interface*.

Question: *How many interfaces are there?*

It has long been readily recognised that cognition interfaces with perception and, subsequently, the external world. It has not been so readily recognised, although it ought to have been, that other interfaces exist which have a bearing on its evolving characteristics, namely, the interface between cognition and the action system, the interface between cognition and the emotion/affect system, and the interface between cognition and the motivation system. Many of these interfaces have been explored independently of one another and not always within the discipline of cognitive science. For example, there is an extensive literature in business and marketing on goal setting and the influence of advertising on consumer behaviour. Motivational and affective systems have been discussed mainly (though not exclusively (e.g., Frijda, 1986; Lazarus, 1991)) in relation to personality formation and identity disorders by social, developmental, and clinical psychologists among others. The interface of cognition with sensory motor activity, approached from a pragmatic point of view, is only beginning to receive more attention in a broader spectrum of cognitive and behavioural sciences (Jeannerod, 1994).

Each of these developments is interesting and valuable in its own right, however, what is needed is a synthesising mechanism capable of associating and adapting all the so illuminated processes and products of embedded cognition. We also need an accurate explanatory model of that mechanism which may yield some form of relevant methodological convergence.

Question: *What is methodological convergence?*

Increasingly, as regards the phenomena of cognition current studies in fields as diverse as philosophy, anthropology, cognitive science, and linguistics appear to anchor on the internal processes which underlie goal management and purposeful action. Below we briefly discuss the thinking behind a sample of current, independent, investigative frameworks. Our intention is to explore how their questioning perspectives condition the insights they arrive at, especially with respect to the importance of the explanatory role played by the intentional action planning capacity within humans. By analysing and attempting to integrate the outcomes of these varying positions we hope to better define a theoretical perspective which can usefully inform the development of a set of CT design principles.

Intentionality

Dennett (1996) links the birth of agency with a degree of complexity within an organism which is sufficient to perform systematic actions, and subsequently, the birth of intentionality with the type of agency that is information-modulated, circumstances-dependent, and goal seeking. In other words, intentional agents are rational agents who favour what is good for them, and whose actions are, therefore, driven by good reason (see also Anderson, 1990). Interestingly, Dennett traces the origins of the term 'intentionality' to medieval philosophers who based it on the arrow aiming analogy (intendere arcum in). He then brings two different senses of 'intentionality' to the common denominator of 'aboutness' (which entails the concept of 'targeting an object'): 1) the lay sense that refers to a motivating factor in goal seeking behaviour, and 2) the philosophical sense that refers to the representational capacity of an organism (which entails a perceiving agents ability to distinguish one thing from another and attend to it). His perspective represents one good example of how reference to goal/action planning serves to support his explanation of intentionality as a cognitive mechanism necessary to the emergence of consciousness.

Meta-representation

Sperber (1997), introducing the difference between human intuitive beliefs (those grounded in perception and in spontaneous inference from perception) and human reflective beliefs (derived by virtue of a meta-represensentational capacity), starts off by noting that

> "[t]he overall function of a cognitive system is to allow the organism to adjust its behaviour to a changing environment. For this, a cognitive system must contain representations of actual states of affairs, a data-base, so to speak. It must also contain representations of behaviours to be engaged in by the organism, representations capable of guiding these behaviours, in other terms, plans. The simple link between data and plans consists in having the triggering of every plan-guided behaviour conditional on the addition to the data-base of a specific datum. For instance, if a representation of cat approaching is added to the data-base of a mouse, this activates a flight plan"   (Sperber, 1997: 67-8)

In more complex organisms capable of meta-representing representations of states, the question arises as to which representations are actually placed in a data-base and, therefore, have the potential to guide behaviour. Sperber sees only intuitive beliefs and those reflective beliefs that have been validated (i.e. recognised and endorsed as being true of and/or relevant to the world of interest and dissociated from the embedding metalevel beliefs) as possible candidates for inclusion in this data-base. From Sperber's perspective it is reasonable to hold the view that the goal of cognition is to amass as much evidence as possible for the validity of one's beliefs. Sperber and Wilson (1986) further argued that the degree to which held assumptions about the world are modified in this process, i.e. strengthened or weakened, determines the optimal relevance of communicative intentions which can be derived from linguistic and ostensive non-linguistic discourse. While they explicitly downplay the importance of goal/action planning in determining relevance they nonetheless cannot deny reference to it in so far as it implicitly represents the motivation for knowledge database expansion.

Clearly, although not necessarily contradictory, there is a difference between Dennett and Sperber's concern for the importance of goal/action planning in supporting their relative arguments. We conjecture that this difference stems a priori from the difference in their specific starting perspective. That is to say their assumptions about what it is which is of central importance imposes a specific set of relevance values on the contributing components of their investigation before the investigation even begins.

Semantic primitives

Anna Wierzbicka has been empirically exploring the relationship between meaning, culture, and language in search of semantic universals in language and thought. She has recently proposed (1992) a mini language of thought derived from a hypothetical set of semantic primitives[3], the existence of which she has been able to establish in a large number of languages. This mini language of thought has its own grammatical categories and syntax comprised of nouns, determiners, adjectives, and verbs. The sentences in the universal language of thought are, according to Wierzbicka (1992:10) something like 'I think this', 'I want this', 'You do this', 'This happened', 'This person did something bad', or 'Something bad happened because of this'. As noted in Gorayska (1993), other concepts are also proposed, within a broader context of Cognitive Linguistics, as prime candidates for commonly distributed structures of experience, which are thought to be generated by early experience of our bodily functions. These include constructions such as 'source-path-goal', 'part-whole', 'centre-periphery', 'scalarity', 'links', or 'figure-ground' (Lakoff, 1987, Langacker, 1987). Upon examination both sets of primitives appear to have a clear connection with goal/action planning activity. Given this apparent connection, if one accepts the premise that the structure of language mirrors the structure of the human mind (as does Wierzbicka and Lakoff among others) it is not surprising to find that there exists strong empirical evidence, emerging from corpus based linguistic research, which supports the view that the core of human cognition is essentially constituted by the mental processes that deal with goal management and intentional action. Yet again, an attempt to explain a particular cognitive phenomena, in this case the universality of basic linguistic structure, has led to a different perspective on the explanatory value of the goal/action planning capacity of humans. Here it emerges as a fundamental cognitive process which lies at the core of semantic construction.

Pragmatic acts

Finally, in contrast to Wierzbicka' semantic orientation, Jacob Mey (1993), arguing against Searle's (1969) narrower notion of *speech acts*, has introduced the broader notion of *pragmatic acts* (acts which are not reduced to verbal expressions) in order to explain the processes which govern the effective use of language. These meaning laden communicative acts are partially linguistic and

---

[3] Wierzbicka has been investigating the existence of semantic primitives since the early 1970's. She has so far established a set comprising 'I', 'you', 'someone', 'something', 'this', 'the same', 'good', 'bad', 'think', 'want', 'know', 'say', 'feel', 'where', and possibly 'part', 'become', 'imagine', and 'world'.

partially behavioural. When we perform these acts, we aim, both linguistically and non-linguistically, to control the way in which people respond to our communication. We do this by setting up scenarios that we hope will greatly increase the probability of inducing certain types of verbal and non-verbal response (referred to as take-ups) in others. Contradistinct to natural environments, such constructs are always goal/task oriented because the setup conditions afford a finite set of actions which in turn entail a set of goals. Thus, when we choose to take up the 'bait', we pursue more readily those goals that can be easily satisfied by the actions afforded by the salient objects and processes within the set up. Pragmatic acts are therefore equivalent, with respect to communication, to the act of fabrication, with respect to tool development in the material environment. By virtue of their existence, these acts suggest that language and action systems must have co-evolved to meet the requirements for effective human output. The analogy can be further extended to include natural language (in particular its written form) as a spontaneously evolving technology which externalises the mind, amplifying and, at the same time, constraining its internal operations (see further Olson 1994 and Haberland this volume). Within Mey's approach to explaining the pragmatics of communicative behaviour there appears to be an implicit reliance on the role of goal/action planning in humans which is not dissimilar to that of Wierzbicka. However, here the emphasis is felt more strongly with respect to the non-verbal aspects of communication.

Question: *What is being converged upon?*

Intentional behaviour on the part of a perceiving agent can only emerge within a specific environment when the functionality afforded within that environment becomes known by that agent. Subsequently designing that environment in such a way as to optimally facilitate effective intentional behaviour must depend on a clear understanding of the processes which govern how a perceiving agent comes to know the functionality afforded within any environment. The key to understanding this process may lie in the relationship between invariants, affordances, and relevance.

We think it hardly a coincidence that within the controversies between situated cognition (Suchman, 1987; Brooks, 1991, 1998) and symbolic cognition (Newell and Simon, 1972, Vera and Simon, 1993), as well as between sylopsistic symbol systems (Fodor, 1980) and grounded symbol systems (Harnad, 1990) reference is often made to the unfinished work of Gibson (1979, 1977) on the ecological approach to visual perception. What appears to be in dispute is how the identity and functionality of objects in the real world are cognised, remembered, recognised, referenced, and utilised in intelligent action in highly dynamic environments. In other words, how people mentally handle the invariant properties of objects and decide which actions those objects afford.

Gibson argued that when people actively integrate themselves with highly dynamic environments they rely on invariant characteristics within objects which are perceived as constant. For Gibson these invariants reside in optic arrays accessible to the sensory input mechanisms of moving perceivers. A single instance of a static view of an object cannot provide us with enough information to facilitate the establishment of perceived invariants. However, the morphing of a perceived object through multiple views within a specific environment does provide sufficient information to allow us to pick up such invariants. Hence, invariants must be relational in nature. In addition, both negative and positive feedback is necessary to reinforce the perceptual selection of invariants. Hence, as noted by Harnad (1990), the real issue is not what invariants there are but rather how they are being picked up. Can the same argument hold for the phenomenon of affordances?

Question: *How do affordances emerge?*

According to Gibson,

> "...the affordance of anything is a combination of the physical properties of the environment [its substance and surfaces] that is uniquely suited to a given animal - to his nuitritive system or his action."   (Gibson, 1977: 79)

Thus, Gibson says, some surfaces afford standing on, others sitting on, still others walking on or falling of, etc. Some substances afford poisoning, others do not. Such affordances are neither subjective nor objective. For Gibson an affordance is real, not phenomenal. It is an environmental fact which is not defined exclusively at the level of physics. It does not depend on the observer for its existence. However, it is equally meaningless to talk of an affordance without it being related to and conditioned by the perceiving agent. An object or substance can only be valuable relative to a specific action or nutrient system. Thus, Gibson says, an affordance is neither exclusively physical nor exclusively psychical:

> " There has been endless debate among philosophers and psychologists as to whether values were physical or phenomenal, in the world of matter or only in the world of mind. For affordances as distinguished from values the debate does not apply. They are neither in the one world nor the other inasmuch as the theory of two worlds is rejected. There is only one environment, although it contains many observers with limitless opportunities for them to live in it."
> (Gibson, 1977:77)

On this account, misperception (of false affordance or of the presence of a true one) is the result of either insufficient or contrary information in the ambient light, or of a fault in the perceptual system for picking up invariances. According to Gibson, it is not a function of motivated attention:

> "The concept of affordance is somewhat related to these concepts of valence, invitation, and demand [in Gestalt psychology (Koffka, 1935)] but with a crucial difference. The affordance of something does not change as the need of the observer changes. Whether or not the affordance is perceived or attended to will change as the need of the observer changes, but, being invariant, it is always there to be perceived. An affordance is not bestowed upon an object by a need of the observer and by his action of perceiving it. The object offers what it does because it is what it is. To be sure, we define what it is in terms of ecological physics instead of physical physics, and it therefore possesses meaning and value to begin with. But this is meaning and value of a new sort."
>
> (Gibson, 1977:78)

Gibson's account of how affordances for behaviour are perceived couples affordance information with information about the invariant properties of surfaces, substances, and surface layouts. According to him, both are present in the ambient light. He explains further that the invariants of external objects are perceived in relation to the types of action system, which characterise the perceiving agent. To Gibson perception of the environment is thus inseparable from the proprioception of one's own body (1977:79). He proposes that the information about real (rather than abstract or fabricated) external world objects which *are relevant to types of behaviour* (emphasis ours, see further page 32) comes in units functioning as compound invariants which specify benefits and dangers for the given observer and are directly perceived as such. By contrast, the ability to extract other affordances, especially those not commensurate with the observer's body, has to be learnt.

Some proponents of Situated Cognition, Greeno and More (1993) and Greeno (1994), propose an account of affordances which is close to the one postulated by Gibson. Within their framework they postulate that "cognitive activities should be understood primarily as interactions between agents and physical systems and with other people." (Greeno, 1994:49). However, in their view, it is only possible to accept Gibson's idea that affordances are about the environment and are directly perceived on condition the distinction is made between *direct perception* and object *recognition* based on what is already known hence remembered. This broadens the concept of affordances to encompass those that are directly perceived (e.g. pauses or facial expressions in conversations) and those that are recognised (e.g. with an aid of symbolic communication that provide constraints for actions).

Vera and Simon (1993), introduce a different questioning perspective. Defending the physical symbol systems against the proponents of situated cognition, they equate symbols with patterns in internal memory structures. These structures, they say, originate either upon reception of sensory stimuli from the environment or else are produced (as motor symbols) in support of acts upon the environment. This makes possible both comparisons with and acting from past experience. Perceptual processes encode sensory stimuli from the environment and motor processes decode motor symbols into muscular responses called motor processes. These two types of process connect the symbol system with the environment and are themselves bridged by the cue-response mechanism which Vera and Simon call productions. Productions are thus viewed as chunks learned from experience, which reduce often complex sequences of perceptual transduction processes into simple, easily encodable internal representations. These productions (or links between environmental cues and appropriate actions: If cue y then action x) are seen as closely but not entirely related to Gibson's affordances. Where Vera and Simon fundamentally disagree with Gibson is the symbolic nature of affordance-like productions which, they claim, provide a functional description of the world and as such are in the head and not in the external environment (Vera and Simon, 1993:21).

Jeannerod (1994:199) takes the pragmatic view according to which representations of situated actions involve an appropriate distribution of action affording properties within objects in the world (cf. Mey, 1993). That is, affordances are likened to those properties of objects which can be linked to specific motor patterns. These properties may provide either implementation conditions for the associated actions or else constitute goals for those actions.

By contrast, Heft (1989) links the perception of affordances to intentionality (cf. Dennett, 1996). He extends Gibson's original idea about body scaling in the perception of affordances to include an awareness of what an individual can do, i.e. relative to what a person's potentialities for intentional (goal directed) action are. He defines intentional acts in terms of the functional characteristics of the environment which confronts individuals and the physical characteristics of their bodies. Consequently, he acknowledges the existence of a tripartite relationship between goals, actions, and world objects, at the same time stressing, like Mey (1993), the pragmatic role of action in perceptual experience.

Leeuwen et al. (1994) have shed a slightly different light on the subject. They argue that perceiving the affordances of tools requires the monitoring of several higher order complementary relationships: the relationship of (actor–tool) to (actor–target) and both of these to (tool–target):

> "It is essential that the tool combine properties that relate it to both the actor and another object in a manner that allows the actor to handle the object. What is meant is most clearly illustrated by the screwdriver. One of its ends represents a potential complementary with a screw (target object); the other end represents potential complementary with the actor's hand."
>
> (Leeuwen et al., 1994: 176)

What appears to be emerging from the above considerations is that, despite a basic common agreement on what constitutes an affordance, there is an apparent lack of consensus on how affordances emerge and/or are picked up by a perceiving agent. The differences in the proposed explanation seem once again to reflect differences in the various starting perspectives adopted within a wide variety of frameworks that attempt to explain cognition. The situation is reminiscent of the varying perspectives on the relationships inherent within the hammer-person-nail metaphor examined earlier. Like with that aphorism, it may be useful here to try to change our view of how the key components of the central questions interrelate in order to explore how the differences between these positions can be seen to compliment rather than contradict one another.

Question: *Where do affordances reside?*

We agree with Gibson that affordances reside neither in the mind nor in the external world (see also Reed 1987a&b). Affordances can be understood as perceptual contracts between perceivers and the objects of perception. This has been elegantly captured by Walker (1996):

> "You have seen the typical visual puzzles used by psychologists to discriminate between right and left brain dominance (e.g. a Dalmatian dog hidden in a whirl of black and white blotches on a page of white paper). Typically people take a few moments to identify the presence of the dog. However when asked after they have identified the dog, "where is it?" they look baffled and say, "Why it is there in the middle of the picture!" One can then ask well where was it before you identified it and the response is typically "Well it was there all the time I just could not see it." "Oh!" you say, "then can you now look at the picture and not see it anymore". Usually there are gasps of astonishment at how difficult a task this is. At that point it is possible to point out that in fact the dog is not there at all but only a whirl of black and white dots which afford you the possibility imposing your interpretative structure upon it hence deriving meaning.
>
> In other words, perception and knowledge of the dog's presence is a constructed agreement between the individual and the object of perception."
>
> (Walker 1996: 14)

We venture to suggest that the external world provides only a *potential* for affordance (cf. Gaver, 1991); that affordance is neither differentiated nor complete. Affordance potential also exists in individual perceivers. Specific affordances are reified through contact between the affordance potential in the environment and the affordance potential in an individual perceiver. This leads to the construction of a meaningful action trigger. Action, in turn, has a recursive effect both on the motivational state of the perceiver and the environment.

Question: *Is it possible to trace affordances by analysing invariants or, inversely, identify invariants by analysing affordances?*

Following, and homing in on, the remark of Gibson (quoted earlier, pp. 28-29) that compounded units of invariants comprise information which is *relevant* to the types of behaviour of the perceiver, determining how specific affordances are activated can be understood as an instance of how relevance relations are determined. As will be shown below, this process comprises the fine tuning of complexes of goals, actions, and the perceptions of objects. It also involves the processes by means of which such complexes come to be cognised, internalised, recursively modified, and externalised by living organisms in order to ensure their self-regulating equilibria. Consequently, several conditions have to be satisfied for an affordance to emerge.

Question: *Of what practical value is the theoretical position of postulating emergence/perception of affordances as governed by relevance?*

When we tried to illustrate what is novel about the Cognitive Technology approach to the analysis and design of tools (Gorayska and Marsh, 1996), we began to discuss relevance as a possible framework for inquiry. Our analysis of relevance was based on the foundations laid by Gorayska and Lindsay (1989, 1993) who postulated that the lay conception of relevance (as expressed in the natural language term 'relevant') accurately depicted a psychologically real relation by which people cognitively associated goals with effective means for goal achievement.[4]

We argued that this association could proceed in two ways: either by mapping effective action sequences for the purpose of satisfying existing goals, or by generating new goals and determining novel relevance relations for actions by combining raw precepts and previously acquired concepts. These two modes of processing relevance have been distinguished in the literature by two formal definitions which explicitly relate relevance to the operations of goal/action planners.

One definition (Lindsay and Gorayska, 1995:345) captured the pattern mapping processes involved in handling symbolic representations of goals and plans for effective goal driven behaviour:

An object E is [subjectively] relevant to an agent A in some world M if and only if there exists a goal G entertained by A, and E is a necessary element (or

---

[4] For the same conclusion within the subject area of human related database search and retrieval see Frochlish, 1994.

belongs to a set at least one member of which is a necessary element) of some plan P which is operative in M and sufficient to achieve that G.

Since this definition only allowed valid judgements of relevance to occur after successful planning had taken place, an immediate question arose (Lindsay, p.c.) as to what ensured that the actions selected for sequencing were themselves relevant? One proposed and implementationally validated solution to this circularity (Johnson et al., 1996, Johnson 1997) has been an interactive integration of sub-symbolic and symbolic processes in inductive production-rule generation. In this paradigm the relevance of primitive actions, for consideration in effective plan chains, is determined on the basis of goal related feedback. This lead to a different definition of relevance:

An input I is relevant to a goal G when I causes some variation in output which is associated with a change in the values of feedback.
(Lindsay and Gorayska 1994:7)

Relevance is a relation between a single input and a single output variable of a learning system. An input variable I is said to be relevant to deciding the value of an output variable o if and only if a change in the value of I from v to v', for some v and v', while the value of all other input variables remain constant, corresponds to a 'significant' change in the value of o. If, on the otherhand, for all values of v and v', there is no 'significant' change in the value of o then I is said to be irrelevant to deciding the value of o. (Johnson 1997:66)

The sub-symbolic, unconscious processing of relevance has also been discussed by Evans (1996). He has demonstrated experimentally that decisions about what is relevant to the task in hand (in this case the Wason selection task) take place preconsciously, where choices appear immediately relevant. Conscious, analytical thinking about these choices is only a *post factum* rationalisation of the preconscious selection. Evans argues that the immediacy of relevance is induced by linguistic cues which make people attend to some elements within a situation but not others. (Cf. Mey's pragmatic acts.) Following this attentional preference, decisions are subsequently made with regard only to what one is induced to think about, irrespective of whether or not the intuitive, immediate relevance proves correct on hindsight. Although Evans does not explicitly link relevance to goal related actions, this link is nonetheless evident in the encapsulation of gathered data within specific task performance contexts.[5]

---

[5] As Roger Lindsay (p.c.) pointed out to us, based on the evidence from his own experiments on the effects of the natural language on task related behavioural outputs, the fact that the relevance processing mechanism is subject to faulty external priming and can malfunction in effect is a good reason for utilising the notioin of relevance as an important theoretical construct with a high degree of explanatory value. See also his arguments in (Lindsay, 1996).

The account of relevance that is entirely centred on the role of language, and other ostensive communication in cognition, is offered by Sperber and Wilson (1986; reviewed extensively in Yus Ramos, 1998). In their view, any request for the hearer's attention always carries a presumption about the relevance of the intended message. Unlike the above mentioned postulates, Sperber and Wilson explicitly dissociate the processing of relevance from any influence by goal related task performance. Instead, the optimal relevance of any communicative intention is seen as determined by weighing the processing costs against the gains in modifications to the current pool of knowledge. Hence, another proposed definition of relevance is as follows:

> *"An assumption [about the world] is relevant in a context if and only if it has some contextual effects [of strengthening or weakening already held assumptions] in that context.*
> *[...]*
> *Extent condition 1: an assumption is relevant in a context to the extent that its contextual effects are large.*
> *Extent condition 2: an assumption is relevant in a context to the extent that the effort required to process it in this context is small." (Sperber and Wilson 1986/95:122, 125)*

Because Sperber and Wilson hold that the goal of cognition is to modify assumptions about the world which provide input to action planning and associated behaviour, there is an implicit link between relevance driven cognition and goals within their framework, despite their arguments to the contrary. (See further Gorayska and Lindsay, 1993.)

One reason why there exist these differences in accounts of how relevance is processed (i.e. between the proponents of the cost/effort ratio and the goal/action accounts of relevance) is because different accounts address different aspects of relevance relations. For example, Sperber and Wilson are primarily interested in developing a model of cognition capable of interpreting communicative acts as relevant, given the single goal of cognition (that of amassing more accurate knowledge and database assumptions of the external world). Gorayska and Lindsay, by contrast, are primarily interested in what type of relation relevance is *per se* and, consequently, in the necessary and sufficient conditions for processing this relation (i.e., how it can be captured in terms of goal/plan schema sets). Evans addresses the issue of relevance from the standpoint of why rational thinking breaks down in choosing relevant logical puzzle moves, while Johnson et al. are concerned with the processes by means of which problem spaces for effective planning can be generated. Since different accounts of relevance address different aspects of relevance relations, what we need is a function that can integrate these seemingly unrelated efforts.

Question: *Can these efforts to model relevance-driven cognition be themselves integrated by a switch in perspective?*

What is emerging, so far, from the considerations of relevance provides fair grounds to believe that there exists an archetypal relevance processing schema (represented in figure 4). It is also plausible to assume that this schema is bootstrapped when affordance potential in the environment comes into contact with the affordance potential within the individual perceiver. As a result of such contact, meaningful action triggers are defined which may then be preserved in the form of associative relevance links. Triggered activity subsequently has a recursive effect on both motivational states and the environment.

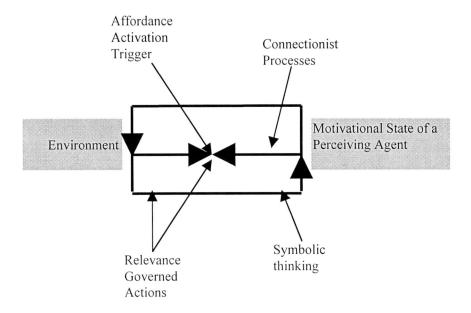

Figure 4. The affordance/relevance feedback loop.

What we think might be of interest here, would be to make a switch away from the current perspectives on relevance, discussed earlier, whilst, at the same time, preserving their positive contributions. People often talk of the extent of relevance, and therefore tend to think that relevance is a scalar predicate (Sperber and Wilson 1986): things can be more or less relevant. But what if we take a different view? What if we assume relevance to be defined as a Boolean type of relation? What if the relevance of a single action or object to the achievement of some first order goal can only be determined as either true or false? Then if we wish to account for what appear to be degrees of relevance (i.e. the extent to which some action or object is relevant), we must first determine exactly which goals are being targeted.

That is, we may have to look for second order relevance relations. For example, an action which directly satisfies a cognitive goal in a complex goal/plan chain has some bearing on the terminal goal in that chain. Since satisfying the cognitive goal per se does not satisfy the terminal one but only contributes to some degree towards such satisfaction, the effective action in question can be predicated as relevant to the terminal goal to the same degree (cf. the probabilistic model of relevance, Keynes 1921).

Apart from these second order relevance relations, other cases where the extents of relevance hold true are those that involve calculations of optimal effectiveness (Gorayska and Lindsay, 1989). Actions or objects are optimally effective depending on how many goals they achieve at any given time, or how many other goals and plans their successful execution causes to fail. Such calculations notwithstanding, what we have come to refer to as *relevance* relationships are the first order primitive relationships between specific goals, their effective plans, and the plan elements that make those plans effective. We see them as Boolean in nature in that they either exist or fail to exist.

This perspective has implications for how the cognitive mechanism that processes relevance may actually work internally. Supposing that every primitive relevance relation is formalised as a logical five place relation:

relevance (X, Goal, Elements, Plan, Agent, Model)

where an *element* is a part of a *plan* inferred from the characteristics of a *goal* entertained by an *agent* capable of implementing the plan, a *model* is the context in which the goal is found, the plan is constructed, and the agent is operative, and x can be an instance of any one of these five parameters (cf. Jaszczolt, 1996). Since we can code such primitive relevance relations digitally [as 0 or 1], we would then be able to create a global relevance metafunction comprising interrelated vectors of any number of iteratively processed complex sets of such relations. An increase or decrease of relevance will be determined by the function, on the basis of positive or negative Boolean instances of the individual primitive relevance relations, while activating affordances will occur for each positive Boolean instance of relevance attribution. Interestingly, cognitive processes themselves can be modelled as relevance-governed, mental-activity schemas on a par with any other goal/plan sets and be subject to the same global principle of relevance ascription and affordance attribution (Gorayska, Tse, and Kwok, 1997). If so, elegant models of adaptive (meta) cognition can be constructed, which are not only capable of learning about the world but also acquiring new learning skills and, in general, processing information more effectively.

Question: *How do we define interrelated vectors of motivational states, environments, and action mediated transitions between the motivation of the perceiver and the environment that help ensure self regulating equilibria in complex, dynamic environments?*

Unlike invariants and affordances, which are objects of perception, relevance operates at the level of action. Changes in the associated environments (current motivational states of the perceiver and the external world) occur as a result of an *ongoing process* of state modifications and alterations, in an attempt to arrive at a satisfactory relevance fit. Take, for example, a single case of satisfying thirst and hunger (figure 5), and further suppose the following scenario. A girl finds herself in an ordinary kitchen, i.e., is currently operating within a universe of perceived objects related to food. This particular environment, being functionally organised around activities related to eating, serves as an effective reminder of her motivational state of hunger. Upon scanning the kitchen for edible food, she selects a pie, and the action of ingesting the pie is triggered. The execution of the triggered action leads to another motivational state of thirst. The kitchen is then perceptually scanned for something to drink. Milk is perceived and selected, which triggers the execution of the drinking action, etc. This process continues until the perceiver reaches the state of full motivational satisfaction in this environment. Needless to say, should any of the necessary items of drink or food not be found in this scenario, cognitive goals would have been generated to accommodate the environmental deficiency.

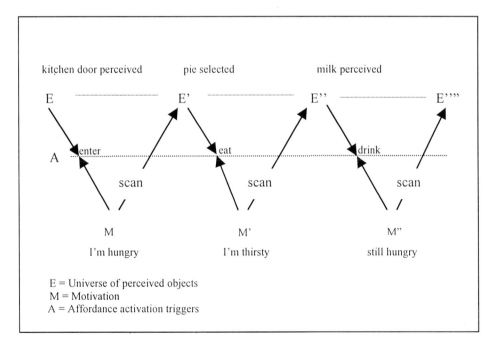

Figure 5. Recursive effects of an ongoing affordance-cum-relevance activation process.

Note that each affordance trigger in figure 5 corresponds to the establishment of a single primitive relevance relation. Iterative applications of scanning, affordance activation, and valuation of output states result either from the execution of old goal/plan chains or from the process of forming new ones. Note, also, that each instance of perceptual scanning of the environment is dependent on the currently operative motivation factor: the selected objects are relevant to the goals and plans being attended to. At this point, perception interfaces with goal related planning, which accounts for the selective nature of attention and selective depiction of the relevant environmental characteristics. Therefore, as we see it, the challenge in formalising the relevance metafunction does not reside only in the complexity of interleaving the attribution of relevance and affordance activation across many contexts and goal/plan sets concurrently. It lies also in providing appropriate interface connections for guiding the content-dependent processes of relevant cognitive (sub) modalities.

METHODOLOGICAL SELF-REFLECTION

We can talk about the relevance/affordance relationship independently of any consideration of CT and its design methodology. On the one hand, the benefit of being able to define affordances in a particular way has given us an explanatory platform for the emergence of relevance. Subsequently, the benefit of being able to account for how relevance is processed gives us an explanatory platform for how affordances emerge. We see the very act of analysing the affordance activation problem as an act of CT enquiry which constitutes one of the central premises upon which CT is built. Since one of the central CT issues is establishing how each current approach to user-centred design can benefit the formulation of a CT methodology, many self-reflective questions immediately spring to mind. Suppose we are able to determine the internal mechanics of an archetypal relevance schema, how will this inform CT? Or, in other words:

Questions: *How will the archetypal relevance schema become fruitful for tool design? How will it meaningfully influence the technology design process, and provide a unified framework capable of accommodating known user-centred design methods?*

The answer to these question will require further investigation. Suffice it to say here, that all the issues we have addressed above have, until recently, been looked at from a variety of perspectives which have mainly benefited the purposes of academic enquiry, business organisations, or industry (Smith et al, 1996). They have not yet been systematically approached from the pragmatic/practical perspective of designing *humane* interfaces in ways that maximally benefit individual humans at the receiving end of technological advance. In order to further the interests of the human user, we first need to fully understand the design process itself. As we have pointed out earlier (Gorayska, Marsh, and Mey, 1998) we ought not to forget that the notion of a relevance/affordance relationship, as discussed here, can only be properly situated in a societal context. This is especially true if we appeal to concepts such as control (those is in power decide what is relevant) ethics (whose relevance is more relevant: that of the producer or of the user of technology), and the meta-issue of locating relevance in the conditions which govern cognitive growth and its expression through environmental awareness. As such the questions we ask will inevitably determine the methodology we arrive at and its usefulness.

In an albeit convoluted way, we have attempted to show that there are always new ways of thinking about old problems (without necessarily having to wait for spontaneous paradigm shifts (Kuhn 1962/96; cf. Buzan and Buzan, 1993)). We have been trying to use such a change in thinking to rethink the questions involved in CT, and to consider the implications of asking these questions. Changing the design perspective through a formal and continuous examination and critique of the way we ask relevant questions – a process we see as a necessary core principle of self-reflection within the CT methodology - may be one way of ensuring new insights and preventing designers from blindly assuming a fixed perspective. A formal self-reflective questioning perspective based on the analysis of relevance/affordance relations offers us a chance to provide a platform upon which to build a practical suit of tools and techniques for humane interface design. To us CT is comprised of that suite, and thus can itself be seen as a tool of design construction.

REFERENCES

Anderson, J. R., 1990. *The Adaptive Character of Thought*. Hillsdale, NJ: Lawrence Erlbaum Associates.

Beynon, M., 1997. Report on the 2nd International Cognitive Technology Conference. *Digital Creativity*, 8(3/4), pp. 160-164.

Biocca, F., 1996. Intelligence Augmentation: The Vision Inside Virtual Reality. In: B. Gorayska and J. L. Mey, eds*., Cognitive Technology: In Search of a Humane Interface*, Amsterdam: North Holland, pp. 59-75.

Biocca, F., 1998. The Cyborg's Dilemma: Embodiment in Virtual Environments. *Proceedings, Second International Conference on Cognitive Technology: Humanizing the Information Age*, August 25-28, 1997, Aizu-Wakamatsu City, Japan. Los Alamitos, CA: IEEE Computer Society, pp.12-26.

Brooks, R. A. , 1991. Intelligence without representation. *Aritificial Intelligence*, 47, pp. 139-159.

Brooks, R. A., 1998. The Intelligence Room Project. *Proceedings of the Second Cognitive Technology Conference, CT'97*, August 25-28, 1997, Aizu-

Wakamatsu City, Japan. Los Alamitos, CA: IEEE Computer Society, pp. 271-278.

Buzan, T, and B. Buzan, 1993. *The Mind Map Book.* London: BBC Books.

Clark, A., 1997. *Being There: Putting the brain, body, and world together again.* Cambridge, Mass.: MIT Press.

Cox, K., J. P. Marsh, and B. Anderson, eds, 1995. *Proceedings of the First International Cognitive Technology Conference, CT'95.* 23-25 August 1995, Hong Kong.

Dennett, D., 1996. *Kinds of Minds: Towards an understanding of consciousness.* London: Weidenfeld & Nicolson.

Engelbart, D., 1963. A Conceptual Framework for the Augmentation of Man's Intellect. In: Howerton, ed., *Vistas in Information Handling. Vol. 1.* Spartan Books. Reprinted in I. Greif, ed., 1988, Computer- Supported Cooperative Work: A Book of Readings, San Mateo: Morgan Kaufmann, pp. 35-66.

Evans, J. St B. T., 1996. Deciding before you think: Relevance and reasoning in the selection task. *British Journal of Psychology*, 87, pp. 223-240.

Fodor, J., 1980. Methodological solipsism considered as a research strategy in cognitive psychology. *The Brain and Behavioural Sciences*, 85(8), pp. 1-5.

Frijda, N., H., 1986. *The Emotions.* Cambridge: Cambridge University Press.

Froehlich, T. J., 1994. Relevance Reconsidered – Towards an Agenda for the 21st Century: Introduction to Special Topic Issue on Relevance Theory. *Journal of the American Society for Information Science*, 45, pp. 124-134.

Gover, W. W., 1991. Technology Affordances. *Proceedings of CHI'91: Reading Through Technology*, New Orleans, Luisiana, April 27 - May 2, USA, pp. 79-85.

Gibson, J. J., 1977. The Theory of Affordances. In: R. Shaw and J. Bransford, eds., *Perceiving Acting and Knowing: Towards an Ecological Psychology*, Hillsdale, N. J.: Lawrence Erlbaum Associates, pp. 67-82.

Gibson, J. J., 1979. *The Ecological Approach to Visual Perception.* Boston, Mass: Houghton Mifflin.

Gorayska, B. and R. Lindsay, 1989. *On Relevance: Goal Dependent Expressions and the Control of Planning Processes.* Research Report 16. School of Computing and Mathematical Sciences, Oxford-Brookes University.

Gorayska, B. and R. Lindsay, 1993. The Roots of Relevance. *Journal of Pragmatics,* 19, pp. 306-312.

Gorayska, B., and J. Marsh, 1996. Epistemic Technology and Relevance Analysis: Rethinking Cognitive Technology. In: B. Gorayska and J. L. Mey, eds., *Cognitive Technology: In Search of a Humane Interface.* Amsterdam: North Holland, pp. 27-39,

Gorayska, B. and J. L. Mey, eds., 1996a. *Cognitive Technology: In Search of a Humane Interface.* Amsterdam: North Holland.

Gorayska, B.and J. L. Mey, 1996b. Of Minds and Men. In: B. Gorayska and J. L. Mey, eds, *Cognitive Technology: In Search of a Humane Interface,* Amsterdam: North Holland, pp. 1-24.

Gorayska, B. and J. L. Mey, eds, 1996c. *AI&Society 10*. Special issue on Cognitive Technology.

Gorayska, B. and J. L. Mey, 1996d. Cognitive Technology. In: K. S. Gill, ed., *Information Society: New media, ethics, and Postmodernism*. London; New York: Springer Verlag, pp. 287-294, (First presented at the International Conference on New Visions of Post-Industrial Society. Brighton UK, 9 July 1994)

Gorayska, B., J. Marsh, and J. L. Mey, 1998. Putting the Horse before the Cart: Formulating and Exploring Methods for Cognitive Technology. *Proceedings of the Second Cognitive Technology Conference*, CT'97, August 25-28, 1997, Aizu-Wakamatsu City, Japan. Los Alamitos, CA: IEEE Computer Society, pp. 2-9,

Gorayska, B., N. Tse, and W. H. Kwok, 1997. *A Goal Satisfaction Condition as a Function Between Problem Spaces and Solution Spaces*. Technical Report TR-97-06. Department of Computer Science, City University of Hong Kong.

Greeno, J. G., 1994. Gibson's Affordances. *Psychological Review*,101(2), pp. 336-342.

Greeno, J. G. and J. L. Moore, 1993. Situativity and Symbols: Response to Vera and Simon. *Cognitive Science,* 17, pp. 49-61.

Harnad, S., 1990. The Symbol Grounding Problem. *Physica,* D 42, pp. 335-346.

Heft, H., 1989. Affordances and the Body: An Intentional Analysis of Gibson's Ecological Approach to Visual Perception. *Journal of the Theory of Social Behaviour*, 19(1), pp. 1-30.

Jaszczolt, K, 1996. Relevance and Infinity: Implications for discourse interpretation. *Journal of Pragmatics*, 25, pp. 703-722.

Jeannerod, M., 1994. The representing brain: Neural correlates of motor intention and imagery. *Behavioural and Brain Sciences,* 17, pp. 187-245.

Johnson, G., 1997. *Neuron to Symbol: Relevance Information in Hybrid Systems*. Ph.D. Thesis. School of Computing and Mathematical Sciences. Oxford-Brookes University, UK.

Johnson, G., J. L. Nealon, and R. O. Lindsay, 1996. Using relevance information in the acquisition of rules from a neural network. *Proceedings of the Rule Extraction form Neural Networks Workshop*, 68-8. AISB 1996. Brighton, UK

Keynes, J. M., 1921. *A Treatise on Probability*. London: Macmillan.

Koffka, K., 1935. *Principles of Gestalt Psychology*. New York: Harcourt Brace.

Kuhn, T. S., 1962. *The Structure of Scientific Revolutions. 3rd edition*, 1996. Chicago and London: Chicago University Press.

Lackoff, G., 1987. *Women, Fire, and Other Dangerous Things: What Categories Reveal about the Mind*. Chicago: Chicago University Press.

Langacker, R. W., 1987. *Foundations of Cognitive Grammar. Vol.1*. Stanford, California: Stanford University Press.

Lazarus, R. S. 1991. *Emotion and Adaptation*. New York & Oxford: OUP.

Leeuwen, van L, A. Smitsman, and C. van Leeuwen, 1994. Affordances, Perceptual Complexity, and the Development of Tool Use. *Journal of*

Experimental Psychology: Human Perception and Performance, 20(1), pp.174-191.

Leontiev, A. N., 1978. *Activity, Consciousness and Personality*. Englewood Cliffs, NJ: Prentice Hall.

Lindsay, R. O., 1996. Cognitive Technology and the Pragmatics of Impossible Plans - A study in Cognitive Prosthetics. *AI & Society* ,10, pp. 273-288.

Lindsay, R. and B. Gorayska, 1994. *Towards a Unified Theory of Cognition*. Unpublished MS.

Lindsay, R. and B. Gorayska, 1995. On Putting Necessity in its Place. *Journal of Pragmatics,* 23, pp. 343-346.

Lueg, C. and R. Pfeifer, 1998. Cognition, Situatedness, and Situated Design. Proceedings of the 2rd International Cognitive Technology Conference, CT'97. August 25-28, Aizu, Japan. Los Alamitos: IEEE Computer Society Press, pp. 124-135,

Marsh, J. and B. Gorayska, 1997. Cognitive Technology: *What's in a Name? Cognitive Technology,* 1(2), pp. 40-43.

Marsh, J., C. Nehaniv, and B. Gorayska, eds, 1998. Humanizing the Information Age. Proceedings of the Second Cognitive Technology Conference, CT'97, 25-28 August, Aizu, Japan. Los Alamitos: IEEE Computer Society Press, pp. 2-9.

Mey, J. L., 1993. *Pragmatics: An Introduction*. Oxford: Blackwells.

Nardi, B. A., ed., 1996. *Context and Consciousness: Activity Theory and Human-Computer Interaction*. Cambridge, Mass. MIT Press

Newell, A., and H. A. Simon, 1972. *Human Problem Solving*. Englewood Cliffs: Prentice Hall.

Olson, D. R., 1994. *The World on Paper: The conceptual and cognitive implications of writing and reading*. Cambridge: Cambridge University Press.

Reed, E., 1987a. Why do things look as they do? The implications of James Gibson's The ecological approach to visual perception. In A. Costall and A. Still, eds, *Cognitive Psychology in Question*. Brighton: The Harvester Press, pp. 90-114,

Reed, E., 1987b. James Gibson's ecological approach to cognition. In A. Costall and A. Still, eds, *Cognitive Psychology in Question*. Brighton: The Harvester Press, pp. 142-173,

Searle, J., 1969. *Speech Acts: An Essay in the Philosophy of Language*. Cambridge: CUP.

Smith, W., M. Rendell, S. Lewandowski, K. Kirsner, and J. Dunn, 1996. The Role of Shared Commitment, Problem Coherence, and Domain Knowledge. *Cognitive Technology,* 1(1), pp. 9-18.

Sperber, D., 1997. Intuitive and Reflective Beliefs. *Mind and Language,* 12(1), pp. 67-83.

Sperber, D., and D. Wilson, 1986. *Relevance: Communication and Cognition*. Oxford: Blackwells.

Suchman, L. A., 1987. *Plans and Situated Action: The problem of human-machine communication*. New York: Cambridge University Press.

Vera, A. H. and H. A. Simon, 1993. Situated Action: A symbolic Representation. *Cognitive Science,* 17, pp. 7-48.

Walker, P., 1996. The art of inspiring students. *The New Academic*, Autumn, pp. 12-16.

Wicker, A. W., 1984. *An Introduction to Ecological Psychology*. Cambridge: Cambridge University Press. First published in 1979 by Wadsworth.

Wierzbicka, A., 1992. *Semantics, Culture, and Cognition: Universal Human Concepts in Culture-Specific Configurations*. New York & Oxford: OUP.

Winograd, T., and F. Flores, 1986. *Understanding Computers and Cognition*. Norwood, N. J.:Ablex Publishing.

Yus Ramos, F., 1998. A decade of relevance theory. *Journal of Pragmatics,* 30(3), pp. 305-345.

Humane Interfaces: Questions of method and practice in Cognitive Technology
J.P. Marsh, B. Gorayska and J.L. Mey (Editors)
© 1999 Elsevier Science B.V. All rights reserved.

Chapter 2

CAN WE CHANGE OUR MINDS?
The impact of computer technology on human cognition[1]

Roger Lindsay

Psychology Department
Oxford Brookes University

INTRODUCTION

This paper examines the belief that computers are able to change the minds of the humans who use them, and that they may have already done so. It begins by trying to establish what is meant by "the mind" in this context, and proceeds to consider the senses in which minds can be "changed". The kind of change supposed to be caused by computers is called "mindchange" to distinguish it from other types of mental change.

In an attempt to give clear substance to the idea of mindchange, cases in which similar claims have been made are brought into consideration. Such cases include the invention of speech, writing, and printed text; technology associated with the measurement of time, and industrial production; and the effects upon mind caused by the use of time-based media such as film and television. The purpose of examining cases of non-computational mindchange is to assemble information about the kinds of mindchange which are alleged to occur, and to review the methodology and evidence which can be used to support such claims.

Technological changes which are at least as dramatic and widespread as the introduction of computers and which are already historically complete, have effects on the human mind conceded to be subtle and subjective in character even by those who believe in them most fervently. It is concluded that there are serious logical and methodological difficulties associated with the idea of mindchange, and thus with the assertion that it occurs:

1. learning, mindchange must be shown to have some exotic, but so far unspecified property if it is to avoid triviality. In particular, it does not seem that mindchange can be coherently interpreted as a causal process

---

[1] This paper arose from a discussion with one of the *Cognitive Technology* volume editors [BG] who noted the widespread belief that extensive use of computer technology can affect human cognition, and suggested that I explore possible methods of testing its truth.

2. While mindchange is of little interest unless it is qualitative and general in its effects, it is unclear how technology which requires a mind changed in this sense, could ever be invented.

3. While mindchange can only be adequately investigated by examining technological changes which are now complete, the mindchange hypothesis seems to imply that mindstates prior to mindchange are not accessible to post-mindchange minds

4. While Literacy Technology seems to provide the best example of a radical innovation in cognitive technology which is now complete, the historical record suggests that post-technology cognitions always remain compatible with pre-literate cognitions.

It is concluded that it is difficult to give a clear interpretation to the idea of mindchange which is both of empirical interest and free of contradiction. Insofar as this can be achieved, there appears to be no evidence that mindchange is associated with computer technology, and the evidence from the introduction of literacy technology suggests that mindchange did not occur.

COGNITIVE PANIC

Nothing is more mutable than mind. Cognitive systems *essentially* model those processes in the world around them which they need to predict. They must accordingly be flexible enough to have their own parameters driven by external change. Language is the transmission of symbol-strings intended to change the mental states of other people. Perception is a process by which physical energy changes mental parameters. The principles of learning are the principles by which minds can be changed. Decision-making is the art or science of allowing accumulated evidence to change a mental judgement, or of preventing it from doing so. Scientific understanding, social cognition, language, perception, learning, decision-making; the idea, and the mechanisms, of mental change are central to all. "Education", "advertising", "propaganda", "psychotherapy", these are the labels we use for technologies developed to change minds. They differ according to whether we value the change produced, and how focused the consequential change is, but all presuppose that mind can be manipulated by external agents who employ appropriate techniques.

In spite of the fact that change is intrinsic to the idea of mind, and that substantial social institutions and huge industries exist with no other object than to bring mental change about, occasionally a wave of cognitive panic is associated with the suspicion that particular kinds of mental change might occur. I use the term "cognitive panic" deliberately to imply a parallel with the "moral panics" which periodically arise concerning football hooliganism or one-parent families (Cohen, 1972). To give examples of cognitive panics: in the 1950s pressure grew for legislation to ban "subliminal advertising" because there was evidence that rapidly presented visual messages embedded in films for example, could influence behaviour without conscious awareness that the message had been received. No one by contrast is concerned that the same message writ large in neon, produces a much greater effect. In the latter case, it is reasoned: message recipients have choice. As message recipients do not believe that their behaviour is affected by the generic injunctions of advertising, the difference between cases is in truth somewhat subtle. In the late 19th century there was serious concern that the development of a mass market for popular novels would produce a qualitative and irreversible transformation in the minds of Victorian youth. The same fear often expressed in almost the same terms, has been expressed in connection first with television, then with videotapes, and most recently with computer games.

An immediate and tempting response to the panicky asseveration that minds might be changed by the fruits of technology is that no mere possibility is involved here, but certainty rather. Information technology changes minds; but then, so does virtually everything else. If exposure to Victorian novels did indeed bring about the feared transformation, it would seem that subsequent generations think themselves no worse for it, and indeed from their new cognitive baseline, resist further changes in exactly the manner of their ancestors. Changed minds can mean changed value systems, and the ancestral form of mind has no way of divining what judgements mutated mindforms will apply to the novel cognitive characteristics they themselves so dread. Can cognitive panic then be dismissed as such, and rational observers content themselves that technology driven changes in mind are differentiated from other such changes only by their source? Or gain comfort from the thought that cognitive relativity logically precludes change from producing any outcome which is absolutely worse?

Things are not quite so simple. Physical technology which changes what it is possible for people to do must also change what it is possible for people to think and plan, if only because thinking and planning are the manipulation of symbolically represented actions (Lindsay, 1996; Weizenbaum, 1976). Cognitive technology has at least the same properties, so that technology in general changes minds in at least one sense which differentiates it from other classes of change agent. Lindsay (1996) has called this technology-driven cognitive empowerment "cognitive prosthetics". Apart from envy however, it is hard to see what legitimate objection parents might have to their children being less blinkered or more mentally able than themselves.

A second possibility refocuses attention on values. A popular idea from anthropology's past is the notion of "modal personality". (Inkeles and Levinson, 1968). According to this view, child-rearing practices, personal values, and social interaction patterns differ across cultures. Consequently, though all cultures are compatible with a wide range of personality types, the average or "modal" personality is not the same in one culture as it is in another. While in one society a gloomy, depressive outlook might be normal; in another paranoid suspicion of people's motives and intentions can prevail; in a third an anxious and neurotic attitude to every choice; and in a fourth an easy-going extrovert love of fun and festivity. If personality is even partly environmentally induced, and if technology can change the external and ideational environment, then in principle at least, technology can change the modal personality of a culture. In some ways the idea of a technologically driven modal personality change comes closest to explaining the cognitive panic associated with the fear that videos or computers might change people's minds. It is no less than reasonable to be concerned if, as a result of playing *Doom* children no longer love or respect their parents; or more extremely, become affectionless psychopaths, willing to kill for the price of the latest game CD.

In fact, personality change is perhaps the least plausible reason for fearing technology as a change agent. Partly this is because people do not show any similar fear of those factors which undeniably do produce dramatic changes in personality, for example: religion, intimate relationships and alcohol. Partly it is because the characteristic personality traits attributed to avid novel readers and "techno-nerds" are quite the opposite of those which might legitimately scare granny (look for these rather, in the nearest bar or rugby football club). Most substantially of all, there do not seem to be inexplicable discontinuities in the transmission of human personality within our culture. If anything, it is the continuity in personality which is remarkable. We do not read poems and plays written a century or two ago and fail to understand the motivations of characters because technology has driven a wedge between them and us. This is what would be expected if technology periodically precipitated sea changes in human personality.

It seems doubtful whether cognitive panic can be coherently related to any systematic changes in the human mind. Possibly it arises from a puritanical fear that every technological boon has a hidden Faustian cost. Or more cynically, from the fact that while novel technoforms remain mysterious to many, rumour of risk both thrives on uncertainty and sells newspapers. Perhaps people inclined towards technophobia or poor at the skills demanded by the new technology, are only too ready to lend a credulous ear to tales that those who traffic with the novel artifacts will inherit loss and damage as their reward. Most prosaically, it is possible that panic settles at random, now on *Listeria* in cheese, now on *Salmonella* in eggs, now on radiation from power lines and now on computer games. Whatever the true cause might be, it seems more sensible to seek an explanation for fear of cognitive damage in the sociology of crowd or media behaviour than on the assumption that wherever there is the smoke of panic, there must be the fire of legitimate grounds.

I shall assume from here onwards, that computers like everything else, are constant causes of mental change in human beings in the usual senses of the terms involved. I shall also assume that technological innovation necessarily produces kinds of mental change which most other features of the environment do not, but that this is not *per se* a cause of concern. The invention of firearms makes possible the planning of an assassination from a long distance, but it is not the possibility of the plan which alarms, but the possibility of the act. Cognitive panic, while a phenomenon of interest in itself, seems to have no coherent or plausible basis, and if anything its interest lies largely in that very fact.

MINDCHANGE

All these things said and granted, the idea persists that some large-scale technological changes produce qualitative shifts in human cognition which are substantial in magnitude, general in their effects and hard or impossible to reverse. The alleged causes of such change have been various. To name but a few: the introduction of writing, printing, or clocks; the industrial revolution or the urbanisation of society; film, television or video, and most recently computers. This idea that technology can initiate some certainly unique and possibly malign mental transformation I shall call, to distinguish it from the less coherent variants dismissed already, the doctrine of "mindchange". Using this terminology, the questions addressed by the present paper are three: 1) 'Is the suggestion that mindchange occurs coherent?'; closely related as every logical positivist will agree is the question: 2) 'By what methodology can the mindchange hypothesis be examined?'; and supposing that some positive answer can be found for these two, the third: 3) 'Does mindchange occur?'

Though the question 'does mindchange occur?' sounds innocent and univocal enough' in fact it has many readings and makes many under-determined presuppositions. Consider the following set of associated questions and issues

1.   Does change in our information processing operations count as mindchange?
2.   Does change in our information processing capabilities count as mindchange?
3.   Does cognitive prosthetics (i.e. the use of technology to change what can be intellectually achieved. See Weizenbaum, 1976; Lindsay, 1996) count as mindchange?
4.   Must mindchange be permanent and irreversible?
5.   Must change in information processing capabilities be qualitative in order to count as mindchange?
6.   Does mindchange imply brainchange? [Readers reacting sceptically might consider this viewpoint: 'The brain changes experience, but what is ignored by many is that experience also changes our brain. While our mental experience can be boosted by drugs, there is also evidence that what we do can cause beneficial changes in the brain'. (Robertson, 1996)].
7.   Can mindchange include changes in "consciousness?
8.   Can mindchange occur with no detectable brainchange and no information processing differences (i.e. changes in consciousness only)?
9.   Can mindchange consist only in affect changes (i.e. in emotional reaction)?

There are simply too many hares here to chase. There is no alternative but to seek to structure the issues in a manner which will capture most of them within a systematic framework, while acknowledging that in so doing, some will be neglected or lost. I begin this process by considering how interpretations of mindchange relate to influential theories of mind.

MODELS OF MIND

The model of mind which has been most influential in western thought is that associated with Cartesian dualism. According to this model, material bodies exist in space, have physical dimensions and are subject to causal interactions. Immaterial minds are temporally, but not spatially located, are dimensionless, and are a-causal. Trivially, mindchange is incompatible with the model. If minds are not exposed to causal influences of any sort, computers cannot cause them to change. In psychology, and for most philosophers, Cartesian dualism was seen off by behaviourism during the first two or three decades of the present century. For behaviourists, the idea of mindchange could be dealt with summarily: no minds and so no mindchange. There is nothing except learning. Learning which systematically produces negative consequences will sooner or later be selected out of an organism's behavioural repertoire. In the behaviourist's universe mindchange does not exist and behaviour change which has undesirable consequences is likely to be reversed. This simultaneously bleak but optimistic picture was in turn fractured beyond repair by the emergence of the information-processing approach to mind which emerged from the mid-1950s onwards, becoming the dominant theoretical approach in Psychology during the 1960s.

Gilbert Ryle's resonant image of the "ghost in the machine" (Ryle, 1949) crystallised in a phrase the anti-mentalist epistemology of Behaviourism. But with the rebirth of mentalism as part of the "cognitive revolution", one or two of the difficulties associated with industrial parapsychology also seem to reassert themselves. If there is after all a ghost in the cerebral machinery, how do you tell if it changes its spots? Are its properties fixed and constant, or does it change like a stormy sky, or move through stages like a butterfly or frog?

The conventional answer to such conundrums probably runs along these lines. The old-fashioned view of mind was that it is a type of "thing", a class of existing objects. Things are characterised by their properties, and anything they do, they do because their properties are what they are. For example, lungs are a type of thing, and their amusing propensity to inflate and deflate while alternately taking in oxygen and discharging carbon dioxide, arises from the properties of their associated musculature, tissue characteristics and component chemical compounds. The mind by contrast is not a thing. It is an abstract expression referring to the properties and potentialities of a complex and flexible set of processes occurring within an equally complex framework of biological structures. This thoroughly modern answer reminds us that referring expressions do not have to refer to objects, and that developments in Psychology and Biology have made us aware of layer upon layer of complexity associated with the human central nervous system and its functions. It does not however, avoid the original question. Christmas and UK universities are also sets of complex processes occurring in association with elaborate structures. But Christmas changed in England when Prince Albert introduced the Christmas tree from northern Europe; and UK universities have changed as a line-management system of decision-making has replaced collegial procedures. (I shall resist pursuing the thought that this latter change has any other connection with mind than a crudely analogous complexity. Those of weaker resolve might be tempted to note an attendant transition from possession to loss).

Though there is no close consensus on matters of detail, most cognitive or information processing theories of mind probably agree about the broad framework involved: hardware, wetware, firmware, software and data. A little more elaborately, minds require:

1. A fixed physical substrate, illustrated by the genetically fixed characteristics of the central nervous system in humans (hardware)
2. A set of physical processes operating within the physical substrate, illustrated by tissue growth and the chemical reactions underlying nervous transmission in humans (wetware)
3. A cognitive architecture which maps a symbolic control structure onto hardware and wetware, illustrated by the relationship between working memory and semantic memory in humans (firmware)
4. A set of control processes which produce determinate behavioural outcomes when activated, illustrated by the routines developed to control performance in a skilled driver or musician (software)
5. A body of data stored in memory or accessible via sensory systems which enable the parameters of control processes to be set and maintained within acceptable limits (data)

If these components are taken as a crude specification of the lineaments of mind, which of them might be expected to change if mindchange occurs? Which components might be expected to, or even could possibly, be changed by exposure to technological novelty?

Genetically fixed hardware can be ruled out right away, as can the biochemistry of wetware. It is remotely possible that these fundamental structures and operations could be affected by technology, perhaps by radiation leakage or chemical contamination. Such effects would not be confined to novels or computers however, but would be equally caused by other classes of artifact from the same physical technology: source: Mrs. Beeton's *Book of Household Management* (printing) and hi-fi systems (electronics). The essence of the mindchange hypothesis is that it is the cognitive content of technology which causes the alleged problem, not the characteristics of the envelope in which it is delivered.

It is rather more credible that cognitive architecture could be modified by intensive interaction with novel technological artefacts extending over lengthy periods of an individual's life and particularly if interactions were heavy during childhood years, when the architecture is presumably established. Evidence that the cognitive architecture is modifiable comes in a variety of forms. At the level of plausibility arguments: if the environment changes so that a given architecture becomes sub-optimal (as the mindchange hypothesis requires if it is to explain why change in the architecture occurs!), it would be an uncharacteristic oversight on the part of the evolutionary process to have so arranged matters that adaptation cannot occur. It is also true that the relationship between hardware and architecture familiar from work in AI is a one-to-many mapping. It is possible, but unlikely that a different relationship is characteristic of biological systems.

In terms of empirical evidence, findings from developmental psychology suggest for example that the characteristics of working memory change with age and experience (Bryant, 1974; Hunter, 1964). Findings have also been reported which suggest that the use of different types of coding process and memory store, underlying employment of visual versus verbal representations, is conditioned by external demand in the form of environmental or task requirements (Paivio, 1972). Differences between individual adults, particularly at the extremes of performance reinforce this picture. Adults who perform well below normal levels in information processing tasks, and performers of exceptional ability often seem to use cognitive strategies which differ considerably from those employed by most of us. Luria (1973) has even documented in some detail the case history of an individual who seems to have re-organised his cognitive architecture in early adulthood when he became the victim of severe brain damage as a result of penetrating missile wounds.

Finally, cross-cultural studies have rarely confirmed models of human cognitive architecture based on data from western subjects. Given the developmental evidence this is hardly surprising. In western educational systems, knowledge is delivered (teaching) and retrieved (assessment) almost exclusively in a verbal mode. This must substantially bias the pattern of demand made upon different representation forms and memory stores. If, as is widely believed, verbal information processing is hemispherically lateralised, (visual coding in the right cerebral hemisphere, verbal coding in the left etc.) the verbal bias in knowledge delivery and representation could even affect macroscopic patterns of brain organisation and use. In many pre-literate rural cultures, visual information is much more important than in western urban societies. Visually presented verbal information is virtually non-existent. This can mean that fundamental features of data used to infer western cognitive architecture, such as semantic organisation of categorised lists in free recall, may be completely absent when subjects from non-western cultures are used (Cole, Gay, Glick and Sharp, 1974). Evidence also exists that bilinguals may organise information in memory in a manner which is substantially different from that observed in monolinguals.

From the perspective of the mindchange advocate, the catch-22 is that the very evidence which shows that cognitive architecture is probably modifiable, also shows that variation in the organisation of cognitive architecture is perfectly normal. If prolonged human computer interaction caused the development of a non-standard cognitive architecture, this would not of itself constitute mindchange, as there is almost certainly a considerable degree of architectural variation in the normal population. Nor would it be a matter of concern that the particular form of the variation was unique or unusual if it was simply a functional adaptation to a novel pattern of ecological demand. For mindchange of this kind to generate alarm, it would need to have some other property. It would be quixotic in the extreme to fear that as a result of extensive interaction with computers, you or I are coming to organise our mental structures and operations in a fashion which is more effective for interacting with computers. What kind of novel and supplementary property, whose effects extend beyond functional adaptation, could give rise to justifiable concern?

Suppose that the cognitive architecture which was optimal for interacting with computers was sub-optimal for, or even incompatible with, effective interaction with other people. Wouldn't adaptation to computers then reduce our social competence? What if interaction with computers taught us to disregard feelings and emotion, because computers don't have them. Might we then not come to ignore mother's cries and anguish as we approach her with the axe, because we have learned to treat feelings as matters of no significance?

If this scenario was a likely one, then evolution would presumably have its long-term say. Emotionally inept computer nerds would fail to win partners and reproduce; would languish in prison because of casual matricide and would become victims of many other selective pressures. But it isn't even remotely plausible. For one thing the procedures for modelling and understanding feelings are established pretty early on in life, well before most people interact with PCs. For another, social and sexual motivations are likely to be very hard to override, just because of their intimate connection with reproductive behaviour. Then again, why should people become socially inept because they spend more time interacting with complex electronic systems? Social interaction involves complex modelling, presumably the very skill being practised in using complex computer programmes. It would perhaps be more reasonable to worry about the gardener, spending days and weeks interacting with passive inanimate plants, becoming used to wielding the scythe and axe. Isn't this where the real danger would lie? There are other relevant considerations also: as philosophers interested in the "other minds" problem have emphasised, we never directly experience the emotions and experiences of other people but attribute to them a mental life akin to our own because we recognise them as agents of the same kind. Computers are not agents of the same kind. So fearing that we will cease to treat people appropriately because we write articles on the word processor, is a bit like worrying that we might try to peel the cat because we spend a few hours a week preparing carrots and parsnips for a casserole. Anyway: the primary assumption itself is suspect: interaction with people sensitises while interaction with inanimate systems brutalises. No need to worry then about prison warders, or concentration camp guards. It's just the AI researcher and the payroll clerk who are at risk.

As we move from relatively fixed aspects of mental structure, to variable processes and data, we also move from aspects of mind which we expect to remain fixed, at least in the short-term, and in particular individuals, to aspects in which change is the normal case. Of course control processes determining behavioural outcomes change when we interact with computers, but this is just to say we learn to use them more skilfully. Of course the data we process changes from moment to moment as we watch the computer screen; but this just means that we see and understand what we are doing. This type of change is simply the kind of change which accompanies normal learning and perception. It begins to look as if, though technological artefacts can change our minds in a variety of ways in which it is quite natural for minds to change, there is no mechanism for mindchange itself, that profound, irreversible, and general change which some have feared accompanies the dissemination and extensive use of new technology.

A-CAUSAL ASPECTS OF MIND

Up to this point, we have made the assumption that if computer technology produces mindchange it does so as a cause-and-effect process, with computer technology as the cause and mindchange as the effect. However, analysis of the physical basis of mind and the types of causal interaction which can affect it seems to rule this approach out. If computer technology causes mindchange, then either it does so by affecting brain tissue through radiation or chemical pollution or it alters "mental software". In the former case, mindchange is not intrinsically caused by computer technology, but by the physical characteristics of the screens or other subsystems used to implement it. On the other hand to say that computer technology causally affects mental software is to say no more than that perception and learning are involved in its use. While the *content* of perception and learning may damage people, for example if they become exposed to pernicious propaganda or unwholesome pornography, this is not a causal consequence of the technology *per se* and at best is an argument for greater censorship or control, not for neo-Luddism.

Can it be concluded that if mindchange is not a causal process then it does not occur? There is one other possibility worth exploring which arises because both computer technology and human minds are cognitive systems. Humans plan and solve problems by using mental processes which resemble computation. It seems almost certain that some types of mental computation use systems of symbolic representation such as "mental models" (Johnson-Laird, 1983; 1993). The relationship between the mental model used by a problem-solver, and the system it is intended to model is not a causal relationship, and yet the features of the model, and the pattern of resemblances between the model and what is modelled are crucial determinants of problem-solving and planning effectiveness. Many psychological studies show that problems can be made easy, or well-nigh impossible to solve by changing the way in which they are mentally represented: the so-called "structural isomorphism" problem (Kotovsky, Hayes and Simon, 1985; Reed, 1987). Is it possible that interaction with new technoforms, such as computers in our own time, changes the way in which we represent the world, or the range of representations available? And could changes in representational capability produce mindchange?

Let us examine the possibility first. There is a great deal of evidence from the history of science which suggests that new symbolic models are commonly developed and productively applied to new phenomena. Neils Bohr's model of the atom supposed that electrons orbited the nucleus as planets circle the sun, thus applying the "novel" Copernican model of the solar system. Most recent developments in physics have used mathematical models which themselves are Twentieth Century inventions. Closer to home, many types of formal logic have been used to model aspects of human cognition or computer behaviour in AI research, most of them developed since 1850. The "computer model" of the human mind itself, which still forms the conceptual bedrock of cognitive psychology, became available only after the Second World War. Crudely, scientific explanation works like this: a body of unexplained phenomena is either brought within the domain of science by showing that it can be modelled using some already-familiar symbolic apparatus, or by "custom-building" a new one. Once researchers become accustomed to the new system it too becomes part of an expanded repertoire available for future applications.

There is no reason to doubt that novel technology can provide new mental models which allow already representable phenomena to be represented in different ways, and previously unrepresentable phenomena to be represented for the first time. There may be more doubt, attached both to the question of whether changes in representational format repertoire (**RFR**) can produce mindchange, and to the question of whether **RFR** changes have any special connection with technology. If mindchange is produced by change in **RFR** might it not arise from the geometry of Euclid, or the syllogistic of Aristotle; the analyses of Macchiavelli or the plays of Shakespeare? When the human repertoire of "ways of seeing things", of mental models, is expanded by creative developments in the humanities, the fact is universally applauded as positive, beneficial, and humane. Why should new models from another source be greeted with concern and suspicion?

Though loose ends hang free on all sides, I intend to set matters of theoretical interpretation aside at this point simply because I doubt that a stronger framework which could prune their number can be justified by evidence. The main conclusions which I think can be drawn from discussion up to now are these: if mindchange occurs then it does not result from physiologically or biologically unusual structures or events, nor from the *form* of operations or processes at the information processing level. If it occurs, then it occurs because of changes in the *content* of information processing operations, which can be best characterised as changes in the **RFR**. Mindchange, if it is to be differentiated from other and everyday kinds mental adaptation, must have at least the following distinguishing features:

1. Qualitative in form
2. Content dependent
3. Not readily reversible
4. Relatively general in its effects (no-one will worry if even a radical mental modification only affects performance under narrow and extraordinary circumstances)

I shall leave hanging the issue of whether technological change is for any reason particularly liable to produce such changes, my own inclination is to think not but I do hold this belief with such fervour that I wish to bear the reader with me unwillingly. I am prepared to be so cavalier with issues of no little substance, because I think that yet weightier matters are to hand, and that in dealing with them, perspectives may shift on issues which now seem troublesome. Let us turn then to methodology.

METHODOLOGY AND MINDCHANGE

A search for needles amongst hay is at its most challenging when needles cannot be distinguished from snarks. Indeed if a seeker is truly ignorant of the nature of the sought it is unclear that "search" is an appropriate term for whatever is occurring. A method of detecting mindchange accordingly presupposes some prior idea of what mindchange is. I have tried to develop a theoretical framework within which such ideas can be formulated in earlier sections of this paper. Negative conclusions loom more definite than their positive counterparts:

1. It is pointless to look for anatomical or biological correlates as it is highly unlikely that underlying brain processes are in any way physically distinctive
2. It is equally unlikely that mindchange is associated with unique modifications in cognitive architecture.
3. Changes in cognitive operations within a relatively standard cognitive architecture and mediated by standard brain processes are accommodated by normal processes of perception and learning and are therefore unlikely to be identifiable via their form.

The broad positive implication of this analysis is that if mindchange exists, the most plausible way of identifying it is via content. What this means quite bluntly, is that mindchange is most likely to result from a change in the way in which objects or events are represented, or as a change of the manner in which operations arc applied to mental representations. There are two ways in which changes of this kind might manifest themselves: changes in consciousness (or in the way in which the world is subjectively apprehended), and changes in behavioural outcome (or changes in observable performance). Both are attended by chronic methodological difficulties. While changes in consciousness are never directly accessible to external scrutiny; neither do changes in behavioural product commonly allow the mechanisms of their production to be unambiguously inferred.

The fact that consciousness is not observable does not entirely remove the possibility of evidence from that source. Subjective accounts might exist in which the fact that mindchange has occurred is reported, or its nature described. Helen Keller's moving account of her discovery of the possibility of linguistic representation, when as a blind and deaf child she was first taught the tactile sign for the sensation of cold water, is a case in point. Similar descriptions exist from adult illiterates, as they come to make sense of the hitherto uninterpretable world of writing. The same kind of reports do not seem to exist for computer skills. It is instead common to find accounts of an arduous induction into a formalist and if anything unnatural mode of cognition, the potential of which is only slowly and progressively discovered. This is rather closer to the model of acquiring a skill such as driving or typing, than to achieving a qualitative shift in mode of representation. The absence of thrilled and breathless reports of dramatic subjective change accompanying early exposure to the PC proves nothing; but like the silent dog in the night it suggests a great deal. It might be rejoined that excited reports of consciousnesses radically transformed by computer use do not occur because while other cognitive changes are perceived as positive, effects of computer technology are malign. First person lamentations do not seem to occur either however, nor litigation for damages against employers. It is a conspicuous feature of mindchange attribution that it is invariably claimed to affect not the claimant, but others more susceptible. This does nothing to enhance its plausibility.

There are incidentally, a number of conceptual worries buzzing like flies around the idea of mindchange. Let us call the mindstate (**MS**) which precedes mindchange **MS1** and the post-mindchange state **MS2** for the purpose of describing them. We have until now supposed that mindchange might consist simply in a supplementation of the cognitive repertoire, a new addition to the tool kit, a broadening of the range of representation modes. This is actually rather too anodyne to fill the bill, and as we saw in section **4.** turns the idea of mindchange from a source of concern to a welcome and liberalising experience, akin to the effect of literature or drama. If the user can choose whether to use the **MS2** representational scheme, or can learn that it is appropriate for some problem-solving contexts but not others, then mindchange becomes no more alarming than any other learning experience. The negative content attributed to mindchange requires that **MS1** is qualitatively different from **MS2**, *and that the difference is irreversible*, or at the very least not under voluntary control. Another way of expressing this is that **MS2** must be incompatible with **MS1**.

The conceptual difficulties now begin to emerge. Mindchange assumes that the **MS1** - **MS2** shift is induced by technological change. The originator of the technology which induces mindchange must presumably have been in **MS1** when the invention was conceived. It seems to follow either that the conception of the technology and some of its uses is possible without **MS2**, or that **MS2** is possible without the technological catalyst. Interestingly enough, something like this idea has been proposed by academic researchers seeking to explain the phenomena of technological change. Constant (1984) for example makes the following claim:

> "In the case of both firms and individuals, community practice defines a cognitive universe that inhibits recognition of radical alternatives to conventional practice. When abrupt transitions in technological practice do occur, as happens from time to time, they are almost always the work of people outside, or at least on the margins of, the conventional community."
>
> (Constant, 1984: 30)

According to Constant's theoretical analysis, **MS** constrains or determines how problems are solved, and is itself constrained or determined by "community practice". On this analysis, mindchange is caused by a prior change in community practice. Community practice is in turn seen as operating like a Kuhnian scientific paradigm (Kuhn, 1962), that is to say as dictating the framework within which events are perceived and actions planned, resisting falsification but accumulating anomalies and counter-examples etc., until catastrophically replaced by a new paradigm. Constant can now account for cognitive immunity from the current technological paradigm by allowing some individuals to operate outside the cognitive community: "on the margins". The price Constant pays for this get-out clause is that in order to explain how community practice can change, (via mindchange in cognitively marginal individuals), Constant has to allow that **MS** is a predisposing rather than a determining factor. Community practice is thus like a plague transmission vector: it can account for the distribution and spread of cognitive change, but not for its occurrence. Translated into the conceptual currency of our present debate, Constant's viewpoint might suggest that technology capable of inducing mindchange (from **MS1** to **MS2**) is generated by individuals whose minds are in **MS2** all along. In the end this is not a satisfactory solution. It explains **MS1** by cognitive pressure from the community, only to admit that **MS2** might have some other cause. If **MS2** then why not **MS1**? It also suggests that all mindstates which might be induced by future technology are already present in the community though perhaps with low frequency. Where on earth did they come from? At the very least some further cause which determines the initial distribution of mindstates is required by Constant's model. To enable this problem to be conveniently referred to let us call it the "Source Problematicity" problem.

The "Constant Gambit" of shifting the causal determinants of **MS** outside the individual and into the community is at first sight attractive. Certainly it appears to side-step the difficulties associated with locating plausible mechanisms by which cognitive change having substantially more inertia than conventional learning can be brought about, either within or outside the mechanisms of normal learning. Unfortunately, the problems are pushed back a stage rather than being solved, as community practices must arise from, and be mediated by individual cognitive systems.

In addition to the problem of how technologically induced mindchange can arise, there is also a parallel problem of understanding when it has occurred in the past. How can someone in **MS2** understand the mindstate of someone in **MS1**? This problem we will call the problem of "Projective Opacity". It is a particularly vexing difficulty in historical contexts because the doctrine of mindchange requires the abandonment of the methodological principle that the past can be understood entirely in terms of principles and mechanisms discoverable from the study of the present. This is the foundation stone of almost all historical enquiry. The projective opacity problem has been noted for example in connection with the historical change from non-literate to literate culture in mediaeval Europe:

> "Literacy is unique among technologies in penetrating and structuring the intellect itself, which makes it hard for scholars, whose own skills are shaped by literacy, to reconstruct the mental changes which it brings about."
>
> (Clanchy, 1979: 149)

The uniqueness claim at the beginning of this quotation is obviously false if changes induced by computer technology may have the same character. In principle any cognitive technology can raise similar problems; it is merely a historical accident that for quite a few centuries the introduction of non-electronic text-technology was the only technological change which was both cognitive and left physical traces. If the advent of literacy did indeed induce mindchange, then it must be somewhere between possible and likely that the development of speech, perhaps the first intrinsically cognitive technology, did so as well. In the case of speech, neither first hand accounts of the impact of such changes as occurred, nor interpretable effects of modified behaviour, can be expected to have survived. It is possible that in the post-speech mindstate, feats of co-operative planning (farming; earthwork and stone circle construction, for example) became possible which could not have occurred in the mindstate which preceded speech. Without an independent index mark demarcating the **MS1/MS2** boundary such speculations must remain idle. There is far more room for optimism however, with respect to those historical innovations in cognitive technology which do leave definite traces of their arrival. In these cases there is a real prospect of discovering correlated changes in human performance or achievement.

MINDCHANGE AND COGNITIVE TECHNO-HISTORY

When we began to investigate the idea of mindchange induced by computer technology, we noted that a related but somewhat more vulgar and insubstantial phenomena, which we labelled "cognitive panic", had arisen in connection with other novel technoforms such as printed literature, television, and computer games. While we concluded that cognitive panic was baseless, it was admitted as a possibility that some kind of technologically driven, qualitative change in the content of cognition might occur. Though there is no recognised body of first-hand evidence that this kind of cognitive transformation is associated with computer usage, it was noted that accounts of the subjective impact of other kinds of cognitive change such as linguistic signing, and literacy acquisition, do exist.

Interpretation of behavioural evidence for computer induced mindchange is also problematic. This is partly because of the recency of the technology, which makes it difficult to know whether any change which is under way is just beginning, in full spate, or is fully completed. The latter seems unlikely, if only because a hefty proportion of the population has still avoided direct exposure to computers. More serious is the following problem. The availability of computers is bound to cause differences in the way people solve problems: after all, that is what tempts people to use them. So how can changes in performance caused by mere employment of computer technology be differentiated from any changes in performance caused by mindchange resulting from computer use? Superficially, the problem seems easy to solve - establish how a sample of computer users solved problems in some domain before computers were available. Then ask them to solve test problems from the same domain, without using computers, but after they have become experienced computer users. Suppose contemporary subjects solve problems differently from people in the pre-computer era. Is this mindchange, or just new organisational or analytic habits? This same question persists even if we test people on problems they haven't worked on with computers. Experience of using a word processor might change the way I go about composing a sonnet, even if I have never composed a sonnet using a word processor. If these are not difficulties enough, consider what tasks should be used to seek evidence of mindchange if we do elect to examine behaviour not directly "contaminated" by computer use. Without a clear idea of the cognitive changes involved, how is it possible to predict what behaviours it might be expected to affect?

Two conclusions might be drawn from this discouraging collection of considerations. One is that given the intellectual obstacles to establishing satisfactory evidence for mindchange, it is unlikely that those who believe that it occurs have adequate, or indeed any satisfactory grounds for their belief. The second, closely related conclusion is that if mindchange can be proven to occur, it is unlikely that this can be done at the present time with respect to mindchange induced by computer usage.

A more positive line of thought is this. We have noted several times that computers are not the only type of cognitive artefacts to which humans have been exposed, there is a substantial series of others running from the discovery of speech to the invention of video-recorders. If there is satisfactory evidence for mindchange, it is more likely to be in connection with a past and completed cognitive transformation than one which is still in progress. It is also encouraging that the features which might be expected to characterise mindchange: qualitative nature, resistance to reversal, generality of effects, problematicity of cognitive source, and projective opacity, have also been claimed to be associated with non-computational technological change.

The methodological strategy which seems most appropriate in the light of discussion so far seems to be this. Locate an example of major, and now-complete technological changes which have occurred in the past, and which have possessed a definite cognitive dimension. Seek evidence that mindchange has occurred in connection with these types of technology. Examine the evidence so as to establish:

1. Its adequacy as an existence proof for mindchange in general (and)
2. A model to predict the effects of computer-induced mindchange in particular.

Let us begin by reviewing the possibilities. These appear to be plausible candidates:

1. Spoken language
2. Written script
3. Monotheistic religion
4. Time measurement
5. Printing
6. The industrial revolution
7. Film, TV, Video

Though their social and cognitive impact was undoubtedly profound, both Spoken language (1) and Monotheistic religion (3) occurred so far back in time, and leave such sparse and unreliable traces that they must be set aside. Each of the other changes in cognitive technology has a case to be made for it. A case in point is Time measurement (4). Lewis Mumford and Joseph Weizenbaum have both drawn attention to the far-reaching consequences of the technology associated with time measurement, originally the monastery clock:

"The instrument presently spread outside the monastery; and the regular striking of the bells brought a new regularity into the life of the workman and the merchant. The bells of the clock tower almost defined urban existence. Time-keeping passed into time-serving and time-accounting and time-rationing. As this took place, eternity ceased gradually to serve as the measure and focus of human actions...[The clock] dissociated time from human events and helped create the belief in an independent world of mathematically measurable sequences: the special world of science"   (Mumford 1963: 14-15)

"The clock had created literally a new reality....the trick man turned that prepared the scene for the rise of modern science was nothing less than the transformation of nature and of his perception of reality....this newly created reality.... rests on a rejection of those direct experiences that formed the basis for, and indeed constituted, the old reality. The feeling of hunger was rejected as a stimulus for eating; instead one ate when an abstract model had achieved a certain state, i.e., when the hands of a clock pointed to certain marks on the clock's face"   (Weizenbaum 1976: 25)

If magnitude of effect was the only selection criterion in play, it would be hard to pass over time as a suitable case study in cognitive technology and its consequences. There are other considerations which make it less suitable however. It is characteristic of technology that its effective cultural transfer mode is person to person. (Laudan, 1984). Even contemporary technology like computer systems is most effectively disseminated by demonstration, not for example by manuals and handbooks. This means that much of the relevant evidence concerning the physical aspects of time measurement technology, and most of the evidence concerning who was affected is unavailable. "Irrecoverability" is a frustrating but near-universal feature of technohistory (how was Stonehenge erected? how were the Egyptian Pyramids built? How did the Moors make Damascus steel? etc.). It arises from the extent to which technological knowledge is maintained as craft lore by a specialist group, by the fact that skills and techniques cannot readily be expressed in, or acquired from text, and from the fact that the model or diagram is more commonly the preferred way of supplementing linguistic understanding than written text. The consequence is that technoforms which are both ancient and highly complex are not ideal for our present purpose.

The Gutenburg Press (5. Printing) is often claimed to be the wellspring of much of modern thought, and the direct cause of universal literacy and education in the West. Certainly the technological revolution it initiated had massive cultural consequences in terms of:

> "The flood of cheap literature which, like the modern Babylon itself, no living man has ever been able to traverse, which has sprung up and continues to spring up, with the mysterious fecundity of certain fungi, and which cannot be accounted for in its volume, variety, and universality by any ordinary laws of production."   (Author unknown, 1859. Cited in Anderson 1991:1)

It is also fortuitous that of necessity, printed text leaves a record of its own cognitive content. Is printing technology not an ideal testbed for mindchange hypotheses? There are two reasons to be doubtful, the first is that it is questionable whether printing *per se* is likely to induce any cognitive change which is not caused by forms of script-based text which already existed. The second is that though printing technology may have massively increased the resources available to the already literate, it is sometimes questioned whether it greatly expanded their number. Anderson (1991) for example argues both that it was only with the dissemination of printed visual images in Victorian times that true mass communication was achieved:

> "In the early and mid-nineteenth century the printed image more than the word itself represented a cultural break with the past, for it demanded neither formal education nor even basic literacy. The new inexpensive printed image thus became the first medium of regular, ongoing, mass communication."
> (Anderson, 1991: 3)

More surprisingly, Anderson also believes that such mass audiences were achieved only by producing content which was accessible without dramatic cognitive adjustments on the part of the readers:

> "The appeal of the new pictorial magazines derived as much from the readers' long-held social, moral, and aesthetic values as it did from the efforts and ideologies of publishers, editors, writers and artists. Moreover other kinds of popular imagery, expressing radical consciousness or alternative taste, survived or developed concurrently......Thus the emergence of a formative mass culture - at least in its visual forms - was not a process of wholesale repression or replacement."
> (Anderson, 1991: 4)

The Industrial Revolution (6.) is perhaps most frequently cited as the midwife of contemporary forms of consciousness and sensibility. Unfortunately it is not one technological change but a myriad such changes, all bound up with changes in social and political organisation. While there is no denying the momentousness of the historical phenomena, nor the crucial role of technology in producing them, nor yet the fact that cognitive change was a probable consequence, there is no real possibility of tracing threads of connection amid this welter of complexity.

The cultural commentator most widely known for his beliefs that dynamic media based upon image transmission (7. Films, TV, Video etc.) have wrought some dramatic cognitive transformation in humans, is the Canadian author Marshall McLuhan (McLuhan and Fiore, 1989; Stearn, 1968). The difficulty with McLuhan's writings lies in extracting definite claims about the precise form the alleged changes take. McLuhan's style is elliptical, impressionistic, and apothegmatic. This is not necessarily a fault, but it does make McLuhan's work unsuitable for present purposes, even though it seems to provide tantalising support for the belief that something remarkably akin to cognitive change is going on. More helpful attempts to concretise the nature of the alleged changes have been made by other commentators:

"The aesthetics as well as the accessibility of culture have been transformed by these new technologies. The shift from theatre to film and television, and from concerts to records, tapes, and compact discs, is far more than technology assisted audience enlargement. Instead, performance, a unique event, becomes a product that can be endlessly reproduced...... ......Not only is the economy of the culture industry radically influenced by new technologies; not only as a result, are individual aesthetic responses reshaped in ways which appear to undermine Kant's belief that aesthetic judgements are able to mediate between the objective world of science and the subjective world of morality; but the very idea of literacy itself is transformed. Visual sensibility and oral skill are clearly likely to be more highly prized than literary merit when telecommunications permit instantaneous face-to-face interaction, the global village of the headline writers. The 30-second soundbite is mightier than the elegantly drafted minute; the television documentary more persuasive than the finely written essay."   (Gibbons et al., 1994: 102)

Again the very scale of the technology involved threatens to overwhelm. There is not just one change, but a host of changes, all interacting in complex ways and as with computers, abutting against the cognitive forms which we ourselves employ. It is clear that there is no shortage of potential technologically-based agencies of cognitive change. The difficulty lies in locating an instance, which is of sufficient magnitude to be likely to have operated as a change agent, but sufficiently restricted in its effects to examine without contending with a host of secondary and more remotely repercussive sequalae. And of course, the technological change agent we want must leave behind interpretable evidence of the course of its operations. Only one item survives from our candidate list (2) Written script; fortunately this residual instance of cognitive technology provides a good fit to the selection criteria we have developed.

MINDCHANGE AND THE TECHNOLOGY OF LITERACY

Let us try to reformulate the mindchange hypothesis to fit the case of literacy technology; I am going to insist upon the use of this unattractive label to remind us that function-oriented, artifact-based cultural innovations are technological, regardless of the physical structure and superficial complexity of the artefacts involved. And technology which supports and enhances mental operations including memory and communication, rather than physical skills, is cognitive technology. So written script is a form of cognitive technology and will be called literacy technology (or at least **LT** for brevity). Some important hypotheses associated with the theory that **LT** causes mindchange are set out below as two main hypotheses, each accompanied by a number of subordinate implications. It is assumed for the purpose of constructing these hypotheses that mindchange requires a transition between qualitatively different mindstates, and that qualitatively different mindstates are mutually incompatible. The rationale for this is that purely quantitative differences in cognitive performance can be accommodated within normal mechanisms of learning, and that compatibility interpretations such as class inclusion (e.g. **MS2** includes **MS1**) are effectively quantitative. For mindchange to be inferable from physical evidence it is also essential that some cultural productions (e.g. inventions, ideas, communications) be uniquely (or at least with some discriminating probability) associated with each mindstate.

1. LT causes qualitative cognitive change (**MS1** —> **MS2**) in individuals:

    a. Changed individuals will be aware of altered cognitions
    b. Individuals will be in either **MS1** or **MS2**
    c. **MS1** individuals will not fully understand **MS2** productions
    d. **MS2** individuals will not fully understand **MS1** productions

2. LT causes qualitative cognitive change in communities:

    a. Change transfer will take time
    b. Cultural productions incompatible with **MS1** will increase in frequency as change transfer proceeds
    c. Cultural productions incompatible with **MS2** will reduce in frequency as change transfer proceeds

The richest source of evidence on the cognitive impact of **LT** seems to be Clanchy (1979). Clanchy himself sometimes seems to hold a version of the mindchange hypothesis and his view that literacy penetrates and structures 'the intellect itself', and that later scholars must 'reconstruct the mental changes which it brings about' (Clanchy, 1979: 149) has already been quoted. However the evidence which Clanchy reviews does not seem to lend support to the idea of mindchange at all.

Let us consider hypothesis (1). It has already been noted that adult illiterates who belatedly acquire literacy skills, not uncommonly report the dramatic impact this makes upon their mental life. However, the impact seems to result entirely from gaining access to the cultural facilities and communicative opportunities available in a literacy based culture, not from the cognitive change *per se*. Literacy might well seem a tedious and insipid body of skills if it were shared by no-one thesis of his book. On the contrary Clanchy's evidence suggests that the cognitive changes associated with **LT** were partial, and piecemeal and extended over a timespan, of the order of centuries. What might seem to be a qualitative change between the beginning and end of this sequence, would of course, be experienced by no single individual. Let me use Clanchy's evidence to illustrate this point.

To begin with, the idea of a unitary **LT** is a historical fiction. Reading and writing are nowadays seen as intimately related, but this was not so when the technology was introduced. The writer was usually unable to read, and the reader unable to write:

> "Throughout the Middle Ages the writer remained a visual artist, and the reader a specialist in the spoken word. Medieval reading (lectio) was primarily something heard rather than seen until the invention of printing, and writing (scriptura) often continued to be admired for its calligraphy rather than its textual accuracy." (Clanchy, 1979: 230)

Even so, it might be supposed the difference between vocalised speech and silently apprehended text must surely have been sufficiently stark to gain notice. Again not so, most people's encounters with text were via a vocal rendition of it by one of the few possessing reading skills:

> "the medieval recipient prepared himself to listen to an utterance rather than to scrutinise a document visually as a modern literate would. This was due to a different habit of mind." (Clanchy, 1979: 214)

Even the surviving term "reading" as in "reading Psychology at Oxford", would according to Clanchy, originally have meant "being read aloud to". Silent reading emerged as a much later cultural and cognitive development.

Hypothesis (2) is more plausible, but the timescale involved is much greater than anything required by Constant's Kuhnian idea of cognitive change: it is cross-generational not an inter-individual, synchronic pattern of transmission from the eccentric margin to the cultural mainstream. Cognitive change within a "cultural cohort" was gradual and the post-literate mindstate coexisted peaceably alongside the mindstate it was to largely replace:

> "writings seem to have been thought of at first as subsidiary aids to traditional memorising procedures and not as replacements of them. A new technology usually adapts itself at first to an existing one, camouflaging itself in the old forms and not immediately realising its potential." (Clanchy, 1979: 256)

One piece of suggestive evidence comes from the legal process of conveyancing or transferring property from one person to another. In the pre-**LT** era an unsubstantiated oral contract required supplementary evidence in the form of a transfer of some physical object such as a doorknob, to provide substantive proof that the transaction had occurred; this was known as "livery of seisin".

transfer of some physical object such as a doorknob, to provide substantive proof that the transaction had occurred; this was known as "livery of seisin". Forensically, this procedure was quite unnecessary once a written and signed contract existed. In practice however:

> "Because writing was only an ancillary aid for laymen, it did not immediately sweep away traditional non-literate ways of doing business. Reliance upon symbolic objects and "livery of seisin" in conveyancing of property persisted. Writing was converted into the spoken word by the habitual practice of reading aloud, and of listening to or making an "audit" of a statement, rather than scrutinising its text on parchment. Clerks and scribes themselves were slow to comprehend the full potentialities of documentary proof, as their inconsistencies in signing and dating documents demonstrate."   (Clanchy, 1979: .263)

The picture which emerges from the historical record is quite different from the one which might be expected on the mindchange hypothesis. Where the mindchange hypothesis requires sudden switches in cognitive state, the facts suggest gradual and cumulative change. Where the mindchange hypothesis requires incompatibility, the facts suggest coexistence. Where methodology insists that dissociations exist between cultural productions and mindstates in order to test the mindchange hypothesis, the mindstates seem not to be discrete and mutually exclusive structures within an individual but continuously evolving processes operating over a timespan which makes comparison meaningless because of the multitude of covarying factors.

Of course it is possible to reject LT as a model for computer driven mindchange on the grounds that the magnitude of the latter may be substantially greater. This is possible but not really plausible. Yates (1966) has charted the massive differences between how memory skills were used and taught in mediaeval times, with reliance on mnemonic strategies and the systematic use of mental imagery, and the virtual disappearance of such techniques from the modern curriculum. Similarly, Baddeley (1976) discusses the disappearance of the Eighteenth Century "Syllabary", or text promoting memory by presenting visual illustrations of the component syllables of words or phrases which it was considered important for the young to learn. A different kind of evidence comes from independent psychological reports of investigations of individuals with extraordinary memory capabilities. The first of these studies was carried out in Russia on a reporter from a Moscow newspaper. The other was carried out and reported in the USA.

> "One was the subject of Luria (1969) the other was studied by Hunt and Love (1962). These two men were similar in several respects including the fact that the places where they spent their early lives were only thirty-five miles apart."
> (Klatzky, 1975)

The coincidence is striking. It is greatly mitigated once it becomes clear that both men were born and raised in isolated Jewish settlements in the Soviet hinterland, in communities in which literacy was rare and education entirely based upon memorisation skills. The mindstate produced by what was effectively a mediaeval programme of education, produced a pattern of performance sufficiently distinctive from the cultural norm to attract the attention of psychologists in two different continents. Though this contrast between mindstates is undeniably extreme, the reports do not suggest that either individual experienced any difficulty in comprehending the cultural productions of the 1960s.

Another tack is to argue that LT is too extreme or atypical a cognitive change to model the effect of computers. Again, the evidence from the history of technology provides little comfort. In most cases novel technologies coexist quite comfortably alongside the artefacts and practices they replace, e.g. replacement of water wheels by rotary steam engines as power sources in the late 18th and early 19th centuries, or replacement of piston engines by turbojets in the 20th century (Constant, 1980; Price, 1984; Laudan, 1984). The rate of substitution seems to depend much more on social and economic factors than on anything to do with cognition; for example the:

> "wars that cut off France from Spanish barilla, Germany from Chilean nitrate and Russian oil, and the United States from natural rubber have in each case drastically changed the economies of the respective resources and their use and thus induced technological developments which eventually replaced them."
>
> (Weingart, 1984: 134)

CONCLUSION

The conclusions from this investigation of the belief or concern that computers may change our minds, may be variously projected as a source of comfort or disappointment. In a trivial sense computers do change our mental powers and abilities, and that is why we use them. There are a number of more extreme and alarmist interpretations of the idea of mental change which require change to be qualitative, substantial, generalised, irreversible and associated with negative adaptive consequences. The negative adaptation feature is rejected early on because it seems to violate essential preconditions of learning. Theories of catastrophic cognitive change are difficult to coherently formulate because of paradoxes associated with the idea of mental transition from an initial state to a second and incompatible one. When a coherent interpretation is available, even more serious difficulties are presented by the challenge of deducing testable consequences. The problem of unequivocal evidence is so severe in the case of cognitive effects of computers, that it is concluded that proponents of this view cannot base their beliefs upon any direct evidence that such effects occur. When the more general claim that cognitive technology can precipitate dramatic mental change is evaluated, the evidence suggests that different technological solutions to the same problem are cognitively compatible, but that elaborations of a preferred technology over long periods of time can exaggerate apparent differences between it and a displaced rival.

REFERENCES

Anderson, P., 1991. *The Printed Image and the Transformation of Popular Culture.* Oxford: Clarendon Press.

Baddeley, A. D., 1976. *The Psychology of Memory.* New York: Basic Books.

Beeton, Mrs. I., 1861. *The Book of Household Management.* London: Cape.

Bryant, P., 1974. *Perception and Understanding in Young Children: An Experimental Approach.* London: Methuen.

Clanchy, M. T., 1979. *From Memory to Written Record.* London: Edward Arnold.

Cohen, S., 1972. *Folk Devils and Moral Panics.* London: MacGibbon and Kee.

Cole, M., J. Gay, J. A. Glick, and D. W. Sharp, 1974. *The Cultural Context of Learning and Thinking.* London: Methuen.

Constant, E. W., 1980. *Origins of the Turbojet Revolution.* Baltimore: Johns Hopkins Press.

Constant, Edward W., 1984. Communities and hierarchies: Structure in the practice of Science and Technology. In R. Laudan, ed*., The Nature of Technological Knowledge: Are models of Scientific Change Relevant?* Dordrecht: D. Reidel, p. 30.

Gibbons, M., C. Limoges, H. Nowotny, S. Schwartzman, P. Scott, and M. Trow, 1994. *The New Production of Knowledge.* London: Sage.

Hunt, E., and T. Love, 1972. In A. W. Melton and E. Martin, eds*, Coding Processes in Human Memory.* Washington D. C.: V. H. Winston and Sons.

Hunter, I. M. L., 1964. *Memory.* Harmondsworth: Penguin Books.

Inkeles, A., and D. J. Levinson, 1968. National Character: the Study of Modal Personality and Sociocultural Systems. In G. Lindzey and E. Aronson, eds, *The Handbook of Social Psychology, Volume Four.* Reading Mass.: Addison Wesley.

Johnson-Laird, P. N., 1983. *Mental Models.* Cambridge: Cambridge University Press.

Johnson-Laird, P. N., 1993. *The Computer and the Mind: An Introduction to Cognitive Science.* London: Fontana.

Keller, H., 1956. *The Story of My Life.* London: Hodder and Stoughton.

Klatzky, R., 1975. Human Memory. San Francisco: W. H. Freeman.

Kotovsky, K., J. R. Hayes, and H. A. Simon, 1985. Why are some problems hard? evidence from the Tower of Hanoi. *Cognitive Psychology*, 17, pp. 248-94.

Kuhn, T., 1962. *The Structure of Scientific Revolutions.* Chicago: University of Chicago Press.

Laudan, R., 1984. *The Nature of Technological Knowledge: Are models of Scientific Change Relevant?* Dordrecht: D. Reidel.

Lindsay, R. O., 1996. Cognitive Technology and the Pragmatics of Impossible Plans - A study in Cognitive Prosthetics. *Paper Presented to the International Pragmatics Association International Pragmatics Conference,* Mexico City, July 4-9.

Luria, A. R., 1973. *The Man with the Shattered World: the history of a brain wound.* London: Cape.

Luria, A. R., 1969. *The Mind of a Mnemonist.* London: Cape.

McLuhan, M. and Q. Fiore, 1989. *The Medium is the Massage.* New York: Simon and Schuster.

Mumford, L., 1963. *Technics and Civilisation.* New York: Harcourt Brace Jovanovich.

Paivio, A., 1972. *Imagery and Verbal Processes.* London: Holt, Rhinehart, Winston.

Price, D. J. De Solla, 1984. Notes towards a Philosophy of Science/Technology Interaction. In R. Laudan, ed., *The Nature of Technological Knowledge: Are models of Scientific Change Relevant?* Dordrecht: D. Reidel.

Reed, S. K., 1987. A structure-mapping model for word problems. *Journal of Experimental Psychology: Human Memory and Cognition*, 13(1), pp. 125-39.

Robertson, I., 1996. Keep taking the smarties. *The Guardian newspaper*, London: Tuesday September 17th.

Ryle, G., 1949. *The Concept of Mind.* London: Hutchinson.

Stearn, G. E., 1968. *Hot and Cool: A Primer.* Harmondsworth: Penguin Books.

Weingart, P., 1984. The Structure of Technological Change. In Rachel Laudan, ed., *The Nature of Technological Knowledge: Are models of Scientific Change Relevant?* Dordrecht: D. Reidel.

Weizenbaum, J., 1976. *Computer Power and Human Reason.* San Francisco: W. H. Freeman.

Yates, F. A., 1966. *The Art of Memory.* London: Routledge and Kegan-Paul.

Humane Interfaces: Questions of method and
practice in Cognitive Technology
J.P. Marsh, B. Gorayska and J.L. Mey (Editors)
© 1999 Elsevier Science B.V. All rights reserved.

Chapter 3

COMPUTERS AND PSYCHOSIS

Richard W. Janney

University of Munich

PROLOGUE

The idea for this paper originated in a conversation with a psychotherapist in Germany a few years ago, who was treating a computer program engineer who had started beating his computers. The man lived alone, with little social contact, in an apartment with four PCs, one in each room. He rarely left home; and when he did, it was usually only to go to his office, where there were two more PCs. He had come for help because, after having beaten his computers for several weeks, he had begun to feel as if he were abusing his family. The psychotherapist was on the verge of giving up. The patient insisted that he wanted to cooperate, but he could not, because he could not understand the relevance of the psychotherapist's questions about his feelings and desires. They didn't compute for him; he was unable to respond to questions of almost any kind that didn't allow clear, either/or, yes/no, digital types of answers. He had come to think that he was a computer.

COMPUTERS AS PROSTHESES

The idea of computers as mental prostheses was implicit fifteen years ago in an article published in the *Journal of Pragmatics*, in which Trevor Pateman (1982: 237) argued that "computer programs are things to think *with*, not things which think ... this is their virtue" (1982: 237). In the same issue of the *Journal*, Jacob Mey (1982: 212) emphasised the need for developing artificial intelligence technology that works *for us*, in our service, helping us to perform our tasks, and not simply technology designed to meet its own needs or intended to replicate, compete with, or replace human thought. These were the beginnings of the view, which is now an underlying assumption of Cognitive Technology, that computers can be regarded as tools for prosthetically extending the capacities of the human mind.

In this paper, somewhat in the spirit of Umberto Eco's (1984) discussion of the functions of prostheses in modern life, I will suggest that it is important to consider what our use of the computer as a mental prosthesis implies for us, its users. It is important, I will claim, to understand how computers influence the human mental capacities that they extend. I will argue that enthusiasm for computers as potential extensions of the mind should not blind us to the fact that all extensions of human faculties have their price. Eco has pointed out that prostheses have 'deceptive properties'. In this paper, I will claim that computers and computer programs, as presently designed, tend to force users to engage in a psychotic communication process that can have important psychological effects on heavy computer users. The paper, we could say, is about the *psychopragmatics* of the human-computer interface. It is intended to encourage discussion about what can be done in Cognitive Technology to address the problems pointed out.

PROSTHETIC BIASES

Following Eco (1984: 208), any device that physically replaces a part of the body (an artificial hand, denture, hip joint, heart valve), or that artificially extends the range of action or efficiency of some *function* of the human body (a hearing aid, magnifying glass, telescope, telephone, computer), can be regarded as a type of prosthesis. Despite the growing importance of technological prostheses in modern life, the trouble with prostheses in general - and here, computers are no exception - is that, as Eco says, they are rarely functionally *neutral*. A fully equivalent prosthetic replacement for a part of the human body, that is, is rare; and a fully equivalent extension of a complex, multifunctional process like human thought is impossible, given the present state of research on artificial intelligence.

In replacing or extending something, a prosthesis generally also modifies its functions in some way (Eco, 1984: 210). Prostheses are usually more specialised than the parts of the body they replace, and their own *restricted* functions tend to become privileged over the more complex or less specialised functions of the original, which are lost or can only be imperfectly imitated. Hence, early artificial hands replaced the grasping functions of real hands at the cost of eliminating thermic and tactile sensory functions, early telescopes extended depth of vision but reduced breadth of vision, and the telephone extended the distance at which people could speak at the cost of eliminating their ability to see each other. In all these areas, of course, and in many others, technology constantly improves, and increasingly life-like functions are added to the original prostheses. And this is a goal of Cognitive Technology: to encourage the development of computers and programs that work increasingly naturally for human users and meet *their* needs rather than technology that simply forces them to adapt to *its* needs.

But at the present time, in my view, certain important, basic psychological questions are not being asked about human-computer interaction: above all, the question of what happens to the human *mind* at the interface with the mechanical prosthesis, where the two have to communicate with each other in order for a prosthetic extension to take place. Which capacities of the mind are extended by this interaction, and which are not? And what happens to the mental capacities that are *not* extended? What is the psychological price of the bond between humans and computers? I believe that presently, computers prosthetically extend our cognitive 'reach' at the cost of partly paralysing our emotional and conative 'grasp' of things. I am interested especially in the psychological *magnifying* and *reducing* effects of computers on the mind (Eco, 1984: 208).

COMPUTERS AS PARTNERS: A PRAGMATIC VIEW

An important characteristic of computers as mental prostheses is that they have to be given a lot of information and commands before they can be of any use to us. This distinguishes them from earlier, simpler prostheses. In order to *do* anything with a computer, that is, we first have to *communicate* with it; so that prior to being a prosthesis, a computer, we could say (unlike an artificial hip joint), is a type of *partner*: a second-person 'you' to whom a first-person 'I' (the user) implicitly addresses messages.

Yet, from a pragmatic point of view, there are certain problems with this 'I'-'you' relationship that tend to undermine the notion that users will ever be able to communicate naturally with computers. If we adopt an intentionalist account of meaning, for example, as in traditional speech act theory, where intentionality is regarded as a precondition for meaningfulness of reference, we must more or less conclude that almost everything a computer communicates to us is meaningless. A computer has no intentions; therefore, its references, even if produced in the form of linguistically decodable locutionary acts or logical propositions, have no illocutionary force (cf. Pateman, 1982: 228 ff.). And by the reverse logic, since a computer lacks intentions itself, it cannot recognise or process the intentions of a human user. This deprives the user's input into the computer of its illocutionary force as well, and partly explains why a command to a computer does not have the same illocutionary force or perlocutionary effect as the speech act of 'commanding' has in human interaction. We could say that because a computer lacks intentionality, it is incapable of producing or processing felicitous speech acts, and is hence incapable of producing, or engaging in *cooperative discourse*. Its propositions, however 'true', can never be 'sincere'.

The absence of intentions in computers tends to undermine the pragmatic basis of human-computer communication. To the extent that computers lack *sincerity conditions*, they become obscure partners. A user cannot assume that the output of a computer in any given instance will be (1) that which is required at the stage at which it occurs in the exchange , (2) as informative as required for the current purpose of the exchange, (3) relevant to what is immediately happening in the exchange, or (4) clear and unambiguous in the context of the exchange. Without being able to appeal to cooperative principles of some type - maxims of quality, quantity, relation, manner, etc. - people find it difficult to maintain the presuppositional basis of communication with a computer. Especially in cases where the computer does something unexpected, an inexperienced user can have trouble producing reliable implicatures about what is 'meant' by what the computer 'does'.

COMMUNICATING WITH COMPUTERS: AN INTERACTIONAL VIEW

A point not often enough emphasised in pragmatics is that, psychologically speaking, intentionality is a *motivational* property of behaviour - that is, an intrinsic property not of language or of logic but of human *will* and *action*. Hence, in human communication, we do not usually infer others' intentions from the ideational *content* of their utterances in isolation but from perceived *relationships* between their utterances, themselves, and ourselves in particular contexts. According to Paul Watzlawick, Janet Beavin and Don Jackson's (1967: 51) second axiom of communication, acts of human communication not only convey *factual information* but also impose *relational constraints* on partners' behaviour. These are sometimes called the *report* and *command* aspects of communication, and together, they form the basis of all successful human interaction (cf. Ruesch and Bateson, 1951: 179-181).

Following Watzlawick, Beavin and Jackson (1967: 52-53), there are certain similarities between the report and command aspects of human communication and the information and instructions fed into computers in human-computer communication. In order to multiply two figures, for example, a computer needs information (data: e.g., the two figures) and instructions about what to do with this information (commands: e.g., the instruction to multiply them). These latter instructions provide metainformation; their main function, that is, is to convey information about what to do with information (1967: 52-53).

Human communication, somewhat like human-computer communication, also relies on message *content* ('you're stupid') and on *relational metainformation* about how, in the broadest sense, the content is to 'be taken' ('I'm serious', 'this is only a joke'). And this latter type of information is no less important for human speakers than the former. According to Watzlawick, Beavin and Jackson (1967: 53), in fact, "the ability to metacommunicate appropriately is not only the *conditio sine qua non* of successful communication, but is intimately linked with the enormous problem of awareness of self and others."

In human-computer communication, however, the computer tends to be an uncommunicative, passive partner, without awareness of itself or others. It processes incoming reports and commands from its human user, but provides feedback to the user mainly only in the ideational *report* mode, without providing accompanying relational metainformation signalling how the user is 'to take' or 'to understand' its responses. Moreover, as a partner, the computer typically recognises neither the *need* for this second type of information nor the possibility that its reports may be *misunderstood* by the user. This further erodes the pragmatic foundations of human-computer communication. The user, in this situation, is forced to supply the missing relational information by an act of empathy or imagination. But without the possibility of negotiating meaning with the computer, the user can never be sure to have fully understood its reports.

This is of course a highly anthropomorphic way of looking at computers. It is clear that computers do not operate on human principles and that communication with them cannot be compared with communication between humans. And there is not much to 'negotiate' with a computer in the first place. Nevertheless, many problems of human-computer interaction, I believe, stem from the user's natural, psychological *need* to imagine the computer as a 'you' to whom information and commands are addressed. The 'I' of human communication and of human self-consciousness requires, at the very least, an *implicit* 'you' in order to define itself as an independent agent and envisage itself as being able to make meaningful statements in and about the world.

It is hence little wonder that computer users tend to speak of their computers as if they were people. The social 'self' requires the possibility of projecting itself empathically into an 'other'. We could perhaps regard the anthropomorphisation of computers by users as a modern psychic survival strategy. Almost against our will - and certainly contrary to our reason - we empathise, at times, with our computers. This is how, especially when it is hard to understand what is required of us by a computer program, we sometimes have the mildly schizoid feeling that the program knows what we are supposed to know, but it can't tell us what this is because it doesn't know what we don't know what it is (cf. Laing, 1970: 56).

To summarise before going further: we presently can only get computers to function as extensions of our minds by communicating with them. And the fact that we have to communicate with computers in order to do things with them tends to make it at least as natural for us to think of them as *partners* as to think of them as extensions of *ourselves*. But normal human communication is not possible with a computer. As an interlocutor, a computer has no emotional life and no will; it neither possesses nor recognises human intentions, and it has no sense of conventions of human communication or of how to cooperate in interaction with a user. It has to be told what it knows and told what to do with what it knows, and it doesn't get a 'point' because it is incapable of making pragmatic inferences. A computer is incapable of empathy. It does not know that it can be misunderstood; and when it is not understood, it does not recognise this and cannot engage in the renegotiation of meaning with the user. Thus, from the user's side of the human-computer interface, the computer is a problematical partner.

COMPUTERS AS PSYCHOTICS: PSYCHIATRIC CONSIDERATIONS

A drawback of present computers as prosthetic extensions of the mind, in my opinion, is their sheer *alienness* as communication partners: the fact that we cannot establish empathic relations with them. The 'you' to whom the 'I' implicitly addresses its communication is not there. I think that users will continue to have identity problems in relation to computers until software designers find ways of making computers produce more cooperative, conventional, natural communication - or, alternatively, find ways to drastically reduce the amount of communication that is necessary with computers. With partners of almost any other kind (including animals), we can usually imagine at least some type of partly shared intersubjective context; with computers, however, we are separated by a gulf that almost defies description.

The closest analogy to this situation in human communication is communication with schizophrenics. The characteristics attributed to computers as partners at the end of the preceding section would apply to schizophrenic partners as well. *Dementia praecox* , invented as a diagnostic concept by Emil Kraepeling in 1896 for what is now called *schizophrenia*, is described as "a peculiar destruction of the inner cohesiveness of the ... personality with predominant damage to the emotional life and the will" (cf. Sass, 1994: 14). Schizophrenics, like computers, tend to suffer from a radical imbalance of cognitive and emotive mental capacities, with a strong proclivity to the former. They lack an inner unity of thought, emotion, and motivation.

Schizophrenics' thoughts often appear to be uncoupled from their feelings and desires. There is a tendency among schizophrenics to describe their thoughts as mechanical processes, or to imagine that their minds are controlled by mechanical devices that have been implanted in their brains by others (bugs, microphones, loud speakers, tape recorders, computers, etc.). Many schizophrenics display what psychologists call 'flatness of affect', and seem to be nearly devoid of emotion and desire. The psychiatric term for the radical separation of cognition from emotion in schizophrenia is *intrapsychic ataxia;* and it is a built-in feature of computers.

Other prominent characteristics of schizophrenia are asociality, indifference, introversion, detachment from the world, and what is sometimes called 'cognitive slippage'. This is an unanchored quality of thinking, or a loss of the normal goal-directedness of thought, and it works itself out in schizophrenic acts of speech that fail to follow conventional conversational expectations (cf. Sass, 1994: 77-78). As with computers, we often cannot know if a schizophrenic's utterances are meant cooperatively, and we often cannot be sure that they are required responses, informative responses, relevant responses, or clear responses in the contexts in which they appear. As a result, in attempting to communicate with a schizophrenic, as in attempting to communicate with a computer, we sometimes have difficulty making accurate pragmatic implicatures. The necessary groundwork of shared pragmatic presuppositions and the necessary assumed intentionality of the schizophrenic's utterances are often missing, making it difficult, in cases of doubt, to infer what is meant by what is said.

Moreover, many schizophrenics, like computers, tend to respond to questions by only giving reports of their momentary inner states, failing to provide the additional relational information that would be necessary for fully understanding the implications of what they say in the context. Like computers, schizophrenics often do not tell us how to process the content of their communication. Their speech is often overconcrete or overabstract, and repetitive or stereotyped. The *poverty of content* of schizophrenic speech and its *tangentiality* (where a question is answered, but not in the desired sense), in fact, are used to discriminate schizophrenics from manic-depressives (cf. Rochester and Martin, 1979: 40). They can also be used, however, to discriminate answers of computers, in certain situations, from answers of normal human interlocutors. Computers often give too little information or too much; and they often provide answers that are irrelevant or tangential to the intended question.

Other common communication disturbances of computers and schizophrenics are *derailment* (jumping from one topic to another), *loss of goal* (failure to follow a chain of thought through to a logical conclusion), *perseveration* (persistent repetition of words and/or ideas), *poverty of speech* (absence of unprompted talk; a tendency for replies to be brief and unelaborated), *incoherence* ("word salad", or speech so severely disorganised as to be incomprehensible), *semantic dissociation* (use of neologisms), *literalism* (inability to recognise or to perform indirect speech acts), and *disrupted or restricted gestalt perception* (difficulty grasping the 'point' of the partner's statements or questions).

SHARED PSYCHOTIC BONDS

What are the implications of this for computer users? Almost everyone who has had contact with heavy computer users has at some time met individuals with communication disturbances vaguely like those described above: computer users who seem somehow disconnected from the external world, uncoupled from themselves, and indifferent to others in a way that seems vaguely similar to the style of operation of the computers with which they interact.

Is it possible that constant interaction with machines with schizophrenic communication characteristics, like computers, can result in psychosis? From the literature on schizophrenia, we know, at any rate, that there is a striking tendency among family members of certain types of schizophrenics to develop schizoid pathologies themselves. The psychiatric term for this is *Shared Psychotic Disorder (Folie à Deux)*, and it refers to "a delusion that develops in an individual who is involved in a close relationship with another person (sometimes termed the 'inducer' or the 'primary case') who already has a psychotic disorder with prominent delusions" (DSM-IV, 1994: 305).

The psychiatric term for abnormalities that do not fully qualify as 'schizophrenic' but sometimes occur as shared psychotic disorders in relatives of schizophrenic patients is *schizoid*. It was proposed in 1910 by Eugen Bleuler to describe a recurring constellation of partly contradictory symptoms including *coldness, indifference, asociality, hypersensitivity, obstinacy, vacillation, rebelliousness, timidity,* and *introversion* (cf. Sass, 1994: 76). Some heavy computer users seem to have symptoms like those described in Louis Sass's (1994: 77) account of the schizoid personality: "Seldom do such people feel in harmony with their bodies or with the environment, and typically, their emotions do not flow in a natural and spontaneous way; instead, they seem forced or stiff, and others may find them cold and unfeeling, perhaps overly cerebral or calculating. Often they will seem detached, "as if something unnatural and strange divided them from the world", and others are liable to sense something not entirely genuine in their behaviour and emotional expression. In fact, many schizoids convey an "as-if" quality, giving the impression that they are only role-playing - perhaps to caricature themselves, to mock those around them, or simply to give an appearance of seamless normality. But beneath the apparent coldness, these people can be excessively sensitive, thin-skinned, and self-deprecatory, highly vulnerable to slights and criticism. Sometimes they will seem docile, submissive, and awkward, at other times arrogant, superior, or rebellious. They have, in any case, an aloof, vaguely mysterious air, suggestive of a realm of experience hidden away from others."

THE USER'S DILEMMA: SELF-AMPUTATION AS ADAPTATION

More than thirty years ago, Marshal McLuhan (1964) provided an account of human adaptations to prostheses that continues to be relevant, I think, to describing shared psychotic disorders like those described by Sass (1994). Physiologically, McLuhan said, there are abundant reasons why all prosthetic extensions of ourselves - and especially electronic extensions of the nervous system - tend to create states of numbness (1964: 52). Numbness, he said, is a response of an organism that is attempting to maintain equilibrium in the face of an irritating overload in some sensory or psychic mode. It is a strategy resorted to by the body or the mind when the cause of irritating input cannot be avoided.

There are two prototypical forms of this sort of adaptation: physical shock and psychic trauma. In both, a generalised numbness increases the threshold of perception of all kinds. Following McLuhan (1964: 52), we protect ourselves from irritating, overloading, inescapable input by a strategy of *autoamputation*. If the coordination of the senses is threatened seriously enough by the irritating input, the central nervous system reacts by automatically closing the offending receivers. That is, it cuts out, shuts off, numbs, or amputates the receiving sensory or mental function, in extreme cases, blocking perception of irritating input to the point that the victim seems immune to pain (in shock) or sense (in trauma). The removal of the irritant through the autoamputation of the receiving sensors becomes our comfort (1964: 53).

The interface between a prosthesis and a human being is almost always characterised by irritation. In the case of a wooden leg, it is the irritating pressure of the wooden socket against the human flesh of the natural leg. In the case of a denture, there is the irritating pressure of the plastic rim of the denture on the human gum. In the case of the computer, I have suggested in this paper, it is the irritating psychic pressure of the unnatural, autistic, cognitive operating style of the computer and the flexible, integrative, cognitive-emotional-conative operating style of the normal human mind. At all interfaces between humans and prostheses, McLuhan claimed, the result of an inescapable irritation is a numbing self-amputation on the human side.

Just as the natural leg or the gum become insensitive to physical irritation at the interface with their prostheses, the mind becomes insensitive to the psychic irritation - which is the absence of psychic unity - at its interface with the computer. The main irritant is the computer's impassionate, impassive, unresponsive, schizophrenic quality as a partner in communication - the fact that while it has possibilities for processing cognitive information, it has no means of processing human emotions and desires. Presently, it is not the computer that adapts to the user, but the user who adapts to the computer, by amputating parts of his or her emotional and motivational psychic 'self'. The result, in extreme cases, as suggested earlier, is *intrapsychic ataxia*, a schizoid disorder ironically shared with the computer, in which the user suffers a loss of psychic inner cohesiveness, and an impoverishment of his or her emotional life and will. It is perhaps only a hollow consolation in this connection that, as Marshall McLuhan remarked, "self-amputation forbids self-recognition" (1964: 52).

It seems to me that an important future goal of Cognitive Technology will have to be to encourage the development computer technology that reduces our need for psychic self-amputation. But this, I believe, will require more studies aimed at finding out where the prosthesis 'pinches', so to speak, and progress will depend on discovering and describing the sources of sensory and psychic irritation at the human-computer interface. It should be clear, at any rate, that the simple continuation of present research focused exclusively on discovering new applications and markets for computer technology is not the answer. A one-sided extension of users' cognitive capacities, at the expense of their emotional and motivational capacities, is technological madness.

REFERENCES

DSM-IV, 1994. *Diagnostic and statistical manual of mental disorders. 4th ed.* Washington, DC: American Psychiatric Association.

Eco, U., 1984. *Semiotics and the philosophy of science.* London: Macmillan.

Gorayska, B. and J. L. Mey, eds, 1996. *Cognitive Technology: In search of a Humane Interface.* Advances in Psychology 113. Amsterdam: Elsevier.

Janney, R. W., 1996. E-mail and intimacy. In: B. Gorayska and J.L. Mey, eds., 1996, *Cognitive Technology: In search of a Humane Interface*. Advances in Psychology 113. Amsterdam: Elsevier, pp. 201-211.

Janney, R. W., 1997. The cold warmth of communication in computer networks. In: W. Nöth, ed., 1997 *Semiotics of the media*. Berlin/New York: Mouton de Gruyter.

Laing, R. D., 1970. *Knots*. London: Bellknap.

McLuhan, M., 1964. *Understanding media: The extensions of man*. New York: McGraw-Hill.

Mey, J. L., 1982. Introduction: on simulating machines and lisping humans. *Journal of Pragmatics,* 6, pp. 209-224.

Nöth, W., ed., 1997. *Semiotics of the media*. Berlin/New York: Mouton de Gruyter

Pateman, T., 1982. Communicating with computer programs. *Journal of Pragmatics,* 6, pp. 225-240.

Rochester, S. R. and J. R. Martin, 1979. *Crazy talk: A study of the discourse of schizophrenic speakers*. New York: Academic Press.

Ruesch, J., and G. Bateson, 1951. *Communication: The social matrix of psychiatry*. New York: Norton.

Sass, L. A., 1994. *Madness and modernism: Insanity in the light of modern art, literature, and thought*. Cambridge, MA: Harvard University Press.

Watzlawick, P., J. Helmick Beavin, and D. D. Jackson, 1967. *Pragmatics of communication: A study of interactional patterns, pathologies, and paradoxes*. New York: Norton.

Humane Interfaces: Questions of method and practice in Cognitive Technology
J.P. Marsh, B. Gorayska and J.L. Mey (Editors)
© 1999 Elsevier Science B.V. All rights reserved.

Chapter 4

THE NATURAL AND THE ARTIFICIAL IN LANGUAGE AND TECHNOLOGY[1]

Hartmut Haberland

Department of Languages and Culture
University of Roskilde

POINT OF DEPARTURE

This paper takes its point of departure the question "what is natural about so-called natural languages?" Probal Dasgupta is to be credited for pointing out that many linguists fall victim to the "naturalness fallacy", as I elsewhere have argued for sociolinguistics (Haberland, in press). In discussing the relationship between Cognitive Technology and Pragmatics, and thus between systems and language users, one might be tempted to refer to the "naturalness" of language as opposed to the "artificiality" of computer programs as an explanatory factor (Haberland, 1996). It ain't necessarily so.

'NATURAL' HUMANS, 'ARTIFICIAL' MACHINES

As David Good has pointed out, conversation or face-to-face interaction is the "basic model from which all other forms of human communication ultimately derive" (1996: 80). Even when dealing with computers, and trying to understand how it is possible for humans to engage in something that at least resembles communication with these heaps of wired metal, we always go back to what we know existed before we invented computers: good old plain communication between people. We apply a basic communication model (sender, channel, receiver) and replace one of the parts by a machine. As with any other analogy, we notice similarities – without similarities we would not be able to use Human–Human communication as a model of Human–Machine communication at all. And we also notice differences – if there were no difference, we would not talk about a model, but about simple identity. The question is only, what exactly is the difference.

There are obvious differences, most of them trivial. One of the reasons why we cannot have face-to-face interaction with computers is that computers do not have a face. With machines, we use different input devices than those we are used to with

---

[1] This paper is a revised version of Haberland (1998).

humans: keyboard, mouse, some pointing device. This is true, but technologically transitional and not so important unless it has deeper consequences.

A much more important difference is the lack of symmetry in human–machine interaction. Two humans conversing with each other could at least *in principle* enjoy a symmetrical relationship, while a human and a machine who interact, cannot. In a sense, they do not even communicate with each other: the human communicates with the machine, not vice versa. Far from every user is a programmer, but in principle every user could be, which means that they wield a power over the machine that the machine does not have over them. On the other hand, a computer will always be alien to the human communicating with it. We cannot empathise with computers, hence we cannot understand them by trying to take their role in interaction. This makes computers often unpredictable, and gives them a power of a different kind over the user: since the users often cannot change the computers' ways, they will try to appease them. Through this built-in asymmetry, the human part in the interaction is privileged in principle, but often forced to submission in practice. This asymmetry is where the 'naturalness' argument usually comes in: Human–Human–Interaction is different from Human–Machine–Interaction because communication between humans is natural while communication that involves a machine is not (it is technological or artificial).

In the following, I want to deconstruct this assumption – to a certain extent. I want to suggest that the borderline between the 'natural' and the 'artificial' even in communication involving humans on both sides is not as clear as one sometimes would wish. This has important implications for the analysis of communication processes that involve humans only on one side. If Human–Human communication is only 'natural' with certain qualifications, the two types of communication processes are not separated by a clear dividing line. We are rather talking about a difference in degree. This does not mean, though, that the difference is only a small one, it may in fact be quite significant.

'ARTIFICIAL' AND 'NATURAL' IN SEMIOTICS AND LINGUISTICS

The term 'natural language' has its tradition in semiotics and modern linguistics. But the discussion about what is 'natural' in language goes even further back in history. The Sophists of Greek antiquity were the first in Europe to ask questions about what was given by nature and what was merely conventional, that is given by agreement. Their overall concern was probably in showing that societal institutions were human-made, hence not 'natural', but in applying their investigations to language, the approach was seriously hampered by the fact that hardly any aspects semiotics or linguistics had been developed at that stage. The issue got thus side-tracked into a discussion about whether word meanings are natural or conventional, and into the construction of 'natural' explanations of word meanings (cf. Steinthal, 1890; Matthews, 1990). These first etymologies can only provoke smiles from us today (Plato's dialogue Cratylus contains some nice examples), and the whole discussion seems outdated, since we have agreed that sign meanings are conventional. The whole issue as to whether language was natural or not was not taken up again for a long time.

Rudolf Carnap was one of the founding fathers of pragmatics and one of the first to define the notion. In 1958 he referred to 'pragmatics' as "investigation[s] which refer explicitly to the speaker of the language – no matter whether other factors are drawn in or not" (1958:79). For Carnap, 'speakers' are one of the three 'principal factors' in each situation in which 'a language is employed', the others being linguistic expressions and what the speaker intends to designate by these expressions. In clarifying the scope of this framework of semiotics, Carnap refers to a distinction between the 'natural' and the artificial; this framework is said to apply to all languages, "either historical natural ones or artificial ones" (1958:78). For Carnap, the basic difference between natural and artificial languages is that the former are 'given by historical fact', hence can be described by empirical investigation, while the latter are 'given by the construction of a system of rules' only.

The need for the term 'natural' as opposed to 'formal' language became even clearer a few years later, when the study of formal languages and their syntax and semantics became an important field of investigation in its own right and linguists had to specify which of their results, like those pertaining to the famous Chomsky hierarchy as explained in Chomsky (1963), are valid for natural languages, which for formal languages, and which for languages *tout court*. But by 1970, Richard Montague questioned the validity of the distinction between the two types of language, at least as far as their theoretical description was concerned. He started his paper *English as a formal language* by stating, "I reject the contention that an important theoretical difference exists between formal and natural languages" (1970:189). For Montague, the construction of a theory of truth was the central goal of 'serious' syntax and semantics, hence formal and 'natural' languages could basically be described with the same descriptive tools and should, therefore, not be considered as vastly different.

Another source of the use of the term 'natural' is in sociolinguistics, where certain sociolinguistic states (like diglossia and, by some, even societal bilingualism) are considered less 'natural' than others, hence transitional and unstable. Language planning, although its importance as a factor of language change is acknowledged, is often seen as interference with the natural flow of language development. Since the language system in the Saussurean tradition is considered an arbitrary mapping of forms on meaning, it can only be understood as having evolved naturally, not as being designed to fulfil a function. This assumption of the naturalness of language as a corollary of the Saussurean *arbitaire du signe* is what Probal Dasgupta has called the "naturalness fallacy".

The traditional point of view does not imply that language or languages are either natural or artificial. On the contrary, both 'natural' languages and 'artificial' languages are acknowledged, and within the realm of 'natural' language, natural and artificial phenomena are distinguished. The traditional view assumes that there is a 'natural' state of language (if untampered with), and that this 'natural' state of a language, guaranteed by the arbitrariness of the basic structure, is the starting point for its description: languages can have more or less artificial extensions, but

Languages seen as natural phenomena	Languages seen as artificial phenomena
grown, not created, developed, not designed	planned, designed, human-made
not planned and not under conscious control	monitored and consciously controlled
spontaneous	subject to planning
Cannot be changed from the outside, but change due to their inner dynamic	change according to external decisions
passively and naturally acquired in primary socialisation	actively learned through education
biology as model science	engineering as model science

Table 1: Characteristics of language as a natural vs. artificial phenomena

their basic meaning-coding system constitutes their natural core which cannot be affected by conscious interference Table 1 tries to set up a picture of this traditional view.

CHALLENGING THE TRADITIONAL VIEW

The traditional view gives languages as natural phenomena a privileged status vis-à-vis their artificial extensions. Maybe not even this is historically correct: it has been suggested that 'artificial' writing could be at least as old as 'natural' speaking, since we cannot know if the earliest hominids used their vocal organs for symbolic expression prior to their producing visible marks on stone and the like. This is, of course, speculative; but it is easier to argue why the traditional view is problematic, viz. that there is a naturally developed core in human language that is barely affected by conscious design. The idea of a natural core of language can only be maintained if we consider language use as external to the language system proper. The key idea that helps us to understand this is that human beings are not just natural, biological creatures that live in an artificial, technical environment which they have created. Neurobiologists point out (e.g. Changeux 1985) that our biological basis is not simply unaffected by the environment shaped by humans; the relationship goes both ways. Hence we cannot simply divide phenomena pertaining to humans into biologically given, natural ones and human-created artificial ones. When we realise that artificial phenomena shape phenomena perceived as natural, the latter's naturalness can be doubted seriously.

The distinction between the natural and the artificial also disregards that human beings live in a society that they have not created individually, but collectively.

The fact that they do not have created society (or its manifestations like language) individually may sometimes lead them to assume that these have not been created at all, or at least not by anything human; hence they must have been there all the time, must be 'natural'. What human beings *have* created, and know that they have created, must then be of a totally different order, be 'artificial'.

All linguistic manifestations are tools of the human mind, and as such they are partly devised consciously, 'planned', partly internalised and spontaneous. Not even Good's example of face to face conversation is fully spontaneous and 'natural'. The asymmetry which is so obvious in Human–Machine–Interaction where the Human agent is privileged (since humans can program machines, and machines cannot program humans) is also present in apparently innocent face to face encounters. Only an idealised dominance-free dialogue in the sense of Habermas (which always has been conceived as an ideal model, not an empirically observable fact) could be truly natural and symmetrical; concrete humans that interact are always under constraints and outer pressure which usually puts one of the interlocutors in a position of power.

Even in sociolinguistics, doubt is growing about the feasibility of a distinction between the 'natural' and the 'unnatural', given that historical sociolinguistic states are always under some conscious control from humans. This does not, however, mean that 'natural' sociolinguistic states exist, as if language, if untampered with, could develop fully spontaneously and beyond the control of the societal mind. Naturalness is an analytic construct, not something that will unfold by itself when one leaves one's language alone.

THE PERVASIVE NATURE OF CONSTRAINTS ON INTERACTION

One could not even say that the difference between Human–Human interaction and Human–Machine–Interaction lies in the fact that Human–Human–Interaction can be analytically *conceived of* as symmetrical and Human–Machine–Interaction cannot. The true difference is that the constraints that work on the two kinds of communication are of different types. Constraints that define the degrees of freedom allowed for human interlocutors with humans are usually given by societal conditions at large, by 'the fabric of society'. In Human–Machine–Interaction, these conditions are superseded and partly blurred by constraints of a purely technical kind, that is constraints that are down-to-earth man-made. Focusing too much on these technical constraints has given researchers for a long time the wrong impression that the problem we have to solve is to overcome meaningless and dysfunctional technological constraints only in order to make Human–Machine interaction more natural. But this naturalness does not even exist in the basic face-to-face interaction processes, and assuming that it exists is again the result of the workings of the naturalness fallacy. Cognitive Technology has pointed out to us that since the models incorporated in technological tools in their turn shape the mind that created them in a manner not very different from the way 'other minds' work back on us in Human–Human communicationn. It is therefore important to see which other constraints these systems work under.

The difference between these two kinds of constraints becomes clear in the comparison of the different forms of face-to-face interaction on the one hand as studied in 'natural' sociolinguistics, and the emerging patterns of Human–Machine dialogue we know from Artificial Intelligence on the other. In the latter, the clumsy constraints of the early days (where trivialities like buffer sizes prevented the system from approaching anything that could even look like interaction between humans, as already pointed out by Hein, 1981) have given way to constraints that more and more resemble those encountered in interaction between people. Questions like who has access to information and initiative and who controls turn-taking and who monitors interruptions and overlap, gradually become meaningful even when the one side of the interaction is represented by a machine.

Focussing on language use (communication and interaction) removes the need to assume the existence of a residual 'natural' system within language which is a precondition of language use, but not shaped by language use in return.

REFERENCES

Carnap, R., 1958. *Introduction to symbolic logic and its applications*. New York: Dover. [German edition 1954]

Changeux, J. P., 1985. *Neuronal man*. New York: Oxford University Press. [French edition L'homme neuronal 1983]

Chomsky, N., 1963. Formal properties of grammars. In: R. D. Luce, R. R. Bush and E. Galanter, eds, *Handbook of Mathematical Psychology*, Vol. 2, New York: Wiley, pp. 323-418

Good, D., 1996. Patience and control: The importance of maintaining the link between producers and users. In: B. Gorayska and J.L. Mey, eds, 1996. *Cognitive technology: In search of a humane interface*. Amsterdam: Elsevier, pp. 79-87,

Haberland, H., 1996. Cognitive technology and pragmatics. Analogies and (non-) alignments. *AI&Society*, 10, pp. 303-308.

Haberland, H., 1998. Natural language and artificial technology – It ain't necessarily so. In: J.P. Marsh, Ch.L. Nehaniv and B. Gorayska, eds, *Proceedings, Second International Conference on Cognitive Technology: Humanizing the Information Age*, August 25-28, 1997, Aizu-Wakamatsu City, Japan. Los Alamitos, CA: IEEE Computer Society, pp. 27-30.

Haberland, H., 1999 (in press). Small and endangered languages: a threat to the language or to the speaker? In: A. Ph. Christidis, ed, *Proceedings of the Conference "Strong and "weak" languages in the EU: Aspects of linguistic hegemonism. Thessaloniki*: Center for the Greek Language, Linguistics Section.

Hein, U., 1981. Interruptions in dialogue. In: D. Metzing, ed., *Dialogmuster und Dialogprozesse*. Hamburg: Buske, pp. 73-95.

Matthews, P., 1990. La linguistica greco-latina. In: G. C. Lepschy, ed., *Storia della linguistica I*. Bologna: Il Mulino, pp. 187-310

Montague, R., 1970. English as a formal language. In: B. Visentini et al., eds, *Linguaggi nella società e nella tecnica.* Milano: Edizioni di Communità, pp. 189-224,

Steinthal, H., 1890. Geschichte der Sprachwissenschaft bei den Griechen und Römern mit besonderer Rücksicht auf die Logik. *Erster Teil.* 2. Auflage. Berlin: Dümmler.

Humane Interfaces: Questions of method and practice in Cognitive Technology
J.P. Marsh, B. Gorayska and J.L. Mey (Editors)

Chapter 5

UNDERSTANDING USERS
The Knowledge-Level of Analysis

Alonso H. Vera

The University of Hong Kong

INTRODUCTION

Amongst its goals, Cognitive Technology (CT) proposes to create a new set of methodologies for understanding the interrelationships that are possible between humans and machines. In contrast to traditional Human Computer Interaction (HCI) approaches, the proposed goal of CT is one of creating tools that further culture, society, and human interaction. The CT view attributes the problems of HCI to a misguided focus on making smarter machines rather than smarter humans. This problem is seen as compounded by practitioners' lack of awareness of the subjective roles they play in their "science" (Gorayska and Marsh, 1996).

I will argue that the main problem with computer technology today has little to do with general issues of the relation between researcher, humans, and the environment, but instead with the specific lack of application of user-centred design methodologies. It also has little to do with attempts to anthropomorphic computers. Current research in HCI is directed toward developing interfaces that assist humans where they are limited (e.g., working memory) and that intelligently support activities at which humans are better (e.g., decision making). The main reason why today's technology does not seem particularly suitable for common human use is not that the methodologies of HCI have failed but that they have seldom been used. When they have been carefully applied notable success stories have resulted (see Landauer (1995) for evidence on this issue).

Methodologies such as cognitive modelling allow us to characterise the cognitive mechanisms, processes, and constraints involved in the performance of specific tasks. If these tasks happen to be technology-based, then these methodologies shed light on how our cognitive processes are enhanced or impeded by the technology. Granted, it tells us little about the socio-cultural impact of new technologies but I would argue that those effects are largely independent of the evolution of our cognitive facilities. So, although there has been and will continue to be significant social and cultural change as a consequence of technology, it does not mean that social change translates into genuine changes in our cognitive make-up.

THE HCI RESEARCH APPROACH

Using my own recent research experiences in applied HCI, I will argue that when HCI methodologies are properly used, tools that are specifically suited for the target users' needs --that is, tools that help novices acquire the task easier and experts to perform it better -- can be successfully developed. Making better humans may or may not be possible, but understanding our cognitive processes and developing tools to support them definitely is. The methodologies provided by some 20 years of HCI research are the stepping stone to achieving better cognitive technologies.

Learnability and usability are the two principal variables that determine interface quality. An interface that is easier to *learn* requires less training time and post-training support on the part of the software provider. Furthermore, an interface that is easier to *use* once it has already been learned will be preferred over systems that do not permit similar levels of expert performance. These two advantages are achieved by analysing the specific tasks users perform with the system. Combining task-analysis with knowledge about the cognitive facilities and limitations of typical users yields the parameters required to create a good interface.

To understand the importance of computer interfaces, it is perhaps useful to think of human social interaction as a metaphor for interaction with computers. Today, it is widely accepted that the brain is the source of higher human cognitive capacities. Understanding the brain and its functions has progressed quickly in the past few decades. We now know, for example, that many functions such as language, emotion, and even particular kinds of knowledge are localised in specific areas of our cortex. Advances of this kind, however, have not changed the fact that understanding aspects of human behaviour such as motivation, dedication, leadership, analytical skills, and so on, is not in the realm of neuroscience. These capacities fall under the domain of fields that are in the business of understanding and predicting human *behaviour*, such as cognitive science, psychology, sociology, anthropology and economics.

The situation is much the same with computers. Until the mid 1980s, computer users were primarily scientists and computer/software developers. Personal computers changed this, and, in the past 10 years, we have seen computers move from labs into just about every imaginable setting. The minute computers were no longer being used by the developers themselves, learnability and usability became major concerns. Human-Computer Interaction, as a field of research, was born when people who were not computer scientists or software engineers began using computers in order to increase productivity.

Just as humans make decisions, computers provide decision support. They also provide external representations of knowledge, training, models of data, particular ways of achieving goals, and so on. These are all activities which are best understood at the "knowledge" level rather than at a binary level. Whereas developers are somewhat like neuroscientists -- their job is to understand the underlying mechanisms by which a system functions --it is the job of HCI researchers to understand how systems will perform in relation to their users. It should be noted that this is not a question of understanding how the interface should look any more than understanding human behaviour is about understanding a person's face.

The interface of a system is not just the superficial perceptual characteristics of screen content. A system's interface refers more broadly to its functional and interactive qualities, and much less to the look of what is on the screen. The interface is really the knowledge-level of the system. It is the level which determines how well the system matches the user's expectations of the task, how well it provides quick access to the most frequently performed functions, and how well it presents sequences of required actions in ways that functionally correspond to users' representation of the task. These knowledge-level variables greatly affect the learnability and final usability of the system.

HCI METHODOLOGIES - GOMS

Research in the field of Human-Computer Interaction provides methodologies for prototyping and testing machine interfaces before they are used by people. This involves applying what is known about cognitive mechanisms and the way humans interact with computers to create models of computer users that can be used to test new interfaces.

A number of techniques have been developed by Human-Computer Interaction researchers that yield what are called "engineering models of human performance" (see John and Kieras (1994) for an extensive review and comparison of these tools). Like their physical science cousins, these models allow *a priori* prediction of human performance on computer tasks. They can also be applied consistently to a wide variety of tasks and they yield useful approximations of expected behaviour. One such task analysis technique that has gained significant empirical support in recent years is GOMS (Card, Moran, and Newell, 1983). GOMS is an acronym for *goals, operators, methods, and selection rules.*

GOMS is a technique that allows researchers and software designers to describe a computer-based task (e.g. using MS Word or an ATM) at a level of detail which yields predictions about user learning and performance. A GOMS model begins with the concept of a top-level goal which the user seeks to achieve, and a series of unit tasks that the user performs repeatedly until there are no tasks left. A goal is achieved by executing a method, which consists of a series of steps in which either a low-level operator is called to perform an action, or a subgoal is called to accomplish a subtask. An operator may be one of three types of things: *perceptual*, such as reading a display; *motor*, such as moving and clicking a mouse; or *cognitive*, such as making inferences from available data.

Methods are organised as a series of sequential steps to be performed to achieve a goal. A step may invoke a new goal to be accomplished, in which case the method for that subgoal is executed much like a call to a subroutine, or a step may invoke an operator, which contains implicit procedural and declarative knowledge that has not been further analysed. A step may also invoke a memory operation of storing an item in working memory, recalling an item from working memory, or retrieving an item from long-term memory.

In those cases where there is more than one method which can accomplish a goal, selection rules are written which decide which method is appropriate given the current unit task, the current state of the user's information, and the current state of external factors such as the display interface. Selection rules may also reflect a user's individual preference for one type of operation over another in various circumstances; however, the rules for choosing among methods should be clear in a well-designed interface. In GOMS, selection rules are tested in parallel, and, at any given time, exactly one of the rules must have a condition that is true. The result is a directed acyclic graph of goals and subgoals whose terminal nodes are low-level operators which capture the actual behaviours performed by the user.

The construction of a GOMS model is based on task analysis, which itself requires the application of a number of techniques. First hand data from computer users in the selected domain must be collected. This typically involves getting in-depth interviews as well as detailed protocols of task performance. This information is then integrated with task-specific characterisations of expert knowledge (e.g., training manuals). The process is an iterative one where the researcher goes back and forth between model and data in order to maximise the model's predictive fit.

USING HCI METHODOLOGIES TO DEVELOP BETTER INTERFACES

The initial learnability of a system and its eventual expert-level usability tend to be inversely correlated. Striking a balance between the two requires an understanding of the task performed by the end-user. Task-analysis tools such as GOMS provide the appropriate level description needed to characterise users' interactions with the system. The results of this sort of analysis can and should be integrated with interface *design* efforts that affect the more visual characteristics of the interface.

HCI methodologies such as GOMS have been successfully applied in numerous projects. The author has been involved in a number of such projects including development of an on-line banking system for an interactive television channel, a ship-board radar station for an aerospace company, an automation support interface for the U.S. Postal System, and a system that helps companies send and track their own packages through a major shipping company. All of these projects have been successful as measured empirically by pre/post usability comparisons. An overview of two of these studies is presented below. The goal is to demonstrate that the careful application of existing HCI methodologies yields interactive technologies that are better suited for human use.

AN INTELLIGENT INTERFACE FOR RADAR OPERATIONS

As described in Vera and Rosenblatt (1995), the investigators studied the task of Radar Operators monitoring air and sea traffic on board a ship. The task is very interactive, between the operator and other members of the crew, as well as between the operator and the radar console itself. The work used GOMS to model the task of the human operators. Although it is a methodology that was originally developed to address routine expert behaviour in non-interactive tasks, recent work has indicated that this methodology also yields excellent results when applied to interactive tasks (John, Vera and Newell, 1994; Gray, John and Atwood, 1993; Endestad and Meyer, 1993).

The overall goal of this project was to develop a user model-based *intelligent agent* that could provide guidance and assistance in fast-paced and information-rich computer task, specifically, ship-based radar operations. are independently functioning software entities that achieve complex, intelligent behaviour (i.e., learning, problem-solving, reasoning, and so on) in specific, narrowly constrained domains or tasks. Intelligent agents represent a promising direction for research in human-computer interaction. The basic idea is for complex system interfaces, such as those on aeroplanes or in air-traffic control towers, to have built-in agents that can assist users in their tasks. Intelligent agents that have recently been created are essentially interactive expert systems, programmed for one specific function (e.g., Maes, 1994). This research put forward a new approach for agents based on user models, allowing them to observe and track user actions as well as predict situations where the user will need assistance.

Attempts to create broad and robust models of general human behaviour have not been successful. More recently however, research in the field of Human-Computer Interaction has yielded new ways to model human behaviour on specific kinds of tasks. If such models can be built into intelligent agent software, these agents should be able to perform the tasks in human-like ways. Perhaps more importantly, these agents would also be able to provide assistance to a user because they would be able to track and anticipate the user's behaviour. Intelligent agents consequently represent a whole new class of computer-based interactive technology. They are software programs specifically designed to interact with human users in a way and at a level which is specifically relevant to the task and user.

A number of approaches to developing intelligent agents have recently arisen. They can be broadly characterised as systems that acquire knowledge about specific areas, either through programming or built-in learning mechanisms. We developed a different approach to the problem in which the agent's knowledge is based on a human cognitive model. Instead of programming the agent with specific knowledge, the agent is given a model of how a human would perform the specific task. The agent is thus less like an expert system and more like an active participant in the activity. As part of an interface, such an agent would be able to track the users behaviour, provide assistance and guidance when needed, and even learn (i.e., update its models of the user) from novel user behaviour.

To work co-operatively with a user, an automated agent must be aware of what goals the user is trying to achieve, and where he is in the process of achieving them. Furthermore, the efficacy of agent-user co-operation and communication is greatly enhanced by an understanding of the other's current priorities and beliefs. Examples of such agent tracking can be seen in various arenas, including education (e.g., intelligent tutors that track student activities), training (e.g., intelligent participants in interactive battlefield simulators), and entertainment (e.g., interacting characters in a virtual reality setting such as a mystery novel). The need for intelligent user-interfaces becomes greater in high pressure occupations such as air traffic control and radar operations; it is in such domains, where the agent must respond in real-time, that we have concentrated our research efforts.

"An important idea which has recently been resuscitated in the cognitive sciences is that cognition can be distributed. All the cognitive processes associated with completing a task do not have to reside in *one* head -- cognition involves more than the manipulation of internal representations. Environment and external representations actively affect our behaviour and cognitive processes. External knowledge is no longer seen as just a memory aid or something to be internalised, but rather as something that structures and limits our cognitive behaviour, alters the outcomes of processing isomorphic tasks, and changes the nature of tasks."   (Hutchins, 1995)

Currently, the main limitation of the distributed cognition approach is the lack of a process model. A theory of external knowledge/representation without an adequate explanation of the process is incomplete – it does not allow prediction of the actual flow of control between internal and external knowledge as a task is performed. In order to create such a process model, the notion of conceptualising internal and external representation as distinct entities in the process of cognition must be extended to include the actual interaction between external and internal control of behaviour. Through records of observation of individuals working together and with their environment in real-world tasks, we have accumulated data regarding how a larger system, including internal and external influences on behaviour, can be described in a way that may eventually lead to an adequate process model of interactive tasks.

The Radar Operations project can be seen as an extension of the GOMS task analysis methodology to a complex, distributed cognitive task. The GOMS model we developed addressed how complex tasks can be successfully performed through the interaction of external cues, external representations and memories. The characteristics of GOMS are ideally suited for modelling distributed cognitive tasks. In the first place, GOMS captures user goals as well as device goals; these goals can be represented as internal or external in the analysis. Second, the defined goal-structure in GOMS makes explicit the process by which an expert co-operates with other experts and with his or her environment. Third, the GOMS model explicitly describes how the flow of information demanded by a given task moves from inside the head to out-in-the world, and back. Hence, this use of the GOMS methodology involves not only a claim that cognitive behaviours are the total interactions among users, memories and external representations, but also makes explicit when and how these interactions take place.

An agent that will serve as an intelligent assistant must be able to perform plan recognition, i.e., observe the user's actions and deduce what his beliefs, intentions, and goals are based on those actions. Research in plan recognition has mostly focused on quasi-static domains where real-time constraints and uncertainty were not considered, rendering them inappropriate for tasks where reactivity is crucial (Dousson, Gaborit and Ghallab, 1993). Plan recognition systems operate in a top-down, goal-oriented fashion, maintaining hypotheses concerning other agents' beliefs, desires, and intentions (Bratman, 1987), so that means-ends analysis may be conducted to infer subsequent actions (Peck and John, 1992; Tambe and Rosenbloom, 1995).

Modelling tools such as GOMS create a knowledge-level description of a task (Newell, 1982) and provide a hierarchical structure for decomposing goals into increasingly finer details, thus providing the means to predict the user's goals, beliefs, and priorities, and therefore his actions (Gray, John and Atwood, 1993). However, in contrast to other systems, no planning or searching need take place to deduce the next action within a GOMS model; decisions are made by means of selection rules, thus preserving the reactivity of the agent (John, Vera and Newell, 1994). Our methodology emphasises a reactive data-driven approach as more appropriate for a highly dynamic domain where priorities and actions often change from one moment to the next based on the occurrence of a new event.

When developing a model of a dynamic, real-world task, it is of critical importance to capture and retain the qualities that allow humans to perform the task as well as they do. This research demonstrates that GOMS can capture reactivity in a natural way which results in sequences of behaviours like those produced by humans in similar tasks (see also John and Vera, 1994). This research demonstrated GOMS's power to predict behaviour in highly interactive domains and showed that GOMS is especially useful at making predictions about human behaviour at the functional goal level.

GOMS models derive their reactivity from the organisation of their methods and selection rules. At any given moment in a model's behaviour, the goal stack is relatively shallow because there are very few chained methods that get called as a sequence. Thus, these models behave in a very "situated" way, avoiding criticism such as those of Suchman (1993) and Agre (1993) that current AI systems are inherently non-reactive. Reactivity is not achieved by forcing the model to check for changes in the world (e.g., new orders or contacts) within each method, but instead by returning to the top-level goal after completing a portion of prioritised sub-tasks. The top-level method can then check for changes in the world. Avoiding long linked sequence of methods allows the model to check for important changes in its environment in a way that does not overload working memory nor unnecessarily interrupt routine behaviours. These model are thus able to combine the routine nature of expert behaviour with the demands of real-world interactivity.

Learning is also an important aspect of an intelligent agent, so that it may with time increase its knowledge about the task domain and about the methods and preferences of individual users (Maes and Kozierok, 1993). Implementing an agent in an AI architecture such as Soar (Newell, 1990) or ACT-R (Anderson, 1993) would allow it to learn to correct its own internal model based on observation of real-world activity.

Learning in an intelligent agent takes two forms: improving the model of the task and improving the model of the user. Reinforcement learning techniques can be used to capture a large degree of individual variation between users by rewarding advice that is accepted and punishing advice that is refused; however, they tend to learn somewhat slowly so that the user must extensively train the agent before it becomes useful as an assistant. This approach takes maximum advantage of the structure of the task as captured within the model. The task model can be made more accurate with time as the probabilities and utilities of the various possible outcomes are updated based on actual experience.

The current status of this work is that we have developed a computational model of a ship-based radar-station operator's task. Using GOMS, it is shown that, to a large extent, the radar operator's tasks are of a highly routine nature. The model characterises the operator's goals as well as the methods he uses to accomplish them. A simulated execution of the model in a sample scenario predicted the operator's responses with a high degree of accuracy, and furthermore provided details of those actions that were not explicitly stated in the scenario description. Based on this model, those portions of the task where an intelligent agent would be most able to assist the operator in the performance of his duties were identified. The decision making and information gathering aspects of the operator's task that can be assisted by an intelligent agent are described, as are the structural characteristics necessary for an intelligent agent architecture to fulfil this role. The next phase of this project involves integrating the knowledge model of the task into the Computer Assisted Virtual Environment (CAVE) interface being developed by our collaborators.

As the complexity of computer applications increases and the amount of information available in such systems grows, users of these systems are becoming increasingly overwhelmed by the task of processing all the information that is delivered to them. Providing intelligent interfaces that can assist in the interaction between human and computer can increase productivity, reduce errors, and make the task more enjoyable for the user. Although GOMS has not typically been used as a cognitive modelling tool because it is descriptive rather than explanatory, it allows researchers to characterise human performance on routine tasks that require expert knowledge. Expanding the range of tasks to which tools such as GOMS can be applied is therefore an important activity with respect to developing technologies which are better suited for human use within the context of specific tasks.

A SOFTWARE INTERFACE FOR SHIPPING AND TRACKING PACKAGES

It is worthwhile to ground this discussion further by introducing another recently undertaken interface development project where user-centred design was used to restructure a computer-based task. The goal of this second project was to improve the usability of a system used by customers of a large express shipping company. PackageCo (not the company's real name) gives customers who send more than five packages per day a dedicated computer system which allows them to prepare their own airway bills, commercial invoices, and package labels. This system, which I will call PackageCo Solution, also allows them to download package information directly into the shipping company's computer, which then dispatches someone to pick up the package. Customers can track their packages by logging into the company's computer.

Just as the 1980s witnessed a transformation in the role of computers in the workforce, the 1990s are witnessing a new transformation with the movement of company automation to the consumer level. The early steps of computerisation involved putting a computer on each employee's desk. In many cases, it also involved the development of task specific software. This, for example, was the case for earlier versions of PackageCo Solution, which were developed for in-house use allowing PackageCo employees to send and track packages as well as to provide information about packages to customers. PackageCo is now pioneering the second transformation: providing task specific computers and software to *customers*. This presents both new challenges and great opportunities. The challenges come in the form of interface design, especially at the knowledge level. The target users, the customers, have different knowledge, goals, skills, etc. than the original users. The product therefore has to be re-structured to reflect these user characteristics.

It was necessary to re-conceptualise the task from a user-centred perspective: From the user's point of view, the *package* is the primary mode of entry into system. The top-layer of the system should be designed with the assumption that the user has a package (or packages) to ship or track. Other functions of the system should be secondary. For example, commercial invoices, commodity types, dim weight, and so on, are parts of the task that, from a knowledge-level point of view, are related to the mechanics of shipping. They are not related to the user's task goals but rather to PackageCo's shipping goals. The software consequently needed to be restructured so that the functions of the system revolved around the user's goals. This entailed relocating interface characteristics or functions that were not on the critical path or that unnecessarily consumed cognitive resources (e.g., attention, reading, decision-making).

A simple path analysis using GOMS indicated that the set of functions available to the user during performance of the most frequent tasks was too broad. The typical user's goal is simply to send packages or track packages; these are the two main functions of the system comprising approximately 80% of its use . Low frequency functions, such as using the Database and Reporting (the system can keep and compile shipping information for a given period of time), should therefore be separated into independent functional units. These kinds of activities are functionally distinct from package-specific goals in that they have more to do with maintaining the system and performing routine upkeep operations.

Assuming that the user's entry-point into the system is a package to send or track, the system should have one format for entering package information, regardless of whether the end function is shipping, tracking, reporting, or database entry (one method for multiple goals, in GOMS terms). That is, whether the user is sending, tracking, reporting, or whatever, there should only be one "form" for entering information about packages. The software should take care of transferring information from this general form to the shipping label, commercial invoice, or database -- it should intelligently guide the user through the task. The appearance of the information-entry screen does not have to resemble the final printed output.

The only reason for the look of the screen to resemble the look of the printed output would be to make it easier for the user to check and correct errors. However, because of the interactive advantages of electronic media over printed media it makes sense to take advantage of the usability enhancements provided by computers. The system could have a *print preview* option, similar to word-processing software in order to check the form for errors after it has been completed in a simplified and interactive form.

The current manual for the software indicates that there are multiple paths (methods) to achieve a given function. For example, the user can begin a new shipment by either clicking on the SHIPPING box on the first menu screen, selecting SHIPPING from the pull down menu, or pressing Alt + S using the keyboard. These three types of options are available for many of the functions (though not all). This multi-option approach has two benefits, but also a number of drawbacks. The benefits are that it allows for users that do not have a mouse or do not like to use one (although this system runs only on a 486 machines or higher meaning that few if any user will not have a mouse). It also allows users to change from one method to another as they become more experienced and their performance improves.

On the other hand, presenting users with these options may lead them to use one in some instances, another in other cases, and yet a third for other functions. This may not seem initially problematic, but *consistency* is one of the most important interface characteristics at the functional level (Howes and Young, 1996). Consistency is what allows users to make inferences about new commands they have not learned (e.g., "If Alt + S works for Shipping, then maybe Alt + T works for Tracking"). Consistency in the interface takes advantage of the fact that the capacity to generalise from one instance to another is one of the central cognitive mechanisms by which humans learn. Furthermore, having multiple methods to achieve a goal increases (triples, in this case) the amount of perceived learning faced by the novice.

A final point with respect to specific characteristics of the interface concerns the terminology used. The actual functions of some of the key words currently being used for interface commands are not likely to match users' typical lexical access for the terms. COMMODITY, for example, almost certainly has less meaning for the typical user than for a PackageCo employee. Looked at from the user's perspective, the task is typically to do something with a package (usually shipping it, sometimes tracking it) and therefore it may make more sense to think of it as CONTENTS of the package, rather than commodity types. This follows the more general recommendation that the system should be restructured to present 'the package' as the entry point to the system and the system's terminology should be adapted accordingly to reflect the user's goals.

Research in human-computer interaction indicates that one of the main characteristics that makes systems easier to learn is interactivity. Other interface attributes such as "windows" and file-cabinet metaphors are helpful but not to the same extent as interactivity. The fact that computers, which are very complex tools, can generate their own behaviour in response to human input is what makes them accessible to the average user. The version of the software evaluated for this study does not take advantage of this capacity in order to facilitate learning and usability. Most existing software systems being used around the world today still under-use or misuse this characteristic.

There are numerous functions that could be facilitated in this way. Perhaps the most important one is alerting the user to errors or omissions. The current version of the system informs the user that an error has been made (like trying to move to another field when a required field has not been filled in) by presenting a text line at the bottom of the screen. Observation of users conducted for the purpose of this study indicated that even experienced users often fail to notice the error message and needed to search the interface looking for the cause of the problem. More interactive cues such as colours, greyed-out areas, flashing areas, pop-up boxes, or any other form of simple perceptual marker should be used to differentiate required information from optional information and to alert the user to errors. This takes advantage of the fact that computers are better than printed media (e.g., paper airway bills) at attracting users' attention to relevant functional areas.

The problem with marking particular fields as optional or required is that they change depending on the nature of the shipment. For example, if a shipment contains only printed matter, then the commercial value field does not need to be filled, whereas if the content is anything other than printed matter, it does. On printed media such as airway bills and commercial invoices, it is therefore difficult to clearly demarcate optional and required fields. However, computer interfaces which can respond contingently to particular user inputs easily solve this problem. Creating contingent goal paths, where subsequent screens change depending on the information previously entered, is a straight forward way to enhance usability by allowing the interface to behave "intelligently".

A more interactive system greatly reduces the cognitive resources required for the user to achieve the task. To the extent that the user needs to search the interface to find the next relevant action to execute, more learning is required in order to improve performance. Instructions draw attention away from the area of the display which is functionally relevant to the next task. For example, when a message prompting the user for additional information appears in a command line at the bottom of the screen the user's attention is drawn away from the box in which the information needs to be entered. Furthermore, once attended to, the text on the screen is processed automatically, even when the user is familiar with it. If, on the other hand, searching is reduced or removed completely by having the system cue the user with respect to the next required action, then performance improves, but the amount of information the user has to learn does not increase.

One of the most important characteristics of PackageCo Solution is that it is not a stand-alone system -- it allows users to login to the mainframe to upload and download information. This feature is currently being underused as a potential channel for passing information to the end user. This channel could be used to provide the user with information about new products, software system upgrades, usability tips, and even customer support. Most of these can be accomplished fairly automatically, involving little or no specific attention to individual users by PackageCo, thereby reducing the need for expensive customer support.

There is another potential advantage to having customers electronically connected to the PackageCo mainframe. Having "tethered" users allows PackageCo to gather very useful information about its customers. When a software company releases a new version of a program, user feedback is slow and limited. It is slow because users' goal are primarily task oriented -- they need to get something done, and software problems are an impediment, but dealing with them is not on the goal path. They are also limited because users typically have, at best, only a rudimentary understanding of the nature of the problem and are thus unable to report it in a useful way. On the other hand, having users connected to the system allows the interface analyst to get direct information about the systems usability and learnability without troubling the user. PackageCo's connection with their customers is an example of a general phenomenon that we are seeing more and more of. The same is true of the World Wide Web, intranets, and client-server architectures; all of these provide invaluable opportunities for researchers to gain a deeper understanding of users' knowledge and patterns of cognitive activity.

To work co-operatively with a user, an interface must match the goals the user is trying to achieve. As the complexity of computer applications increases and the amount of information available in such systems grows, users of these systems are becoming increasingly overwhelmed by the task of processing all the information that is delivered to them. Providing intelligent interfaces that can assist in the interaction between human and computer can increase productivity, reduce errors, and make the task more enjoyable for the user. This approach, combined with a restructuring and slight reduction in the functions available to the user, yields a significantly more usable product.

CONCLUSIONS

I have described two studies in which established HCI modelling methodologies and user-centred design were used to create tools more suited to users' tasks. The Radar Operations task involves dealing with a complex and fast-paced environment. Providing computer-based support for this task requires a solution that aids the user where he/she needs it most, in this case, support of working memory and plan execution. To get at this solution it was necessary not only to capture the task-knowledge from the user's perspective but also to design an electronic assistant that embodies that knowledge. The second study presented here investigated how to adapt a system that was originally developed for experts in the task of shipping packages, for use by new users with no expertise in that area. Re-structuring the software to reflect the new users' goals and knowledge required applying user-centred design methodologies to conceptualise the shipping task from their perspective. The overall goal of these two studies was to provide more intelligent interfaces, carefully designed around users' understanding of the task.

Methodologies that have been tried and found to be useful are the most important tools we have. As proponents of the CT view argue, the effects of new technologies on our human abilities and competencies are likely to be negative unless we, as researchers, make an active effort to avoid it. I have argued that this is true, not because we lack good methodologies to assess the impact of new technologies on human activity, but because we have failed to use those we do have. The two examples provided here hopefully show that careful application of these methodologies can result in tools that are well suited to the user's task and that serve to improve not only task performance but also the user's experience in performing the task.

The goal of applying HCI methodologies is not, in principle, to make things *easier*, but rather better tuned to user needs. I would argue that these HCI tools cannot be accused of creating new problems or unduly raising performance standards, as in the vacuum cleaner example in Gorayska and Mey (1996: 9). There is little doubt that the general argument they make is correct: making things easier makes people less able. Our vigilance should consequently be focused on understanding the skills and performance levels demanded by tasks so that we might ask ourselves, before creating a new tool for the task, whether we are affecting these in negative ways. However, this vigilance should not prevent us from applying the useful methodologies we have available to improving those tools which we deem to be necessary. It is real interface improvements associated with performance and usability that will eventually lead to more humane technologies.

Technology changes the way we live in profound ways: how we spend our time and the nature of our daily activities are widely affected by the tools we create for ourselves. Cars have "transportationalised" us to the extent that many people cannot imagine life without them. How deep is this change though? Has it really affected our physiology? Are our legs weaker, or our perceptual abilities to navigate our bodies around while on foot lessened? Probably not. Our tools change our activities, how we spend our time, but they do not change our underlying cognitive and physical make-up. Nevertheless, to the extent that there are certain activities we must engage in, our time on them should be spent constructively. The tools we build to support such activities should be designed to maximise performance and usability. I hope I have convinced the reader that we already have the methodologies at our disposal to achieve this.

REFERENCES

Agre, P. E., 1993. The Symbolic World View: Reply to Vera and Simon. *Cognitive Science*, 17(1), pp. 61-70.

Anderson, J. R., 1993. *Rules of the mind*. Hillsdale, N.J.: Lawrence Erlbaum Associates.

Bratman, M. E., 1987. *Intentions, Plans, and Practical Reason*. Cambridge, M.A.: Harvard University Press.

Card, S. K., T. P. Moran, and A. Newell, 1983. *The psychology of human-computer interaction*. Hillsdale, N.J.: Lawrence Erlbaum Associates.

Dousson, C., P. Gaborit, and M. Ghallab, 1993. Situation recognition: representation and algorithms. *Proceedings of the International Joint Conference on Artificial Intelligence*. AAAI Press.

Endestad, T. and P. Meyer, 1993. *GOMS analysis as an evaluation tool in process control: An evaluation of the ISACS-1 prototype and the COPMAsystem*. Technical Report HWR-349, OECD Halden Reactor Project, Instituut for Energiteknikk, Halden, Norway.

Gray, W. D., Bonnie E. J., and M. E. Atwood, 1993. Project Ernestine: A validation of GOMS for prediction and explanation of real-world task performance. *Human Computer Interaction*, 8(3), pp. 209-237.

Gorayska, B. and J. L. Mey, 1996. Of minds and men. In: B. Gorayska and J. L. Mey, eds, *Cognitive Technologies: In search of a humane interface*. Amsterdam: Elsevier/ North Holland, pp. 1-24.

Gorayska, B. and J. Marsh, 1996. Epistemic technology and relevance analysis: Rethinking cognitive technology. In: B. Gorayska and J. L. Mey, eds., *Cognitive Technologies: In search of a humane interface*. Amsterdam: Elsevier/ North Holland, pp. 27-39.

Howes, A. and R. M. Young, 1996. Learning Consistent, Interactive, and Meaningful Task-Action Mappings: A Computational Model. *Cognitive Science*, 20(3), pp. 301-356.

Hutchins, E., 1995. How a cockpit remembers its speeds. *Cognitive Science*, 19(3), pp. 265-288.

John, B. E. and D. E. Kieras, 1994. *The GOMS family of analysis techniques: Tools for design and evaluation*. Technical Report CMU-HCII-94-106, Human-Computer Interaction Institute, Carnegie Mellon University.

John, B. E. and A. H. Vera, 1992. A GOMS analysis for a graphic, machine-paced, highly interactive task. *Proceedings of the Conference on Computer Human Interaction*. New York, N.Y.: ACM Press.

John, B. E., Alonso H. V., and A. Newell, 1994. Toward real time GOMS: A model of expert behaviour in a highly interactive task. *Behaviour and Information Technology*, 13(4), pp. 255-267.

Landauer, T. K., 1995. *The trouble with computers: Usefulness, usability, and productivity*. Cambridge, MA: MIT Press.

Maes, P., 1994. Agents that reduce work and information overload. *Communications of the ACM*, 37(7), pp. 30-40.

Maes, P. and R. Kozierok, 1993. Learning interface agents. *Proceedings of the International Joint Conference on Artificial Intelligence*. AAAI Press.

Newell, A., 1982. The knowledge level. *Artificial Intelligence*, 18, pp. 87-127.

Newell, A., 1990. *Unified theories of cognition*. Cambridge, M.A.: Harvard University Press.

Peck, V. A. and Bonnie E. J., 1992. Browser-Soar: A computational model of a highly interactive task. *Proceedings of the Conference on Computer Human Interaction*. New York, N.Y.: ACM Press.

Suchman, L. A., 1993. Response to Vera and Simon's Situated action: A symbolic interpretation. *Cognitive Science*, 17(1), pp. 71-76.

Tambe, M. and P. S. Rosenbloom, 1995. RESC: An approach to agent-tracking in a real-time, dynamic environment. *Proceedings of the International Joint Conference on Artificial Intelligence*. AAAI Press.

Vera, A. H., and J. K. Rosenblatt, 1995. Developing User Model-Based Intelligent Agents. *Proceedings of the Seventeenth Annual Conference of the Cognitive Science Society*. Hillsdale, N.J.: Lawrence Erlbaum Associates.

*Humane Interfaces: Questions of method and
practice in Cognitive Technology*
J.P. Marsh, B. Gorayska and J.L. Mey (Editors)
© *1999 Elsevier Science B.V. All rights reserved.*

AUGMENTATION, MEDIATION, INTEGRATION?

Barbara Gorayska
Jonathon P. Marsh
Jacob L. Mey

COMMENTARY

The need for Methodological clarification in design begins to emerge from the arguments presented in the previous section. If the results obtained from CT investigations into tool/mind co-evolution are to be at all legitimate, it is of paramount importance that we first commit ourselves to a certain view of the mind and what is meant by mind-change. Only then can we agree on what level, and what kind of change is appropriate to our investigations. Having done so, we then need to make sure that the methods we use suit the purpose and are properly applied.

The chapters in this section elaborate on the issue of methodological clarification in greater detail. In discussing the changes which have occurred in humans as a result of technological development (both in the realm of the tools themselves and on the level of qualification and design), the various authors invite the reader to reflect further on the fluidity of the boundary between the natural and the artificial. It would appear that in times of technological explosion, this commonly accepted intuitive distinction is neither immediately obvious nor methodologically useful.

One particularly interesting development is taking place on the linguistic front. Is the language that emerges in human-machine interactions still human, and 'natural' (whatever that means)? We are dealing with a general problem here: that of the effects of computerization on the mental activity of humans. By way of example, Kelly Wical, a scientist working at the California-based ORACLE Inc., has remarked on automated indexing and its possible consequences as follows:

"As automated indexing becomes available, we will begin to depend on it. It will encourage people to write plainly without metaphors or double entendres that might confuse search engines. After all, everyone wants people to find what they have written." (From an interview with Steve G. Steinberg in *Wired* magazine, May 1996: 183)

The case is analogous to the instruction figures found on Danish tax return forms, or on the back of Russian envelopes, which require people to form their figures (for the purpose of automated return or automatic recognition of the postal code) in accordance with some pre-set patterns of writing (e.g. don't bar your '7's, don't close your '4's on top, etc.). What this indicates is that the mind and its products are forced to adapt to the requirements of the technology, rather than the other way around: adaptivity rather then adaptability, in Mey's terminology (1994).

We could equally well put into question the commonly held belief that what is usually thought of as 'natural' in human-to-human language is indeed free from design. What, then, is design and how does it manifest itself? If we take the view, as Tripp does, that anything that has a purpose, structure, model cases and arguments that explain and evaluate it, is subject to design, then theories, ideas, science as such, and indeed human language itself must be designed.

The problems of design specification and methodological clarification associated with the blurring of the distinction between the artificial and the natural, are amplified when one tries to distinguish clearly between the real and the virtual with respect to the interactions between internal and external worlds. Current advances in media culture appear to confirm the relationship between *the brain, the body,* and *the environment* as a dynamically integrated continuum rather than as a collection of interacting but separate systems (Clark, 1997). It stands to reason that the continuum (of the brain, the body, and the environment) can be "interfered with" in a variety of ways, depending on how the technology which serves to augment it, is designed.

In order to successfully, and humanely, interact with computers, we need to be ourselves, and not succumb to the temptation to be 'like machines' (Mey. 1984; Gorayska, 1994). For example, the awe-inspiring potential of a computerized memory for storing and retrieving information is not something humans need to emulate, or even envy. Humans do not just *augment* knowledge. They work with it as a tool. They *mediate* knowledge. That is to say, using the computer as a medium, they apply knowledge to their own functional uses. However, if this mediating process is to be entirely successful, it has to be *integrated* into the whole human pattern of interaction; perhaps, even into the human 'wetware' of the brain via prosthetic chips which replace or augment some of its functions (the 'silver paths' that W. Gibson prophesies about: see the *Foreword,* above). Such a vision is squarely within the domain of CT: it begs the question of how to guide such development according to truly *humane* principles. Thus, the questions emerging here are:

- *What are the relative effects of prosthetic tool intervention at different points in the brain-body-world continuum?*
- *To what degree is prosthetic tool intervention a process of mediation rather than augmentation?*
- *What happens when the process of tool intervention is out of step with the needs of either the user, or the world, or both?*

- *What design methods can we use to ensure that prosthetic tool intervention occurs humanely?*

CHAPTER SUMMARIES

Chapter 6
Frank Biocca
The Cyborg's Dilemma

In his contribution to this volume, Frank Biocca attends to the Cartesian duality of body and mind in the context of the recent advances in Virtual Reality. He shows how the unique forms of communication offered by digital technology, in particular the process of progressive embodiment which allows us to think through our technologically extended bodies, change our sense of mind/body cohesion. He points out that processing of digitized information has become portable to the point that our personalities can be easily distributed throughout the material world. Similarly yet conversely, our physical bodies can be made present as control mechanisms within virtual worlds. Consequently, questions such as 'Who am I?', 'Where am I?', and 'What happens to me when I engage in new technologies?' become profoundly significant to the scientific and social inquiry agenda. Biocca discusses significant design challenges in the construction of virtual environments, especially with respect to immersive virtual reality systems, which are posed by the progressive embodiment of the user inside the interface. Supporting his argument with evidence of the progressive evolution of the user into a cyborg of the Cyberspace, the author draws our attention to the fact that, in order to ensure that prosthetic tool intervention occurs humanely, it is now necessary to formulate an explanatory theory of presence.

Chapter 7
Kari Kuutti
Cognitive Tools Reconsidered: From Augmentation to Mediation

Kari Kuutti draws our attention to the fundamental fact that internal cognitive processes, shaped by artifacts, are manifested in, and transformed by, the cultural context. Going beyond a simple augmentation of cognition, he sees the tool user's mind as constituted by tool mediation. What is needed to ensure humane tool design, therefore, is a set of design rules and standards derived from and related to the dynamics of functional organs. This, he maintains, can only be achieved by studying the actual learning dynamics of systems-in-use, and not by providing analytical definitions of such use apriori.

Chapter 8
Benny Karpatschof
The Meeting Place of Cognition and Technology

Benny Karpatschof analyses the relationship between the technological and cognitive spheres from the perspective of his theory of externalization. Two topics are considered: the evolution of cognitive technology and the related demand for increased human capacity in the form of personal competence. Since cognition and technology have been inseparable since humans first appeared, the way these two interrelate can be seen as a constitutive characteristic of our species. Human activity has always been mediated by tools and signs which, once produced, have been transferred to others within a given cultural community as objective, non-personal entities. The evolving complexity of tools has caused an increase in the cognitive demands placed on tool users, often resulting in cultural revolutions, when the knowledge culture accelerates out of step with the tool culture. For example, the currently ongoing evolution of information technology is changing the societal structure away from the need for qualification toward the need for competence. How these transitions happen cannot be studied effectively by a conglomeration of independent disciplines. If we want to study the mind by scrutinising its externalisations, we must recognize the externalisation process as being directly linked to the concurrent process of internalisation whereby we are systemically confronted with an externalized picture of ourselves and the way we think.

Chapter 9
Will Fitzgerald and Eric Goldstein
What Do You Know? Evaluating Honesty of Affordance in Cognitive Tools

In their chapter, Will Fitzgerald and Eric Goldstein pose some fundamental questions such as: 'What is affordance?', 'What is capability?', 'How can we measure whether an affordance leads to a capability, or whether a capability is realised by an affordance?', and 'Are there useful quantitative and qualitative measures by which the honesty of affordance' within a tool or an environment can be assessed? In other words, 'Can we establish how difficult it is to achieve one's goal using a tool'? By way of example, an application of the proposed methods for evaluating the establishment of humane requirements in World Wide Web search engines and internet browsers is discussed.

Chapter 10
Steven D. Tripp
The Design of Cognitive Tools

The related evolution of ideas and artifacts is examined by Steven Tripp from a different angle. The author starts off by considering the Science of Design, based on Simon's distinction between the natural sciences and the sciences of the artificial, and proceeds step by step towards his conclusion that there exists a *Design of Science* which reverses Simon's distinctions. If scientific theories are knowledge designs, in the sense that they have a purpose, structure, model cases, and arguments that explain and evaluate them, then it is more appropriate to talk about two kinds of design rather than two kinds of science: the design of artifacts and the design of ideas.

Chapter 11
Jacques Vidal
Cyberspace Bionics

Jacques Vidal reflects on the computer revolution which, unlike earlier communication technology, has transformed, rather than extended, the range of human experience. For him the challenge that faces developers of computer network environments for information transfer is the intelligent integration and cooperation of information. It is conceivable that the success of such development will result in the eventual emergence of a shadow society of software robots, inclusive of user agents capable of taking into account the dynamically changing mental states of the user. As the dialogue between humans and machines becomes ever more intimate and natural, one goal driving human machine communication is the creation of a bridge between human bodily perception and cognition and the capabilities of the computer, thus once again blurring the borderline between the real and the virtual. Vidal argues that our capacity to increase the intimacy of interaction between humans and machines can be furthered by biocybernetic research. Earlier projects on 'bionic interfaces' worked by regulating biofeedback to task performing humans; current research is exploring the use of measurable biological signals, amplified by real-time computer processing, to assist in controlling vehicles, weaponry, and other biometric systems for authentication and control in major social institutions. These include systems capable of dealing with hand geometry, face recognition, and retinal scans. Future developments in biocybernetic technology include the possibility of direct brain-computer interfaces. The author discusses the methods and experimental conditions required to assess the potential use of brain signals in furthering our understanding of the cognitive processes that take place in real time during human-computer interactions. When attempting to fully integrate and utilize brain signals in human-machine interactions, a related CT design issue of crucial importance must be addressed, viz.: How do we design the technology so as to ensure that the machine is elevated to the status of a true brain prosthetic, rather than remain a fundamentally alien piece of supporting hardware which brings its own set of non-human demands to the interaction?

Chapter 12
Myron Krueger
Cognitive Space

To round out this section, Myron Krueger argues that contrary to common assumptions, intellect cannot be equated with the faculty of abstraction. Because of this common belief, people have neglected the physical aspects of design in creating interfaces. Thus, it is not surprising that perceptual design metaphors, in spite of their well-known advantages, have largely failed to deliver ergonomically sound interfaces. In contrast to the use of perceptual metaphors, Krueger suggests that a better cognitive fit between humans and machines can be achieved through immersive representations of programmable virtual worlds. Worlds which involve all of our senses, including smell, touch, and movement, thus allowing us to function within information spaces of our own creation. Since memory and logic are located in our bodies, interfaces to computerized tools ought to take advantage of humanity's heritage as spatial beings. While traditional endeavors within virtual reality have been directed towards making real environments virtual, the present chapter suggests how we might consider making real space more interactive. He argues that space can be permeated with information by superimposing projected information on real objects. As every surface around us becomes usable for memory and communication, the new culture that emerges may radically change not only the way in which we obtain knowledge, with respect to what we need to know and when we need to know it, but also the very way we think about knowing.

REFERENCES

Clark, A., 1997. *Being There: Putting the brain, body, and world together again.* Cambridge, Mass.: MIT Press.
Gibson W., 1984. *Neuromancer.* London: Harper Collins, p. 289.
Gorayska, B., 1994. How to lose the soul of language. *Journal of Pragmatics,* 22, pp. 529-547.

Mey, J. L., 1984. *'And ye shall be as machines. Reflections on a certain kind of generation gap'.* Journal of Pragmatics, 8, pp. 757-797.

Mey, J. L, 1994. Adaptability. In: R. E. Asher, ed*., The Encyclopedia of Language and Linguistics I.* Oxford: Pergamon Press. pp. 25-27,

Humane Interfaces: Questions of method and
practice in Cognitive Technology
J.P. Marsh, B. Gorayska and J.L. Mey (Editors)
1999 Elsevier Science B.V.

Chapter 6

THE CYBORG'S DILEMMA
Progressive embodiment in virtual environments [1]

Frank Biocca

Media Interface and Network Design (M.I.N.D.) Lab
Michigan State University

"The intrinsic relationship that arises between tools and organs, and one that is to be revealed and emphasized – although it is more one of unconscious discovery than of conscious invention – is that in the tool the human continually produces itself. Since the organ whose utility and power is to be increased is the controlling factor, the appropriate form of a tool can be derived only from that organ." *Ernst Kapp, 1877, quoted in* Mitcham, 1994, p. 23

MINDING THE BODY, THE PRIMORDIAL COMMUNICATION MEDIUM

In the twentieth century we have made a successful transition from the sooty iron surfaces of the industrial revolution to the liquid smooth surfaces of computer graphics. On our computer monitors we may be just beginning to see a reflective surface that looks increasingly like a mirror. In the virtual world that exists on the other side of the mirror's surface we can just barely make out the form of a body that looks like us, like another self. Like Narcissus looking into the pond, we are captured by the experience of this reflection of our bodies. But that reflected body looks increasingly like a cyborg.[2]

---

[1] ©1998 IEEE. Reprinted, with permission, from Proceedings oftheSecond International Conference on Cognitive Technology, August 25 – 28, 1997, Aizu, Japan, pp. 12-26. Los Alamitos: IEEE Computer Society Press.

[2] Those readers familiar with McLuhan's work will see the echo of McLuhan's warning about the "Narcissus trance" that our technologically "amputated" senses present us. But here, I argue that rather than technological "amputation," I have a form of technological adaptation.

This article explores an interesting pattern in media interface development that I will call progressive embodiment. Each progressive step in the development of sensor and display technology moves telecommunication technology towards a tighter coupling of the body to the interface. The body is becoming present in both physical space and cyberspace. The interface is adapting to the body; the body is adapting to the interface (Biocca and Rolland, in press).

Why is this occurring? One argument is that attempts to optimize the communication bandwidth of distributed, multi-user virtual environments such as social VRML worlds and collaborative virtual environments drives this steady augmentation of the body and the mind (see Biocca, 1995). It has become a key to future stages of interface development. On the other hand, progressive embodiment may be part of a larger pattern, the cultural evolution of humans and communication artifacts towards a mutual integration and greater "somatic flexibility" (Bateson, 1972).

The pattern of progressive embodiment raises some fundamental and interesting questions. In this article we pause to consider these developments. New media like distributed immersive virtual environments sometimes force us to take a closer look at what is fundamental about communication. Inevitably, theorists interested in the fundamentals of communication return in some way or another to a discussion of the body and the mind. At the birth of new media, theories dwell on human factors in communication (Biocca, 1995) and are often more psychological than sociological. For example when radio and film appeared, Arnheim (1957) and Munsterberg (1916) used the perceptual theories of Gestalt psychology to try to make sense of how each medium affected the senses. In the 1960s McLuhan (1966; McLuhan and McLuhan, 1988) refocused our attention on media technology when he assembled a controversial psychological theory to examine electronic media and make pronouncements about the consequences of imbalances in the "sensorium."

Before paper, wires, and silicon, the primordial communication medium is the body. At the center of all communication rests the body, the fleshy gateway to the mind. Becker and Schoenbach (1989) argue that "a veritable 'new mass medium' for some experts, has to address new senses of new combinations of senses. It has to use new channels of information" (p. 5). In other words, each new medium must somehow engage the body in a new way. But this leads us to ask, are all the media collectively addressing the body in some systematic way? Are media progressively embodying the user?

The senses as channels to the mind

Each of us lives within ... the prison of his own brain. Projecting from it are millions of fragile sensory nerve fibers, in groups uniquely adapted to sample the energetic states of the world around us: heat, light, force, and chemical composition. That is all we ever know of it directly; all else is logical inference (1975, p. 131) (see Sekuler and Blake, 1994 p. 2).

The senses are the portals to the mind. Sekuler and Blake extend their observation to claim that the senses are "communication channels to reality." Consider for a moment the body as an information acquisition system. As aliens from some distant planet we observe humans and see the body as an array of sensors propelled through space to scan, rub, and grab the environment. In some ways, that is how virtual reality designers see users (Durlach and Mavor, 1994). Many immersive virtual reality designers tend to be implicitly or explicitly Gibsonian: they accept the perspective of the noted perceptual psychologist J.J. Gibson (1966, 1979). Immersive virtual environments are places where vision and the other senses are meant to be active. Users make use of the affordances in the environments from which they perceive the structure of the virtual world in ways similar to the manner they construct the physical world. Through motion and collisions with objects the senses pick up invariances in energy fields flowing over the body's receptors. When we walk or reach for an object in the virtual or physical world, we guide the senses in this exploration of the space in same way that a blind man stretches out a white cane to explore the space while in motion. What we know about the world is embodied, it is constructed from patterns of energy detected by the body. The body is the surface on which all energy fields impinge, on which communication and telecommunication takes form.

The body as a display device for a mind

The body is integrated with the mind as a representational system, or as the neuroscientist, Antonio Damasio, puts it, "a most curious physiological arrangement ... has turned the brain into the body's captive audience" (Damasio, 1994). In some ways, the body is a primordial display device, a kind of internal mental simulator. The body is a representational medium for the mind. Some would claim that thought is embodied or modeled by the body. Johnson and Lakoff (Johnson, 1987; Lakoff and Johnson, 1980; Lakoff, 1987) argue against a view of reasoning as manipulation of prepositional representations (the "objectives position"), a tabulation and manipulation of abstract symbols. They might suggest a kind of sensory-based "image schemata" that are critical to instantiating mental transformations associated with metaphor and analogy. In a way virtual environments are objectified metaphors and analogies delivered as sensory patterns instantiating "image schemata."

In his book, *Decartes' Error,* the neuroscientist Damasio explains how the body is used as a means of embodying thought:

"...the body as represented in the brain, may constitute the indispensable frame of reference for the neural processes that we experience as the mind; that our very organism rather than some absolute experiential reality is used as the ground of reference for the constructions we make of the world around us and for the construction of the ever-present sense of subjectivity that is part and parcel of our experiences; that our most refined thoughts and best actions, our greatest joys and deepest sorrows, use the body as a yardstick"

(Damasio, 1994)

Damasio's title, *Descartes' Error,* warns against the misleading tendency to think of the body and mind, reason and emotion, as separate systems.

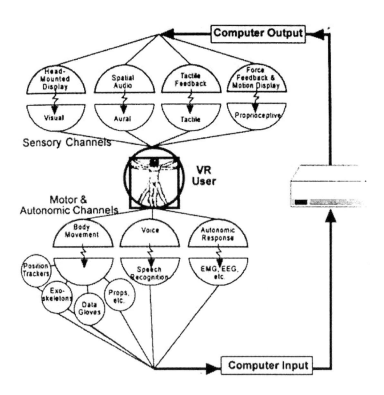

Figure 1. Range of possible input (sensors) and output (effectors) devices for a virtual reality system.

The body as a communication device

The body is also an expressive communication device (Benthall and Polhemus, 1975), a social semiotic vehicle for representing mental states (e.g., emotions, observations, plans, etc.) to others. The body emits information to the senses of other bodies, whether intentional or not (Ekman, 1974). Observers of the physical or mediated body read emotional states, intentions, and personality traits by an empathic simulation of them (Zillman, 1991). The body transmits information to other bodies through a kind of affective contagion.

Thinking of the body as an information channel, a display device, or a communication device, we emerge with the metaphor of the body as a kind of simulator for the mind. But as in a simulator, the software and the hardware cannot be cleanly separated; they both contribute to the fidelity of the simulation.

EMBODIMENT: THE TELEOLOGY OF INTERFACE DESIGN

If the body is the fundamental communication hardware, a simulator for a mind, what is its relationship to media made of steel, plastic, or silicon? Instead of pulsing blood, pulses of electrons and light animate these media. McLuhan long ago pointed out that modern communication interfaces attach themselves to the body. In the words of McLuhan, "media are extensions of the senses."

The relationship of a human to an interface can be one of a body to an environment, or of one brain to another through a kind of conversation. McLuhan's vision of media environments is a slightly different vision than the one advanced by Licklider (1960) in his famous article on "man-computer symbiosis." For him, "man-computer symbiosis" is a subclass of "man-machine systems." The computer was not to be treated like other machines because it was "intelligent." This intelligent partner could be engaged in a kind of conversation. The disembodied human brain would be coupled to a machine brain rather than to cognitive environments:

> "The hope is that, in not too many years, human brains and computing machines will be coupled very tightly, and that the resulting partnership will think as no human brain has ever thought and process data in a way not approached by the information-handling machines we know today. "
>
> (Licklider, 1960,: 4)

In a view of the computer as giant brain, widely shared in the 40s and 50s, we see another version of Descartes' error. This coupling was of one brain to another. The communication between human and machine was one of conversation. The conversation was with a large disemboded electronic brain, seen either as a peer, slave, or competitor. Instead of a mind communicating through a body to another body, we have only two disembodied conversations, a sterile coupling of abstract symbol generators. It is the symbol manipulating vision of early artificial intelligence, rather than the situated embodiment of intelligence augmentation (Biocca, 1995). At the close of this century, the development of advanced computer interfaces appears to be increasingly characterized by what we might call progressive embodiment. Progressive embodiment is defined as the steadily advancing immersion of sensorimotor channels to computer interfaces through a tighter and more pervasive coupling of the body to interface sensors and displays.

This pattern of progressive embodiment is most evident in the discourse, research, and development of advanced immersive virtual reality, augmented reality systems, and wearable computers (Biocca and Delaney, 1995; Durlach and Mavor, 1994). Writings growing out of early conferences on virtual reality and cyberspace enthusiastically welcomed the coupling of the body to virtual reality interfaces:

The trajectory of Western thought has been one moving from the concrete to the abstract, from the body to the mind; recent thought, however, has been pressing upon us the frailty of that Cartesian distinction. The mind is the property of the body, and lives and dies with it. Everywhere we turn we see signs of the recognition, and cyberspace, in its literal placement of the body in spaces invented by the mind, is located directly upon the blurring of this boundary, this fault (Novak, 1991, p. 227).

Evidence that virtual reality was creating a tighter integration of sensors and displays with the body gave rise to this kind of pronouncement. Figure 1 displays the range of virtual reality devices and their connection to sensory channels or the motor and autonomic channels. The evolution of these devices is the evolution of the progressive coupling of sensors and display devices to the body. The vision of such a system foresees some applications where the body of the user is to be completely immersed in the interface, and the mind is set floating in the telecommunication system – in cyberspace. Like a body entering a sink, a bath, or a pool, communication demands and contexts will determine how much the body needs to be immersed in the electric-cool waters of cyberspace.

There is a teleology to human-machine symbiosis. Advanced communication interfaces are designed to assist users in those times when total embodiment is desired for information intensive communication (e.g., sensorimotor training in flight, battle, sports, etc.; certain forms of entertainment where simulations of the past places, telepresence to existing places, and the subjective experience of others is critical). Total immersion is the goal. There has been some temporary retreat from the aggressive pursuit of this vision because of the immaturity of the display and sensing devices. Early attempts to immerse the body in these immature technologies have led to imperfect mapping of the body to the interface. Physiological reactions of the body to this imperfect mapping have taken the form of simulation sickness (Biocca, 1992); (Kennedy et al., 1992) and visuomotor adaptation (Biocca and Rolland, in press).

Virtual reality is an immature technology. But simulation technologies are developing rapidly. Figure 2 shows the classes of variables that are critical to the continued refinement of virtual environments and progressive embodiment. Looking only at the evolution of the hardware and operation systems of virtual reality interfaces, we can characterize the design of progressive embodiment by developments in the following classes of variables:

Sensory engagement

Clearly the senses are connected to the interface. But how? How should we define this aspect of embodiment? Past theorists of virtual environments have attempted to define the degree to which the senses are connected to the displays of the interface. Upon analysis most of these definitions prove to be flawed. For example, Sheridan (1992) states that physical presence (defined below) may be related to the "amount of sensory information" in the interface. On the surface this seems acceptable. But this definition suggests using "information" as the unit of measurement. How does one measure the variable "amount of sensory information." It has been known since perceptual experiments in the 1950s that information theory measures of "information" (Shannon and Weaver, 1949), especially of perceptual information, are not usable because we are unable to predict chunking and other structural information. One "bit" of perceptual information is not definable in any useful way.

In another attempt to define properties of the interface Steuer (1995) arrays interfaces according to their amount of "vividness." This concept is also flawed. It confuses independent and dependent variables by defining a property of the interface, the computer, in terms of the effect of this property on the user. As a result it is difficult to operationalize.

I will use the term, sensory engagement, to define the degree to which the senses are engaged or connected to the interface. The amount of sensory engagement is defined and measurable using the following dimensions:

Number of sensory channels engaged by the virtual environment

Not all senses are channels for information for virtual environments. For example, the nasal and oral senses tend to be underutilized, and coverage of the haptic and tactile senses is highly limited (see Biocca and Delaney, 1995; Durlach and Mavor, 1995). Media have not evolved that far. So in some ways, we are partially disembodied when interacting with most media. Interfaces can easily be classified as to the number of sensory channels they address. There is also a trend towards increasing the number of sensory channels that are connected to the interface. In this century displays for the visual and aural senses have been steadily perfected. For example, the silent film evolved another display channel and became the "talkie." In the last twenty five years sophisticated tactile and proprioceptive devices have been incorporated into some simulators, and in the last few years nasal displays are beginning to evolve from the crude aroma releasers of a few decades ago to more sophisticated devices (Krueger, 1997). In the process of progressive embodiment, more of the senses are entering cyberspace. If we look at the trajectory of interface development, it is fair to say that at some point all the senses may be connected to cyberspace for certain intensely sensory experiences.

Increasing sensory fidelity of displays and range of sensory cues within each sensory channel

Our knowledge of the senses is being directly applied to the design of increased fidelity (e.g., (Biocca and Delaney, 1995; Durlach and Mavor, 1994). So for each sensory channel we can theoretically define the level of sensory fidelity for that channel. Sensory fidelity can be defined in terms of the pattern of energy impinging on the senses. Sensory fidelity is the degree to which the energy array produced by a mediated display matches the energy array of an unmediated stimulus. The quantification and measurement of the increasing match of the mediated display to an unmediated stimulus is easier for some sensory channels (i.e., the visual), than for others (i.e., olfactory). Good examples of commonly used measures in the visual channel are resolution and color fidelity, two quantifiable properties of array of light on a visual display.

Over time virtual environment designers hope that display devices will approach and exceed the full sensory capabilities of each sensory channel. At the moment, even the most advanced displays, those for the visual channel, for example, fall short of the full capabilities of human vision (Durlach and Mavor, 1995; Kocian and Task, 1995).

Increased saturation of the sensory channels engaged by the virtual environment and suppression of sensory channels not engaged

In an effort to fully embody the user in the virtual environment, the capacity of those senses engaged by the system must be immersed in the representation of the virtual world.

Level of sensory saturation is defined as the percentage of the sensory channel occupied by stimuli (information) from the virtual as opposed to the physical environment.

For example, when a user looks at a typical monitor only a fraction of the visual field is occupied by stimuli from the virtual environment. But monitors are becoming progressively larger, and VRhead mounted displays are moving to larger fields-of-view. The ambition is to saturate the field-of-view of the user with the virtual environment. A similar pattern of progressive saturation is found in other sensory display systems. The bandwidth of each sensory channel is being steadily taken up by stimuli from the virtual world.

When users use media it is often done in a setting that suppresses stimuli from the physical environment. We can call this phenomenon *sensory suppression of the immediate environment.*

Sensory suppression of the immediate environment is caused by features of the interface or the user's environment that dampen, eliminate, or minimize the impact of stimuli on the sensory channels not engaged by the interface or by the part of a sensory channel not saturated by the interface.

A good example of sensory suppression is the environment of the typical movie theater:

- The mediated environment, the movie screen, especially in IMAX theaters, saturates the visual channel (i.e., field of view) of the user so little of the immediate environment, the theater, is visible.

- Dimming the lights makes the screen (the mediated environment) dominant, and suppresses visual information from the parts of the physical environment that are not displaying mediated information (i.e., the people seated beside you, the curtains on the walls, etc.).

- Sound volume and social rules about making noise suppress sound from the ambient physical environment.

- Soft comfortable seats and temperature controls suppress awareness of the haptic and proprioceptive channels.

The interface, the environment, and social rules during interface use are all designed to immerse the users' senses in the virtual environment of the movie screen. Communication flows to parts of sensory bandwidth not immersed in cyberspace are suppressed and decreased.

Motor engagement

The body's movement and activity is increasingly part of the interface (Biocca and Delaney, 1995; Durlach and Mavor, 1995). It can be argued that historically the body enters cyberspace with the creation of the humble mouse (Bardini, 1997). Why not use the keyboard someone might ask? The keyboard was primarily a symbolic input device for textual "conversation" with the computer. The keyboard did not map the movement of the body in space to cyberspace. So it was conversational input, not a somatic input. Over time more of the body's morphology and motion are being captured by the position trackers, motion capture systems, and other sensors, vivid 3D representation of the user, direct manipulation, and machine analysis of user intention (task selection).

Number of motor channels engaged by the virtual environment

Progressive embodiment can be seen in the number of interface sensors that map the motion of the body including joysticks, head trackers, eye trackers, facial motion systems, etc.

Resolution of body sensors

Sensors, like displays, are capturing finer and finer resolutions of body motion and physiological activity, e.g. fine finger movement, lip movement, etc.

Sensorimotor Coordination

One of the most important factors in immersing the user's body into the interface is sensorimotor coordination. It is the essence of feedback, especially the kind of feedback we experience in our interaction with the physical environment. Sensorimotor coordination is defined as the degree to which changes in body position correlate immediately and naturally with appropriate changes in sensory feedback. The presence of lag in immersive virtual reality systems between motor movement and sensory feedback is a significant source of simulation sickness and decrements in human performance (Held and Durlach, 1991).

EMBODIMENT: THINKING THROUGH OUR TECHNOLOGICALLY EXTENDED BODIES

The process of progressive embodiment is occurring at a time when there is increasing social integration of the interface. Social integration means that the interface is being integrated into everyday activity at work, home, and on the street. Increased social integration of the sensorimotor interface into everyday communication is giving rise to longer and more contextually varied access to cyberspace. The interface enters the social sphere via easier coupling with the body through miniaturization, portability, and wearability.

In most virtual environments systems, but especially in immersive virtual reality systems, progressive embodiment of the user inside the interface presents significant design challenges.

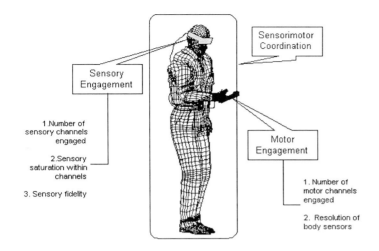

Figure 2. The users are progressively embodied in virtual environment interfaces through evolving technologies of sensory engagement, motor engagement, and sensorimotor coordination.

Designing a space for bodily action

How do we create the illusion of a stable and coherent spatial environment with at least most of the sensory properties of the physical world (i.e., visual space, auditory space, tactile resistance and pressure, smell and appropriate free floating molecules, etc.)?

Design of other intelligent beings

The space the body enters cannot be a ghost town, as many early VR worlds were in the early 1990s. So the challenge is to create the perception of other intelligent beings. These issues are normally found under the discussion of the design of agents and avatars, and of virtual humans.

The most pressing design issues are:

1. The design of body morphology.

Here the concern regarding embodiment focuses on the design of the shape of represented beings, especially the engineering of their motion (Badler, et. al.1991).

2. Expressiveness of the body.

Here the debate over embodiment dwells on the capability of the represented being to communicate the full range of human and non-human expression. Concern often focuses on the engineering of an expressive face from the 3D geometry of avatars and agents.

3. Perceived intelligence via bodily action and expression.

The only evidence we have of another being's intelligence is the motion, motor behavior, and symbolic behavior of that being. By directly controlling the motion and behavior of an avatar, a human operator provides the intelligence in real time. Barring the expressive and kinematic inadequacies of avatar embodiment, the intelligence of human embodiment is perceived quickly. The challenge, best expressed by Turing, but evident in the work of previous designers of automata is to have an agent that somehow possesses or creates the illusion of intelligence.

The ambiguity of intelligence can be a source of pleasure and not necessarily a flaw in virtual environments. As Randy Walser pointed out early in the design of VR environments (Walser, 1991), part of the pleasure in VR narrative environments might come from not quite knowing when a dynamic form is either an object, an avatar, or an agent. The challenge to the user's expectations about the correlation of morphology with intelligence might be a source of great art in virtual environments.

Clearly animation can communicate all of the above to a satisfactory– if not ideal – degree. Didn't Disney already do this? Have we not achieved the illusion? The real challenge is not achieving these goals under controlled point of views and interactivity such as that of a third-person voyeur (i.e., as in the way film and animation present us with intelligent behaviors). Nor is it experiencing second-person interaction in the way some video games allow the user to experience the interaction of a puppet with other apparently intelligent i.e., intentional, puppets. The challenge is giving the user full first-person interaction with other intelligent beings animated by a complex expressiveness.

Design of the represented body

The represented body is referred to as the avatar of the user. In immersive virtual reality systems the avatar is not the small puppet used in standard computer interfaces, those regular computer monitors on which an iconic representation of the self is moved in a world via a mouse or joystick. In immersive VR the whole interface defines the boundaries and shape of the body by defining the boundary between inside and outside, between the part of the VR world that is "me" and the part that is "the world" (see Loomis, 1992). Both, of course, are just perceptual illusions generated on a head-mounted display (HMD). For example, users wearing a head-mounted display look down and readily accept the floating virtual hand of the immersive VR systems as their own. A part of the continuum of light in the HMD, a visual illusion, is given the distal attribution of "me" and the rest "other." From coherent patterns of energy impinging on the senses (i.e., the proximal stimulus) the virtual world is divided into "self" and "environment". In immersive VR, more so than in any other medium before it, the representation of the user's body is a psychologically profound issue. This is especially true when the systems map the user's body directly to the first person experience of a full virtual body, as virtual body that provides feedback about the location of limbs and head in space. As I will discuss later, the design of this virtual body may be the source of a number of current psychological problems in coupling of the body to immersive VRsystems.

USER EMBODIMENT AND THREE FORMS IN WHICH THE BODY "FEELS" PRESENT IN THE VIRTUAL ENVIRONMENT

Embodiment plays an important role in the design of virtual environments   , especially collaborative virtual environments (e.g., (Benford, et al., 1995). In immersive virtual environments the environment surrounds the body, often engulfing the senses, and, therefore, the mind. We sometimes speak of sound environments, architectural environments, natural environments, etc. All suggest fields of stimuli that somehow engulf one or more of the senses.

Embodiment of the user is a critical dimension of the program for intelligence augmentation that motivates the advancement of virtual reality systems (Biocca, 1995). The phrase intelligence augmentation describes the design theory that communication technologies can be cognitive prostheses amplifying or assisting cognitive processes or by developing cognitive skills. This postulate has a long history in telecommunication and human-computer interface design. In one form of another it is an implicit or explicitly goal in the work of Vannevar Bush (1945), Douglas Englebart (1962), Douglas Licklider (1960; Licklider and Taylor, 1968) and numerous others (see also Howard Rheingold, 1985).

This leads us to ask of ourselves and the VR design community, if embodiment contributes to intelligence augmentation what does it mean to be embodied? In other words, what are the psychological effects of goals of embodiment in virtual environments? Most commonly the psychological effects or goals of progressive embodiment can be expressed as various forms of what is called *presence*.

PRESENCE: EMERGENCE OF A DESIGN GOAL AND THEORETICAL PROBLEM

Telepresence: Origins of the design of presence

Emergence of the design goal and theoretical problem of presence

The concept of presence is central to theorizing about advanced virtual environments such as immersive virtual reality (Barfield et al., 1995; Lombard and Ditton, 1997; Sheridan, 1992; Steuer, 1995). For example, a leading VR journal out of MIT enshrines the psychological goal of presence rather than the technology of virtual reality by calling itself Presence.

In its more general use the term presence has referred to a widely reported sensation experienced during the use of virtual reality specifically, but also found during the use of other media. Users experiencing presence report having a compelling sense of being in a mediated space other than where their physical body is located (e.g., Slater and Usoh, 1993). Because we automatically construct models of the space around us (Bryant, 1992) more sophisticated analyses have suggested that we simply think of presence as a form of perceptual externalization or distal attribution. When media are involved the space constructed from the energy impinging on the sense is generated from mediated stimuli rather than unmediated stimuli (Loomis, 1992).

The *Random House American Heritage Dictionary* definition of presence refers to a "spirit inside a body" or to "immediate proximity in time and space." In telepresence, this sense of "immediate proximity" is no longer immediate environment and source of sensation, but "transported" using technology to a location that is not in the same place as the physical body. Presence is sometimes called telepresence to emphasize the use of communication media for transportation. In its original formulation in the NASA and robotics community, telepresence meant the illusion of being transported via telecommunication systems to a real, physical location experienced synchronously (e.g., Minsky, 1980). The user's body was linked via an interface to sensors on a robot. Telepresence has since been generalized to a sense of transportation to any "space" created by media (e.g., Steuer, 1995). The shorter and more common term, presence, has been generalized to the illusion of " being there" whether or not "there" exists in physical space or not. This generalization of the term allowed theorists of presence to include the fantasy environments of narrative and game designers as well as the abstract iconic representations of scientific visualization.

The desire for physical transcendence and the control of sensory experience

Biocca, Kim, and Levy (1995) argue that goal of virtual reality, presence, is part of an ancient desire to use media for transportation and experience "physical transcendence" over the space we live in and to experience an "essential copy" of some distant place, a past experience, or the experience of another person. These basic kernel concepts of the "physical transcendence" of the body and space, and the "essential copy" of bodily experience are intertwined into discussions that animate the pursuit of presence. We see a desire to use media to move beyond the limits of body and the sensory channels. This desire for physical transcendence is clearly visible in the work of one of the most revered pioneers in computer graphics and VR, Ivan Sutherland:

> "A display connected to a digital computer gives us a chance to gain familiarity with concepts not realizable in the physical world. It is a looking glass into a mathematical wonderland.... There is no reason why the objects displayed by a computer have to follow the ordinary rules of physical reality... The ultimate display would, of course, be a room within which the computer can control the existence of matter."   (Sutherland, 1965, p. 506, 508)

Presence as transportation of senses via telecommunication (i.e. tele-phone, tele-vision)

The engineering and computer science use of the term telepresence, or presence, started as a telecommunication design goal and has evolved into an intriguing theoretical problem and philosophical issue (e.g., Biocca, 1996; Loomis, 1992). The concept can be found in the HCI literature first as "telepresence," the illusion of being present in a distant location (e.g., Minsky, 1980), but the word "presence" appears by itself at the same time (Corker, Mishkin, and Lyman, 1980). The word telepresence meant using sensors and effects to link the body of the user via telecommunication channels to a robotic system. The robot would move when the user moved. Sensors, such as cameras and force detection devices, would provide feedback to the user. The user would sense what the robot "senses." In a phrase, the user would be remotely embodied in the robot. Telepresence is about the telecommunication of the body, the transmission of sensory and motor data. According to some of the early users of the term, the conditions for telepresence would be met when:

At the work site, the manipulators have the dexterity to allow the operator to perform normal human functions. At the control station, the operator receives sufficient quantity and quality of sensory feedback to provide a feeling of actual presence at the work site (Akin, Minsky, Theirl and Kurtzman (1983) quoted in Held and Durlach, 1992).

Influential definitions of telepresence reflect this origin. For example, the treatment of presence by robotics pioneer Tom Sheridan (1992) defines telepresence as the feeling of a teleoperator being phenomenally "there" at the remote site of operation.

Why a theory of presence has become necessary

The arcane and somewhat philosophical concept of presence became more theoretically urgent with the arrival of immersive virtual reality (See the first volume of the journal *Presence*). Practical design problems made issues of conceptualization and measurement critical (Held and Durlach, 1992; Sheridan, 1992; Zeltzer, 1992). Presence was a design goal of virtual reality. The difference between virtual reality and other media was defined as a difference in the level of presence (e.g., Steuer, 1995). It can be argued that advanced forms of virtual reality only differ from previous media in quantity and quality of presence. While the design of virtual reality technology has brought the theoretical issue of presence to the fore, few theorists argue that the experience of presence suddenly emerged with the arrival of virtual reality. Most see the illusion of presence as a product of all media, and that virtual reality is the medium that at this point in time can generate the most compelling sense of presence (Biocca and Levy, 1995; Lombard and Ditton, 1997; Steuer, 1995). But with the arrival of virtual reality, the creation of the sensation of presence becomes more of an explicit design goal.

Intense sensorimotor feedback from headtracking in virtual reality made people aware of their bodies

The experience of a much higher level of sensorimotor feedback and first person perspective generated the head-tracked (Meyer, Applewhite, and Biocca, 1992) head-mounted display that helped bring the whole issue of presence to the fore. The interactivity resulting from the sensorimotor coordination of the moving head with visual displays created a sensation not found with non-headcoupled media like film and television. *Users became aware of their bodies;* their head movements altered what they saw. Immersive virtual reality immediately distinguished itself from other media when users reported a strong sense of "being there" in the virtual environment. Early user's of VR systems where struck by the compelling sensation that their bodies were in a different place (e.g., Rheingold, 1991). For some, the experience was powerful. They felt they were no longer in the lab, office, or entertainment center, but "there," inside the virtual world. It was hoped that this surprising experience could be made more compelling.

This medium was interactive in a profoundly natural way. The world was now all around the user's body. With advanced virtual reality technology, users and designers sought to increase this sensation of presence, pursuit of which has become the sine qua non goal of many immersive virtual environments, labs and companies. The day-to-day design of presence has temporarily outstripped the theory of the presence. In the history of science we have often seen the design of technology outpace our understanding of the principles that make the technology function. Designers know that presence is something their users experience, but don't know exactly what it is. What is presence? This is one of the important questions in VR design. Most discussions of presence thus far (e.g., Barfield et al., 1995; Heeter, 1992, 1995; Lombard and Ditton, 1997; Steuer, 1992; Zeltzer, 1992) can be subsumed into the following conceptualization of three forms of presence.

Being There: The Sense of Physical Presence in Cyberspace.

Clearly the sense of presence was not created just for use with virtual environments. But as Loomis (1992) points out, presence is a basic state of consciousness, it is part of the attribution of sensation to some distal stimulus, or more casually, to some environment. A topic that has traditionally been discussed by philosophers and perceptual psychologists as "externalization" and "distal attribution" is now a practical matter of virtual environment design. It has even been proposed that VR might be used to study the classic epistemological topics of consciousness (Biocca, 1996; Lauria, 1997).

When we experience our everyday sense of presence in the physical world, we automatically generate a mental model of an external space from patterns of energy on the sensory organs. In virtual environments, patterns of energy that simulate the structure to those experienced in the physical environment are used to stimulate the same automatic perceptual processes that generate our stable perception of the physical world.

As Loomis (1992) points out, the mediation of virtual environments leads us to reconsider how the active body mediates our construction of the physical world:

> "The perceptual world created by our senses and the nervous system is so functional a representation of the physical world that most people live out their lives without ever suspecting that contact with the physical world is mediated; moreover, the functionality of perception impedes many reflective individuals from appreciating the insights about perception that derive from philosophical inquiry. Oddly enough, the newly developing technology of teleoperator and virtual displays is having the unexpected effect of promoting such insight, for the impression of being in a remote or simulated environment experienced by the user of such systems can be so compelling as to force a user to question the assumptions that the physical and perceptual world are one and the same."
>
> (Loomis, 1992, p. 113)

Note that Loomis says that all "contact with the physical world is mediated," by which he means the primordial communication medium, the body. The default sense of "being there" is the basic state of consciousness in which the user attributes the source of the sensation to the physical environment. We have been present in this environment for so long and it is so natural, that the idea that presence might be a psychological construct is only raised by philosophers and perceptual psychologists. The experience of compelling virtual environments has disturbed this common complacency. The discussion of virtual reality and the strong sense of being there that it generates is often accompanied by questions about the stability of our perception of the physical world (e.g., Lauria, 1997). If the senses can be so easily fooled, then how can we trust the day-to-day experience of physical reality? This is the century old insight born of all illusions, especially in dreaming where we directly experience interaction of the body and the mind as the primordial simulator.

Where are you? : Oscillations in the sense of presence

The compelling sense of presence in virtual environments is unstable. At best it is fleeting. Like a voice interrupting a daydream in the imaginal environment, presence in the virtual environment can be interrupted by sensory cues from the physical environment and imperfections in the interface (Slater and Usoh, 1993; Kim and Biocca, 1997).

At one point in time, users can be said to feel as if they are physically present in only one of three places (see Figure 3): the physical environment, the virtual environment, or the imaginal environment. Presence oscillates among these three poles.

The physical environment (distal immediate)

Here users are attentively constructing a mental model of the physical space (Bryant, 1992), responding and attending to cues in the physical non-mediated environment as the user plans and guides engagement with the natural world.

The virtual environment (distal mediated)

Users are primarily constructing a mental model of the virtual space and responding to and attending to cues in the virtual mediated environment. Presence in the virtual environment can be readily engaged, but can rarely be maintained at the same level as presence in the physical environment.

The imaginal environment (minimal attention to distal stimuli)

Dreaming and daydreaming reveal that there is another place we can be present, the imaginary environment. We can say that the user is present in the internally simulated, imaginal environment when the user:

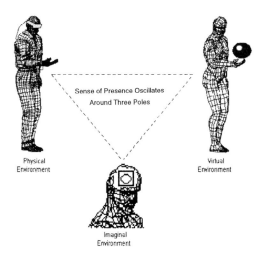

Figure 3: Users' sense of presence is not stable but labile. They variously feel present in the physical environment, virtual environment, or in the imaginal environment (e.g., dreaming, day dreaming).

- has withdrawn focal attention to incoming sensory cues,

- is attending to internally generated mental imagery,

- has diminished responsiveness to sensory cues from either the physical environment or the virtual environment.

In dreams, and to a lesser degree in hallucinations and daydreaming, it is apparent that the mind is capable of producing very compelling spatial environments. In these environments, we have conscious experiences of moving through space (e.g., running down a busy street), interacting with others (e.g., talking with friends), and manipulating objects (e.g., throwing a ball). Clearly in a dream state we are present in a spatial environment. But it is also clear that this environment has nothing to do with technology.

But dreams use what I call the mental simulator, the generator of mental imagery that makes of cognitive resources used in perception (Farah, 1984; Kosslyn, 1980). But unlike states of presence in virtual and physical environments the mental spatial simulation is not based on incoming sensory stimulation but is mostly constructed from memory. I say mostly because there is evidence that in dream states, the mental simulation is responding to some environmental stimuli and somewhat random stimulation from the spinal system.

From a design viewpoint, physical presence is critical in applications that must involve spatial cognition, the transfer of spatial models from the virtual environment to the physical environment, or for sensory bombardment and escape from the physical environment. Applications where physical presence is critical include architectural walkthroughs, battle simulations, engineering design, and some entertainment rides.

BEING WITH ANOTHER BODY: DESIGNING THE ILLUSION OF SOCIAL PRESENCE

For many theorists, communication is essentially the connection of one intelligence with another. In this view, communication is the experience of another being. Even in the telecommunication model of Shannon and Weaver (1949), where communication is an abstract relationship between two machines, the source and receiver of communication are most often interpreted as one intelligent being connected to another.

For many face-to-face communication is an ideal that media technologies attempt to replicate (Palmer, 1995; Rafaeli, 1988; Schudson, 1978). In an elaborate book length attempt at a taxonomy of all present and future media, Ciampa (1989) presents all media as vain attempts to recover the immediacy of face-to-face communication. Michael Heim (1993) in his discussion of virtual reality interfaces takes this one step further. He inserts the ideal of face-to-face communication into the general notion of inter-face, "a mysterious, nonmaterial point where electronic signals become information":

> "In ancient times, the term interface sparked awe and mystery, The archaic Greeks spoke reverently of *propsopon,* or a face facing another face. Two opposite faces make up a mutual relationship. One face reacts to another, and the other face reacts to the other's reaction, and the other reacts to that reaction, and so on ad infinitum. The relationship then lives on as a third thing or state of being."   (Heim, 1993, p. 77)

The ideal of the face-to-face interaction is the background against which comparisons are made for all technologies that link two humans together. It is against this background of immediate or non-mediated communication that the concept of social presence has been discussed (Short, Williams, and Christie, 1976; Rice, 1993). Typically, mediated communication is depicted as mechanically convenient, sometimes appropriate, but ultimately a limited substitute for face-to-face communication. If mediated communication is an inadequate substitute for face-to-face communication, then to what degree does a medium simulate the face-to-face presence of another? Or to what degree does a user feel the social presence of another?

The institutional context for the discussion of social presence has usually been organizational communication: communication in workgroups, business, and other settings involving decision-making, negotiating, and work coordinating groupings of human beings. This discussion is found most often in the context of computer supported cooperative work (CSCW) (e.g., Walther, 1996). Issues of presence, how much, how little, and what kind are mapped to social psychological and sociological discussions of group harmony, social hierarchy and status, interaction satisfaction, deception, etc.

There are two practical design problems that have always been there in the design of media:

Transporting and displaying patterns of energy (e.g., light of video, the sound energy of a telephone) to generate the illusion of another (e.g., puppets, pictures, and avatars)

This is the perennial quest of telecommunication, the transportation of the senses. How can we use telecommunication technology to collapse space and storage devices to collapse time so that communication between two distant human beings is possible? At present, further advancement of this long standing design goal takes the form of the design of social virtual environments populated by avatars who display the real time transmission of some of the body's communication cues (e.g., morphology, motion, sound, and physical force).

Creating an artificial other (robots and animals)

Creating an artificial other is the age-old, God-overthrowing dream of human creativity, (i.e., robotics, artificial intelligence, etc.), the desire to create a device that can mimic the morphology, motion, and communication behaviors of intelligent sentient beings (i.e., humans, animals, etc.) or serve their creators in the performance of menial tasks (Sheehan and Sosna, 1991). In virtual environments this social presence is the social presence created by agents.

On the surface the goal of social presence seems simple enough. But the design of truly interactive social presence is horrendously complex. The symbol of this challenge is the Turing test. It some ways it is only a limited challenge, because it requires little embodiment of the other -- the computer only types text messages to the "judge" who determines whether the other is an artificial intelligence or a human intelligence. A convincing, fully articulated being may be more challenging, and given the technology of the day, beyond the possibility that Turing imagined. But the presence of another body make the Turing test easier. If convincing morphology is present, less intelligence may be required to fool the user into believing that a human intelligence is "present." Users may be fooled by convincing morphology and believe an artificially intelligent agent is really a humanly directed avatar.

Definition of social presence

In past research it has been useful to consider what aspects of social presence are supported in media such as the telephone or email systems (Short, Williams, and Christie, 1976; Rice, 1993). Researchers in this tradition have listed social cues and semiotic devices that are present or absent in a particular technology. The emphasis has been on the consequences of the absence of such cues on comprehension, collaboration, and other forms social interaction. Discussion focused on whether the glass of social presence was half-full or half-empty.

But if we dig a little deeper, we find that social presence may be a little more complicated and interesting than this initial discussion. The perception of social presence might be defined as:

> *The minimum level of social presence occurs when users feel that a form, behavior, or sensory experience indicates the presence of another intelligence. The amount of social presence is the degree to which a user feels access to the intelligence, intentions, and sensory impressions of another.*

How does this definition help us? As Husserl (1973) pointed out, we have phenomenal access to our intelligence, intentions, and sensory impressions. The perception of the other is the empathetic simulation of internal states of another "if we were there in the space" over there. The simulation of the other is based on bodily motions and cues. It occurs so easily that we fail to see the artifice of it all. A few, like severe autistics, cannot do it at all. Others overdo it when they anthropomorphize animals, the sun, plants, and other physical phenomena. Given the thousands of years of anthropomorphic projection, it is perhaps not surprising when recent research reminds us that we tend to anthropomorphize computers and treat them as "social actors" (Reeves and Nass, 1996).

Rather than seeing social presence as a partial replication of face-to-face communication, we should more generally see social presence as a simulation of another intelligence. The simulation is run in the body and mind of the perceiver, and models the internal experience of some other moving, expressive body. It is a simulation because the simulation occurs whether or not the moving object has intelligence or intentionality, whether the "other" is a moving human being or an animation composed of nothing more than moving patterns of ink. The definition above suggests that social presence applies to the mediated experience of *all forms of "intelligence."* This perceived intelligence might be another human, a non-human intelligence such as an animal, a form of artificial intelligence, an imagined alien or a god.

Hyperpresence

The definition of social presence also opens up other possibilities. It also suggests that although mediated social presence should be measured against the yardstick of face-to-face communication between two human beings, it may be possible to develop a medium in which one feels *greater "access to the intelligence, intentions, and sensory impressions of another" than is possible in the most intimate, face-to-face communication.* One aspect of what might be called *hyperpresence* (Biocca, forthcoming) may be possible in the social presence domain as well.

Of course, it is hard for us now to imagine a medium that can create greater intimacy than face-to-face communication. But this misses the point of social presence and the very artifice of the body itself. In face-to-face communication the body is used to communicate one's sensory experiences, observations, and inner states to another. The body is the medium for this transfer. Communication codes such as spoken language and non-verbal codes such as facial expression, posture, touch, and motion are used. But, for example, inner states might be communicated more vividly through the use of sensors that can amplify subtle physiological or non-verbal cues. These can augment the intentional and unintentional cues used in interpersonal communication to assess the emotional states and intentions of others.

IS THIS BODY REALLY "ME"? SELF PRESENCE, BODY SCHEMA, SELF-CONSCIOUSNESS, AND IDENTITY

The definitions of telepresence (Biocca and Delaney, 1995; Sheridan, 1992; Steuer, 1995) imply that telepresence is possible because the subject of presence, defined as the subjective sense of being somewhere, is not the physical body of a person. Specifically, Loomis (1992) and Heeter (1992, 1995) refer to the "phenomenal body" and "self," respectively, as the subject of presence, and imply that the phenomenal body or the self does not always correspond with the physical body.

This phenomenal body or body schema has certain properties: e.g., perceived shape and size, perceived relative location of the limbs and senses, etc . Beyond this there is also an internal model of the self: e.g., perceived qualities or traits that "cause" behavior, perceived states, etc. So inside the virtual world there is more than a computer graphic representation of the self, there is an internal subjective representation of the self, that is a model of the self's body and a model of one's identity.

Self-presence is defined as users' mental model of themselves inside the virtual world, but especially differences in self-presence due to the short term or long term effect of virtual environment on the perception of one's body (i.e., body schema or body image), physiological states, emotional states, perceived traits, and identity.

Self-presence refers to the effect of embodiment in the virtual environment on mental models of the self, especially when that model of the self is foregrounded or made salient. As with other forms of presence, designers share the assumption that increases in self-presence are correlated with higher levels of cognitive performance, and, possibly, emotional development. In the words of Socrates, the goal to "know thyself" is a worthy journey -- it may be the only journey!

Questions of identity formation and self-consciousness are very broad issues pertaining to the formation of the individual. Most processes are by no means unique to virtual environments. But the interaction with computers raises some interesting questions in this domain (e.g., Turkle, 1985). So in assessing the role of virtual environments in influencing self-presence, we should concentrate on those aspects of the environment that are radically different from the physical world.

Two issues emerge as most pertinent to virtual environments as opposed to physical environments. Both pertain to the effect of progressive embodiment, that is, the embodiment of the user's body via close coupling to the interface and representations of coupled body via first person avatar geometry and behavior.

Embodiment in an avatar and the effects of mental model of the self

When the user is embodied in an avatar two things are occurring:

1. the mental model of the user's body (body schema or body image) may be influenced by the mapping of the physical body to the geometry and topology of the virtual body,

2. The virtual body may have a different social meaning (i.e., social role) than the user's body.

The latter, the social meaning of the avatar, is situationally or environmentally dependent. For example, a "cowboy" avatar will have different social meaning in historic "wild west" environment, a "New York Bar" environment, or inside a pickup truck in a contemporary southern rural environment. The social role of avatar body is partially determined, but not defined, by its geometry and kinematics. Implicit and explicit social norms that may be partially idiosyncratic to the virtual environment and imported from the user's social environment finalize the social-semiotic role and identity of the avatar. Issues of class, gender, occupational role, body type, etc. are raised when considering this aspect of embodiment. The social meaning of body morphology and social role and its effect on the self-schema is a rich area. But most aspects of it (e.g., stereotyping) are not particularly unique to virtual environments, and only partially under the control of designers. For this reason, I will not pursue it further here.

Rather I will pursue a topic more unique to virtual environments. The interaction of the virtual environment with the user's body schema in immersive virtual environments may have a number of implications for the design of virtual worlds. We can say that in almost any virtual environment system with any significant level of embodiment, there are three bodies present: the objective body, the virtual body, and the body schema. These three bodies may be present even in comparatively primitive, non-interactive virtual environments like standard television (Meyers and Biocca, 1992). The objective body is the physical, observable, and measurable body of the user. The virtual body is the representation of the user's body inside the virtual environment. The body schema is the user's mental or internal representation of his or her body.

Our body schema is a not stable, but labile (Fisher and Cleveland, 1968; Fisher, 1970). The use of media can radically alter one's body schema. In virtual and augmented reality systems, changes in the location of the represented head or hands can significantly distort the body. Biocca and Rolland (in press) found that a small displacement of vision in an augmented reality system triggered disruptive visuomotor adaptation (Welch, 1978), or to put in another way a recalibration of the body schema. When the users exited the virtual environment and reached for objects in the physical environment, they exhibited significant distortions in hand-eye coordination. A short anecdote will make this clear. The first subject in the Biocca and Rolland experiment was drinking a cola prior to beginning the study. As the end of the study, she reached for her cola and quickly raised it to drink only to discover that she was about to pour it into her eyes! In this case, the coordinate system of the visual system and the motor system (specifically, the hands) had adapted to the geometry of the virtual body, which had a different structure. The objective body was now "out of sync."

Distortions in body schema can also result from exposure to implicit representations of the self, even in non-immersive environments like television. Meyers and Biocca (1992) found that exposure to videos that emphasized an ideal body shape for women led to distortions in the their body schema. The saw themselves as thinner than the young women in the control group.

There are other ways in which the objective body and phenomenal body may be in conflict. Virtual environments cannot perfectly synchronize and map the moving physical body of the user with the user's virtual body or avatar. Representations of the body are never completely free of some form of mismapping between user action (motor outflow) and sensory feedback (sensory inflow). This mismapping often leads to some form of intersensory conflict. Intersensory conflict, or the mismapping of the moving body, is believed to be the source of simulation sickness (Biocca, 1992), a form of motion sickness experienced by some users of immersive virtual reality.

What are we to conclude about embodiment and the design of avatars? It appears that embodiment of the user in virtual environments may not be a trivial design question. Problems such as intersensory conflict suggest that the design of the user's avatar should not be seen as some virtual environment equivalent of the selection of clothing or costume, especially in immersive virtual environments. It appears that embodiment can significantly alter body schema. Metaphorically, we might say that the virtual body competes with the physical body to influence the form of the phenomenal body. The result is a tug of war where the body schema may oscillate in the mind of the user of the interface (see Meyers and Biocca, 1992).

THE CYBORG'S DILEMMA

As we approach the beginning of the next century, the problem of embodiment and the representation of the body has become a central problem in a number of overlapping, intellectual debates. Most appear to be directly or indirectly stimulated by the progressive development of technologies of the body, especially the development of new sensing and display devices. In the neurosciences the development of sensing devices such as MRI, CAT, and PET scans has contributed to a discussion of the role of body in fundamental representational processes associated with reason and emotion (e.g. Damasio, 1996). In the design of artificial intelligence, embodiment is debated in discussions of the role of body, its function in ongoing representations of the external world, and its role in plans and action (e.g., Haber and Weiss, 1996; Johnson, 1987; Lakoff, 1987; Lakoff and Johnson, 1980). In the humanities, a concern over embodiment, fanned by feminist studies, debates the representations of the body, mostly as circulated in media technologies such as film, TV and the Internet, and its effect on social roles and identity. Here we see Foucault-influenced (Foucault, 1980) debates about "technologies of the body."

Another version of our concern with the progressive embodiment is becoming visible. The evidence of this concern can be found in our fascination with the idea of the cyborg, the interface of the physical body with technology (e.g., Gray, Figeueroa-Sarriera, and Mentor, 1995). The level of progressive embodiment found in advanced forms of virtual environment technology can be characterized as a form of cyborg coupling, the body coupled with its technological extensions. This coupling, I have suggested, is progressive. It is increasing over time and the body is getting tighter and more integrated into every life (e.g., miniaturization, ubiquitous computing, and wearable computing). This soma-technic coupling is beginning to highlight what I call the cyborg's dilemma, a kind of Faustian bargain between us and our technological alter-egos:

The cyborg's dilemma: *The more natural the interface the more "human" it is, the more it adapts to the human body and mind. The more the interface adapts to the human body and mind, the more the body and mind adapts to the non-*

human interface. Therefore, the more natural the interface, the more we become "unnatural," the more we become cyborgs.

In this article I have suggested ways in which the interface is becoming more "human": in virtual and augmented reality, for example, the interface's sensors and effectors are increasingly mapped to the body's senses and motor systems; in the design of agents and avatars the interface presents itself with a human face; and once inside the interface the user's body is experienced in digital form. These are the immediate sources of the cyborg's dilemma.

But my characterization of the cyborg's dilemma also raises a number of important issues. First, my description might suggest that there is an escape from the cyborg's dilemma. Some might feel that we can reject the new technologies and avoid the uncertain choices and changes implied by the cyborg's dilemma. It is not that simple. Anyone who believes that there is a "natural" place where the body is not wedded to technology may be embracing both technology and self-deception. Cyborg theorists point out that "we are already cyborgs." We may have been cyborgs for centuries. The cyborg's dilemma is present in our acceptance of the most primitive technologies: in a piece of clothing, in a wrist watch, in a baseball bat, in short, in all technologies that attach themselves and augment the body.

Secondly, it raises questions of what is "natural" about our relationship to our technology. We tend to think of technology as something alien, not a reflection of ourselves. Maybe we have been designed to be cyborgs. It may be our nature, therefore "natural," to embrace our technologies. What do I mean? A number of scholars have pointed to the similar neurological, cognitive, and structural substrates shared among language, fine motor movements, and tool use (see Gibson and Ingold, 1993). It may well be that the human brain and body evolved to fully inhabit these externalizations of mental processes and amplifications of the body that are our technologies. We are inhabiting and building what Popper (1972) calls the third world, a world that is not the first world, the self, or the second world, the physical world, but the stamping of human form on matter and energy. In the cyborg there may be part of an evolving harmony of the self with the humanly design and extended forms of physical matter and energy.

In his classic essay, "The role of somatic change in evolution," Gregory Bateson (1972) outlined what he called "an economics of somatic flexibility." In the push for somatic flexibility in response to pressures in the environment, he posited three classes of beings: adjusters, regulators, and extraregulators. Humans were the classic example of the class he called "extraregulators." Extraregulators achieve "homeostatic control outside the body by changing and controlling the environment" (p. 362). Evolution, he said favored the "extraregulators" who pushed the "locus of control" for the somatic change to engineered changes in the environment. In this way they achieved greater level of somatic flexibility. There is much detail in this argument to work out and I cannot attempt it here. But if this perspective on human and technological evolution is on the right track, it says something significant about the relationship of the body to technology. It suggests that we are designed to be cyborgs, to achieve a tighter and tighter coupling of our minds and bodies with the externalizations of ourselves, that part of the physical world that is mixed with human forms, that part that is our technology.

Thirdly, the cyborg's dilemma raises profound questions about the locus and stability of our individual identity. The pursuit of presence and the telecommunication of the body pushes a tight coupling of the physical body and the computer interface. To the degree that cognition and identity are embodied in the simulations run by our sensors and effectors, then the mind in advanced virtual environments becomes also adapted to a mediated body, an avatar, a simulation of the cyborg body. Observing the day-to-day movements of our consciousness between the experience of our unmediated body and our mediated virtual bodies, we may come to ask: Where am *"I"* present? footnotes

REFERENCES

Arnheim, R., 1957. *Film*. Berkeley: University of California Press.

Badler, N., B. A. Barsky, and D. Zeltzer, 1991. *Making them move: Mechanics, control, and animation of articulated figures.* San Mateo: Morgan Kaufmann.

Bardini, T., 1997. Bridging the gulfs: From hypertext to cyberspace. *Journal of Computer Mediated-Communication On-line*, 3(2). Available: http://207.201.161.120/jcmc/vol3/issue2/bardini.html

Barfield, W., D. Zeltzer, T. Sheridan, and M. Slater, 1995. Presence and performance within virtual environments. In W. Barfield and T. A. Furness, III eds, *Virtual environments and advanced interface design*. New York: Oxford University Press, pp. 473-541

Bateson, G., 1972. *Steps to an ecology of mind*. New York: Ballantine Books.

Becker, B. L., and K. Schoenbach, 1989. *Audience responses to media diversification : Coping with plenty*. Hillsdale, N.J. : L. Erlbaum Associates.

Benford, S., J. Bowers, L. Fahlen, C. Greenhalgh, and D. Snowdon, 1995. *User embodiment in collaborative virtual environments*. Paper presented at CHI'95.

Benthall, J., and T. Polhemus, eds, 1975. *The body as a medium of expression*. New York: E. P. Dutton and Co.

Biocca, F., 1992. Will simulation sickness slow down the diffusion of virtual environment technology? *Presence*, 1(3), pp. 334-343

Biocca, F., 1996. *Can the engineering of presence tell us something about consciousness?* Paper presented at the 2nd International Conference on the Science of Consciousness, Tuscon, AR.

Biocca, F., 1995. Intelligence augmentation: The vision inside virtual reality. In B. Gorayska and J. Mey, eds, *Cognitive Technology*. Amsterdam: North Holland, pp. 59-75

Biocca, F., forthcoming. *Presence of mind in virtual environments: Immersing mind and body into virtual environments. Media Interface and Network Design* Lab, Michigan State University, East Lansing, MI

Biocca, F.,, and B. Delaney, 1995. Immersive virtual reality technology. In F. Biocca and M. R. Levy, eds, *Communication in the age of virtual reality.* Hillsdale, NJ: Lawrence Erlbaum Associates, pp. 57-124.

Biocca, F., and M. R. Levy, eds, 1995. *Communication in the age of virtual reality.* Hillsdale, NJ: Lawrence Erlbaum Associates.

Biocca, F., and J. Rolland, in press. Virtual eyes can rearrange your body: Adaptation to visual displacement in see-through head mounted displays. *Presence.*

Biocca, F., T. Kim, and M. Levy, 1995. The vision of virtual reality. In F. Biocca and M. Levy, eds, *Communication in the age of virtual reality.* Hillsdale, NJ: Lawrence Erlbaum Associates, Inc., pp. 3-14.

Bryant, D. J., 1992. A spatial representation system in humans. *Psycoloquy,* 3(16), http://bion.mit.edu/ejournals/b/nz/Psycoloquy/3/psycoloquy.92.3.16.space.1.br yant

Bush, V., 1945, July. As we may think. *The Atlantic Monthly,* pp. 101- 108.

Ciampa, J., 1989. *Communication, the living end.* New York: Philosophical Library.

Corker, K., A. Mishkin, and J. Lyman, 1980. *Achievement of a sense of operator presence in remote manipulation.* Tech. Rep. No. 60. UCLA School of Engineering and Applied Science, Biotechnology Dept.

Damasio, A., 1994. *Decartes' error: Emotion, reason, and the brain.* New York: Grosset/Putnam.

Durlach, N., and A. Mavor, 1994. *Virtual reality: Scientific and technological challenges.* Washington: National Research Council.

Ekman, P., 1974. *Unmasking the face.* Englewood Cliffs, N.J.: Prentice- Hall.

Englebart, D., 1962, October. *Augmenting human intellect: A conceptual framework.* Summary report, contract AF 49(638)-1024 Stanford: Stanford Research Institute, pp. 187-232.

Farah, M., 1984. The neurological basis of mental imagery: A componential analysis. *Cognition*

Fisher, S., 1970. *Body image in fantasy and behaviors.* New York: Appleton-Century Crofts.

Fisher, S., and S. Cleveland, 1968. *Body image and personality.* NewYork: Dover.

Foucault, M., 1980. *The history of sexuality.* Translated from the French by Robert Hurley. 1st Vintage Books ed. New York : Vintage Books,

Gibson, J. J., 1966. *The senses considered as perceptual systems.* Boston: Houghton-Mifflin.

Gibson, J. J., 1979. *The ecological approach to visual perception.* Boston: Houghton-Mifflin.

Gibson, K., and T. Ingold, eds, 1993. *Tools, language, and intelligence: evolutionary implications.* New York: Cambridge University Press.

Gray, C. H., H. Figeueroa-Sarriera, and S. Mentor, 1995. *The cyborg handbook.* New York: Routledge.

Haber, H., and G. Weiss, eds, 1996. *Perspectives on embodiment.* New York: Routledge.

Heeter, C., 1992. Being there: The subjective experience of presence. *Presence,* 1(2), pp. 262-271.

Heeter, C., 1995. Communication research on consumer VR. In F. Biocca and M. R. Levy, eds, *Communication in the age of virtual reality.* Hillsdale, NJ: Lawrence Erlbaum Associates, pp. 191-218.

Heim, M., 1993. *The metaphysics of virtual reality.* New York.

Held, R., and N. Durlach, 1991. Telepresence, time delay and adoption. In S. Ellis, M. K. Kaiser, and A. C. Grunwald, ed., *Pictorial communication in virtual and real environments.* London: Taylor and Francis, pp. 232-245.

Husserl, E., 1973. *Cartesian meditations.* The Hague: Martinus Nijhoff.

Johnson, M., 1987. *The body in the mind.* Chicago: University of Chicago Press.

Kennedy, R. , N. Lane, M. G. Lilitenthal, K. S. Berbaum, and L. J. Hettinger, 1992. Profile analysis of simulator sickness symptoms: Applications to virtual environment systems. *Presence,* 1(3), pp. 295-302.

Kim, T., and F. Biocca, 1997. Telepresence via television: Two dimensions of telepresence may have different connections to memory and persuasion. *Journal of Computer Mediated-Communication On-line,* 3(2), Available: http://207.201.161.120/jcmc/vol3/issue2/kim.html

Kocian, D. F., and H. L. Task, 1995. Virtual coupled systems hardware and human interface. In W. Barfield and T. A. Furness, eds, *Virtual environments and advanced interface design.* New York: Oxford University Press.

Kosslyn, S. M., 1980. *Images and mind.* Cambridge, Mass: Harvard University Press.

Krueger, M., 1997. *Virtual vaporware: Olfactory stimuli in VR.* Presented at Virtual Reality Universe, San Francisco.

Lakoff, G., 1987. *Women, fire, and dangerous things.* Chicago: University of Chicago Press.

Lakoff, G., and M. Johnson, 1980. *Metaphors we live by.* Chicago: University of Chicago Press.

Lauria, R., 1996. Virtual reality: An empirical-metaphysical testbed. *Journal of Computer Mediated-Communication On-line,* 2(1), Available: http://207.201.161.120/jcmc/vol3/issue2/lauria.html

Licklider, J. C. R., 1960, March. Man-computer symbiosis. *IRE Factors in Electronics,* HFE-1, pp. 4-11.

Licklider, J. C. R., and R. W. Taylor, 1968, April. The computer as a communication device. *Science and Technology,* pp. 21-31.

Lombard, M., and T. Ditton, 1997. At the heart of it all: The concept of presence. *Journal of Computer Mediated-Communication On-line,* 3(2), Available: http://207.201.161.120/jcmc/vol3/issue2/lombard.html

Loomis, J. M., 1992. Distal attribution and presence. *Presence,* 1(1), pp. 113-118.

McLuhan, M., 1966. *Understanding media* . New York: Signet.

McLuhan, M. and E. McLuhan, 1988. *Laws of media: The new science* . Toronto: University of Toronto Press.

Meyer, K., H. Applewhite, and F. Biocca, 1992. A survey of position trackers. *Presence*. 1(2), pp. 173-200.

Meyers, P., and F. Biocca, 1992. The elastic body image: An experiment on the effect of advertising and programming on body image distortions in young women. *Journal of Communication*, 42(3), pp. 108-133.

Minsky, M., 1980. Telepresence. *Omni*, 2, pp. 44-52.

Mitcham, C., 1994. *Thinking through technology*. Chicago: University of Chicago Press.

Munsterberg, H., 1970. *The photoplay: A psychological study*. New York: Dover. (Originally published in 1916).

Novak, M., 1991. Liquid architectures in cyberspace. In M. Benedict, ed., *Cyberspace: First steps*. Cambridge, MA: MIT Press.

Palmer, M., 1995. Interpersonal communication and virtual reality: Mediating interpersonal relationship. In F. Biocca and M. Levy, eds, *Communication in the age of virtual reality*. Hillsdale, NJ: Lawrence Erlbaum, pp. 277-302.

Popper, K., 1972. *Objective knowledge*. Oxford University Press

Rafaeli, S., 1988. *Interactivity: From new media to communication*, Sage Annual Review of Communication Research: Advancing Communication Science, 16. Sage: Beverly Hills, CA

Reeves, B., and C. Nass, 1996. *The media equation: How people treat computers, television, and new media like real people and places*. Stanford, CA: CSLI Publications

Rheingold, H., 1985. *Tools for thought*. New York: Summit Books.

Rheingold, H., 1991. *Virtual reality*. New York: Summit Books.

Rice, R. E., 1993. Media appropriateness: Using social presence theory to compare traditional and new organizational media. *Human Communication Research*, 19(4), pp. 451-484.

Schudson, M., 1978. The ideal of conversation in the study of mass media. *Communication Research*, 5(3), pp. 320-329.

Sekuler, R., and Blake, R., 1994. *Perception*. (3rd ed.). New York: McGraw Hill.

Shannon, C. and Weaver, W., 1949. *The mathematical theory of communication*. Urbana: University of Illinois Press.

Sheehan, J., and Sosna, M., 1991. *The boundaries of humanity: Humans, animals, machines*. Berkeley: University of California Press.

Sheridan, T. B., 1992. Musings on telepresence and virtual presence. *Presence*, 1(1), pp. 120-126.

Short, J. Williams, E., and Christie, B., 1976. *The social psychology of telecommunications*. London: Wiley.

Slater, M., and Usoh, M., 1993. Representations systems, perceptual position, and presence in immersive virtual environments. *Presence*, 2(3), pp. 221-233.

Steuer, J., 1995. Defining virtual reality: Dimensions determining telepresence. In F. Biocca and M. R. Levy, eds, *Communication in the age of virtual reality.* Hillsdale, NJ: Lawrence Erlbaum Associates, pp. 33-56.

Sutherland, I., 1965. The ultimate display. Information Processing 1965: *Proceedings of the IFIP Congress 65*, 2,. Washington, DC: Spartan Books, pp. 506-508

Turkle, S., 1984. *The second self : Computers and the human spirit.* New York : Simon and Schuster.

Walser, R., 1991. Elements of a cyberspace playhouse. In S. Helsel, ed., *Virtual reality: Theory, practice, and promise.* Westport: Meckler.

Walther, J. B., 1996. Computer-mediated communication: Impersonal, interpersonal, and hyperpersonal interaction. *Communication Research*, 23 (1), pp. 3-43.

Welch, R.B., 1978. *Perceptual modification: Adapting to altered sensory environments.* New York Academic Press.

Zeltzer, D. (1992). Autonomy, interaction, and presence. *Presence*, 1(1), pp. 127-132.

Zillman, D. (1991). Empathy: Affect from bearing witness to the emotions of others. In J. Bryant and D. Zillman, eds., *Responding to the screen: Reception and reaction processes.* Hillsdale, NJ: Lawrence Erlbaum.

Humane Interfaces: Questions of method and practice in Cognitive Technology
J.P. Marsh, B. Gorayska and J.L. Mey (Editors)
© 1999 Elsevier Science B.V. All rights reserved.

Chapter 7

COGNITIVE TOOLS RECONSIDERED
From augmentation to mediation

Victor Kaptelinin

University of Umeå, Sweden

Kari Kuutti

University of Oulu, Finland

INTRODUCTION

The idea that computer tools "augment", "amplify", or "enhance" human cognition has been deeply ingrained into our way of thinking about computers. The concept of augmentation is almost as old as computer tools themselves and dates back at least to the works of Douglas Engelbart (1963, reprinted in Greif, 1988). Augmentation is an attractive idea: probably, one of the most important factors underlying the current fascination with computer technology is that people want to become more capable and powerful by using a system. There is also a sense of truth in it: when watching an expert user of a system (for instance, a UNIX system administrator, an engineer working with a CAD package, or a graphics designer creating images with a drawing tool) "fly" through complex manipulations and transformations with amazing ease one can almost see that some augmentation or amplification is taking place. It also corresponds to our own experiences: even if we are not such expert users, it is very frustrating when a computer tool is not suitable for a particular task we know it would make much easier. As cognitive technologies, computers promise a lot.

On the other hand, in real life the promise of augmentation seems hard to fulfil. More and more, recent commentators on the use of computer systems are becoming sceptical with respect to augmentation, especially in terms of increased work productivity. Thomas K. Landauer's book (1995) casts a deep shadow over claims that the use of computers increases productivity. By drawing on a number of published empirical studies from business economy, Landauer is able to show convincingly that it is practically impossible to show any connection between productivity and the dramatic increase in use of computers in organisations. This conclusion is supported by a number of other studies where the extent of computer use has been observed. For example, in a recent empirical study conducted in large

Finnish companies it was found that a sizeable amount of time needs to be devoted to getting systems functioning properly:

> "The results show that currently about 10% of working time is spent on activities which are not directly related to user's tasks, but which tackle the implementation of the PC-technology. Initially more than 50%, and currently 20-40% of the total time at a PC is spent learning new features, solving breakdowns, and helping fellow users."   (Heikkilä, 1995: 26)

These figures are rather alarming: There is hardly any other technology in wide use today where one third of a user's time is dedicated to dealing with problems related to the technology itself. One of the reasons for the situation is obviously that the systems we have are not good enough for their intended purposes, as is unanimously testified to by two respected members of the system design community:

> "The real problem is simple enough: the systems are not simple enough. They are too complex, have too many features, give the user far too many options. Almost all users use their computer for only a few operations. Nevertheless, their machines and minds are loaded up with a vast junk pile of options, commands, facilities doodads, and buttons, most of them superfluous to the user and there just because somebody knew how to program it. Having this mountain of stuff available usually means that doing even the simplest operation can be extraordinary difficult."   (Landauer, 1995: 127)

> From VCRs to clock radios, designers are adding every button, switch, and other power user doo-dad they can in the mistaken belief that the true power of technology is to be measured in the number of features and controls rather than impact on people's lives. Our computer software has tracked the trend. Systems and applications are festooned with every wangdoodle imaginable, offering users plenty of power to blow themselves up, while at the same time inhibiting them from accomplishing their task."   (Tognazzini, 1996: 221)

It is almost a joke to talk about augmentation when dealing with this sort of commentary. There is a heavy tension in augmentation: a strong and intuitively convincing promise on the one hand, and a huge gap between the promise and the situation in real life, on the other.

It would not be much of an exaggeration to say that we don't know yet how to properly design systems for augmentation. It might be reasonable to take a closer look at what is actually meant by augmentation and try to learn from that. That is the main purpose of this paper. In the rest of this paper we elaborate on ideas formulated by one of the authors elsewhere (Kaptelinin, 1996b) and further explore the concept of augmentation and the problems related to theorising around it. First, we introduce some current approaches to the augmentation of human cognition, which are based on two main assumptions, namely, that: (a) there are some "native" cognitive capabilities of human beings, and (b) these capabilities can be enhanced by structural expansion of unaided individuals, that is, providing human beings with artefacts that would complement native human capabilities within a larger scale and more efficient cognitive system. Second, we put these assumptions under scrutiny and provide evidence against both of them. We criticise the augmentational approach and show how this position leads to both theoretical and practical problems. Third, we present an alternative -- a mediational approach -- which from the very beginning focuses on the interaction between the individual and the world. We show that by using the ideas underlying the mediational perspective it is possible to both deepen our understanding of the role of cognitive tools in human activity and avoid the problems which plague the augmentational approach. In the final section we discuss the consequences of adopting the mediational approach. It is concluded that such an approach can be used as a conceptual framework within which to understand the rationale behind some of the rules-of-thumb suggested by the software design community.

WHAT IS MEANT BY "AUGMENTATION"?

Since design for augmentation is considered difficult, it seems logical to start with asking how the augmentation actually takes place, that is, with focussing on the specific mechanisms involved and on what the nature of "augmented cognitive systems" is. Surprisingly enough, despite its importance this area has not recently received much attention within HCI studies or elsewhere within the studies on computer technologies. The only recent title on augmentation, relevant to our present inquiry, recognised by the standard reference ACM Guide to Computing Literature is a reprint of one of Douglas Engelbart's articles originally published in the 1960s (Engelbart, 1963/1988). Probably, the only area in which the ideas of augmentation are currently being actively applied and developed, is virtual reality (see Biocca 1996). Thus the field has been mostly dominated by cognitive psychologists, resulting in what we call here a distribution approach. In our opinion, it is possible to identity three different perspectives on augmentation in the existing literature, namely, (a) the theoretical framework developed by Engelbart, (b) a group of approaches falling in the general category of "distributed systems", and (c) a virtual reality - oriented approach recently proposed by Biocca (1996) .

Engelbart

More than 30 years ago Douglas C. Engelbart developed a conceptual system intended to provide a basis for the research and development of technologies that would augment human intellect (Engelbart, 1963/1988). At the core of his conception of augmentation is the notion of the H-LAM/T system (Human using Language, Artefacts, and Methodology in which he is trained):

"Our culture has evolved means for us to organise and utilise our basic capabilities so that we can comprehend truly complex situations and accomplish the processes of devising and implementing problem solutions. The ways in which human capabilities are thus extended are here called augmentation means, and we define four basic classes of them:

1. Artefacts — physical objects designed to provide for human comfort, the manipulation of things and materials, and the manipulation of symbols.

2. Language — the way in which the individual classifies the picture of his world into the concepts that his mind uses to model that world, and the symbols that he attaches to those concepts and uses in consciously manipulating the concepts ("thinking").

3. Methodology — the methods, procedures, and strategies with which an individual organises his goal-centred (problem-solving) activity.

4. Training — the conditioning needed by the individual to bring his skills in using augmentation means 1, 2, and 3 to the point where they are operationally effective." (Engelbart 1963/1988,: 38)

Engelbart's conceptual system is amazingly rich and elaborated, especially if we take into account the time when it was created. Engelbart does not want to study isolated augmentation, but he sees his attempts to develop augmenting systems as one step in the continuum of general cultural artefacts, and he demands, that "the H-LAM/T should be studied as an interacting whole from a synthesis-oriented approach". He is also well aware of the dynamics related to the use of artefacts.

There are also some ambiguities in Engelbart's approach. He never makes it completely clear if a H-LAM/T should be conceived as one holistic system or two interacting systems. Also, the dynamics of the use situations are hidden behind "training" which is never explained. It is possible to point out some other inconsistencies and uncertainties in the conceptual system developed by Engelbart. It is worth noting, however, that most later attempts to conceptualise augmentation are far less sophisticated and thorough.

The distributed systems approach

Currently, the dominant approach in studies of augmentation seems to be associated with an attempt to understand how cognition is distributed between human minds and artefacts (Cosmo, 1992; Norman, 1991, 1993; Pea, 1993; Perkins, 1993; Salomon, 1993a, 1993b). Most approaches to distributed cognition follow generally the same sequence of steps. Typically, they start with differentiating between two entities: (a) a person whose cognition is not supported by any artefacts, and (b) the same person taken together with objects, usually tools, which support or perform some cognitive functions. In other words, the distribution of cognition between individuals and artefacts is viewed as creating a larger scale cognitive system by complementing "native" human cognition with external resources.

The next step of the analysis is to identify the limitations of native human cognitive capability and, then, to define the external components of "cognition at large". Finally, the analysis is focused on how the two cognitive systems -- one of the unaided individual and one of the individual augmented by artefacts -- affect each other. There are three questions addressed by most studies of distributed cognition:

a)   Does the fact that cognition is distributed mean that the border between the individual and the world should be reconsidered?

b)   What are the specific kinds of artefacts which actually or potentially augment human cognition?

c)   What is the impact of the distribution of cognition on the human mind?

Following the same sequence of analytical steps does not mean, however, coming to the same conclusions. In fact, the whole spectrum of possible answers to the above questions is represented in studies of distributed cognition. According to Norman (1991), the performance of the individual with artefacts represents the "system view", which should be differentiated from the "personal view" (the latter corresponds to the individual's perspective on what he/she is actually doing). Another position calls for a differentiation between the two meanings of the "individual". For instance, Perkins (1993) introduced the concepts of "person solo" and "person plus". The former corresponds to the individual without any artefacts, while the latter corresponds to the individual taken together with available external resources.

There is also a wide variety of views on the specific limitations of native human cognition that is, the limitations which should become the targets of artifact-based augmentation. Typically, a general model or taxonomy of human cognition is introduced, and then it is claimed that cognition should be augmented by designing artefacts to overcome the limitations associated with the identified structural components or functions. The differences the between proposed approaches lie in which specific model of human cognition is taken as a starting point. Some suggestions for the most promising ways to augment human cognition include: supporting decomposition of complex problems into sets of more simple ones, supporting task performance with representational artefacts in order to help bridge "the gulf of execution" and "the gulf of evaluation" in the action cycle (Norman, 1991), enhancing short term memory and long term memory (Cosmo, 1992), and providing needed knowledge, accessible representations, retrieval paths, and construction arenas (Perkins, 1993).

Finally, different positions have been expressed regarding the impact of artefacts on human cognitive capabilities. One of them states that the human components of augmented cognition are the same, no matter what the increase in overall cognitive performance. Norman (1991) wrote: "... artefacts do not actually change an individual's capabilities. Rather, they change the nature of the task performed by the person." (Norman, 1991: 19). (Later on Norman has come to a less unambiguous position, as suggested by the very title of his more recent book – "Things That Make Us Smart", Norman, 1993.)

According to Salomon (1993b) however, individual and distributed cognitions "... interact with one another in a spiral-like fashion whereby the inputs of the individuals, through their collaborative activities, affect the nature of the joint, distributed system, which in turn affects their cognitions such that their subsequent participation is altered, resulting in subsequent altered joint performances and products." (Salomon, 1993b: 122).

Biocca

Biocca (1996) looks at augmentation from a virtual reality (VR) engineer's point of view. He sees that VR has inherited Engelbart's goal of "augmenting human intellect" but recognises that theories about it are not very well developed:

> "The conceptualisation of intelligence augmentation has sometimes been wanting — the technology was claimed to assist or augment human thinking. How it will assist thinking is not always specified. The conceptualisation has been, for the most part, sketchy — more a design goal than a psychological theory."   (Biocca 1996,: 63)

For Biocca, VR is a media technology, and he tries to conceptualise how this new medium may influence the interaction between humans and their environments. He differentiates between two principal ways of interaction: amplification, where tools amplify the mind, and adaptation, wherein the mediated environment alters the mind. In amplification a human interacts with the environment through the medium in an "amplified" way but his or her cognitive structures remain unaltered, while in adaptation the environment and the used medium influence the human, and his or her cognitive structures or mental processes are altered in the interaction. Biocca's own position with respect to these two main modes remains a bit unclear: on the one hand he is positive that adaptation exists, on the other he seems to be unsure if the phenomenon can be constructively used in augmentation.

BASIC ASSUMPTIONS OF THE AUMGENTATION APPROACH

Despite the variety of specific concepts of augmentation described above, it would be safe to conclude that the original idea by Engelbart (1963/1988) is still underlying most of the thinking in this area. Probably, with the exception of the recent work by Biocca (1996), the basic assumptions underlying existing approaches can be summarised as follows. First, there is a set of some "native" cognitive capabilities of human beings which make it possible for people to solve certain kinds of problems. Second, these capabilities are limited, meaning that some problems are too difficult for people to solve. Third, the limitation of "native" human capabilities can be overcome to some extent if a "hybrid" cognitive system consisting of an individual human and an external means is designed. If true, such systems would be able to solve more difficult problems than unaided individuals could on their own. So, in terms of performance the new cognitive system would represent an augmentation of human cognition.

These assumptions and conclusions seem quite natural and intuitive. We believe, however, that these apparently convincing statements can be questioned, and that is what we focus on in the two following sections. We start with a discussion of the assumption of the existence of some "native" human cognitive capabilities, and then proceed to consider the notion of augmentation as a structural extension of unaided cognition.

THE SOCIAL NATURE OF HUMAN ABILITIES

In this section we are going to take a closer look at an idea which recurrently emerges in discussions of the basic strategy for augmentation. This is the notion of "natural" human cognitive abilities, which seems to be one of the basic assumptions supporting the augmentation approach ever since it was formulated by Douglas Engelbart (1963/1988), Its central role is illustrated by Engelbart's claim that "Increasing the effectiveness of the individual's use of his basic capabilities is a problem in redesigning the changeable part of the system. " (p. 43) and that "Thorough redesigning of the system requires making an inventory of the basic capabilities available." (p. 50).

In the history of psychology there have been several attempts to define an ultimate set of basic cognitive capabilities of human beings, but this project is still far from being completed. Moreover, as we shall see shortly, there are reasons to believe the goal of making such a list is probably not realistic and cannot be attained at all.

A growing body of research, including, cross-cultural studies of cognition and studies of the role of schooling in cognitive development (see Cole, 1996), have shown that one of the most important factors shaping cognitive functioning are the social practices in which human beings are involved. In particular, IQ tests have been proven to be inappropriate tools for measuring cross-cultural differences, as there appears to be no common scale of intelligence applicable to all cultures. Of course, the brain "hardware" imposes important constraints on how people process information, but within these limits there are enormous possibilities for qualitative and quantitative differences between (and within!) individuals. Brain mechanisms provide a basis for cognitive functioning but do not define its content. It is culture and development which are the major determinants of what and how people think.

Let us consider two examples of skills that play a crucial role in human cognition: reading skills and arithmetical skills. Of course, the way people read through various texts, how many words they can recognise, or how difficult the calculations they can perform are, are related to the architecture of the brain and the eye. However, those skills are too much greater extent determined by social and cultural factors. The human brain had evolved to its present capacity long before the time when writing systems and arithmetic were invented. Therefore, reading and math are not, strictly speaking, "native" human capabilities. They, as well as other "basic human capabilities", are acquired by humans from the culture. While "natural" mechanisms are heavily engaged and not everything can be appropriated from cultural environments (as failed attempts to realise social utopias have clearly demonstrated), culture is the most important source of what is considered basic human capability. According to Michael Cole (1996), "... ontogenesis is a process of co-construction among factors conceived of as biological, social, and psychological that periodically gave rise to "bio-social-behavioural-shifts" which take place within the medium of culture." (p. 337).

The notion of basic cognitive capabilities being determined by culture have direct implications for the design of cognitive tools. First, this notion suggests that cognitive technologies should be culture-specific. Perhaps the decision support systems, idea processors, or information visualisation systems appropriate for one culture would be less effective or even useless in another culture. For instance, cultural norms and procedures related to group decision making are different in Japan and the US (Nakakoj, 1993). It probably means that efficient use of decision support systems (DSS) in one country should be considered as a strong evidence *against* using the same system in a different cultural context. In other words, the "native" capabilities of individual and collective "actors" are different in different cultures, and so should be the technologies intended to enhance those capabilities.

To make matters worse, most cultures are anything but homogeneous environments. Usually they consist of subcultures, sub-subcultures, etc. Differences between them should also be taken into consideration. It might eventually turn out that the set of basic capabilities to be supported and enhanced by cognitive technologies should be established for every individual user (a human being or an organisation).

Second, the diversity of cultures is neither the only nor the most difficult problem which should be taken care of. Even more important is the fact that culture is constantly affecting people. Through learning human beings acquire new skills and abilities, thus expanding the repertoire of their basic capabilities. In other words, people develop, and therefore, the same person might have different basic capabilities at different stages of his/her development.

Third, the very introduction of a new tool means that its users can be involved in new cultural practices, and thus acquire new skills, meaning, and problem solving strategies. It means that augmentation of human capabilities with a tool is an intervention that can change the augmented capabilities themselves. These changed capabilities should be augmented in a different way, possibly with new or modified technologies, which, in turn, can result in changes of the capabilities, and so forth, This "augmentation/ transformation" cycle is, in a sense, similar to the notion of "task/artifact" cycle introduced by Carroll et al. (1991). According to the latter, new artefacts not only help to solve existing problems in a more efficient way, but also change the task itself. Therefore, new artefacts are needed to support the complete the new task, etc. In both cases, that is the"augmentation/transformation" cycle and the "task/ artifact" cycle, understanding of the nature of developmental cycles can help to avoid an unrealistic attitude towards creating a tool which would solve all problems in a certain area once and for all. Instead, system developers should adopt a developmental perspective on cognitive technologies. For instance, they might consider making a system flexible and open enough, so that it can be modified in the future to meet the developing needs of its users (e.g., Henderson and Kyng, 1991), or try to anticipate developmental changes and implement a range of solutions, so that one of them can be selected depending on which specific scenario comes true.

Fourth, the most important feature of human beings which differentiates us from other animals is the ability to create and use tools. If this capability is considered a basic one, then using artefacts should be understood not only from the point of view of an enhancement of "native" human capabilities but also as a modus vivendi of one of the most basic capabilities of human beings. This capability cannot be accounted for if a distinction between "native" human facilities and their external augmentation devices is the starting point of analysis.

To sum up, most current attempts to consider distributed cognition as an expansion of "native" information processing structures usually do not take into consideration the fundamental fact that internal cognitive processes are also being shaped by artefacts (see also, Biocca, 1996). In fact, the cognitive capabilities of human beings in general not only manifest themselves within a cultural context but are actually transformed and shaped by that culture. The fact that human capabilities are acquired through developmental changes shaped by endlessly diverse social cultural environments, makes it difficult, if not impossible, to create a taxonomy of basic capabilities to be augmented with artefacts. Of course, people do use artefacts to enhance their potential, and it is important to help them with appropriate technologies. However, in the interest of establishing effective design methods such enhancement, or augmentation, should be analysed within a larger context. People not only put their existing cognitive potential to use trying to achieve a higher performance level, they also transform themselves through participation in social practices. This crucial aspect of using artefacts is usually missing within the augmentation approach.

PROBLEMS WITH UNDERSTANDING AUGMENTATION AS A STRUCTURAL EXTENSION OF UNAIDED COGNITION

There are several conceptual and theoretical problems with the augmentation approach (for more detailed discussion see Kaptelinin, 1996b). Firstly, most conceptualisations of augmented cognition ignore the difference between the two kinds of boundaries: (1) the boundary between the individual and the world and (2) the boundary between internal and external. This is rather obvious in the case of approaches differentiating between a *person* and an augmented cognitive *system*.. In other words, the boundary between the person and the means of augmentation is the individual's skin. (i.e., "skin" as a metaphor, a symbol of the boundary between the internal and the external.)

Therefore, the difference between "individual" and "internal" in human cognition, which appears to be of critical importance for understanding how human cognition is distributed, is basically ignored, when the analysis begins with the distinction between unaided and augmented cognition. Such analyses do not provide an account of individuals dynamically extending themselves by including parts of their environments.

Secondly, augmentational accounts of distributed cognition consider both human minds and artefacts as information processing units complementing each other within the framework of the whole system. In other words, an essentially symmetrical relationship between human beings and artefacts is assumed. The ultimate outcome of studies of distributed cognition is formulated as the design of more efficient cognitive systems which would augment human cognition. This view misses the fundamental fact that there are human beings who augment their cognition.

Thirdly and finally, the heavy structural focus in the analysis of distributed cognition mostly ignores the developmental aspects of the distribution.

The above critical comments on the view of distributed cognition as a structural expansion of unaided, "native" human cognitive capabilities, call for a different perspective which could help to overcome the limitations of the structural augmentation approach. This new perspective should provide an account of the following aspects of distributed cognition:

- The dynamic integration of internal and external resources within the changing boundaries of the individual
- The mechanisms underlying the impact of artefacts on internal cognitive processes and structures
- The central role of the individual in creating and handling distributed cognitive systems
- The developmental transformations of distributed cognition

It is obvious, that to meet the above requirements one should look for a conceptual system which considers the human mind as a part of the context in which it exists. There are several candidate approaches. In the next section we discuss an alternative to the augmentation approach, based on a cultural-historical perspective in the design of cognitive tools, which emphasises the role of culture and development.

TOWARDS A MEDIATIONAL PERSPECTIVE IN DESIGN OF COGNITIVE TOOLS

In our opinion, many conceptual problems related to the understanding of computer tools and their role in human cognition can be resolved if instead of the augmentational perspective discussed above a *mediational* one is adopted. More specifically, we propose that the conceptual system of cultural-historical psychology, an approach originally developed in Russia, and a closely related conceptual framework of activity theory be applied to the analysis of computer tools and their role in human cognition.

The foundations of cultural-historical psychology and activity theory (which are sometimes considered together as the "cultural-historical activity theory", or CHAT, see Cole, 1996) were developed in Russia by a number of psychologists, most notably Lev Vygotsky and his disciples (Vygotsky, 1978; Leontiev, 1978). It is currently an international perspective underlying interdisciplinary studies in a variety of areas, including development, education, and human-computer interaction (Bødker, 1991; Engeström, 1987; Kuutti, 1996; Nardi, 1996; Cole, 1996).

The theoretical construct of cultural-historical psychology, most relevant in the present context, is the Vygotskian distinction between natural and higher mental functions (Vygotsky, 1978). The natural, "native" mental capabilities of human beings are slowly being transformed into higher order ones via the process of mediation. For instance, human memory is not limited to the direct retrieval of needed information. Instead, an elaborated system of semantic tools, including language and other culturally developed means, underlies the efficient functioning of human memory.

Also, Vygotsky differentiated between technical tools and psychological tools (see Engeström, 1987). The former ones help people change things, while the latter ones are used by individuals to change other people or themselves. Therefore, the notion of mediation, according to cultural-historical psychology, can be used to explain the mechanisms underlying the cultural determination of basic human capabilities, discussed in the previous section. Culture provides tools which are used by human beings in their external activities oriented towards things or other people. This way external activities become externally mediated and change their structure accordingly. Through the internalisation of mediated external activities internal activities become mediated, too (that is, natural mental functions are transformed into higher order mental functions).

Vygotsky defines some conditions for the successful acquisition of new mental abilities by introducing the ideas of "inter-psychological" and "intra-psychological" functions (Vygotsky, 1978). According to Vygotsky, new human abilities are acquired in two steps, or, on other words, they emerge twice in the process of development. First they appear as distributed between people (as inter-psychological ones) and then as appropriated by individuals (as intra-psychological ones).

Therefore, cultural-historical psychology identifies the potential impact of tools on human cognition not in terms of augmentation, that is, enhancing some "native" capabilities, but in terms of re-mediation (cf. Cole, 1996), that is, introducing new forms of mediation. This conclusion seems to be directly relevant to the current problems of designing cognitive tools.

First, the mediational perspective on computer tools imply that it is of crucial importance for a successful design of a cognitive tool to study how people utilise existing technologies. Since appropriating of a new tool can be considered a restructuring of the existing mediational system, the tool should be designed so that transition to its use is as smooth and graceful as possible. Only too often designers come up with new "amazing" systems or system features that look very attractive if considered on their own, but which fail because they are incompatible with what people actually use.

Second, the mediational perspective emphasises the social nature of development (including cognitive development). Therefore, cognitive tools should be intended to be used not only by individuals working alone, but also by communicating and collaborating groups.

Finally, we believe the notion of functional organs, developed within the framework of activity theory (Leontiev, 1978; Kaptelinin, 1996a, Kaptelinin, 1996b) provides a useful theoretical construct for the understanding and designing of computer tools.

Activity Theory is usually associated with the name of Alexey Leontiev, the student of Vygotsky, who came to formulate the principles of this approach in the 60s and 70s (Leontiev, 1978). The main idea behind Activity Theory is that psychological analysis should focus on goal-oriented human *activity*, which mediates the interaction between the individual and the world. Activity includes both external and internal components, which are organised into an integral whole and which can transform into each other.

We would like to mention only a few ideas of Activity Theory relevant to this paper. First, Activity Theory views the difference between internal and external processes as of secondary importance compared to the integration of these processes within human activity as a whole. Second, Activity Theory emphasises the crucial importance of tool mediation in the individual appropriation of socially accumulated experience. Third, activities are hierarchically organised according to the motives, goals, and actual conditions of the individual. Fourth, activities undergo various kinds of development.

From the above perspective, distribution of cognition is, essentially, a mediation. Artefacts, which are considered as tools in the broad sense, are integrated into both external and internal human activities. Below we will discuss one idea of Activity Theory, which, from our point of view, may shed some light on the mechanisms underlying distributed cognition. This is the concept of *functional organs*. created by individuals through the combination of both internal and external resources.

One implication of the notion of functional organs is that distribution is always functional. It takes place only within functional subsystems. Such subsystems are integral parts of the individual, who makes ultimate decisions on when to use functional organs and whether they have to be updated, modified, or even completely abandoned. Such functional organs are dependent of the history, context and situation of use at least as much as on the functionality of the system.

PROSPECTS FOR THE FUTURE

Some may think that from a design point of view the distinction we make between augmentation and mediation approaches is merely semantic. This is not the case however: there is a deep difference in the issues which are brought into focus during the design process. From an augmentation point of view one sees two systems: a human with "basic cognitive skills" that shall be connected with an "augmenting" system that is seen in it's full glory — say, a word processor with 600 commands; together they are capable of doing wonders. Where is the focus? Not on the human, that is always the same and can thus be bracketed out. In the connection between systems, then? Well, the theory does not explain that — better to leave that issue for training. The natural focus of design is thus on the system.

In contrast, from a mediational perspective there is only one system to be seen: a human already equipped with many kinds of functional organs, developing against a cultural background and situated in a personal history of interactions with the world. Besides this one system there is nothing else to be seen. A place for a computer tool with a set of functionalities is there, but it is totally opaque. There is a possibility that some of the hidden functionality can be used to transform the human system in order to enable it to perform a task, but it is only a potential. To realise the potential, a situation has to be organised where the person interacting with the material can recognise a possibility and create a new functional organ or extend an old one for the new purpose. Hence, within a mediational perspective the focus is on transformations.

The existence of two symmetric information processors/cognitive systems has been the dominant micro-level theory of HCI for a long time. Although not the only reason, the lack of a proper conceptualisation of use situations has been a factor contributing to the emergence of current monster systems like the ones mentioned in the introduction to this paper. If the perspective of mediation is adopted in system design it will cause a shift in focus. Instead of ultimate functionality, ultimate utility and usability will be the major goal. The dynamics of learning how to use a system – a topic still beyond the scope of our current usability design and testing – will become very central. How a person can first create functional organs within a system and then how the number of them can be increased in a natural way and how already existing organs can be further enlarged, will be a major question in system design. There is no use in designing 600 word processor commands without providing some way for them to be easily assimilated into new functional organs when needed.

The current problems with systems, of course, have long been recognised by the design community, and different remedies have already been suggested to improve the learning of systems; including some design rules that are consistent with the theoretical framework of functional organs presented in this paper. Let us consider just a couple of rather arbitrary examples.

Example one: The International Organisation for Standardisation (ISO) has for years been developing a standard with a code number ISO 9241 which defines a set of characteristics inherent to user friendly systems. Part 10 of this standard is concerned with "Dialogue Principles" and consists of the following seven principles: Suitability for the task, self-descriptiveness, controllability, conformity with user expectations, error tolerance, suitability for individualisation, suitability for learning. These sound good and indeed would potentially support the situational creation of functional organs, but unfortunately, beyond that the standard cannot give much advice to a designer on how these goals might be achieved in practice. Instead of analytical definitions and explanations, only general examples are provided.

Example two: Bruce Tognazzini suggests "successive disclosure" (Tognazzini 1996) that contains advice like

- Never present an expert-user option in such a way that normal users must learn all about it in order to know they don't need to use it.
- Do not require advanced techniques to perform nonsophisticated functions.
- Features the new user needs should be "within arm's reach".
- Features new users do not need should be placed in the background.
- Design software so people unfamiliar with the task domain can learn it.
- Begin in a familiar domain.
- Offer familiar tools and behaviours.
- Give people an intellectual upgrade path.

(Tognazzini, 1996: 263-287)

These excellent rules are slightly more practical than those in the ISO standard, but still very general. Also here most of the rules can easily be related to the dynamics of functional organs: one has to design situations so that the possibility of using some functionality in mediating an interaction with actual material for a particular purpose can easily be recognised.

Thus the design community is already making progress in the right direction. The problem is that in both cases we have only rules-of-thumb available; a weak and unsystematic means of supporting proper design practices. We believe, however, that the mediational approach we suggest gives us a sound conceptual foundation upon which a more analytic design approach can be built. By situating our study of the actual learning dynamics of systems-in-use within this framework we can start to figure out how these rules-of-thumb may be developed into a coherent and systematic body of knowledge to help us design useful and usable cognitive tools.

REFERENCES

Biocca, F., 1996. Intelligence Augmentation. The Vision Inside Virtual Reality. In B. Gorayska and J. L. Mey, eds, *Cognitive Technology: In Search of a Humane Interface*. Amsterdam: North-Holland, pp. 59-75.

Bødker, S., 1991. *Through the interface: A human activity approach to user interface design*. Hillsdale, NJ: Lawrence Erlbaum.

Carroll, J. M., Kellogg, W. A., Rosson M. B., 1991. The task-artifact cycle. In J. Carroll, ed. *Designing Interaction: Psychology at the Human-Computer Interface*. Cambridge: Cambridge University Press,

Cole, M., 1996. Cultural Psychology: *Once and Future Discipline*. Harvard University Press.

Engelbart, D., 1963. A Conceptual Framework for the Augmentation of Man's Intellect. In Howerton, ed., *Vistas In Information Handling. Vol.1*. Spartan Books. Reprinted in Greif 1988, pp. 35-66.

Engeström, Y., 1987. *Learning by Expanding: An Activity-Theoretical Approach to Developmental Research*. Helsinki: Orienta-Konsultit Oy.

Greif, I., ed., 1988. *Computer-Supported Cooperative Work: A Book of Readings*. Morgan Kaufmann, San Mateo, CA.

Heikkilä, J., 1995. *The diffusion of a learning intensive technology into organisations. The case of personal computing*. Helsinki School of Economics and Business Administration, Report A-104.

Henderson A., Kyng M., 1991. There's no place like home: Continuing design in use. In: J.Greenbaum, M. .Kyng, eds, *Design at Work: Cooperative Design of Computer Systems*. Hillsdale, NJ: Lawrence Erlbaum.

ISO 9241 Standard, Part 10: Dialogue principles. International Standard Organization, Geneva.

Kaptelinin, V., 1996a. Computer-Mediated Activity: Functional Organs in Social and Developmental Contexts. In Nardi, ed, 1996. *Context and Consciousness: Activity Theory and Human-Computer Interaction*. Cambridge, Mass. MIT Press

Kaptelinin, V. 1996b. Distribution of cognition between minds and artefacts: Augmentation or mediation? *AI and Society*, 10, pp. 15-25.

Cosmo, R. B. 1992. Constructing Knowledge With Learning Tools. In Kommers, Jonassen, and Mayes, eds, *Cognitive Tools For Learning*. Springer.

Kuutti, K., 1996. Activity Theory as a potential framework for human-computer interaction research. In Nardi, ed, 1996, *Context and Consciousness: Activity Theory and Human-Computer Interaction*. Cambridge, Mass. MIT Press.

Landauer, T. K., 1995. *The trouble with computers. Usefulness, Usability, and Productivity*. Cambridge, MA, MIT Press.

Leontiev, A. N., 1978. *Activity, Consciousness, and Personality*. Prentice Hall. Englewood Cliffs, NJ.

Nakakoj, K., 1993. *Position paper for the InterCHI'93 Workshop on Cross-Cultural Perspectives on Human-Computer Interaction*.

Nardi, B. A., ed., 1996. *Context and Consciousness: Activity Theory and Human-Computer Interaction*. Cambridge, Mass. MIT Press

Norman, D., 1991. Cognitive Artefacts. In J. Carroll, ed., *Designing Interaction: Psychology at the Human-Computer Interface*. Cambridge University Press.

Norman, D., 1993. *Things That Make Us Smart: Defending Human Attributes in the Age of the Machine*. Addison-Wesley. Reading, Mass.

Pea, R. D., 1993. Practices of Distributed Intelligence and Design for Education. In Salomon, ed., *Distributed Cognitions: Psychological and Educational Considerations*. Cambridge University Press.

Perkins, D. N., 1993. Person-Plus: A Distributed View of Thinking and Learning. In Salomon, ed., *Distributed Cognitions: Psychological and Educational Considerations.* Cambridge University Press.

Salomon, G., 1993a. Editor's Introduction. In Salomon, ed., *Distributed Cognitions: Psychological and Educational Considerations*. Cambridge University Press.

Salomon, G., 1993b. No Distribution Without Individual's Cognition: A Dynamic Interactional View. In Salomon, ed., *Distributed Cognitions: Psychological and Educational Considerations*. Cambridge University Press.

Tognazzini, B., 1996. *TOG on Software Design*. Addison -Wesley, Reading, MA.

Vygotsky, L. S., 1978. *Mind and Society*. Harvard University Press. Cambridge.

Humane Interfaces: Questions of method and practice in Cognitive Technology
J.P. Marsh, B. Gorayska and J.L. Mey (Editors)

Chapter 8

THE MEETING PLACE OF COGNITION AND TECHNOLOGY

Benny Karpatschof

Psychology Department
University of Copenhagen

INTRODUCTION

In this paper I want to analyse two topics. The first concerns what appears to be a technological phenomenon, the evolution of *Cognitive Technology*. The second concerns the demand, created by this evolution, for an increase in human capacity in the form of personal *competence,* a concept I shall characterise by the qualities of *self-organisation* and *self-instruction*.

TOOLS AND SIGNS AS RELATED MEDIATORS OF HUMAN ACTIVITY

This paper is dedicated to the relation between the technological and the cognitive, a relation between two areas seen until a few decades ago as very distant from one another. The former is usually included in the realm investigated by natural science, the latter forms a part of the realm studied by psychology. I shall start by showing that technology and cognition have been inseparable since humans first started using tools. The relation of these two phenomena is thus a constitutive characteristic of our species. This will become clear when we compare the form of human activity, on the one hand, with the activity of other non-human species on the other.

Animal activity is founded on pre-wired instincts modified by learning[1]. It can be explained in terms of interacting with a circuit of particular signals emitted from an ecologically relevant source and a preprogrammed set of actions activated by a release mechanism.

When we compare this circuit of animal activity with the human one, we see that it is fundamentally *immediate;* by contrast the latter is fundamentally *mediate*. Animal activity[2] is certainly mediated by signals; and stretching our language, we

---

[1] In Lorenz' theory (1967), an instinct is characterized by the predefined type of stimulus, the *key stimulus*, that triggers the reaction, and the release mechanism, the *Innate Response Mechanism*.

could call these signals 'immediate mediation'. These immediate mediations are, however, bound to the present and to the sensory input given. In contrast, human mediation is qualified by its mediate character: it is full mediation.

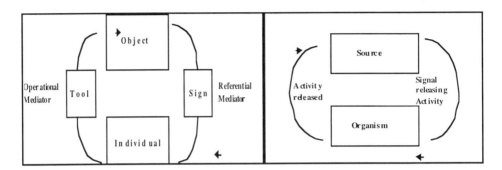

Figure 1: Human Activity compared to Non-human Activity

Whereas animal activity is governed by a simple feed back principle, human activity is mediated by two types of entities which appear to be largely absent in other species. I shall call these entities *tools* and *signs*, respectively.

Tools are artefacts produced by human beings to facilitate a certain *operation* within a specific goal- directed action that is a constituent of human activity. Thus, the tool is characterised by a certain *functional value*. The tool is thereby a culture-specific *operational mediator*. The tool is a piece of hardware that is not a part of the inborn morphology of the individual; its production and use are, furthermore, not defined by a piece of software that is pre-wired or simply programmed through an individual learning process. Therefore we need signs in order to use tools.

Signs are processes or objects, produced or selected by a human being in order to communicate *meaning* with respect to a certain object or phenomenon. Furthermore, meaning is the quality of the sign endowed with a certain potential *for referring to something else*. The sign is thereby a culture-specific *referential mediator*.

Now, tools and signs are not merely collateral categories of human culture. They are not independent entities. They presuppose one another.

Clearly, the production and use of a tool, being a cultural entity, can not be prewired as an instinct or individually developed in a simple learning process. The ways of producing and using a tool can only be transmitted culturally, that is by means of signs. On the other hand, there would be no reason to create signs if not in order to communicate the culturally defined *meaning* of tools and operations.

An especially important class of signs consists of those which express the meaning of tools. Here, tool meaning can be defined as the (meta-) functional value

---

[2] The proto-actions are here excluded as unavoidably disturbing precursors modifying, but not defining, the essence of animal activity.

of referring to the functional value of the tool. For instance, the meaning of the word "spear" is the potential of referring to the functional value of the spear tool, that functional value being the killing of game.

We have now introduced two complementary mediators of human activity, tools and signs. In fact, these two categories of mediators are placed in a kind of circuit, consisting of the afferent and the efferent side of activity.

My rough anthropological sketch is no doubt somewhat unfair to the higher vertebrates, especially our near relatives among the apes, but the basic distinction is, in my opinion, correct.

When we look at human activity in the diagram, it is apparent that the mediators on both sides, the afferent sign and the efferent tool, are the bearers of respectively the reference (the mediated perception forming the category of cognition) and the operation (the mediated implementation of activity forming the category of technology). This, then, is the first approximate formulation of the meeting place of these two categories. If we understand the sign as a psychological entity and the tool as an entirely technological one, we have, however, simplified the picture in a rather destructive way. Both mediators have, on the one hand, a psychological function, and on the other hand, a technological one.

On the one hand, the fundamental function of both mediators is psychological insofar as they are mediators of psychological processes. As psychological mediators their capacity to be used must be *internalized* by the active subjects in question.

On the other hand, tools are produced as cultural objects, and oral signs are produced as cultural phenomena (later scriptural signs are also produced as cultural objects). Thus, both tools and signs are *externalised* mediators that can also be understood as societal rather than psychological entities.

In this way, an anthropological dialectic arises between internalisation and externalisation; this dialectic concerns tools as well as signs. (see fig. 2)[3] In this diagram, I have replaced the earlier, primitive circuit of human activity with a more refined one. Here the interplay between the human actor and the activity is transposed to an interplay between the individual and the society of which he or she is a member.

The arrow from person to society is called *production,* insofar as society can be conceived as a major human product. The reverse arrow, from society to person, is called *appropriation,* as the very development of the essential quality of a person, that is his or her personality, is the result of this process. Thus, these are the main forms of human activity.

---

[3] This dialectic was clearly pointed out by Vygotsky (1978, 54) who wrote:
"....[T]he basic analogy between sign and tool rest on the mediating function that characterizes each of them. They may, therefore, from a psychological perspective, be subsumed under the same category. We can express the logical relationship between the use of signs and of tools using the schema in [the] figure [below], which shows each concept subsumed under the more general concept of indirect (mediated) activity."

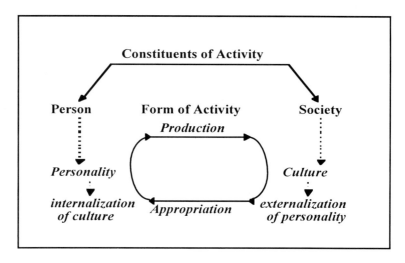

Figure 2: The constituents and forms of activity

I have constantly used the term 'human activity' without defining what I mean by this concept. Hence, to complete this introduction, a formal definition should be given:

> "**Human activity**: a socially organised life process, the constituents of which are acts of individual persons."

THE TENDENCY TO PROGRESSIVE EXTERNALIZATION IN TOOLS AND KNOWLEDGE

When we study the history of humanity, a certain characteristic aspect of cultural evolution catches our eye; viz., a tendency to progressive externalisation. The emergence of tools and of signs are processes that are logically bound to one another. The tools, the material culture, presuppose a language to express the meaning, the specific function of a specific tool, whenever this function becomes complicated beyond a certain level. Also, the part of material culture related to the making of tools presumes a way of transferring this know-how. Thus, the material culture presupposes a cognitive culture, or as I prefer to call it, a knowledge culture.

The Stone Age Culture

Now there is a remarkable difference between the initial stages of the earlier and later constituents of culture. From the beginning, that is from the Paleolithicum on, material culture has been externalised. Whenever a person produced a tool, this tool could be transferred to another person without the consent or even participation of the original tool-maker. Having been produced, the tool takes on an objective, non-personal entity.

For the counterpart of material culture, that is knowledge, the case is different. A piece of knowledge, the know-how of making and using the tool, is by definition person-bound. Of course, this personal knowledge too, can be transferred to other people. This is the basic function of a sign-based knowledge culture[4].

This transfer is, however, of a different kind than the material transmission of a tool. Personal knowledge as a person-bound phenomenon which has this meaning system as its primary vehicle of transference from one person to another. At the same time, the whole meaning system is, in itself, person-bound, as long as it is limited to the original oral language.

While the notion of person-bondage applies to oral language (and the cultural meaning system), it is not to be confused with the category of subjectivity. The oral language, and the cultural meaning system based on it are not subjective, but objective entities. They exist and function in an objective and societal way rather than a subjective and individualistic way. The characteristic of being person-bound is thus not attached to any societal functions, but only to their ontological foundation as the exclusive personal bearer of linguistic and cognitive competence.

This restriction to persons has no grave consequences, as long as the culture is homogeneous and is organised primarily along the lines of a sexual division of labour. Such is the case for Stone Age cultures, the cultures of the hunting-gathering and Neolithic farming societies. With the emergence of more highly developed cultures in what is called the Bronze Age, a more complicated technical and organisational structure arose in the Middle East.

The Bronze Age Culture

To coordinate the diverse contributions of the different occupations of farmers, artisans, and soldiers, and to organise the flow of products and services based on these more or less voluntary contributors, a specific class of administrators was needed.

Their function was basically to ensure the smooth material transferral of goods produced and services delivered; but in order to ensure that the organisers themselves are properly organised, their sign-based work could not be limited to oral language as such communication system is person-bound and thus severely restricted to direct person-to-person communication.

Now, the only way to ensure a transfer of meaning that is *not* person-bound, is to develop a sign system that has the same superiority over oral language as manual tools have possessed from their very beginning; that is, the superiority of *externality*. The leap from a person-bound to an externalised sign system was, in Bronze Age cultures, represented by a jump from oral language to writing. In the

---

[4] This is, however, not the only function, of the category of signs. In addition, there is an internal function, that of being the building blocks from which to construct the internal representation of the personal knowledge system.

parallel cultural evolution of the pre-Columbian cultures, the leap was bound to the invention of the *Quippu* system of representing numbers through knots.

The consequence (as well as the driving force) of the emergence of writing systems was an additional division of labour. One that was much more influential than the initial diversification into different types of material work. Now, there was instituted a major split between the material or physical labour of the manual workers and the cognitive or intellectual work of the administrative and ruling classes.

The manual workers communicated by means of oral language alone, and even their training, their acquisition of necessary skills, was a simple learning by doing. That is to say, a learning process based partly on the visibility of the ongoing work at the workplace and partly on oral instructions.

By contrast, the administrative workers, the scribes, could not be trained in the same way. The product of their work was generally not present and therefore not visible, just as the meaning of their job was not transparent (being itself a mediation). Furthermore any writing system, even a so-called *iconographic* one, is not immediately understandable. For this reason, the administrators had to be trained in specific institutions, dedicated, not to *immediate production*, nor even to the *mediative processes that is administration*, but to *mediating the skills and functions of mediation* itself.

With the evolution of the script, the meaning system was transformed from a person-bound to a passively externalised status. This had far reaching consequences for the division of labour, the distinction between manual and intellectual work, and the development and distribution of culture.

The very blooming of the first high cultures was thus based on a rise of the knowledge part of culture[5]. Knowledge was elevated to the status of a tool which, from the beginning, had been the hallmark of material culture. Now both parts of the culture had an equal degree of externalisation, having risen above their person-bound status. This degree I shall call passive externalisation.

THE CULTURE OF INDUSTRY

The qualifier 'passive' in the term 'passive externalisation' now needs to be to explained. This is best done by examining the next cultural leap, the transition to an Industrial Culture. This "leap" materialised over a rather prolonged period, from the late Middle Ages to the beginning of the nineteenth century; it represents a new round in the competition between the material culture and the knowledge culture. Material culture took another leap, thus regaining the lead over knowledge culture that it had in the beginning, that is during the Stone Age. The leap in question is the shift from simple tools to machines, that is, from passive externalisation to what I shall call *active externalisation*.

---

[5] The cultural implications of writing have been stressed by Goody (1986).

The development of machines 'transforming heat into motion' (Sandfort, 1962) meant that material technology was raised from the status of a passively externalised *hand tool* to that of an actively externalised *automaton* taking over the motoric work that was until then the monopoly of the artisans skilled in the specific craft.

A machine is characterized as being not only an external product of a person's activity, and thus of his or her skill but also as an externalisation of the activity itself. The machine does, in fact, externalise the operations of the original, pre-industrial worker, as its operations are *external*, mechanical imitations of the internal operations of its human predecessors.

A passive externalisation is merely a supplement to the activity of the worker. It is still him or her that performs the job, with the tool serving as only a passive means to enhance that performance. The machine, however, transcends that limitation by taking over the very operation of the (literally) former worker. It should be noted that I do not assert that the machine is taking over the activity itself; that is certainly *not* the case. The way *human activity* is defined, it presupposes the presence of a *motive*, an intention to fulfill a certain objective; hence, the activity as such remains attached to the person working with the machine (Karpatschof, 1992).

The status of the knowledge system did not change as a result of this change on the scale of externalisation. That, however, does not imply that the knowledge system itself was unaffected during this process of industrialisation. An important contributing factor to such change was the mechanisation of the production and distribution of written material by means of *typography*; an ever more externalised way of "manufacturing" printed matter. A combined cause and effect of the industrial revolution was the explosive growth of natural science. Also other societal changes, such as those happening in the areas of politics and religion, were able to be quickly and widely distributed by means of the printing press.

Just as the invention of writing brought about basic changes in the class structure in antiquity, the invention of machinery is linked to similarly important transformations in the societal structure of industrial culture. This structure has been described by Marx as constituted by two classes, the working class and that of the owners of the means of production, (such as machinery). A feature of this class structure, distinguishing it from the previous societal formations of slavery and feudalism in antiquity and the Middle Ages, seems to have escaped Marx' keen attention, viz.: the simultaneous process of on the one hand, the degradation and dequalification of mechanised labour, and on the other, the elevation of "qualified" labour.

This double movement has its origin in, what I have called the technological threshold of qualification (Karpatschof, 1985). By this I mean the way valuable labour skills are defined by the actual states of the industrial externalisation within a specific area of work operation[6]. As soon as a particular operation is externalised,

---

[6] In the economic theory of Marx the concept should be defined as: The level *of work qualification relevant to production* and therefore of sufficient value to pay what amounts to the necessary living expenses for the worker.

the corresponding skill will have become obsolete, useless, and valueless, or better expressed: its value falls below the technological threshold of qualification. As soon as the value reaches this low point, the worker is ousted by the much faster and much more productive machine. It was this degradation of entire professions (such as the weavers) that was at the basis of the class struggle of the *Luddites* (as this heroic, but unfortunate people were called after their just as unfortunate leader who tried to stop mechanisation by breaking the machines).

In the short term, the rage of these workers, doomed to starvation by the automation of their former crafts, was, of course, without much effect. Furthermore, in the long run the effect was not that prophesied by Marx in his famous *misery theory*. On the one hand, whenever work qualifications fall below the present level of technological qualification, the upgrading of the machinery is accompanied by a relative deskilling of the worker. On the other hand, any worker relevant to the new mechanised form of production must be made to rise above that same level of *technological qualification*. This means that, as soon as the technology advances by taking over the old skills of the pre-industrial workers, the workers controlling the new machinery have to be trained above the level of their previous qualification.

Thus, the dark side of the coin is the annihilation of mechanised human labour, implicating, at least in the beginning, the annihilation of human workers. The coin's bright side embodies the logical counterpart of the technological threshold of qualification. This type of industrial labour does not just consist of pre-mechanised operations, not just of skills that happen to be above the transient externalisation level, it incorporates the knowledge necessary to govern the machines. Precisely because the industrial machines were nothing but mechanical assemblies of moving parts performing mechanised operations, the owner of the factories had to pick up foremen, "work leaders", to supervise the machines. The reasons were even more compelling than in the case of the supervision of the slaves and feudal peasants of the earlier cultures.

Thus, the workers that could only do what the machines could ceased to be part of the work force. In order to stay within the work force, workers had to become much more competent than the machines; for instance, they now had to understand how the machines were functioning.

This implied that the industrial workers not only had to be trained, but also educated. This, again, implied that the limits imposed on schooling as a privilege for the leading classes of society had to be transcended. Universal schooling in the industrial countries was now a societal necessity. In order to rise above the machine, above the technological threshold of qualification, the worker had to appropriate the kind of knowledge that had been the monopoly of the privileged classes for 4,000 years. The division of labour and of society resulting from the split between manual and intellectual labour was not abolished, but its effect were strongly reduced.

While mechanisation of a trade may seem a rather simple matter, the really complicated task consists in training the industrial workers to control such machinery.

An indirect result of the industrial revolution, from its onset in early 19th century Great Britain to some 20 years ago, has thus been a hitherto unseen improvement in education, health, material and cultural living standards, as well as the legal and political rights of the industrial workers. Technological improvement had to be followed by an improvement in the cognitive capabilities of the workers, inasmuch as refined machinery is in need of a refined working staff.[7]

The dramatically increased cognitive demands on the workers carried with it the establishment of a general educational system. For the first time in history, schools were not solely the secondary socialisation agencies of small elite groups of scribes or clerks, dependent on the church or a ruler. They became universal institutions impacting all citizens. Hence, learning by merely doing became just as insufficient for the Sumerian scribe as it is for the industrial worker.

In fact, the development of the so-called welfare state that took place between and after the world wars in Europe and North America can be seen as a consequence of the heightened value and influence of the working class. In this perspective both the fascist, and communist states must be seen as blind alleys[8].

THE CULTURE OF INFORMATION TECHNOLOGY

From about 1970[9] on, we have witnessed a new transition: from the *industrial* society to the *information* society, from industrial culture to information culture. The crucial element of this transition was the emergence of modern information technology (IT). With the emergence of this technology, a whole new wave of automation began, comprising also the cultural skills and intellectual knowledge that during the industrial era had been the benchmark of qualifications beyond the technological threshold, and resulting in a whole new range of cultural products.

How can we understand this new category of cultural products situated in the interface between material culture and cognitive culture? What is happening can be seen as another round in the previously described fight between these two parts of the culture, or as I shall prefer to say, between the *technical system and the knowledge system*. Once more, the knowledge system is getting even with the

---

[7] This analysis is, of course, in opposition to the theory of *scientific management*, developed by Taylor (1911). Similarly Ford assembly line philosophy represents a blind alley, no matter how effective this much more radical type of *scientific management* has proven to be in the development of work organization..

[8] Moore (1973) has analyzed three ways to industrialization: viz., democracy, communism, and fascism. These three ways represents the result of the relative power of the various classes in the preindustrial society, that is the landowners, the peasants, the bourgoisie and the workers.

[9] The change became more or less official in 1982, with Japan's dramatic announcement of its its intention to develop a so-called fifth generation of computers.

technical system, due to its elevation from the category of passive to the category of *active externalisation.*

Until now, the knowledge conserved and expressed in books had merely been a passive instrument for performing a certain activity. Just like the hand tool of the Stone Age, the book, of its own accord, is totally unable to perform any operation whatsoever. Information technology has changed all that. IT can perform any (series of) operation(s), through its externalisation of what used to be understood as intellectual labour.

This impressive development has led to the common misunderstanding of Artificial Intelligence (AI): the adherents to this discipline often assume that the new technology produces a literal copy of the human, having (or at least, soon obtaining) the same intellectual and other mental capacities as the human being that performed the activity before AI (Karpatschof, 1992). This misunderstanding was caused by the awe over the new technology that could perform activities that formerly were exclusively within the reach of humans. However, "activity" in a computer is merely a system of *externalised operations;* hence, no piece of IT can perform any kind of *human activity*, as the *intentional motive* is lacking. As far as the single operations *are concerned*, no *intentional goal* is attached, and therefore such operations lack the specific characteristic of the operations that are constituents of human activity. Thus, the operations of IT should rather be compared to those of the industrial machines, performing certain, well-defined mechanical tasks.

The present state of affairs represents, however, an even more sweeping change in the status of the material and the cognitive culture than their mere equality in the degree of externalisation. The very name of the phenomenon, *Information Technology*, serves to indicate the current societal revolution which is characterised by a rapid fusion of these two aspects of culture.

Just as in the days of the Luddites, we are presently witnessing the annihilation of whole sections of human labour and the concomitant degradation of the workers expelled. Likewise, we see how innovative and self-organising cadres are now by definition elevated above the new threshold of technological qualification, a threshold which at present is defined by the job functions best suited for immediate automation. Furthermore, the future will then be bound by what can, in principle, be automated.

Also at this time, we see a reversal of rising industrialism, with its tendency toward a more egalitarian society. This movement, as expressed in the ideology of the Enlightenment and of socialism and in the evolution of democracy, public health, welfare and education, is now being turned back and its adherents crushed.

The cultural development, just described, can be understood in terms of my theory of externalisation, as shown in the diagram below (see fig. 3).

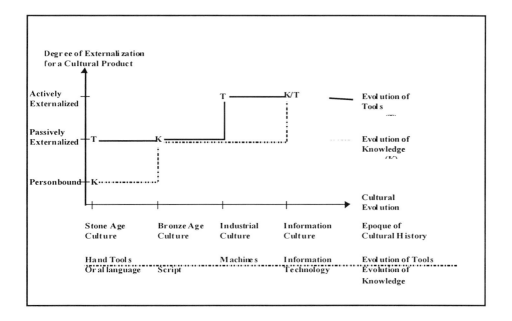

Figure 3 The Evolution of Tools and Knowledge

In Figure 3 the race between knowledge culture (k), here depicted as a solid line, related to, but emulating and periodically catching up with the knowledge culture (T) here depicted as a broken line, (T) a broken line (K). The catching up happened first in the dawn of the Bronze Age, and again now in the era of Information Technology.

COMPETENCE IN THE INFORMATION SOCIETY-SELF ORGANIZATION AND SELF-INSTRUCTION

It thus seems evident that a new major step in cultural evolution is being taken right now. Of the prior steps, the first was anthropogenic in nature: it brought us tools and language. The second step was the evolution of a writing system. The third was the invention of automatic machines. The fourth and most recent one is the evolution of information technology, in which the same transition is taking place in the meaning system that earlier took place in the technical system of industrialism: a transition from a passive to an active state of externalisation. With the transition from oral to written language, the meaning system was elevated to the independent, externalised status of a tool. Both systems are supplements: in the first case to intellectual, in the second, to manual work.

When industrialisation took place, the technical system once again surpassed the meaning system by transcending its merely passively externalised status. It is this lead that is being caught up to by the knowledge system. A book has no effect, except through the ways it may influence our thoughts, and thereby possibly even our deeds. In contrast to this restricted function, IT now automates many intellectual functions in much the same way that the industrial machinery earlier mechanised manual functions.

Also at this time, the threshold of qualification within the production process is raised above the skills of millions of workers; as a consequence, the victims are not restricted to manual workers, but also belong to the clerical and intellectual professions.

Faced with this alarming picture, one could ask whether our current mass unemployment is just a transitory phenomenon, as was the one referred to in the case of early industrialism. Alas, such is not the case. The employees fired are certainly falling victim to a dramatically heightened level of required "qualifications" in IT. To rise above this threshold of technological qualification is, however, only to obtain a short respite. What is needed now to keep a job is more than qualification; the necessary quality is *competence*.

My colleague O. E. Rasmussen defines the concept of qualification in the following way:

> **Qualification**: A qualified personal performance is an unfolding of knowledge, insight and values, which systematises a complicated occurrence in such a way that a specified state or objective is achieved. When we speak of qualifications, we are dealing with the way in which we as human beings systematically unfold knowledge, insight and values (Rasmussen, 1995:7).

Qualification is thus the ability that delivers rule-bound work, the repetition of well-known performances; what it does not ensure, however, is innovation and flexibility. These features demand another, quite different quality, *competence*, defined by Rasmussen in the following way:

> **Competence:** A competent personal performance is an assembling of ideas that creates perspective, while ordering and organising a complex occurrence in such a way as to make sense of it (ibid:8).

The new division of labour in the IT-culture thus makes computerised technology take over the functions which demand merely *qualification*. By contrast, *competence* is certain to *absolutely* exceed the threshold of technological qualification. Those employees who only *relatively* exceed the threshold of technological qualification may maintain their jobs for a while, but only until their present qualifications are matched by computer technology.[10]

---

[10] The argumentation for such an absolute limit for automation is found in (Karpatschof 1984 and 1985)

Consequently, we can model the outlines of this new, stratified IT-society in the following way:

1. The High Priest (possessing competence)
2. The Temple Servants (possessing still useful qualifications)
3. The Outcasts (possessing no useful qualifications)[11]

Figure 4: The IT-Temple and its strata

The upper class, the high priests, correspond to what Reich (1991) calls the symbol analysts, whereas the subordinate class of temple servants consists of two groups, the routine and the service workers in Reich's analysis. At the bottom, there is the vast mass of the unqualified; the people that have been eliminated by the system, the outcast of the temple.

With regard to what currently corresponds to the 'high priests' (the new class of leadership), the decisive problem is how to get access to this privileged class. What is the secrete formula, and how does one acquire the capacity needed to be thus selected?

In reports from corporate and governmental studies (Commission of the European Communities, 1993) on job qualification and vocational training, two qualities keep coming up:

1. Self-organisation

   - The ability to organise one's own work, either alone or in self-organising teams.
   - The combination of intellectual skills (Zuboff, 1988), motivation, and creativity to initiate and implement new activities.

2. Self-instruction

   - The ability to organise one's own training when certain new qualifications are needed.
   - The combination of the capacity of defining, finding, and appropriating whatever knowledge is needed to realise a certain project.

---

[11] (Ibid.)

PERSPECTIVES FOR A COGNITIVE TECHNOLOGY

In this historical sketch, I have stressed the fusion of the material and the cognitive culture, or in my own terms the technical and the knowledge culture. The very phrasing of the concept *Cognitive Technology* bears witness to this tendency.

In this light, *Cognitive Technology* is not just one more ad hoc discipline like AI. Rather, it is an expression of the metamorphosis of contemporary technology. This tendency is already an established part of the status quo. Thus Microsoft Inc., one of the most characteristic representatives of Cognitive Technology, has in less than two decades expanded to be one of the largest corporations in the world.

It would, however, be practical to distinguish between Cognitive Technology in this broad sense, and another, quite narrow sense, which refers to the corner of this fusion area in which the most characteristic integration is taking place[12]. Examples of which are human-computer-interfaces, translation programs, and individually programmed hearing aids defined on the basis of psychoacoustical parameters,

Now, a technology generally needs a basic science as a foundation of its activity of construction and implementation. In the case of *Cognitive Technology,* it would be natural to conceive of what is called Cognitive Science as being such a science. When this new science was launched in the last decade, it was received with great expectations, and it was a widespread view that Cognitive Science was the science of the future.

Cognitive science was originally loosely defined as an assembly of a most diverse group of individual scientific disciplines:

Looking now at this list of constituents it is really no wonder that this Frankenstein monster of a science should have had very serious problems of coherence, not to mention identity. Cognitive science today is, if anything, just a forum of communication between the scientists from the constituting disciplines cooperating in projects of Cognitive Technology in the strict sense. The 'science' as such has remained a postulate.[13]

---

[12] That cognitive technology is a yet rather immature area of scientific study is shown by a search on a database covering the monographs of the last 10 years. PsycLIT 87-97 had only two records on cognitive technology, the first of which happened to be (Gorayska & Mey 1996), while the second was a book on psychiatric rehabilitation (Spaulding 1994) I have not been able to fetch the latter book yet, but it scarcely appears to be an essential representative of what I have defined as the kernel area of cognitive technology.

[13] A search on a database covering the last 10 years showed the following picture of the referred 767 books: The large majority had the term 'cognitive science' not in the title, but only in the name of the scientific institution of the author, probably as a strategy for fund raising. A much smaller part had the term in the title, but only as a catchword, as the content evidently was mono-disciplinary within a traditional discipline. A few books were interdisciplinary in the sense that the content was bi-disciplinary of a traditional type, especially neuro-psychology or psycho-linguistic Only 2 of the more than 700 books were truly interdisciplinary: Roitblat & Meyer (1995) and Sperber, Premack &

```
Computer Science
Logic
Epistemology
Cognitive psychology
Neuroscience
Linguistics
Organisation theory
```

Figure 6: Disciplines contributing to cognitive science

Evaluating the experiences from the last decade, there is maybe no reason to lament the futility of the cognitive science enterprise. In contrast to the belief that the constituting disciplines were arbitrary confinements of knowledge and cognitive science the natural, all-encompassing discipline, reality seems to be the other way round: the constituents are the natural and viable entities, whereas cognitive science is an arbitrary composition.

On the basis of my theory of the fusion and externalisation of cultural development, one could wonder why this is so.

I shall not go into a detailed theory of science here, but will only stress two points. The first is an explanation of the non-coalescence of the constituent disciplines of cognitive science. The second point is the real scientific relevance of Cognitive Technology.

Point 1: The non-coalescence of the constituent disciplines of cognitive science

According to my theory of science (Karpatschof, 1997), any major scientific discipline like the physical sciences, the biological sciences, psychology or the social sciences is defined as the theory field of a corresponding pre-established object field. Since cognitive science spans the totality of possible major theoretical fields, it is no wonder that it should have had such painful problems of coherence. Not only is the span of cognitive science all-encompassing, but it has in addition another problem built into its very definition. The constituent disciplines have been deprived of their very integrity right from the start. Thus, psychology is only admitted in respect to its cognitive part, the social sciences only in respect to linguistics and organisation theory; and so on. Unlike poor Dr. Frankenstein, the constructors of cognitive science have taken some spare parts from diverse sciences; but the composition is already defective due to an ad hoc cannibalistic decomposition of the constituent disciplines.

Premack (1995), but both titles reveal a comparative perspective. Thus, not in a single case do we find a genuine integration of the constituent disciplines.

Point 2. The real scientific relevance of Cognitive Technology

What then is the real perspective of Cognitive Technology? There is an aspect of the externalisation tendency in cultural development that has not been mentioned until now. Parallel to the tendency to externalise human activity into tools and techniques, there is a reverse tendency of re-internalisation. That means that whenever we have produced some artifact or externalised knowledge, we have the opportunity of a confrontation with this external picture of ourselves.

Thus the rise of a mechanical technology from the late Middle Ages was the material precondition of the development of a scientific physiology. When Harvey had the bright idea of understanding the heart as a pump, he did so on the basis of the construction of a pump that already was an externalisation of human activity, namely the activity of moving a liquid.

In the process of reinternalization, we make what appears to be a category mistake of reducing human abilities and processes to human artefacts. This reductionism is, however, sometimes fertile or even correct; whenever the artifact is already an externalisation of human abilities and processes.

Thus the thesis of strict AI, that there is no fundamental difference between the human mind and the computer, is a gross exaggeration of the plausible thesis that we have constructed the computer as an externalisation of mental tasks, and that we therefore have an opportunity of studying aspects of these tasks in their externalised form.

In this light, Cognitive Technology not only has the necessary task of finding inspiration from disciplines such as cognitive psychology and linguistics. It has also a great potential of inspiring those disciplines.

REFERENCES

Commission of the European Communities, 1993. *Commission Memorandum on Vocational Training in the European Community in the 1990s*, Bruxelles.

Goody, J., 1986. *The Logic of Writing and the Organisation of Society*, Cambridge: Cambridge University Press.

Gorayska, B. & Mey, J. L, eds, 1996. *Cognitive Technology: In search of a humane interface*, Amsterdam: Elsevier Science Publishing Co, Inc.

Karpatschof, B., 1982. Artificial Intelligence or Artificial Signification, J. Pragmatics, 6, pp. 293-304.

--- 1985. Grænsen for automatisering (The Limit of Automation), *Psyke & Logos*, 5, pp. 201-220.

--- 1985. Informationsalderens vidensbegreb (The Concept of Knowledge in the Age of Information) In: T. Söderquist, ed., *Informationssamfundet* (The Information Society), Copenhagen: Philosophia.

--- 1992. The Control of Technology and the Technology of Control, *Activity Theory*, 11(12), pp. 34-40.

--- 1997. *Human Activity - Contributions to the Anthropological Sciences - from a Perspective of Activity Theory*. (MS submitted for the Ph.D. degree to the Psychology Department, the Faculty of Arts, University of Copenhagen).

Leaky, R. E., 1981. *The Making of Mankind*. London: Michael Joseph Ltd.

----. 1982. *Human Origins*. New York: Lodestar Books.

Lee, R. B., 1979. *The !KungSan - Men, Woman and Work in a Foraging Society*. Cambridge: Cambridge University Press.

Lorenz; K., 1963. *Das sogenannte Böse, Wien*: Dr. G. Boroth Schoeller Verlag.

---. 1967. *On Aggression*, London: Methuen & Co.

---. 1971. *Studies in Animal and Human Behaviour, vol.II* London: Methuen.

Moore, B., 1973. *Social Origins of Dictatorship and Democracy*, Harmondsworth: Penguin, 1966.

Rasmussen, O. E., 1995. *A Strategy for the Development of a Theory of Organisational Leadership and Administration In: Danish Psychological Yearbook, 1995*. Copenhagen: Musæum Tusculanum.

Reich, R. B., 1991. *The Work of Nations*, London: Simon & Schuster.

Roitblat, H. L. & Meyer, J. A., eds, 1995. *Comparative approaches to cognitive science*. Cambridge (MA): MIT Press.

Skinner, B. F., 1974. *About Behaviorism*, New York: Alfred A. Knopf.

Sandfort, J. F., 1962. *Heat Engines. Thermodynamics in theory and practice*. London: Educational Series Inc.

Spaulding, W. D., ed., 1994. *Cognitive Technology in Psychiatric Rehabilitation*, Lincoln (Nebraska): University of Nebraska Press.

Sperber, D., Premack, D. & Premack, A.J., eds, 1995. *Causal Cognition: A Multidisciplinary Debate*. New York: Clarendon Press/Oxford University Press.

Vygotsky, L. S., 1978. *Mind in society*. Cambridge, Mass.: Harvard University Press.

Zuboff, S., 1988. *In the Age of the Smart Machine - the Future of Work and Power*. Oxford: Heineman.

Humane Interfaces: Questions of method and practice in Cognitive Technology
J.P. Marsh, B. Gorayska and J.L. Mey (Editors)

Chapter 9

HONESTY OF AFFORDANCE

Will Fitzgerald

Neodesic Corporation

Eric Goldstein

Institute for the Learning Sciences

INTRODUCTION

Designers of modern "things that make us smart" (Norman, 1993) face an increasingly complex task, made no easier by an insistence that these tools be humane. An important concept in design is understanding the perceived and actual affordances of artefacts. By viewing affordances as acts of communication between designer and user, we can develop criteria for humane tool design. One such criterion we will describe as *honesty of affordance.* Intuitively, honesty of affordance means a tool tells the truth, the whole truth, and nothing but the truth about the capabilities it has. No tool can help but tell some truth; that is, it will always be endowed by its creators (and users!) as having some thing that can be done with it. But it will have honesty of affordance to the degree that affordances indicate some capability desired by the user, and its capabilities are indicated by some affordance, or it is clear that no affordance indicates that capability. Further, developing a theory of what a tool needs to be honest about eases a designer's job of creating humane tools.

AFFORDANCES AND HUMANE TOOLS

Modern design theory for cognitive tools has been strongly influenced by the idea of affordances. These can be defined as the properties of a natural object or artifact which determine how it can be used (Gibson, 1979; Norman 1988, 1993). Although the idea of an affordance is a powerful idea, we will show that it is not quite powerful enough, as currently understood, to help us design humane tools. However, we will show there is a natural way to interpret affordances in artefacts that will allow us leverage in human cognitive tool design.

Essential to the idea of an affordance is the role played by the user of the object. A door may afford opening and closing, but only if there is an agent with the ability to do the opening and closing. For example; a typical door may afford opening and closing only to a person whose hand can grasp its handle, the same door may not afford opening or closing to a dog, and almost definitely not to a snail. See Figure 1.

Also essential are the goals of the user. For example, people in general have the goal of being able to move from one room to the next; hence it makes sense to consider whether the doors in Figure 1. afford opening. Affordances become available as goals become active. For example, if the person in Figure 1. desires to hide a key, he may notice that the top of the door frame will afford hiding small, flat objects such as keys.

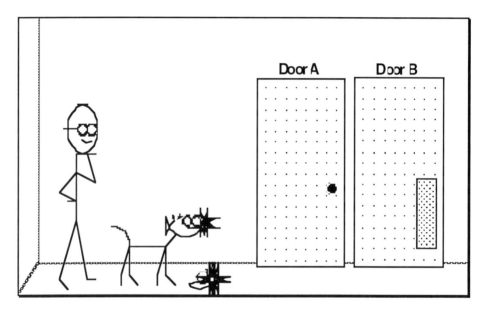

Figure 1: The effect of the observer on affordances

An object also affords some capability due to social convention. A door affords opening partly by virtue of our individual and social experience with doors: things that look like doors almost always afford opening and closing, so its likely that this door-like thing also affords opening and closing.

Thus, affordances are not just properties of an object. They also involve the relationship between an object and an agent and the individual and social history of the agent and other objects perceived to be in the same class. For example, chairs afford support for sitting furthering the goals of resting but remaining somewhat alert. A graphical button on a computer screen affords, at different levels of analysis, pushing and starting some action. This is partly by virtue of the conventions established for human interface guidelines established by computer firms and subsequently internalised by users and partly by virtue of what physical buttons do in the physical world.

The traditional definition of affordances just presented does not provide an immediately clear path towards building humane tools beyond a general prescription to build tools which are cognitively and ergonomically sound that is, provide a good mapping between perceived affordances and actual affordances. There is a way, however, of viewing affordances which can aid in the design of humane tools.

DESIGNED AFFORDANCES AS A COMMUNICATIVE ACT

Affordances in artefacts have the quality that they are designed. That is to say there is a designer involved, choosing which among the potential affordances to include into the artifact in order to meet users' goals. The designer intends some capability and provides affordances which (one hopes) will achieve that capability. The user perceives the affordance and can guess what the designer had in mind. By acknowledging the presence of two minds—that of the designer and that of the user—we acknowledge that effectively designed affordances involve a communicative act. The designer attempts to communicate the capabilities of the design through the affordances, and the user attempts to understand the capacity of the design through its affordances.

Recognising that designed affordances[1] are communicative acts provides new ways of thinking about design and evaluation. For example, because communication can be seen as a planned activity, we may view the mapping of affordances to capabilities as an instance of plan recognition. Likewise, we may examine models of dialog, memory, storytelling, etc., for ways of looking at affordances (e.g., Schank 1982). However, with the theme of creating humane technology, we will ask how we can (as designers) create cognitive tools which communicate more humanely via their affordances.

CREATING HUMANE COGNITIVE TOOLS

As designers and developers of humane cognitive tools, we want our cognitive tools to be good citizens. Whether or not we attribute human qualities to them, we want them to manifest human qualities: we want them to be thought of as kind, polite, loyal and patient, and so on.

(We are trying to be careful in our language. We are not affirming or denying the idea that someday it will be reasonable for a tool to be "really" honest or loyal, etc. Rather, we only desire that they exhibit these qualities. We are not making a claim for their prospective citizenship; rather, we are making a weaker claim. We may, along the way, anthromorphise our tools, but we do so with the purpose of humane-izing our tools, not humanizing them.)

---

[1] From now on, when we mention "affordances," we will mean "designed affordances, " that is, the intentionally designed affordances of human-designed artifacts, unless otherwise stated.

What qualities, then, characterise humane communication, and how should our tools manifest them? Among these qualities are:

- **Candor**. We expect people to be frank with us, to say what they mean. Similarly, we expect our tools to be clear as to what their affordances enable.
- **Sincerity**. We expect people to be genuine in their communication; to believe what they say. Similarly, we expect our tools not to fool us into thinking they can do things they cannot.
- **Artlessness.** We expect people to avoid guile and sham, to speak plainly what they believe. Similarly, we expect our tools to be easy to understand.
- **Veracity.** We expect to believe what people tell us. Similarly, we expect our tools to be believable, and not present false impressions.

Clearly, there are other aspects of humane communication which we have not touched on such as politeness or patience. The qualities discussed all have something to do with *honesty*, which will be the focus of this paper. Being honest is complex, but we examine a number of facets of honesty as they relate to the humane construction of cognitive tools. In particular, we examine how we might evaluate a tool's honesty with respect to how well it honestly communicates its affordances. There are facets of honesty which we will not examine, including being honest in financial transactions (although we don't want our tools to steal from us we will not discuss what this). We primarily consider how cognitive tools should communicate truthfully through their affordances.

SOME STORIES ABOUT HONESTY OF AFFORDANCE

Before considering what it is that cognitive tools communicate, and how honestly they communicate it, it may be helpful to consider several stories that illustrate tools communicating dishonestly through their affordances.

The Dishonest Thermometer

I have an indoor/outdoor digital thermometer at my home. The thermometer has three buttons labelled "Max," "Min," and "Reset." Ordinarily, the thermometer just shows the current temperature, but when you hit the "Max" button, it displays the warmest temperature it has recorded. Then it keeps displaying this temperature. The first time I used the thermometer, I just waited a little while for the display to return to the current temperature—it reminded me of one of those cheap digital watches where after you hit the "date" button, the watch resets itself in few seconds and goes back to telling the time. With the thermometer, nothing happened. So I hit the reset button. The thermometer went back to telling the current temperature, and I thought that was that. However, in fact, I had reset the memory of the maximum and the minimum temperatures to the current temperatures and the thermometer was now displaying the new maximum temperature it had recorded. Apparently you have to hit the "Max" button again to get it to go back to normal. Most of the time, the thermometer blends into the background of my life and I use it simply to tell me the current temperature. On especially cold or warm days when I start fiddling with the "Max" and "Min" buttons I get tripped up and hit the "Reset" button and thus erase the very information I want to record.

The Dishonest Mail Icon

I saw a news story recently about an email program that makes it easy to use PGP encoding, a type of computer encryption used to make email more private. The news anchor described it as "putting your email in an envelope." On the web, I've seen icons which afforded sending email—they show a quick animation of a letter going into an envelope and/or an envelope going into a mailbox. But as the news anchor's comment indicates, envelopes are commonly thought of as a means of privacy—if you don't want privacy, you save money and send a post card. I've noticed that most mailing programs use an icon of an envelope, but it's rare for a mailing program to acknowledge in any way that the email being sent might easily be intercepted and read. Postal mail may be slower, but one usually has a better sense as to whether someone else can read it!

The Dishonest Car

I was recently towing a heavy trailer load with my car. I had never towed such a heavy load before, and I was a bit concerned because I was in a remote rural area late at night. However the car seemed to be doing fine. When we got to a truck stop, I refilled my gas tank and then discovered that the car wouldn't start. Whenever I turned the key, the engine wouldn't turn over Instead, the car would start turning all the dashboard lights on and off in sequence. It then flashed the transmission indicators three times and shut everything down. We looked under the hood, and everything looked okay. All the sequential flashing led everyone who stopped to help to believe that it was the car's computer. I didn't know what to do. I left my hood up (to let others know the car was disabled) and went to eat some food. Much to my suprise the car started right back up! I later found out that the car's transmission had overheated. Leaving the hood up so the car could cool down turned out to be exactly the right thing to do even though I did it for the wrong reasons. My car wasn't damaged much by the incident because the computer sensed the temperature had climbed too high and wouldn't let me start my car. But the whole incident left me annoyed. The car took control of the situation, and didn't give me any choice in the matter. To make matters worse, it did not even explain what was going on.

A TAXONOMY OF COGNITIVE TOOL COMMUNICATION

Important to the understanding of honesty in affordances is an understanding of what it is our tools can, communicate *qua* tools. A taxonomy of tool communication can serve as a checklist against which cognitive tools can be evaluated. The following is an incomplete list what of our tools can tell us, which we illustrate with the stories from above.

- **Functionality:** A cognitive tool should clearly communicate its functionality. They should communicate what they can do for us which goals they can achieve, and how. This is the canonical case of honesty of affordance. In the story of the Dishonest Car, the car never informed the driver about a very important safety feature of the car, that it would shut itself off if the transmission overheated. The story of the Dishonest Thermometer showed a tool which (on the one hand) did not communicate how to achieve a function (return to the normal temperature display) and (on the other hand) miscommunicated what the function of the "Reset" key was thus actively undermining the user's goals of checking the maximum and minimum temperatures.
- **Warnings:** Cognitive tools should also clearly warn us about what can go wrong that is in what ways our goals might be undermined by the tool. In the story of the Dishonest Thermometer, the "Reset" key provided no warning about its effects. Neither does the icon in the Dishonest Mail Icon story indicate that security of the message might be compromised.
- **Repairs:** Cognitive tools, when appropriate, should communicate how to repair a failure. None of the tools in the stories above communicated this. In the story of the Dishonest Car the successful repair (opening the car's hood so that the engine could cool off) was accidentally triggered when the driver wanted to communicate to other drivers that the car was disabled. When the car started, the driver had no idea why the car worked, nor whether it would fail again.
- **Current State:** Cognitive tools should communicate what the current state of the device is. This includes state information the device may have been built to measure (for example, temperature for a thermometer), but it also includes the state of the device *qua* device. For example, once the Reset button had been pressed on the Dishonest Thermometer, the fact that the Maximum and Minimum temperatures had just been reset was not communicated, but had to be induced by the user. Cognitive tools can be very complex devices with multiple parameter settings and selected options. It is important to communicate what these settings and options are.
- **History:** Similarly, a cognitive tool should communicate the history of its use. The Dishonest Thermometer correctly communicated the maximum and minimum temperatures since the last time it was reset (or at least we assume so, although the story does not make this explicit).

- **Projection:** A cognitive tool should also communicate what is likely to happen. This is particularly helpful when it can allow the user to entertain "what-if" scenarios and perform his or her own cost/benefit analysis for action. In the case of the Dishonest Car, the driver had no choice but to stop. He didn't have the option of deciding to drive at the risk of further damage to the transmission; the computer *in loco parentis* protected the driver from himself. But in many cases, it is clearly worth risking further damage to an overheating engine if some particular performance can begot of that engine. A recent marine accident in New Orleans was caused by exactly this problem—a ship's engine shut down before it overheated, even though it would have been much safer and cheaper to have simply run the engine until it destroyed itself thereby gaining an additional period in which the ship could be steered.
- **Rationale:** Often, a user of a tool is asked or required to perform some action without an explanation of that action. Honestly communicating tools should provide an adequate rationale for action. By the same measure, the tool should also communicate the rationale for the actions it takes. In many cases, this will amount to informing the user how it has arrived at an answer or explaining how it itself works.
- **Prerequisites:** Cognitive tools can be complex artefacts for achieving complex goals. If there are a set of plan prerequisites, these need to be clearly communicated to the user, along with their rationale.

These are some of the ways that cognitive tools, *qua* tools, can communicate. They form the basis for evaluating the honesty of their affordances.

EVALUATING HONESTY OF AFFORDANCE

As designers and developers of cognitive tools, we want to be able to consistently evaluate the honesty of our tools in order to improve them. As users and chooses of cognitive tools, we want to be able to consistently evaluate the honesty of affordance of our tools in order to make better market-place choices. The question is, how can honesty be evaluated?

Why a quantitative metric is unlikely to be useful

It would be nice to have a strictly quantitative metric for evaluating honesty of affordance, something as easy to compute as a readability score or ease of reading. It is unlikely, however, that such a metric can be created. There are several problems evident.

- First, there is the complexity of affordances. We claimed above that affordances are complex entities, which change on the point-of-view of the tool user. It is hard to imagine that a quantifiable taxonomy of affordances can be created.

- Second, there is the complexity of capabilities. If a tool's affordances are complex, then so are its capabilities. It's very difficult to quantify the "features" of a tool, which tend to be more of an artifact of a marketing department than a calculated, consistent list.
- Third, there is the complexity of measuring the match between affordances and capabilities. The ways in which a capability is communicated are also complex, and measuring this is difficult in all but the simplest cases. Door A in Figure 1. affords opening to the human; so does Door B; both doors are capable of being opened. It is not easy to see how to measure how well their affordances match their capabilities.

The complexity of the problem belies a simple, quantitative metric. A qualitative metric is possible, however.

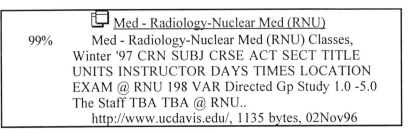

Figure 2: HotBot Search Report on "nuclear winter" (first item)

Qualitative metrics

In the United States, the standard of honesty for courtroom testimony is to tell "the truth, the whole truth, and nothing but the truth." We want such an exacting standard for cognitive tools as well. Given the taxonomy of computer communication given above, we can then proceed in two major steps: a "truth" analysis, and a "whole truth and nothing but the truth" analysis.

The "truth" analysis proceeds in this way:

For each identified affordance of a cognitive tool, Describe its honesty of affordance.

This implies there is a way to identify what the affordances of a cognitive tool are. This is itself a difficult problem, but for most cognitive tools, these will probably be the "interface elements" of the human computer interface: the buttons, labels, toolbars, etc., which interface programmers create.

The "whole truth and nothing but the truth" analysis proceeds in this way:

For each identified capability of a cognitive tool, Describe how honestly it is afforded.

Similarly, this implies there is a way to identify the capabilities of a tool, again, a difficult problem, but one that can be solved to a level of sophistication by creating a list of the "features" of the tool. That is to say, we arrive at a qualitative understanding of a tool's honesty of affordance by examining each of its affordances in turn, and each of its capabilities in turn.

A checklist for evaluating honesty of affordance

The taxonomy of what cognitive tools communicate provides a checklist for conducting the "truth" analysis. A designer or evaluator of a cognitive tool can use such a checklist in two ways. First, the checklist can be used to collect descriptions from the designer or producer of the tool. Second, the checklist can be used to collect descriptions from the potential users of the tool. The first can be used by the designer to diagnose potential problems arising from the affordance. The second can then be compared with the first checklist to provide feedback to the designers about the accuracy of their beliefs about how honest the affordance is.

To conduct a "whole truth, and nothing but the truth" analysis, we need to consider three sets of cases: when a programme capability is hidden (nothing affords the capability), when there is a one-to-one relationship between a programme capability and an affordance, and where there is a one-to-many relationship between the programme capability and the affordance. When there is no affordance for a capability, the tool is not telling the whole truth. When there are multiple affordances for a capability, then the tool is at least in danger of telling more than the truth, perhaps indicating there are more capabilities than the tool actually has.

We turn to a brief examination of a real-world cognitive tool: the Internet search engine Inktomi™, which powers the HotBot search site[2]. We examine this tool not because it is particularly egregious, but simply to illustrate some of the principles describe above.

To use the HotBot Internet search site, a user enters a phrase into a type-in box situated with the expression: [Search] <the Web> for <all the words> _____.
The expressions in <angle brackets> indicate pull down menus. [Search] is the button the user presses to start the search. What we want to focus on is the report which HotBot returns when the search is done. Figure 2 indicates the result of searching for "nuclear winter."

The "1." indicates that this is the first item returned from the search list (also implying it is the best result). The icon indicates that the item points to a page on the Internet, and the underlined title that follows (Med - Radiology ...) indicates the title of the page; the underlining being the standard convention for a hyperlink to that page.

---

[2] <http://www.hotbot.com>

"99%" indicates the confidence level that the page is relevant to the search terms[3]. The text that follows shows the first few lines of the hyperlinked page, and the final line is the URL (Uniform Resource Locator, the address on the World Wide Web), the size of the document, and the date of creation.

Focusing on the search report, we examine how honest it is, in terms of the taxonomy of communication above.

- **Functionality:** As a report, it indicates that (in some sense) this is the best document meeting the search request ("search the Web for all the words 'nuclear winter').

- **Warnings:** No warning is giving that the "99%" confidence level might not reflect relevance to the user. An attempt is made to ameliorate this by providing a bit of context about the page which is linked (its title and first few sentence), but this is first of all not explicit, and secondly, not always enough information to describe whether an item is relevant (for example, this page *could* be a course about the effects of a nuclear winter). By supplying the URL, page size, and creation date, it implicitly warns the reader whether the site is far away (inferable from the URL domain), would take a long time to view (from the size), or out of date.

- **Repairs:** No indications are given how to repair an irrelevant search. As it turns out, searching for <the exact phrase> "nuclear winter" provides many more relevant items. But this is not indicated.

- **Current State, History, Projection:** No indication is given whether the item is still available or is likely to be in the future (the former is relatively easy to discover, but costly; the later is impossible).

- **Rationale:** In terms of honesty of affordance, this is the biggest failing of this tool. Granting that, following some computational procedure, this is the best result of the search query, it leaves completely unsaid what the rationale is for this particular ranking. A score of "99%" affords a belief that this item is a trustworthy result for the search query, but (on inspection), the item is not relevant. (It should be pointed out that similarly high rankings are given to equally irrelevant items on the search report).

- **Prerequisites:** Not applicable.

The single biggest failing of this report is the report of a score of "99%" for an irrelevant item. If this were a singular event, it would be less interesting, but it is a consistent failing of this particular search engine. Some other search engines on the Web do not publish a score. Given that the rationale for a particular score is either too complex to explain, or proprietary in nature, we believe this to be a more honest approach.

---

[3] The score is described in this way: "The score represents HotBot's confidence in the match. A high score is given to the pages that most likely contain the data you are looking for." From <http://www.hotbot.com/FAQ/faq-results.html>, which gives a brief description of the scoring mechanism, which is proprietary.

SUMMARY: BUILDING HUMANE COGNITIVE TOOLS ON CONVERSATIONAL PRINCIPLES

Design is a complex task; perhaps building cognitive tools which are humane is even more complex. But if we take on this task, then it is necessary to develop design and evaluation criteria which reflect how it is we want our tools to be humane. The notion of *affordance* has proven to be a powerful concept for design. Augmenting the idea of affordance to include its communicative aspect (where affordances are viewed as a means of communication between designer and user) allows designers a means by which humane communication can be applied to the design of cognitive artefacts. There are a variety of ways we judge communications; in this paper, we have focused on honesty in communication as a model for honestly communicating the affordances of tools. By designing artefacts that honestly communicate functionality, warnings, current state, and other vital information about themselves, designers can build tools that meet humane principles.

REFERENCES

Gibson, J., 1979. *The Ecological approach to visual perception.* New York: Houghton Mifflin.

Norman, D. A., 1988. *The psychology of everyday things* (The design of everyday things in paperback). New York: Basic Books.

Norman, D. A., 1993. *Things that make us smart: Defining human attributes in the age of the machine.* Reading, MA: Addison-Wesley.

Schank, R. C., 1982. *Dynamic Memory.* Cambridge: Cambridge University Press.

Humane Interfaces: Questions of method and
practice in Cognitive Technology
J.P. Marsh, B. Gorayska and J.L. Mey (Editors)

Chapter 10

THE DESIGN OF COGNITIVE TOOLS

Steven D. Tripp
The University of Aizu

INTRODUCTION

Herbert Simon's (1969/1981) proposal to link the natural sciences and the artificial sciences is well known (see Figure 1). Simon addressed the nature of fields like computer science, engineering, and education by proposing a comparison between the natural sciences and what he called "sciences of the artificial."

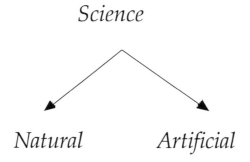

Science

Natural   *Artificial*

Figure 1. Science as Superordinate Category

The four qualities that characterise the artificial or design sciences are: 1) artificial things are synthesised by man, 2) they imitate the appearance of natural things but lack the reality of them, 3) artificial things can be characterized in terms of functions, goals and adaptation, and 4) artificial things are usually discussed in terms of imperatives as well as descriptives. Simon conceived of design as encompassing all kinds of human activity which involve planning.

"Engineers are not the only professional designers. Everyone designs who devises courses of action aimed at changing existing situations into preferred ones. The intellectual activity that produces material artefacts is no different fundamentally from the one that prescribes remedies for a sick patient or the one that devises a new sales plan for a company or a social welfare policy for a state. Design, so construed, is the core of all professional training; it is the principle mark that distinguishes the professions from the sciences. Schools of engineering, as well as schools of architecture, business, education, law, and medicine, are all centrally concerned with the process of design."

(Simon, 1981: 129)

Simon's purpose was to clarify the nature of the "design sciences" as he called them and to suggest how they could be advanced. His hope was that by incorporating some of the rigor of natural science, the design fields, which he considered central to human civilisation, would evolve deeper understanding and better methodologies .

Initially Simon's hopes for incorporating rigorous methods into the design sciences met with some success. His work on the General Problem Solver was one of the earliest attempts at artificial intelligence. The information processing theory of problem solving (Newell, Shaw, and Simon, 1957) aimed to describe a wide variety of behaviours in terms of a limited number of mechanisms. It consisted of a problem space whose elements are knowledge states. A set of generative processes creates new knowledge states and a set of test procedures compare knowledge states to a solution state. They defined a problem thus: Given a set **P** of elements, find a subset **S** of **P**, having specified properties. The elements of both **P** and **S** are knowledge states, and their arrangement in **P** represents the problem space. Finding subset **S** among **P** is thus a matter of moving, by way of generating potential solutions, from one knowledge state to another, until one having the specified properties is found or developed. The problem-solving behaviour involved three subclasses of activity: Problem representation, solution generation, and solution evaluation. Methods of generating solutions were trial and error, means-ends analysis, hierarchical decomposition and hierarchical decomposition-recomposition. In spite of the ability to deal with certain types of problems, this methodology did not achieve the general level of applicability expected of it. Neither did it have much influence on the actual practice of design.

THE PRACTICE OF DESIGN AND ITS IMPLICATIONS

In contrast to the lack of headway in the production of scientific problem solvers, there has been considerable progress in understanding the process of design. This chapter will review some of that progress and then propose a different way of conceptualising the relationship between science and design which will have implications for how we design tools that help people think.

Since the 1970s there has been considerable empirical research into the methods employed by designers in a variety of fields as diverse as architecture, engineering, and computer science. In an interesting comparison, Lawson (1979, in Lawson 1980) studied design-like problem solving in architects and scientists. The problem was to arrange coloured blocks onto a three by four rectangular plan. The objective was to arrange the blocks so that as much blue or red was showing. Certain constraints were combined in a series of problems. The two groups show consistent and different strategies. The scientists tried out a series of possible combinations in order to maximise their information about the problem, in hopes of discovering a general rule. The architects attempted a design based upon a cursory examination of the blocks. If this was not acceptable, the next most likely solution was tried. In other words, the scientists attempted to discover general principles, while architects focused on desired solutions. In a second experiment with the same materials, high school and first year architecture students were tested. Both performed more poorly than the postgraduate students did and neither group showed consistent patterns. Thus the consistent strategies of the architects were not a natural tendency.

Other studies of architectural design followed. Al Wareh and Murta (1979, in Lera, 1983) studied six award-winning architectural firms and discovered two main phases of design. In the first dominant ideas were conceived and checked against constraints. This took a surprisingly short time. In the second phase the design was developed and refined. Chan (1990) investigated the cognitive processes involved in architectural design problem solving. The experimental study of a Ph.D. student in architecture used think-aloud protocols based on videotapes and an information-processing model of cognition. Design problem-solving ability was a function of the number of constraints, associated rules, and presolutions stored in long-term memory. Cornforth (1976, in Lera, 1983) studied architectural design and found subjects alternated between specification and search processes, contrary to standard methods. Designers developed a simple solution with a superficial plausibility and used that to develop a more detailed solution. Downing (1987) studied architects working on a building project. Thematic, analogous and "charged" imagery created a framework of thought. Prototypical solutions prestructured problems (using a design-by-precedent approach), the basic model of involves "conjecture-analysis." Architects have an "image bank" of memorable solutions. Eastman (in Lera, 1983) in a study of general design found a correspondence between representation used and constraints discovered. Instead of generating abstract attributes and relationships, subjects generated a design element and determined its qualities. Foz (1972, in Lera, 1983) studying architectural design found designers used existing known examples to solve problems. Some manipulated 3-D models as if they were reality. The most skilled subject called on precedents, made many proposals, performed more tests, used more analogies deliberately, and was explicitly aware of his creative process. It appeared that whatever the designer was confident of being able to produce was put aside until it was needed. Simmonds (1980, in Lera, 1983) studied twelve graduate students in architecture and found that they too differed in their methods. Some analysed the problem first, some generated solutions, and some looked at resources and constraints. Even among those who analysed the problem first, there were a variety of approaches. Some identified sub-problems and attacked them in order of importance. Others generated a range of alternatives. One persistent problem was the inability to reverse the process of concretisation. More successful students exhibited greater range and flexibility in their decisions. Lastly, Darke (1979, in Lera, 1983) in a study of architectural design found that designers do not start with an explicit list of factors to be considered.

There have been numerous studies of the process of engineering design also. Bucciarelli (1988) took an ethnographic perspective to engineering design and studied design process within an engineering firm. Previous studies had shown that a design team spent less than half of their time on legitimate design acts. He describes a discourse between three engineers and the artifact of design itself and cites three cases of design discourse (specification, naming and decision making). He concludes that artefacts are not the design; they symbolise agreements. Hykin (1972, in Lera, 1983) reported eleven case studies of engineers, concluding that it was impossible to isolate and identify simple design strategies. However, exploration of alternatives led to a clearer understanding of the problem. Engineers expressed a need for a method of recording design decisions. Radcliffe and Lee (1989) studied the design methods used by undergraduate engineering students using the protocols of a design session. Fourteen final-year students worked in groups of two to four members. Two groups received keywords to stimulate design ideas. Two others received an outline of a systematic design method. Subjects could not use information resources well, could not brainstorm and individuals did not follow group processes. Each individual had a unique design methodology. Eleven out of fourteen adopted fairly logical sequences of design processes and this reflected innate abilities enhanced by experience and instruction. As the project continued the process became more opportunistic. There was a correlation between the effectiveness of the design and the efficiency of the designer. Lee and Radcliffe (1990) studied the innate design abilities of first year engineering and industrial design students. Two hundred twenty-six students were studied by retrospective review. Experience improved design skills. Engineering and industrial design students exhibited clear differences of attitude, and this may be reflected in their choice of career. There appeared to be an "engineering way" of approaching design tasks and this tendency was acquired before entering university. Stauffer and Ullman (1988) reported a comparison of the results of several empirical studies into the mechanical design process. They listed 27 global strategies in mechanical design based upon six observational studies. They conclude that actual design performance is not well organised. It is opportunistic. Some results were contradictory—solutions occurred in series and solutions occurred in parallel. They questioned whether design strategies could be independent of domain knowledge. Ullman, Stauffer, and Dietterich (1987, in Guindon, 1990) reported that mechanical engineering designers progressed from systematic to opportunistic behaviours as design evolved.

There have also been studies of the software design process. Curtis, Krasner, and Iscoe (1988) reported a field study of the software design processes for large systems. An anecdotal report of the thinking of the system designer on the design process indicated that the software development is a learning, negotiation, and communication process. Guindon, Curtis, and Krasner (1987) constructed a model of cognitive processes involved in software design through an analysis of the breakdowns in early design activities. Protocols of three experienced designers indicated three main sources of breakdowns: Lack of knowledge, cognitive limitations and combinations of those two factors. The designers exhibited huge individual differences in their design strategies and their design solutions.

Prescriptive models could not account for these findings. Jeffries, Turner, Polson, and Atwood (1981) looked at the processes involved in designing software using a recursive model of the design process. They studied four experienced software designers and five novices and observed a great variety of solutions both within and between levels. Novices lacked processes for solving sub-problems and ways of representing knowledge effectively. Most experienced designer had many digressions. Some used "problem-solving-by-understanding." Kant and Newell (1984, in Guindon, 1990) researched software algorithm design by two computer science Ph.D. candidates who used heuristics such as divide-and-conquer and generate-and-test. They shifted between an algorithm-design space and a geometry space. The problem was novel to subjects and when solution retrieval failed, the designers tried test cases. Visser (1987, in Guindon, 1990), investigating software design, reported that a team of programmers showed opportunistic activities due to economic use of means, postponing decisions, handling familiar components, and changing decision criteria.

Other researchers have investigated general design processes. Adelson and Soloway (1984, 1985, in Guindon, 1990) investigated systems design. Three expert designers' work was systematic and balanced. Balanced meant no part of the design was developed in significantly greater detail than other parts. Unbalanced design was followed only when a part was not familiar. Ballay (1987) studied a general design project. His original sequential model of design (criteria formulation, space organisation, details and structure, appearance decisions, and package release) was revised to become: Criteria formulation, information translation, concept generation, detail refinement, and package release. Carroll, Thomas, and Malhotra (1980) used an experimental design situation to compare spatial and temporal isomorphic design problems. In experiment 1 performance and solution time were superior for the spatial isomorph. In experiment 2 subjects were given a graphic representation of the temporal problem. After discarding subjects who misunderstood the problem, no significant differences were detected between spatial and temporal isomorphs on performance and time. The tendency for temporal subjects to experience comprehension failure was shown to be significant. Thus graphic representation helps problem solution but not problem comprehension. Carroll, Thomas, Miller, and Friedman (1980) also conducted an experimental study of the design of a scheduling problem. Making the inherent structure of the problem explicit to the designers resulted in more stability in the solution trajectory as well as reduced time. Cross (1990) in a study of general design reported designers introspections on how they see their own abilities and how they work. They believed they produced novel, unexpected solutions, tolerated uncertainty, applied imagination, and used drawings and other media to model solutions. Klein (1987a, 1987b) examined various real-world design situations and reported several studies of designers dealing with difficult problems. Ill-defined problems required goal clarification and option development. Recognitional processes played a key role in design decision making as well as problem solving. He found little evidence of systematic use of decision analysis methods. The use of analogs led to comparison-based prediction. Imagery was an important part of the design process. Research was used selectively and only to support preferences. Rapid prototyping was an attractive strategy for designers. Nadler (1989) reported an observational study of outstanding designers (an engineer, architect, commercial artist, physician and lawyer) and showed that they did not follow conventional methods, but used rather a purpose and solution-after-next orientation. He reported that Peterson found outstanding engineers and planners are characterized by open-mindedness, a high tolerance for ambiguity, orientation to purpose, a preference for soft or subjective information, and a facility for working with others. Tovey (1985) looked at three real-world design situations and tried to relate thinking styles and design strategies. Two design strategies were "specification-driven" and "solution-led." Three projects are described. One used a serial analytic strategy, one used a serial analytic-holistic strategy, and the last used a holistic-synthetic strategy. Ballay (1987) offered three views of design:

1. design as a series of information transactions: (i.e. seen as an information processing problem),
2. design as a visual task,
3. design as an ill-defined construction task.

A consequence of this view is that the partially completed product becomes part of the task environment. Because the partially completed product is continually changing, the task environment is continually changing; these changes stimulate new ideas. Rowe (1987) studied designers in action through three case studies. Analysis of the protocols indicated that: First the process is episodic exhibiting movement back and forth between exploration of forms and evaluation. There are periods of speculation and then contemplation. Each episode has a particular orientation that takes on a life of its own. There is a "dialogue" between the designer and the situation. The episodes have an interior logic that is determined by the subject matter and the organisational procedures being used. The problem goes from nebulous to more concrete. There are periods of "blinding" and backtracking. Even when the problem was clearly defined, the designer rarely broke conditions down into their basic components. Secondly, the general influence of initial ideas was observed. Inevitably problem-solvers bring organising principles to the problem. Even when severe problems are encountered, an effort is made to retain the initial ideas. This empirical study of design helps us to understand that it is neither systematic nor unsystematic. Rather is opportunistic, moving back and forth between periods of logical evaluation and periods of creative discovery.

The above data indicates that the process of design is highly individualistic, even among trained designers. Carroll and Rosson's (1985) conclusions from their empirical studies may be applied generally to this data. Based on their studies they argue that the process of design is: 1) non-hierarchical, 2) neither strictly bottom-up nor top-down, 3) radically transformational, involving the development of partial and interim solutions which may ultimately play no role in the final design, and 4) intrinsically involving the discovery of new goals.

THE DESIGN OF ARTIFACTS AND THE DESIGN OF SCIENTIFIC IDEAS

Is there a relationship between the development of artefacts and the development of knowledge? Basalla (1988) studied the development of technology in the form of artefacts differing as widely as barbed wire and transistors. He asserted that technological evolution is not a metaphor: Technology literally evolves. New things that appear in the world are based on something already in existence. His evolutionary theory of technology has four elements: 1) Novelty: the creation of new artefacts. Technology involves the design of original artefacts. 2) Diversity of forms. It is typical that numerous similar solutions to a problem emerge roughly simultaneously. 3) A selection mechanism determining the surviving forms. Various mechanisms, both economic and contingent may be involved. 4) The absence of sudden important discontinuities. Each artifact can be traced to some previous artefacts or to nature. Thus Basalla saw the development of new artefacts as, not the product of entirely systematic processes, but rather a combination of opportunistic creativity and systematic selectivity.

How does this relate to the development of knowledge? Holton (1988) investigated the development of scientific ideas from Kepler to Einstein. He found that there were four mechanisms that could explain the development of scientific ideas. First, there is the mechanism of continuity. In science continuity is the specific operational and quantitative nature of important concepts. The second mechanism, mutation, is the constant opportunity for individual variations. A third mechanism is multiplicity of effort. To assure growth despite the low rate of occurrence of great modifications and the absence of a single master plan, science relies on a large number of individual attempts, from which may emerge those few types that are useful. Finally, a selection mechanism is at work whereby certain useful mutations are incorporated into the continuous stream of science.

Clearly Basalla and Holton have enumerated the same set of mechanisms for both the development of artefacts and scientific ideas. Secondly Holton has suggested that the criterion by which scientific ideas are evaluated is their usefulness, the same criterion by which design objects have always been evaluated.

RECONSIDERING SIMON'S CLASSIFICATION

In light of these similarities, it is possible to reconsider Simon's distinction between the two types of science: artificial and natural. Instead of design being a kind of science, it possible to speak in terms of two kinds of design: The design of artefacts and the design of scientific ideas (see Figure 2). Thus science can be thought of as a kind of design and therefore the tools which help us develop scientific ideas may borrow from the knowledge we have gained of the process of artifactual design.

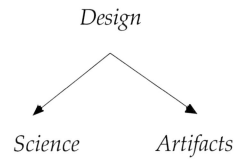

Design

Science   *Artifacts*

Figure 2. Design as the Superordinate Category

WHAT DO WE KNOW ABOUT THE DESIGN OF SCIENTIFIC IDEAS?

Perkins (1986) wrote about the notion of knowledge as design. He proposed that knowledge could be thought of as a kind of design and that there are four design questions we can ask about knowledge objects.

- What is its purpose?
- What is its structure?
- What are the model cases of it?
- What are arguments that explain and evaluate it?

For example, we can treat theories of the solar system as designs. They have a purpose, structure, and model cases. Equally, there are arguments that explain them and allow us to evaluate them.

Similarly, we can also think of claims as designs. Claims are one of the most important sorts of knowledge designs. Scientific theories are claims that have the purpose of explaining or predicting. Mathematical theorems aim to state a relationship in some larger system. Claims can be evaluated according to truth or usefulness.

We can also usefully think about families of knowledge objects as designs. If we think about families of procedures as designs then we will reflect on whether they have common features. Perkins examined the idea of shared resources such as libraries, drinking fountains, rental cars, and public beaches. Such shared resources may be on-site vs. take-away, sign-up vs. anonymous, or fee vs. free We can then stretch families into metaphors. Rental cars may be rental vehicles. Vehicles may be anything that transports us whether physically or virtually. An argument may be a vehicle that carries us toward a goal. There may be justificatory arguments, explanatory arguments, hypothetical arguments, or persuasive arguments. If we think of them like rental cars, then a software tool could provide structured arguments to us, to be used for a purpose and them returned.

In this way, by thinking of knowledge as design we can specify some operations which could be applied to existing knowledge in order to generate new knowledge.

SPECIFICATIONS FOR A KNOWLEDGE DESIGN TOOL

We have seen that traditional notions of design as problem solving have not led to progress in the production of more scientific and systematic design methods. Similarly we have seen that skilled designers do not follow prescribed design methods but instead are opportunistic, moving from the broad overview to local problems and then back, using the information they obtain to redefine the problem. In light of this information Guindon (1990) made the following recommendations for the design of tools which would support a software design process.

- The system should not embody a method that locks designers into strict order of activities.
- The system should support rapid access and shifts between tools to represent and manipulate different kinds of objects.
- It should support easy navigation between these objects.
- The representation languages should support a smooth progression from informal to formal representations.
- The system should support easy editing and reorganisation.
- It should support the identification of the origin of requirements.
- It should support the representation of interim or partial design objects.

Combining these ideas with the data presented previously we can enumerate a set of specifications for a cognitive tool. It should allow us to:

1. Specify a purpose
2. Specify a structure
3. Enumerate model cases
4. Construct arguments that allow us to explain
5. Construct arguments that allow us to evaluate it
6. Expand the idea metaphorically
7. Keep a record of the design history
8. Represent the idea in a variety of ways, such as these from Ballay (1987)
   - Procedural representations
   - Solid models.
   - Matrices
   - Orthographic projections

- Notations
- Perspective drawings
- Dimensions

9. Allow opportunistic movement between views and levels of representation
10. Translate between representation languages
11. Easily edit objects and relationships
12. Customise to allow for individual design styles
13. Support the importation of ontologies
14. Represent incomplete ideas
15. Provide simulation procedures and processes
16. Compare competing ideas
17. Annex discovered purposes.

CONCLUSION

Herbert Simon (1981) wrote that, *"...the proper study of mankind is the science of design...."* I have shown that there is a large literature on the process of design, but limited progress in the "scientising" of design. I have also shown that that by reconceptualising Simon's paradigm, we can borrow from the literature on design to create specifications for a tool that facilitates the design of scientific ideas. From this perspective, we might say that the proper study of mankind is the design of science.

REFERENCES

Ballay, J. M., 1987. An Experimental View Of The Design Process. In W. B. Rouse and K. R. Boff, eds, *System Design.* New York: North-Holland, pp. 65-82.

Basalla, G. 1988. *The Evolution of Technology.* London: Cambridge University.

Bucciarelli, L. L. 1988. An Ethnographic Perspective On Engineering Design. *Design Studies*, 9, pp. 159-169.

Carroll, J. M., and Rosson, M. B. 1985. Usability Specifications As A Tool In Iterative Development. In H. R. Hartson, ed, *Advances In Human-Computer Interaction.* pp. 1-28. Norwood, NJ: Ablex.

Carroll, J. M., Thomas, J. C., and Malhotra, A. 1980. Presentation And Representation In Design Problem-Solving. *British Journal of Psychology*, 71, pp. 143-153.

Carroll, J. M., J. C. Thomas, L. A. Miller, and H. P. Friedman, 1980. Aspects of Solution Structure in Design Problem Solving. *American Journal of Psychology*, 93, pp. 269-284.

Chan, C-S., 1990. Cognitive Processes In Architectural Design Problem Solving. *Design Studies*, 11, pp. 60-80.

Cross, N., 1990. The Nature and Nurture Of Design Ability. *Design Studies*, 11, pp. 127-140.

Curtis, B., H. Krasner, and N. Iscoe, 1988. *A Field Study of the Software Design Process for Large Systems* (STP-233-88). Austin, TX: MCC Software Technology Program.

Downing, F., 1987. Imagery and the Structure of Design Inquiry. *Journal of Mental Imagery*, 11(1), pp. 61-86.

Guindon, R., 1990. Designing The Design Process: Exploiting opportunistic thoughts. *Human-Computer Interaction*, 5, pp. 305-344.

Guindon, R., B. Curtis, and H. Krasner, 1987. *A Model Of Cognitive Processes In Software Design: An analysis of breakdowns in early design activities by individuals* (STP-283-87). Austin, TX: MCC Software Technology Program.

Holton, G., 1988. *Thematic Origins of Scientific Thought* (Revised ed.). Cambridge, MA: Harvard University.

Jeffries, R., A. A. Turner, P. G. Polson, and M. E. Atwood, 1981. The Processes Involved In Designing Software. In J. R. Anderson, ed., *Cognitive Skills And Their Acquisition*. Hillsdale, NJ: Lawrence Erlbaum Associates, pp. 255-283.

Klein, G. A., 1987a. Analytical Versus Recognitional Approaches To Design Decision Making. In W. B. Rouse and K. R. Boff, eds, *System Design*. New York: North-Holland, pp. 175-186.

Klein, G. A., 1987b. Applications of Analogical Reasoning. *Metaphor and Symbolic Activity*, 2, pp. 201-218.

Lawson, B., 1980. *How Designers Think*. Westfield, NJ: Eastview Editions.

Lee, T. Y., and D. F. Radcliffe, 1990. Innate Design Abilities of First Year Engineering and Industrial Design Students. *Design Studies*, 11, pp. 96-106.

Lera, S., 1983. Synopses of some recent published studies of the design process and designer behaviour. *Design Studies*, 4, pp. 133-140.

Nadler, G., 1989. Design Processes And Their Results. *Design Studies*, 10, pp. 124-127.

Newell, A., J. C. Shaw, and H. A. Simon, 1957. *Elements of a Theory of Problem Solving*. Rand Corporation Report P-971.

Perkins, D. N., 1986. *Knowledge As Design*. Hillsdale, NJ: Lawrence Erlbaum.

Radcliffe, D. F., and T. Y. Lee, 1989. Design Methods Used by Undergraduate Engineering Students. *Design Studies*, 10, pp. 199-207.

Rowe, P. G., 1987. *Design Thinking*. Cambridge: MIT.

Simon, H. A., 1969. *The Sciences of The Artificial*. Cambridge, MA: MIT Press.

Simon, H. A., 1981. *The Sciences Of The Artificial* (2nd Ed.). Cambridge, MA: MIT Press.

Stauffer, L. A., and D. G. Ullman, 1988. A Comparison Of The Results Of Empirical Studies Into The Mechanical Design Process. *Design Studies*, 9, pp. 107-114.

Tovey, M., 1985. Thinking Styles And Modelling Systems. *Design Studies*, 7, pp. 20-30.

*Humane Interfaces: Questions of method and
practice in Cognitive Technology*
J.P. Marsh, B. Gorayska and J.L. Mey (Editors)
© 1999 Elsevier Science B.V. All rights reserved.

Chapter 11

CYBERSPACE BIONICS

Jacques J. Vidal

UCLA Computer Science Department and UCLA Brain Research Institute
University of California, Los Angeles, USA
University of Aizu, Japan

INTRODUCTION

It is a safe prediction that, not very far into the next century, computer technology will have dragged a significant portion of human activities into the world we are now beginning to call cyberspace, a world without historical precedent, with a structure that almost invalidates all the familiar space and time boundaries that have been the bedrock of experience for millennia.

At this time, many still perceive the arrival of computers over the past few decades as just the last in a series of industrial events (such as railroads, automobiles or airplanes) that have shaped modern life, or as simply a continuation of the revolution in communications created by the telegraph and the telephone. Certainly, the distant ears and eyes of radio and television have brought the sounds and vistas of other places and other cultures inside our home and enriched life even in the most distant and backward villages. Yet it can be argued that all of these have only extended and not transformed the range of human experience.

By all indications the computer revolution is different and considerably more socially subversive. The computers has progressively expanded it's stature from that of a support tool for the initial actuarial, librarian or scientific interests to invade more and more intimate aspects of human life, thus giving birth to a world of its own. The value added by electronic communication to almost all aspects of human endeavour is making this network a mandatory presence in modern life. Indeed, for future cyberspace citizens this virtual world of electronic information will perhaps become the environment where one might find gainful work, cultural nutrition, learning, entertainment and even social intercourse. Computers are progressively reshaping the way we experience the world.

THE INTERNET

The technological phenomenon that supports this revolution is the wrapping of the world into an increasingly dense electronic communication network, wherein information flows at the speed of light and for which national borders, time zones and physical distances are irrelevant details. The most prominent manifestation of this phenomenon is the Internet. It represents a continually expanding and evolving computer network that nearly doubles in size every year, spans the whole world and progressively claims and moulds to its needs all available transmission media, from ordinary phone lines to satellites or fiber optics links. The Internet makes interactive information distribution, information gathering, commercial transactions and personal communication instantly available across the world for the benefit of governments, academies and commercial companies. At this writing, already some fifty million human users rely on Internet resources to communicate with each other and to access information and services at over ten million hosts around the world.

HISTORICAL NOTE

The precursor of the Internet, Arpanet, was created around 1969 and was sponsored by the U.S. Advanced Research Projects Agency (ARPA) mainly as a research tool for computer scientists and US military and government agencies. The Computer Science Department at the University of California Los Angeles (UCLA), played a key role in Arpanet development and maintained one of the initial servers of the nascent network.

By the nineties, Arpanet had become the Internet and was no longer confined to government and academia. It had muted into a phenomenon of society, an outcome that very few of those who witnessed its birth had anticipated.

The computers or "hosts" that form the Internet, use a common set of communication standards or "protocols " referred to as TCP/IP. Computer messages are split in fixed size chunks of binary symbols called packets, each containing the host of origin, the destination host and a slice of the information being transmitted. Packets are sent through the network as separate packages which will often reach their destination through different routing. Re-assembly takes place at the destination site. These protocols and this packet switching form the critical technologies that the present Internet has inherited from Arpanet.

AGENTS AND COGNITIVE ROBOTS

A recent new frontier in the field of Artificial Intelligence which is beginning to have an impact on the Internet, is that of Intelligent Software Agents; a computer programme category that is still searching for a precise definition or consensus (Wooldridge and Jennings, 1995; Rieker, 1994). While software agents still perform services for human computer users they possess some qualities of autonomy, reasoning and decision making power and are able to independently take initiatives and perform actions. Current implementations of this concept are still limited and typically confined to narrow fields of specialisation. It is likely however that the near future will see a proliferation of autonomous software agents.

One specific characteristic of these agents have is mobility (In contrast with programmes running in a fixed host environment), (Ferguson, 1992). The distributed world of the Internet, epitomises the kind of playground suitable for deploying intelligent agents. Recent computer languages like JAVA and ActiveX have created much excitement precisely because they are well suited to the autonomy, portability and mobility that software agents will require. However, many unsolved problems still remain in the path of development which are among the most ambitious challenges facing Artificial Intelligence and progress has been relatively slow.

It is now recognised that one impediment to agent development is the present communication procedure used on the web the so-called client-server protocol. This protocol implies directional constraints on message passing and regular interruption of connection. Agents will need to communicate with other agents in a peer-to-peer fashion that the client-server concept impedes. The future evolution of Internet protocols is expected to remedy that situation.

Again the US Department of Defense has taken notice and launched a large programme called I*3, for "Intelligent Integration of Information". Its goal is to master new technologies to deal with dynamically changing, potentially inconsistent, incomplete and heterogeneous data sources. In other words agents capable of accommodating conflicting goals, choosing among them and reasoning about the means to reach those chosen. As mentioned earlier these capabilities bring difficult Artificial Intelligence problems in particular the representation of beliefs about present and future situations.

The virtual world into which agents must evolve will also be populated with other agents, whose cooperation will often be necessary in order to accomplish the goal. Cooperation between agents will require the autonomous generation of deliberate messages. In yet another twist of such scenarios, some of these roaming agents may also be hostile, in the fashion of already well known destructive software like viruses, Trojan horses and logic bombs. One line of research is also concerned with the ways, global patterns of behaviour could emerge bottom up, from the cooperation of a multitude of small software entities acting collectively. One can predict the eventual emergence of a shadow society of software robots, with its own indigenous sociology, deeply threaded into human activities. The social impact of these developments is still difficult to predict.

In the context of human-computer interfaces, one particular class of intelligent agents assumes a special significance, those which will embody a model of the user to perform its personalised services. These user agents would operate as the images or alter-ego of their human counterpart. To realistically emulate human intelligent behaviour, a user's agent will likely consist of a whole society of sub-agents interacting and communicating with each other. In "Society of Minds", Marvin Minsky' attempts to explain human intelligence in precisely this distributed multi-agent concept (Minsky 1986). The book provides some good insight on the feasibility as well as the complexity of the task.

Existing implementations of user agents tend to be limited to narrow fields and to the discovery and embodiment of only the static characteristics of their masters for instance. One can find server programmes on the World Wide Web that will advise a user on a choice of musical titles to listen to or buy. This requires a model of the user focused on his or her musical tastes. The necessary data is obtained from an interactive inquiry. The future however is likely to see much more sophisticated autonomous agents, capable of taking into account dynamically the current mental state of the user. This provides one source of motivation for some of the bionic technology to be discussed later.

HUMAN-COMPUTER INTERFACES

A more subtle, but profound and irreversible aspect of the invasion of computers in to the cognitive environment of humans is that the human-computer dialogue is progressively becoming more intimate and natural, often to the point of competing with and even displacing what heretofore would have been reserved for human to human communication.

Only a decade or so ago, dialoguing with a computer usually involved the typing of instructions into a terminal using string oriented and often arcane scripting language. Because of efficiency and low overhead, this is still the option of choice in many situations, especially with experienced users and those people who have invested considerable time in learning to address computers on their own terms, namely professional programmemers.

However for the average user the arrival of graphic user interfaces (GUI's) was a much needed breakthrough. With the development of graphic interface, it became possible to present information in the form of visually identifiable windows and icons. They could themselves be moved and acted upon using natural hand movements and a mouse. The lessons learned made possible the recruiting of a whole new population of computer users in the eighties, following Apple's introduction of first the Lisa and the Macintoshes. The new style of human-computer communication possesses considerably more appeal because it relied on more natural human behaviours and reduced the requirement for memorising a collection of command names.

This process exemplifies one the main concerns of HCI developers to date. Creating an effective bridge between the human brain processes responsible for perception and inductive problem solving and the general symbol-manipulating capabilities of the computer is the goal that drives the developers of human-machine communication systems. The goal is to narrow the gap that remains between the natural boundaries to the human body, namely limbs, special senses and tactile skin, with the input and display mechanisms that can be attached to computers. Indeed the avoided aim of human-computer interfacing is to blur awareness of the frontier between the real and the virtual world.

The major success story of the Internet, the World Wide Web further illustrates the trend. The Web is an immense distributed depository of mostly free information on practically any subject. Documents on the web, which were once limited to text, are increasingly becoming expressed in multimedia. Access is obtained by clicking labels or buttons on the screen rather than laboriously typing in queries. The multimedia technologies that proliferate on the web have made human-computer interaction much more natural and also less threatening for many users. New tools are regularly appearing on the web bringing into the unified realm of the Internet continually improved images and sounds and more recently facilitating real-time communication.

Several research groups are working on exotic interfacing projects financed by multinational companies. One case in point is a project of the MIT Media Lab called "Things That Think". This research consortium involves several MIT professors and some forty corporate sponsors. One of the motivations for which is that the present arsenal of interfacing tools is often a redundant, heterogeneous collection of gadgets. These should shrink and be replaced by more capable unimedia components that are compact and portable. One particularly interesting concept is that of wearable computers, where ordinary articles like footwear and glasses are endowed with intelligent sensors and made part of the human-computer interface. Another is the use of intrabody signaling, using the human body itself as the electrical infrastructure of a local area network. This development and that of appropriate body net protocols is an important part of the MIT programme, along with that of power sources using body motion rather than batteries. Affective computing, the integration of emotional states in the interchange that will be evoked later is also on the project agenda.

VIRTUAL REALITY

Virtual Reality (VR) can be viewed as a step beyond the generic graphic interfaces mentioned above (Stone, 1991). It forms a special class of applications where human-machine interaction is defined by a specific perceptual world designed to create a compelling illusion in which the user can become immersed (Pimentel and Teixeira, 1993; Gigante, 1993). Successful VR systems deliver an interactive sensorimotor experience, that can be realistic enough to cause "suspension of disbelief"(Psotka, 1993).

VR has existed for years with considerable sophistication in flight simulators and many other military and civilian applications such as trainers for truck driving, tank warfare or missile launches. However, by their very nature, these applications did not concern large categories of users. In the nineties however, civilian VR applications became a common sight at computer conventions and gained the attention of the popular media. The emergence was for a great part made possible by the vertiginous increases in computer power that had taken place in the decade, along with dramatic decreases in cost.

New peripheral devices have appeared to facilitate access into the virtual world and to keep out the distractions of ordinary reality. Head mounted displays are helmet like devices that attach to the user's head and project the images created by the computer. Projection can be made from small cathode ray tubes (CRTs), light emitting diodes (LEDs) or liquid crystal displays (LCDs). Natural stereopsis can be emulated by presenting separately to each eye images whose viewpoints are horizontally shifted, letting the user's mind produce realistic three-dimensional views of objects. A process under exploration at the University of Washington, is the Laser Retinal Scanner. This would scan the image directly into the retina, bypassing the display entirely. While still very experimental, this type of research suggests that the roster of possible display technologies is still far from closed.

By using position sensors outside the head-mounted display, the view can be made to respond to changes in the user's visual point of view. This brings a strong sense of reality to the virtual space by making the projected scenery respond to the user's head movements.

Earphone delivery of truly multidirectional sound (i.e., fore and aft, up and down as well as sideways) dramatically add to the realism of acoustical information (Brewster et al., 1994). The sound is filtered so that it appears to emanate from a specified direction and still is delivered through ordinary headphones. The filtering emulates the distortion of the sound caused by the body, head, and pinna, fooling the neurological auditory system. There again, user head position can be fed back to the sound direction, for instance to make it appear as if it is coming from a fixed position in virtual space (Bodden, 1993).

Many body motion detection devices are becoming available. Three-dimensional position trackers can detect the position and velocity of limb movements, allowing "gesture" input (Rhyne, 1987). or communicating hand signals such as those of the Sign Languages for the deaf (Koons et al., 1993). Control gloves and wands, capable of capturing complex movement of hand and fingers, can be used for pushing and grasping virtual objects (Massie T.H. and Salisbury, 1994; Brooks et al., 1990).

These user-controlled devices can also provide sensory feedback. For example, a force-reflecting joystick can be equipped with motors that apply forces in either of two directions (Balakrishnan, Ware, and Smith, 1994: Akamatsu and Sato, 1994). The method can be extended to an entire exoskeleton (Jau, 1988). Tactile-haptic stimulation can be achieved by air jets, vibrotactile devices such as blunt pins, voice coils, or piezoelectric crystals. Electrotactile stimulation can also be achieved via electrical pulses emitted from small electrodes attached to the user's fingers.

At this time, these somatic communication devices have found a number of uses in VR applications predominantly with respect to entertainment and video games. But the most significant impact of VR will come from other directions. In what has come to be known as "telepresence", virtual "hands-on" operation can be conducted in hostile environments such as the sea bottom, damaged nuclear reactors chambers or even on distant planets by controlling human like robots dispatched on the site. This aspect of VR has considerable potential in many areas still in the research stage. For example microsurgery, a surgeon's hand movements can be scaled down to operate on small, and even microscopic body parts while hand and eye feedback is returned to the surgeon at a macroscopic level suitable to normal hand motion.

Another example is in the design of control prosthetics. For years an important motivation for biologically assisted interfacing has been the quest for a compensatory means of physical access for handicapped persons. For instance eye position sensors can instantaneously moves the cursor on a computer screen to the users precise point of observation. Many notable examples exist of control prosthetics which are dramatically enabling for handicapped, but which are often unusable by normal subjects, who lack the need and motivation to master what are often complex and cumbersome devices. Dependency on cumbersome machinery is evidently also an obstacle to the wide proliferation of VR environments and the invention of devices that are convenient and unobtrusive is one of the major challenges facing this field.

BIONIC INTERFACING

Biofeedback and Biocybernetics Control

By the early seventies, several funding agencies of the US Department of Defense had become interested in technologies that would permit a more immersed and intimate interaction between humans and computers and would include so-called bionic applications. These concerns again converged on ARPA. One outcome was a programme proposed and directed by Dr. George Lawrence whose vision guided its evolution during the subsequent years. Initially, its named focus was auto regulation and cognitive biofeedback. Its goal was developing biofeedback techniques that would improve human performance, in particular that of military personnel engaged in tasks demanding high mental loads. The auto regulation research produced some valuable insights on biofeedback, but only indecisive results on its relevance or practicality as a mean to reach the stated goals. A new direction, under the more general label of Biocybernetics, was then defined and became the main source of support for bionics research during the ensuing years. One of the Biocybernetics programme directives was to evaluate the potential of measurable biological signals helped by real-time computer processing, to assist in the control of vehicles, weaponry, or other systems. These more exotic extensions of interface technology will be reviewed below.

Eye gaze direction and eye movement

The voluntary pointing of eye gaze toward an item of interest is a most effortless way to designate the location of a target in the field of vision. For instance, eye gaze can act as mouse or tablet input for selecting, dragging or scrolling items on a computer screen. Furthermore, subconscious eye movements are also of great significance for human-machine communication. For instance, when scanning pictures, the viewer's gaze automatically lingers over key areas, including, in particular, items that elicit emotional interest. Eye-controlled systems have also been designed to provide access to computers for people with severe motor handicaps and whose eye movements are sometimes the only available motor channel input. The eye tracking is typically used to control menu-driven applications from a control screen.

Several technologies are available for dynamic eye position tracking (Young et al., 1975) using either remote or head-mounted apparatus (Schroeder, 1993; Mendel et al., 1993; White et al., 1993). Sophisticated re-calibration systems have been designed to maintain accurate point-of-regard estimates in the presence of significant head displacements. (Mendel, 1993). Some eye tracking systems are technologically quite mature and have made an appearance in at least one consumer product, the Canon 8800 video camera.

Another source of position information is the EOG or Electro-oculogram, the bioelectrical signature generated by the movement of the eyeball. This signal can be measured by electrodes placed next to the eye. The eyeball is polarized and acts as a battery would moving in the eye socket. It creates a large field on the skull that reflects eye position. EOG accuracy as a position indicator is limited by drifts, but it does provide sensitive movement information, including on the small saccades that are always present, i.e. it has an advantage of speed over some of the other methods such as video cameras, but is best used in combination with other approaches.

It should be noted that EOG fluctuations are called "artefacts" by brain wave researchers because they powerfully overshadow the much smaller neuron generated brain signals. Very sophisticated signal processing methods have now been developed to filter out this EOG interference in contemporary brain wave research.

Monitoring emotion

There exist also bionics channels, that in some contexts, are capable of probing significant aspects of human emotion. The interface enhancements mentioned earlier use increasingly natural, but still voluntary and deliberate behaviours to issue commands to a computer. A more intriguing and more controversial direction is the monitoring of behavioural clues and biological signals to acquire unconscious or sub-conscious information reflecting emotional states.

Emotions produce rapid changes in a number of measurable physiological indicators such as blood pressure, heart rate, dilatation or contraction of the pupil in the eye, galvanic skin resistance, and respiration. These indicators can be easily monitored by special equipment using individual probes or perhaps distributed in a computerised body suit. Other approaches may combine emotional clues with cognitive clues such as tracking facial expressions.

A rather unfortunate precedent to instrumental emotional monitoring merits a special mention. The practice of polygraph or "lie detectors" testing, a rather silly practice widely used in the US (over one million are conducted a year, according to some estimates) is an embarrassment to many Americans. It is to their credit that many legislatures, including several American states, ban the practice in civilian life. However, conservative influences have retained its use in some federal agencies such as the US National Security Agency, despite ample evidence that there is no reliable signature of truth or falsehood showing on polygraph displays. Polygraph measurements usually include blood pressure, heart rate, galvanic skin resistance, respiration, abdominal and thoracic. These biological signs are related to emotional arousal in a complex and very subject specific way, but their relation to the goals of a polygraph examination is founded on general assumptions and remains inconclusive. Polygraph results are best viewed as the subjective judgement of the examiner. The fact remains, however, that the introduction of emotional states in the human-machine dialogue is readily feasible and has potential benefits in a number of areas, especially if the process is part of a closed loop with the user. For instance, the provision of emotional feedback in the context of intelligent software tools can be a key to improved self-knowledge and self-control.

Face tracking and lip reading

In ordinary life, many informative nonverbal clues are transmitted by facial expression or by head attitude or motion (Eckman and Friesen, 1977). Indicators of mental states and especially of emotions, can be voluntary or involuntary as well as sometimes intentionally deceptive. Head movements are also commonly used to express hesitation, agreement or refusal.

A considerable body of literature exists that provides a classification and quantification basis for this aspects of nonverbal communication (Ekman and Friesen, 1984). Other research groups have developed the complex computer techniques needed for acquiring facial data. For instance, one team at the CMU Interactive Systems Laboratory has developed a system that can track the face of a subject that moves freely in an experimental room. Tracking relies, in particular, on an elaborate skin color model that allows for changes in lighting and other viewing conditions. The model assumes a Gaussian distribution in 2D chromatic space, and estimates its six parameters for a given subject and lighting environment. The system is to be expanded to the simultaneous tracking of multiple subjects.

Other groups at CMU and UC Berkeley are applying Neural Network technology to track the lip contour dynamically during speech, and merge this information with that from the acoustic track in a visual-acoustic speech recognition system (Campbell, 1988; Bregler et al., 1993; 1994). To port these and many other such behaviours into a human computer interface can be viewed as one component in a larger research agenda which aims to address every significant component in the comprehensive modeling of the user with all of his or her physical, cognitive and social characteristics. In some circles, this perspective elicits serious concerns regarding individual freedom and privacy, but that subject requires a separate forum. One general statement would be that a user model brought to a given degree of intimacy does, in computer communication, play the same role as similar knowledge of and prejudices about one's interlocutor play in ordinary human communication, verbal and non verbal.

Brain waves

Relating the electrical signals emitted by the human brain to the mental state of its owner has been one of the central purpose of neurophysiological research for over sixty years. It has been a long and still frustrating journey for brain researchers. The first reporting by Berger in 1929 of electrical brain waves recorded from the intact skull caused considerable excitement (Berger, 1931). The recordings became known as the Electroencephalogram or EEG. The enthusiasm progressively gave way to the realisation that these electrical signals were considerably more elusive and unpredictable that had been anticipated. Current research, which is critically dependent on modern computer technology, has only recently reached a point that allows a revival of the initial excitement. The results, while still limited, have nevertheless come a very long way to decode brain wave signatures in useful ways.

Brain tissue contains a myriad of active current sources that cause the local electrical potential to endlessly fluctuate with a great deal of variability. Some of the characteristics of the wave trains are somewhat predictable in relation to the electrode site, the activity of the subject, and the presence and type of sensory stimulation. Some of which can be readily identified by eye, and these were for a long time the principal object of EEG research: the recognition of the 10Hz alpha activity and the observation of alpha blocking of sleep versus wake, of barbiturate induced "spindles", and of the 3/sec spike and wave complex of petit mal epilepsy. Indeed, traditionally, the clinical usefulness of the EEG has been mostly limited to assessing the overall condition of the brain such as identifying wakefulness versus REM or deep sleep, as well as to detecting and localising epileptic seizures.

The electrical fluctuations detected over the scalp must be attributed mostly to brain tissue located at or near the skull, i.e., their source is the electrical activity of the cerebral cortex, a significant portion of which lies on the outer surface of the brain below the scalp. The cerebral cortex is a thin layer containing nerve cells or neurones and dendrites, long tubular extensions of neuron bodies which extend toward the surface and branch out laterally for some distance to connect with adjacent neurones and dendrites. Dendrites are electrolytic connectors that propagate electrical fields to the neuron body where they eventually trigger nerve impulses

The surface potentials observed are generated mainly at the dendrites and at the bodies (soma) of brain cells. The peaks and valleys of the waveforms betray polarisation and depolarisation that occurs somewhat in synchrony. A positive variation recorded at the surface would correspond to a region of synchronised depolarisation (greater excitability) underneath and vice versa. To account for the observed amplitudes, one must assume that a large number of underlying neurones in large number are driven from synchrony to disorder on a relatively slow schedule (compared with the time constant of a single neuron). This explains the presence of a power spectrum which displays most of its energy at frequencies around and below 10 Hz. It is generally believed that the neuronal firing themselves are not significant contributors to EEG waves and in fact these waves are present even when all the cells concerned are prevented from firing altogether (Li and Jasper, 1953). By contrast, correspondence between individual waves in the EEG signal and post synaptic potentials recorded intracellularly in adjacent neurones has been well established (Landau, 1967).

This spontaneous EEG activity is also often rhythmic, i.e., its spectral density shows peaks at characteristic frequencies. The analysis of these brain rhythms has retained much of the early attention paid to EEG.

Considerable efforts were spent in the late sixties and early seventies to pry more subtle information from EEG, with the help of computers. Spectral densities and spectral coherence between pairs of channels were measured on relatively short (2 to 10 sec) EEG epochs in order to track short shifts of mental activity. This produced an abundant literature and some interesting results. For instance, it is known that a human subjects' ability to sustain their initial level of performance during continuous auditory or visual monitoring tasks is limited. After only a few minutes on task, particularly in low-arousal environments, performance can deteriorate substantially while the subject fights drowsiness. These in turn cause spectral changes in EEG spectra. One typical study, using tone detection in auditory stimuli, showed that human performance affected by drowsiness tends to fluctuate over periods of 4 minutes and longer and that these performance lapses are accompanied by characteristic EEG changes in the 4 Hz delta and 4-6 Hz theta bands as well as around 14 Hz (the sleep spindle frequency). Furthermore, the transient changes that occur before and after presentations and are good predictors of correct versus incorrect detection of targets. (Makeig and Jung, 1966)

Evoked potentials

A light flash, brief sound, or light touch of the skin generates activity to pathways specific to the sense involved and, in particular, in the corresponding sensory cortex (visual, auditory, or somesthetic). This electrical response as measured by an electrode on the cortical surface is reflected by a nonperiodic waveform buried in the ongoing background activity and covering roughly one third of a second. Again, this results from the synchronous contribution of post synaptic potentials in a large number of neurones in the vicinity of the electrode. The cortical neurones are distributed in layers, each layer in a given area presumably having a particular integrative function. In a direction perpendicular to the cortical surface, cells above one another seem to serve various sub functions for a given sensory modality, while in a lateral direction, the functional properties of the cells exhibit sharp transitions. This columnar organisation was revealed early in the visual and the somatosensory areas by Huben and Wiesel (Huben and Wiesel, 1962) and in the auditory cortex by Gerstein and Kiang (Gerstein and Kiang, 1964). Function and modality vary with the cortical position. Functional specificity in relation to cortical sites is also reflected in the ongoing EEG: sensory stimuli of a given modality will desynchronise localised areas of the cortical surface. Various feature-extracting functions have been found to map on the surface of the cortex, and indeed different stimuli are found to evoke distinct electrical "signatures" on the cortical surface and more diffusely on the scalp beyond. By averaging half a second or so of the EEG signal that followed many repetitions of the same stimulus, such as flashed visual patterns or brief sounds, variations thought of as "noise" were eliminated. The scalp response to the brief flashing of vertical lines would yield a waveform different from that obtained from a set of circles. The presence and stability of these correlates of the sensory modality in the average evoked waveform has been abundantly demonstrated in the early days of brain wave research. (White and Eason 1966; Harter and White 1968; Clynes and Cohn 1968; and Spehlmann 1965)

In the seventies, this Average Evoked Potential or AEP became a source of considerable excitement for behavioural psychologists as well. The waveforms exhibited tantalising regularities that became associated with such concepts as selective attention or novelty. A particular positive deflection of the signal, occurring roughly 300 ms after the stimulus, the "P300", became the object of much attention as it appeared reliably when task significant stimuli were presented at infrequent intervals in a stream of similar events for which the subjects had no task to perform. Deeper analysis proved more elusive but the research showed that large groups of neurones are abruptly called into some level of synchrony, when a sudden, relevant or potentially threatening event occurs.

At about the same epoch, the author headed the Brain Computer Interface Project at UCLA, a component of the ARPA Biocybernetics programme mentioned earlier (Vidal, 1977). Using computer generated visual simulation and sophisticated signal processing, the research successfully demonstrated the possibility of using single-epoch evoked potential without averaging in human-computer interaction, e.g. controlling a robot device). Over the picture of a maze, a cursor was controlled by a successions of turns in four different directions. The decision was transmitted in real-time, solely from the evoked brain signal of the user.

A better grasp of the cognitive signatures present in brain waves had to wait until the development of powerful topographic techniques addressing simultaneously the spatial and temporal distribution of the brain waves on the surface of the brain.

Brain wave topography was pioneered by A. Remond (Remond, 1961; Remond and Ragot, 1978) at the Hospital of the Salpetriere in Paris, many years ago and with interesting results, but a quantitative assessment of key cognitive signatures required both considerable advances in computer technology and new efforts in refining the signal processing methodology and experimental design.

A breakthrough came from a team at the EEG Laboratory headed by A. Gevins in San Francisco (Gevins et al., 1994). It took many years for this group to achieve results which are now nothing short of spectacular. The first realisation was that the spatial resolution, nitially limited to a few electrodes, had to be increased enormously. The meaningful recording of surface maps requires the simultaneous recording of as much as 124 channels of EEG signals. The position of each electrode is first calibrated directly from landmark on cerebral tissue, using Magnetic Resonance Imaging. The recorded signals are de-convolved with an empirical kernel, to minimise the spatial spreading due to bone and scalp, and to lower the focus of the recording down to the underlying brain surface. Brain activity is reconstructed in this manner at half a second intervals.

A typical experiment involves subjects given a visumotor task involving both hands. The task dissection distinguishes successive phases: "prepare to receive information" followed by a stimulus to be recognised, a decision, a presetting of the motor system for the chosen action and finally the motor act itself. A phase of re calibration is added, immediately following feedback informing the subject of his performance level. Multichannel processing consists of time covariance calculations between pairs of channels, and the results are classified with an Artificial Neural Network in relation to each phase of the task. The results, obtained in the form of coloured graphs superimposed on the skull images, by graphic animation can articulate, into connected graphs both spatially and temporally, the succession of cognitive events inherent to the task.

This real-time mapping of brain states, brings brain waves firmly into the realm of human-computer interfacing. However its practical deployment is still somewhat over the horizon. Given the general acceleration of the technology, it is unlikely to remain there for much longer.

EPILOGUE: ECONOMIC AND POLITICAL IMPLICATIONS

The world is clearly in the midst of an unprecedented technological revolution as the millennia comes to an end. But the political context in which this revolution is taking place is disturbingly unstable. As Eric Hobsbawm noted in "The Age of Extreme.":

"No one who looks back on a century in which no more than a handful of states existing at present have come into being or survived without passing through revolution, armed counter-revolution, military coups or armed civil conflicts would bet much money on the universal triumph of peaceful and constitutional change, as predicted in 1989 by some euphoric believers in liberal democracy"

(Hobsbawm, 1994)

Similar predictions are being aired in the late nineties by euphoric believers in the redemptive powers of universally accessible information. Yet, it appears unlikely that the prevailing unrest and ubiquitous conflict will subside any time soon. Irrationality is on the rise everywhere, including the developed world. Many parts of the world are experiencing a social breakdown of unprecedented scale. Even more ominously, in many places an unfocused rejection of modernity and a setback to medieval barbarism is emerging and sometimes take an acute form.

Those are strange conditions indeed to accompany the radical and unstoppable revolution in information technology and telecommunication that is taking place in the developed world. The capability for governments to control the flow of information and the movement of money is rapidly shrinking. Multinational finances and trade companies are acquiring a dominance which bypasses borders and makes short drift of the protective barriers that various constraints have erected in an earlier era. Internet commerce, still in its infancy, is certain to expand exponentially. Instant trading at the speed of light is a novel phenomenon that is viewed as the promise of the future by some and by others as the harbinger of financial crashes that could dwarf any from the past. Whatever the outcome, in the near future the most likely prospect is of the emergence of an enormously powerful supra-national club, deeply involved with the Internet and at ease with advanced technologies. This group will derive its membership predominantly from developed countries. Its numbers will be bare millions in a world population counted in billions. Social cleavage probably cannot be avoided.

In this context, what can be expected from the increasingly intimate interdependence between humans and technology, and in particular, from the bionic enhancements to the human-computer interface discussed in this perspective. It is likely that, at least in the near future, exotic enhancements will play a relatively minor role. Areas that affect commerce such as biometric personal identification are likely to receive increased attention. Biometric systems are being studied in many places for such purposes as owner authentication in banking, social security entitlement, immigration control and even election validation. Modern pattern recognition algorithms and fast database scanning can make the traditionally awkward fingerprint technique both unobtrusive and nearly instantaneous. Hand geometry, face recognition and retinal scans are other approaches that although still experimental are almost ready for large scale implementation. Finally, and in view of our earlier remarks on the fragility of our most cherished humanistic assumptions, one should not discard the concept of chip implantation as unthinkable. It is, after all, currently a most favoured, reliable and even least intrusive way to securely identify domestic animals.

Despite the dangers and the problems looming, these developments and many unforeseen others are on their way and will not stop. These are interesting times. Enlightened human intervention can, sometime and at least locally, moderate the perverse effects that almost always accompany change. This is the best society can hope for.

REFERENCES

Akamatsu, M., and S. Sato, 1994. A multi-modal mouse with tactile and force feedback. *Int. Journ. of Human-Computer Studies*, 40, pp. 443--453

Balakrishnan, R., C. Ware, and T. Smith, 1994. Virtual hand tool with force feedback. In C. Plaison, ed., *Proc.of the Conf. on Human Factors in Computing Systems*, CHI'94, Boston, ACM/SIGCHI.

Berger, H., 1931, Ueber das Elektrenkephalogramm des Menshen, *Arch. Psychiat.* 94, pp. 16-60.

Bodden, M., 1993. Modeling Human Sound Source Localization and the Cocktail-Party-Effect. *Acta Acustica*, 1(1), 43--55.

Bregler, C., H. Hild, S. Manke, and A.Waibel, 1993. Improving Connected Letter Recognition by Lipreading, in *Proc. IEEE Int. Conf. on Acoustics, Speech, and Signal Processing*, Minneapolis.

Bregler, C. and Y. Konig, 1994. "Eigenlips" for Robust Speech Recognition in, *Proc. IEEE Int. Conf. on Acoustics, Speech, and Signal Processing*, Adelaide, Australia, 1994.

Brewster, S. A., P. C. Wright, and A. D. N. Edwards, 1994. A detailed investigation into the effectiveness of earcons. In G. Kramer, editor, *Auditory Display*. Reading, Massachusetts, Santa Fe Institute: Addison Wesley, pp. 471-498

Brooks, F. P. Jr. et al., 1990. Project GROPE - Haptic Displays for Scientific Visualization. *ACM Computer Graphics*, 24(4), pp. 177—185.

Campbell, R., 1988. Tracing lip movements: making speech visible. *Visible Language*, 8(1), pp. 33-57.

Clyne, M. and M. Kohn, 1968. *In Computers and Electronic Devices in Psychiatry*, Kline, N. S. and Laska, E. Eds., Grune and Stratton, N.Y., 206-37.

Ekman, P. and W. V. Friesen, 1977. *Facial Action Coding System*. Consulting Psychologists Press, Stanford, University, Palo Alto.

Ekman, P. and W. V. Friesen, 1984. *Unmasking the face: a guide to recognizing emotions from facial clues*. Consulting Psychologists Press, Palo Alto, CA.

Ferguson, I. A., 1992. *TouringMachines: An Architecture for Dynamic, Rational, Mobile Agents*. Phd thesis, University of Cambridge.

Gerstein, G. L., and N. Y-S. Kiang, 1964. *Exp. Neurol.*, 10, 1-18.

Gevins, A.S. et al., 1994, Electroencephalogr. *Clinical. Neurophysiology*, 90, pp. 337-358.

Gigante, M. A., 1993. Virtual Reality: Definitions, History and Applications. In R. A. Earnshaw, M. A. Gigante,, and H. Jones, eds, *Virtual Reality Systems*, chapter 1. Academic Press.

Harter, M.R., and C. T. White, 1970. Electroencephalogr. Clinical. Neurophysiology. 28(1), pp. 48-54.

Hobsbawm, E. J., 1994. *The age of extremes: the short twentieth century, 1914-1991*. Michael Joseph, London.

Hubel, D. H. and T. N. Wiesel, 1962. *Journal of Physiology*, 160, pp. 106-54.

Jau, B. M., 1988. *Anthropomorphic Exoskeleton dual arm/hand telerobot controller*, pp. 715--718.

Koons, D. B., C. J. Sparrel, and K. R. Thorisson, 1993. Integrating Simultaneous Output from Speech, Gaze, and Hand Gestures. In M. Maybury, editor, *Intelligent Multimedia Interfaces*. Menlo Park: AAAI/MIT Press, pp. 243-261.

Landau, W., M., 1967. *The Neurosciences: A study programme*, Quarton G. C. et al, eds, Rockefeller University Press, N.Y., pp. 469-482.

Li, C. L., and H. H. Jasper, 1953. Journal of Physiology, 121, pp. 117-40.

Makeig Scott, Tzyy-Ping Jung, 1996. Tonic, Phasic, and Transient EEG Correlates of Auditory Awareness in Drowsiness, *Cognitive Brain Research*, 4, pp. 15-25.

Massie, T. H. and J. K. Salisbury, 1994. The PHANToM Haptic Interface: a Device for Probing Virtual Objects. *In Proceedings of the ASME Winter Annual Meeting, Symposium on Haptic Interfaces for Virtual Environment and Teleoperator Systems*, Chicago.

Mendel, M. J., Vo Van Toi and C. E. Riva, 1993. Eye-tracking laser Doppler velocimeter stabilized in two dimensions, *Journal of the Optical Society of America, Optics and Image Science* , (ISSN 0740-3232), 10, pp. 663-669.

Minsky, M. L., 1986. *The society of mind*, Simon and Schuster, New York, N.Y.

Pimentel, K. and K. Teixeira, 1993. *Virtual Reality: through the new looking glass*. Windcrest Books. 279

Psotka, J., S., A. Davison, and S. A. Lewis, 1993. Exploring immersion in virtual space. *Virtual Reality Systems*, 1(2), pp. 70-92.

Remond, A., 1961, *Analyse topologique integree de l'electroencephalogramme, Revue Neurologique,* 104(3), pp. 204-212.

Remond A., and R. Ragot, 1978. EEG field mapping, *Clinical Neurophysiology*, 45, pp. 417-421.

Rhyne, J., 1987. Dialogue Management for Gestural Interfaces. *Computer Graphics*, 21(2), pp. 137-142.

Riecken, D., 1994, editor. *Special Issue on Intelligent Agents, volume 37 of Communications of the ACM.*

Schroeder, W. E., 1993, Head-mounted computer interface based on eye tracking, *Proceedings of the SPIE - The International Society for Optical Engineering,* 2094(3), pp. 1114-1124.

Spehlmann, R., 1965, Electroencephalogr. *Clinical Neurophysiol*ogy, 19, pp. 560-569.

Stone, R. J., 1991. Virtual Reality and Telepresence -- A UK Iniative. In Virtual Reality 91 -- Impacts and Applications. *Proceedings of the first Annual Conerence on Virtual Reality*, London: Meckler Ltd., pp. 40-45

Vidal, J., 1977. Real-Time Detection of Brain Events in EEG, *IEEE Proc., Special Issue on Biological Signal Processing and Analysis*, 65(5), pp. 633-641.

White, C. T., and R. G. Eason, 1966. *Psychol. Monogr.*, whole no. 632, pp. 80-24

Wooldridge, M. and N. R. Jennings, 1995. *Intelligent Agents: Theory and Practice.* (submitted to:) Knowledge Engineering Review.

Young, L. R. and Sheena, 1975. Methods and Design, Survey of Eye Movement Recording Methods, *Behaviour Research Methods and Instrumentation*, 7, pp. 397-429.

Humane Interfaces: Questions of method and
practice in Cognitive Technology
J.P. Marsh, B. Gorayska and J.L. Mey (Editors)

Chapter 12

COGNITIVE SPACE

Myron W. Krueger
Artificial Reality Corporation, USA

Ever since the invention of written language and mathematical symbols, there has been a tendency to equate intellect with abstraction and to look down on the body as a vestigial organ for transporting the eyes and brain around. But the fact is that the brain evolved to serve the needs of the body as it navigated in a three-dimensional world. Many mammals, especially territorial predators have a keenly defined sense of space and indeed of place. Squirrels hide and find their acorns. And, even the lowly bee has developed a language for communicating with its fellows about locations in its environment.

Naturally, humanity has excelled in its ability to understand, remember, and operate in space. When the time came for humanity to create its own spaces in the form of farms, buildings, and cities, one set of organising principles had to do with the logistics of moving objects or conserving materials. However another criterion for design was that the created spaces facilitate the activities that went on within the spaces. So the physical layout of buildings for manufacturing reflected the flow of work through the facility. Yet another criterion was that the designed space should be understandable and pleasing to its human occupants.

As work was transformed from physical into intellectual toil, the modern office evolved to optimise the handling of paper, telecommunications, and face-to-face meetings. However, the spaces created so far are largely generic. Each traditional office looks pretty much like every other: desk, filing cabinets, clock, calendar, and telephone. Only on the desktop itself were the current efforts of the individual represented. Conference rooms and an auditorium are generic spaces for group functions. But on the desktop, the knowledge worker organised his work spatially.

Today, the modern office is changed in only one significant way: upon the heretofore empty desktop now squats a personal computer. On its screen, we are told a virtual desktop has been defined that simulates the function of the real one. On this screen, spatial metaphors are again invoked as useful mechanisms for organising thinking. However, while GUI interfaces exploit the spatial skills of the eye, they ignore or violate those of the body.

It is a bit ironic that the computer simulates the surface that it rests upon. It is also a bit sad that the claim of a virtual desktop is accepted so uncritically by the computer community. At best, the virtual desktop simulates a real one of equal size--about the size of the tray in front of an airline seat. Since physical desks with such stingy surfaces have never even been contemplated, it is odd that we have accepted virtual surfaces that simulate only a small fraction of the area of the real thing.

The other conceit associated with the desktop metaphor is that multiple windows (another spatial metaphor) can be defined on the computer screen. Again, a common sense spatial term is being assigned to a totally inappropriate antecedent.

True, computer windows are rectangular, but that is the end of any similarity. In the real world, you can look through windows. What you see through them is unobstructed. Real windows are disjoint. They do not overlap or occlude each other. Computer windows do.

Computer windows are really pages that lie one on top of each other. The computer desktop typically resembles an unruly heap of paper more than a real desktop which allows distinct piles to be created. While it resembles a stack of papers, the typical PC does not have the resolution to faithfully represent the content of a single page of text on the screen all at once.

While we have come to accept hype from the commercial marketplace, those interested in advancing cognitive technology should not allow themselves to be taken in by it. Especially, they should not be taken in by their own wishful thinking.

At any point in time, we have some good ideas, but our ability to implement them permits us to deliver only a hint of what their real power might be. In the meantime, we do not even chafe at the discrepancy. We do not even notice that the emperor has no clothes. Or, even perhaps in some cases, that he has no genitals.

A fundamental issue that must be addressed before cognitive technology can make good on the human interface community's promise of a spatial interface, is the need for designers, far greater resolution and physical scale than we have today. While 3D graphics and particularly the virtual reality community are constantly screaming for more pixels, that cry is seldom heard from the traditional human interface community.

In fact, these mouseketeers seldom note that the mouse itself is an unsatisfactory pointing device. Contrary to popular belief, one does not point with a mouse. Instead, one performs an anti-intuitive action with the mouse to move a cursor to point intuitively. The idea that pointing would be more understandable with a direct pointing device which has a one-to-one connection between the location of the hand on the desk and the location of the cursor on the screen is not mentioned. The significance of the mouse being a relative as opposed to absolute pointing device is that it takes several actions rather than one to point to an icon on the screen. In addition, this mode of pointing makes no use of the user's proprioceptive memory which would allow him to almost move his hand to the required location without looking. The indirection means that the user must invest much more attention in the act of pointing than he would if he was pointing to a real object in the real world.

There are a number of mechanisms whereby the needed resolution might be delivered, although not rapidly. CRT resolution has plateaued. The current debate has shifted from whether or not flat panel displays will replace the CRT to when they will. In Japan, where space is at a premium, this change is already underway.

But the more interesting question is whether flat panel displays will provide higher resolution and greater size. Existing fabrication techniques have succeeded in creating experimental displays with several times the resolution and several times the size of current monitors. Simply using several flat panels would do as much in the short run, and quite possibly that is one direction that the human interface will go as the cost of these displays comes down in the future. The MacIntosh, for instance, has long had the software capability for driving several screens as extensions of a single desktop.

Efficiency is another issue. People are so used to pull-down menus that they do not realise they are simply a resolution conserving trick that might be unnecessary if we had separate screens allocated for commands. They also do not think to complain about it since the mouse is the only pointing device that is typically available and the user must alternate between its function of pointing or drawing within the application and its other function of selecting and issuing commands. This constant switching between modes causes the user to be endlessly rolling the mouse back and forth between the two parts of the screen. For a sighted person this is a significant inefficiency. For a blind person, it makes GUI interfaces unusable.

Consider an alternative human interface that would be appropriate today for applications which do not require extensive text input and would be natural in the future for any application as speech recognition becomes used to understand commands (Krueger, 1987; 1990). Assume that the existing computer monitor is replaced with a flat panel display that hangs on the wall across the desk from the user. Assume further that the keyboard and other evidence of the computer also disappear from the desktop. Now what we have is an empty desktop with the user's hands resting upon it. A ceiling-mounted video camera looks down at the hands on the desk and superimposes the image of the hands on the application that is shown on the flat panel screen. The image of the index finger of the user's right hand can be used to select objects within the application or to drag or draw objects. The relationship between the action of the hand on the desk and its image on the screen is one-to-one, pointing to an object on the screen is direct. It is natural. It is completed with a single coordinated action, not by a sequence of actions which purport to do the same thing.

Now assume a second screen where many of the most commonly used commands are always displayed. (Overflow commands can be accessed by navigating tree structures as is done today.) The index finger of the left hand can be used to select commands from the second screen. Note that the left hand would only appear on the command screen and the right hand would only appear on the application screen. Since the most used commands are always visible, there is no need to pull down a menu to find them. Since each of the most commonly used commands has a permanent location on the screen, much of the user's pointing action can be performed by physical habit. Both hands can rest near the features they are used to point to, there is no need to constantly go from the workspace to the menu bar and back again. There is still a shift of attention, but no unnecessary physical movement.

As this virtual desktop is as large as the actual desk, the user is again operating in an environment that is matched to his body. The bandwidth between the user and the computer has been increased by the elimination of unnecessary hand movements. It is further increased by the possibility of using the two hands simultaneously by defining both end points of a line, the diameter and center of a circle, the three vertices of a triangle or four control points of a spline curve. Now that speech input technology is affordable and improving in reliability, voice commands will increase the bandwidth even further for those commands that the user has committed to memory.

A second camera looking directly at the user's face and torso is almost certain to be a standard part of the desk environment. Initially, it will be motivated by teleconferencing, but it will also be useful for watching the user. The author has used head and body movements to alter the user's view of three-dimensional objects since 1970. It is helpful, because it is natural. Zooming can be controlled the same way. Computer lip reading has already been used to improve the accuracy of speech recognition.

Currently, the computer experiences the user as keystrikes, mouse clicks and relative mouse movements. Once video cameras and microphones are a standard part of the human interface, the computer can develop an awareness of the user and his colleagues as physical creatures, the desktop and office as work environments, and understand the ebb and flow of the actual work that the user is doing. Initially, this will allow the computer to identify work contexts and thereby to improve speech recognition. It would allow the computer to anticipate entire sequences of actions that are likely to flow as a consequence of a particular word that is said in a phone conversation. It may allow the computer to determine that an incoming call is not important enough to interrupt the conversation that the user is having with his boss at the moment.

Currently, the user interface is totally passive. Nothing happens unless the user invokes it. Thus, for all its power, the computer is still being used like a screw driver. The only way the user's context is reflected is in the different files and applications that are being used. Slowly, the distinctions between applications will fade as the logic of the user's work becomes more important than the vendors' products.

For this process to become successful, the computer must become more aware of the user and how he operates in space for three reasons. First, the user does in fact reside in real space and computer must understand the actions he takes there. Second, the computer will define a virtual space for the user to organise his work in. Third, that virtual space will no longer be viewed through a single tiny porthole. Instead, the user will interact with it as if it was real space.

The virtual space will expand until it fills the user's real space. Clocks and calendars have long hung on the wall providing useful information. Office Post-em's and refrigerator magnets have shown that people like to arrange their information in space--not to confine it to 13" screens. As screens gain resolution and increase in size and number, they will expand to occupy every surface in the office and the home.

Viewed in terms of current CRTs and flat panel displays, such a vision seems impractical; however, there are several independent trends that are likely to provide the capability. The first is the advent of conductive polymers that will allow all of the conventional electronic components such as transistors, diodes, LEDs, photodiodes, and mechanical actuators to be made out of inexpensive materials (Yam, 1992; Brown, 1996; 1997). In addition, these components can be made large (Robinson, 1997). Uniform lighting panels as opposed to very bright bulbs are likely first steps. Animated wall paper and environmental scale information displays will follow.

Another approach is to project the information on every available surface. Video projectors and televisions themselves can now be realised on single chips composed of a million individually deformable mirrors. Scanning lasers offer another way of creating large scale displays. The CAVE at the Chicago Circle campus of the University of Illinois is a 10x10x10 foot room with stereo computer graphic images rear-projected on the walls and the floor (Cruz-Neira et al., 1992). Although it is primarily used for scientific visualisation, it could be used for information display. Its weakness is that the computer's awareness of the user is through tracking the head and the user's hand with sensors that must be connected to the computer by wires. The author's unencumbering video interface could be used to improve the CAVE interface.

The third alternative is to use virtual reality technology. One version of virtual reality is called Augmented Reality. With this technique, virtual information is superimposed on the user's view of the real world by means of a head-mounted display. In the future, these displays will fit within normal eye glasses or even contact lenses (Schneiderman, 1997a&b). While this information could be at a fixed point in the user's field of view, it might be more natural for it to appear on blank walls rather than to float in the air. Blank spaces set aside for that purpose could then be used by any number of individuals to view completely different information simultaneously. This is similar to the recently developed practice of displaying virtual advertising information on billboard spaces in broadcasts of athletic events. The content of that space can then be different in different geographic areas. Ultimately, it can be tailored to the individual consumer. By whatever means, we can be sure that our virtual space of information display and our physical space with real objects will merge.

To the extent that information becomes portable, or, better instantly accessible from any location, information and place which currently are intertwined will become completely independent. This development will alter our relationship with knowledge from our current preparation for life idea of education. Currently, we learn everything in case we need to know anything. In the future, we will switch to what Roger Schank calls just-in-time education. Ironically, this approach will mean that we retain more. As we will only learn what we want to know, what is learned will be connected with a question and often an experience making it easier to remember.

Consider something as simple as looking up a word in the dictionary. Today, the dictionary is a big clumsy book that is probably not in the room when you are thinking about a word and so you do not look it up. If looking a word up was effortless, no matter what the circumstances, we would look up more words and remember more.

However, while portability will make computers independent of space, spatial representations and workspaces will still be important ways of organising our thinking. Currently, there is a considerable amount of activity in visualising abstract information in two dimensions and real objects and phenomena in three. There is even some effort in using three-dimensional representations of n-dimensional information to see if that helps us make sense of it (Noll, 1968). However, there is little effort to construct special spaces that help us organise the information that inundates us or is created by us daily.

Each of the technological trends mentioned will allow us to create and immerse ourselves within an information space of our own creation. Such representations are bound to be of some value given that we remember the locations of hundreds of objects in our homes. Each task could have its own room. Or, each transaction in progress could have its own desktop with its own spatial representation. Thus, we would not have to put things away when we are interrupted in the middle of a task. The entire context would be laid out exactly as we left it when we return to it.

Ultimately, these immersive representations will involve all of our senses. However, even in the near term, sensory involvement can pay dividends. Throughout this essay, the author has emphasised the human's spatial sense. This sense is maximally involved when the person is physically involved in the experience for only then is our proprioceptive sense maximally engaged. Physical involvement may be limited to turning one's gaze to see more; however, it is also useful to turn the head, reach the hand, and move the body.

Physical engagement can go as far as strenuous exertion. We live incredibly sedentary lives which puts our health at risk. Putting more labour back into our work would not only make us healthier, it might make us more alert as well. Working in the same sedentary posture for extended periods of time requires a special temperament. The rest of us may find our attention flagging not from the work, but from the sensory deprivation of an inert body. Even the choice of whether to work sitting down or standing up would offer some relief from the tedium.

The VIDEODESK described earlier is the sedentary form of a more general technology called VIDEOPLACE which perceives the person's entire body (Krueger et al., 1989). Thus, we have a number of applications that the user can operate either sitting down or standing up. The result may even be better problem solving. In the early days of research into the human arousal system, there were studies that showed that the best problem solvers were not those who maintained the highest level of activation. Rather they were the individuals whose level of arousal varied during the problem solving process. While these early results may later have been qualified, we have all had the experience of having the solution to a problem that we were working on come to us during a moment of repose such as while taking a shower.

The author has long wanted to be able to work while taking a walk or even jogging. While he has not pursued this goal with any degree of commitment, self-styled "nomadic" technologist Steve Robertson has added some of the controls that the author had written about so that he could operate his computer while he was riding his bike.

One ingredient that few have missed in the human interface is smell, but a discussion of sensory representation would not be complete without considering it. Indeed, smell has surprising possibilities as a component in cognitive technology. Throughout the ages, many including Marcel Proust has commented on the fact that odours trigger memories. In fact, odour cannot only trigger memory (Proust, 1913-27), it can also improve memory as has been shown in many studies (Engen, 1991). Olfactory memory extinguishes much more slowly that other kinds of memory. In addition, olfactory stimuli can be used to improve human performance (Baron and Bronfen, 1994; Rottman, 1989). There have been a number of studies that show that odours can alter moods (Hashimoto et al., 1988, 1994). However, they can also improve performance at vigilance tasks (Warm et al., 1991) and spatial reasoning tasks (Knasko et al., in preparation).

The creation of such immersive representations will be one of the major challenges of the next few decades. In the past, we optimised the use of the computer. Now, everybody must realise that by far the most expensive component in a computer system is the human user. We must create technology that will allow us to make maximum use of the human intellect. Since spatial memory and spatial action are already built into human cognitive processing, we have to make use of that talent if humans are to increase the amount of useful complexity people can manage with the help of computers rather than forcing them to keep track of needless complexity engendered by computers.

While the discussion has focused on the use of spatial metaphors in the now traditional user interface, that interface is going to fragment as the progression that started with computers being used solely by scientists then led to them being used by programmers and engineers, and now has led to them being operated by users, and will soon lead to computers being used by people going about their everyday lives. The technologies predicted for the office will also be deployed in the home, but there they will be joined by a host of new interfaces that allow computer access while moving around the house, around the yard, in the car, and while hiking in the woods. In addition, the outdoor environment will become more information rich and interactive in the future.

Decades ago, arrays of lights on the sides of buildings scrolled the day's news to be read by pedestrians in the streets below. Today, these signs have been joined by huge video screens that present all sorts of information and entertainment to those nearby. Currently, these displays are objects on the sides of buildings. They will slowly take over every surface of the building, so that the building becomes a sign. It becomes a communication medium. A building will not only make a statement. It will make an endless sequence of the, in every location, once static signs are replaced by programmable displays. Economics currently limits the size of these displays, but we can be sure that every surface in our environment will be eventually covered with information.

A recent development illustrates this trend. Five years ago, German artist Christian Slatter created a sequence of images that were placed along the walls of a subway tunnel. As trains past by, the sequence of stationary static images were perceived as an animation. Since then, a commercial computer-controlled system has been developed for presenting advertising messages to subway passengers in this way.

Thus, our real world will become more virtual. Real space will no longer be a metaphor to be referenced. Rather new kinds of spaces will be invented. These will then be used to help us organise our intellectual activities. Representations that are useful will then find their way into the design of real space.

As information becomes architecture, it will be used for affect as well as effect. The designers of cathedrals were not involved in the optimal use of materials to enclose space. They were trying to elevate the spirit through the buildings they created (Krueger, 1997b).

For over a quarter of a century, the author has tried to create spaces that involve those who enter them in experiences that change their awareness of what is possible and what has always been assumed (Krueger, 1974, 1983, 1991). Movements of their bodies control what they see and hear, but not in the predictable ways that are familiar in the real world. Instead, the body becomes a paintbrush or a musical instrument. The traditional mirror has been replaced by a programmable virtual world in which the image of the person may have completely unexpected effects. He can be joined by a graphic creature that will land on his hand, climb his body, and do a jig on his head. Alternatively, he can have an utterly inhuman abstract shape that metamorphoses as he moves his body.

In this case, the body is no longer a means of navigating space and manipulating the objects within it. The body has become a general mechanism for controlling interactive sensation. A new art form has been created which is not about representing reality, but rather about communicating the essence of our relationship with any reality. Showing that our nervous systems allow us to accept almost any feedback relationship as rewarding as long as we are in control.

Whereas music composes around our auditory expectations, this art form does the same for our expectations about the consequences of our actions. It also intends to communicate and to celebrate the new set of possibilities that we are confronted with. The virtualisation of our world is well underway. To a significant extent, we have always lived in a virtual world of ideas that we could not see. Now we can give them form as we desire.

Animation and interactivity will not only render the static obsolete, but will become the norm in every context that has been mentioned here. The author has created a space in which a graphic fish was drawn on the floor by a ceiling-mounted laser. As people moved around the space, the graphic fish swam after them. This playful experience augurs the day when floors will be used for information display and when buildings interiors and exteriors will be inhabited by graphic creatures that perceive the people who pass by and seek to interact with them.

Outdoor environments are as amenable to interactive display as those indoors. Since 1972, the author has done a series of proposals for interactive buildings in which the lights in the windows responded to the movements of those below or laser drawn representations of individual pedestrians fly around the outside of the building controlled by their movements. He also proposed a five mile long interactive light display on frozen Lake Medota in Madison Wisconsin. Similar proposals were offered for the new Munich airport, for the Ars Electronica Center in

Linz Austria, and the Media Museum in Karlsruhe Germany. The ultimate realisable expression of this idea is to take over the entire skyline of a major city and to make it respond to one or more people. In simulation, impossible projects can be imagined in which the buildings dance with the person's movements, the terrain transforms, and the stars in the sky respond. Such experiences not only decorate but they alter our own consciousness about the world we have created.

To truly take advantage of humanity's heritage as a spatial being, it is necessary to move beyond perceptual metaphor to actual spatial behaviour. We have memory and logic in our bodies. We must tap it all if we are to maximise our cognitive abilities.

REFERENCES

Baron R. A., and M. I. Bronfen, 1994. A whiff of reality: Empirical evidence concerning the effects of pleasant fragrances on work-related behaviour. *Journal of Applied Social Psychology*, 24, pp. 1179-1203.

Brown, C., 1996. "Polymer Material Promises an Inexpensive and Thin Full-Color Light-Emitting Plastic Display," *Electronic Design*, January 8, p. 42.

Brown, C., 1997. "Pumped polymers promise photonic technique," *Electronic Engineering Times*, April 7, p. 34.

Cruz-Neira C., et al, 1992. "The CAVE: Audio Visual Experience Automatic Virtual Environment, *CACM*, June, pp. 64-72.

Engen T., 1991. *Odour Sensation and Memory*. New York: Praeger.

Hashimoto S., N. Yamayuchi, and M. Kawaski, 1988. Experimental research on the aromatherapeutic effects of fragrances in living environments, *Proceedings of the Japanese Architecture Society*, October, pp. 83-84.

Hashimoto S., N. Yamayuchi, and M. Kawaski, 1994. 'Aromatherapy' alters moods, speeds recovery, *Health Facilities Management*, March, pp. 64-66.

Joel S. Warm, W. N. Dember, and R. Parasuraman, 1991. "Effects of olfactory stimulation on performance and stress in a visual sustained attention task. *Journal of the Society of Cosmetic Chemistry*, 42, pp. 199-210.

Krueger M., 1974. *Computer Controlled Responsive Environments*, doctoral dissertation.

Krueger M., 1983. *Artificial Reality*. Reading, Mass.: Addison-Wesley.

Krueger, M., 1987. *VIDEOTOUCH: An Innovative System-User Interface.* SBIR Phase 1 Final Report, September.

Krueger, M., 1990. VIDEOPLACE and the Interface of the Future. In Brenda Laurel, ed., *The Art of Human Interface Design*, Reading, Mass.: Addison-Wesley, pp. 405-416.

Krueger M., 1991. *Artificial Reality II*, Reading, Mass.: Addison-Wesley.

Krueger, M., 1997a. KnowWhere(TM): Virtual Reality Maps for Blind People. *CSUN Conference*, Los Angeles, March.

Krueger M., 1997b. Virtual Spaces and Real Buildings. In Daniela Bertol, ed., *Designing Digital Space: An Architect's Guide to Virtual Reality*, Wiley, pp. 273-284.

Krueger M., K. Hinrichsen, and T. Gionfriddo, 1989. *Real-Time Perception of and Response to the Actions of an Unencumbered Participant/User*, US Patent # 4,843,568 R0379-7433.

Noll M., 1968. "Computer animation and the fourth dimension," *AFIPS Conference Proceedings*, 33, pp. 1279-1283.

Proust M, 1913-1927. *A la recherche du la temps perdu*. 7 volumes.

Robinson G., 1997. "IC effort envisions wall-sized circuits," *Electronic Engineering Times*, March, p. 35.

Rottman T. R., 1989. The effects of ambient odour on the cognitive performance, mood, and activation of low and high impulsive individuals in a naturally arousing situation. *Dissertation Abstracts International*, 50, p. 364B.

Schneiderman R., 1997a. Prospects Brighten for Miniature Displays in Portable Products. *Wireless Design*, July, pp. 27-31.

Schneiderman R., 1997b. Miniature LCD Measures 0.25 inches But Projects to a 20-inch Screen, *Electronic Design*, May, p. 84.

Yam P., 1992. Plastics Get Wired, *Scientific American*, July, p.92.

APPLIED METHODS

Humane Interfaces: Questions of method and practice in Cognitive Technology
J.P. Marsh, B. Gorayska and J.L. Mey (Editors)
© *1999 Elsevier Science B.V. All rights reserved.*

HOW DO WE CONVERT PRINCIPLES INTO VALID AND VALIDATED APPLIED METHODS?

Barbara Gorayska
Jonathon P. Marsh
Jacob L. Mey

COMMENTARY

Having given fair consideration to some of the theoretical issues involved in trying to define a set of methodological principles for CT, we turn now to addressing the question of how to convert those principles into valid (and validated) practices.

Tools are certainly useful, but their practical use is not always straightforward. Referring back to Karpatschof's contribution to this volume, one could invoke the concept of a 'threshold value': a point beyond which qualifications become obsolete such that they lose their value in the market place and have to be replaced by wholly new (sets of) values. By extension, there is a 'cut-off-point' beyond which human values become 'obsolete', i.e., engulfed by the 'values' of technology. To avoid this obsolescence, certain system requirements have to be met in such different areas as assistance to the disabled, education, and in general, humane tool thinking.

The paramount issues here are: control, the role of designers, and the involvement of real users in design. These beg the following questions:

- *How does one ensure that one's own methodological preferences and attitudes do not deteriorate into personal bias or petty professionalism?*
- *How can we avoid reducing input from users to simple 'advice' status, without help from, or recourse to, other resources than those provided by the machine?*
- *Can a third party usefully contribute to the design of first order user-system interactions?*

CHAPTER SUMMARIES

Chapter 13
David Good
On Why the Blind Leading the Blind is a Good Idea

David Good's contribution demonstrates that as designers, in a sense we are all blind. To support his argument he reports on a case study of designing a spatial map for the blind of a London underground station. What becomes apparent in this project is that sighted people are ill equipped to arrive at representations of space that the blind can understand and relate to. What the blind need in order to orient themselves are sound maps of the environment. Such a map can only be successfully drawn, that is, recorded, by other blind people. The challenge for C T is to find methods for facilitating communication between those who share a restricted sensory world, such that real human needs can be met and any undesirable bias avoided.

Chapter 14
Ian Hart
Between the Idea and the Reality: the case for qualitative research

Ian Hart draws on Kearins' (1986) research on the Aboriginal and white Australian children to demonstrate the influence of culture on the development of different types of intelligence. Hart calls for a greater weight to be given to bottom up, data driven, situation embedded methods of testing the impact of computerised media on student learning. He argues that what we need to realise is that students learn *with* media and not *from* media. He postulates that people will always act on what they believe, irrespective of what they may be told, based on sophisticated, quantitative laboratory research. Accordingly, qualitative methods based on the action research feedback "spiral": act-observe-and-reflect, may be better suited to both determining and guiding the cognitive processes involved in tool mediated learning.

Chapter 15
Alex Kass and Joe Herman
Computer Environments Designed to Promote Cognitive Change through the Development of Well Reasoned Recommendations

In their contribution, Alex Kass and Joe Herman ask us to consider a positive side of mind change control through education. They argue that the aim of educational computing systems should be to eliminate cognitive strain, stunting, or maladaptation. However if environments have cognitive impact, we should likewise ensure that cognitive adaptation proceeds in desirable ways, which is the essence of learning. The chapter discusses 'advise systems' that help develop students' habits of mind.

Chapter 16
Colin T. Schmidt and Patrick Ruch
Evolution of Man's Needs and Technological Progression: Pragmatic Foundations for a Relational Coupling

Colin Schmidt and Patrick Ruch attempt to renew interest in the traditional field of Technology Assessment, whose goal is to achieve objectivity through consensus validation. The fundamental question on the design agenda is now 'Who are we and what do we want to become?' This agenda is examined from the viewpoint of dialogism, with a particular focus on pragmatic issues.

Chapter 17
Muneo Kitajima
Successful Technology Must Enable People to Utilize Existing Cognitive Skills

Muneo Kitajima argues that successful CT must enable people to utilise existing skills. For this to happen, CT must satisfy the demands made by those skills, especially as they are realized in the satisfaction of action goals. He shows how a correct mapping of goals into actions will enable users to act skilfully in solving problems, whereas contrariwise, an unsatisfactorily formulated goal, or the wrong mapping of subgoals onto final goal will result in longer reaction times and/or failure to accomplish the task. The experiments show an application of text comprehension skills on interactions with graphically based interfaces, and a model for those interactions called LICAI (Linked model of Comprehension based Action Planning and Instruction taking) is presented.

Chapter 18
Douglas Herrmann, Virgil Sheets, Justine Wells, and Carol Yoder
Palmtop Computerized Remembering Devices: The Effectiveness of the Temporal Properties of Warning Signals

In their contribution, the authors provide empirical evidence that we cannot always change human mind states by the use of tools. They report on a series of experiments in which they tested the usefulness of remembering devices for prospective execution of the user's intended actions. They found that, through no fault in design, devices which externalise intentions are not always dependable. Whether the user attends to the warning signals or not varies according many extraneous variables such as time of day, degree of fatigue, and motivation. As these psychological aspects of human memory become better understood, it may become possible to modify future designs to help humans avoid such problems.

Chapter 19
John Sillince
User Designed Contextualisation Method for an Argumentation Support Tool

John Sillince presents a method for the design of an electronic meeting system that will enable argumentation. The method incorporates a variable for estimating the strength of each argument proposed, and thus controls each turn taken by the debate. The problem is how to design this variable such that it will pick up pragmatic clues, indicating any contextual information. The innovative aspect of this approach is its involvement of the real user in the design and testing, an aspect which is also stressed by David Good in his contribution to this volume.

Chapter 20
Wolfgang Halang
Cognition Oriented Software Verification

Wolfgang Halang takes the view that, if the task of software verification is to be successfully accomplished, then the intrinsic problems and fundamental principles of safety licensing software must include the human element. This issue becomes especially acute in the case of real time computer automated safety systems that deal with computerised automation. He points out that there is a real and growing concern for safety of these systems which, if not fault free, can cause loss of human life and environmental disaster. Arguing for a greater simplicity of trustworthy verification by means of diagrammatic and graphical programming paradigms, Halang presents an ergonomic, yet highly rigorous method called 'diverse back translation'. The method is based on cause-effect tables and block diagrams that are easily understood by non-programmers, yet prove rigorous and accurate enough to overcome the enormous code complexity such systems typically entail.

Humane Interfaces: Questions of method and practice in Cognitive Technology
J.P. Marsh, B. Gorayska and J.L. Mey (Editors)
© *1999 Elsevier Science B.V. All rights reserved.*

Chapter 13

ON WHY THE BLIND LEADING THE BLIND IS A GOOD IDEA

David A. Good

Faculty of Social and Political Sciences
University of Cambridge

INTRODUCTION

In understanding how new Information and Communication Technologies (ICT) can be used to provide tools which extend human capacities in ways which are in accord with a wide range of human concerns, the Cognitive Technology (CT) agenda sets a hard task. We not only need to invent possible technologies, but we also need to predict the possible shapes of human mentality, and to make a judgement as to the social, political, cognitive and affective desirability of those different shapes. Imagine, if you will, the difficulty of predicting what the impact of writing systems and widespread literacy would be before those systems had been invented. Of course, inventions evolve into their final form over a period of time. Hence discovering what must be included for adherence to any design criteria, including the CT one, must be the result of a gradual approximation. However even with this allowance the demands CT sets are potentially hard to meet.

One way of easing that demand would be to consider the development of tools which are designed to help those who are affected by some disability or impairment which impedes their engagement in what are taken to be everyday human activities. At the very least, this permits a clearer focus on what is being attempted, and how any burgeoning technology satisfies the CT goals.

This paper reports on one such technology, the aim of which is to help blind people cope with the demands of navigating places and spaces which are unknown to them. It is still, as yet, at an early stage in its development, but the early trials have been promising. Even if the early promise of this particular device proves to be ultimately unfulfilled, I would argue that the approach used in its development is instructive with respect to the CT agenda.[1]

---

[1] This chapter draws heavily on unpublished work conducted in collaboration with John Barrable and Richard Bennett of the New Media Research Centre at the University of Portsmouth on the development of acoustic maps. This chapter reports on their work as much as mine, except that they bear no

A BRIEF HISTORY OF MOBILITY AIDS FOR THE BLIND

The catastrophic loss of sight at any stage in one's life, or the absence of sight from birth in cases of congenital blindness causes many difficulties. While those in the former group will, as Hull (1990) reports, experience a tremendous psychological trauma on losing their sight which goes far beyond the practicalities of daily life, the greatest practical problem which faces both groups is how to move safely around in the world.[2] The importance of mobility is recognised in the various devices which have been developed to assist the blind in moving around. These fall into two broad categories. One type, that might be called prospective aids, seeks to prepare the blind person for the novel environment through the use of maps or verbal descriptions. The other, that might be called contemporaneous aids, is designed to provide additional or enhanced information about the environment as he or she travels through it.

Prospective Aids

A map is the prospective aid with which we are all familiar. It is a visual form which provides through both iconic and conventional features a representation of a place or space. While maps can be used while traversing an dynamically as directional guides, an equally common practice is to familiarise oneself with a map and thus with what is in prospect, and then set off with an idea in mind about the place one is about to encounter. The idea or representation can then be drawn on to guide oneself moment by moment.

In a similar way, verbal descriptions of a place can provide both procedural knowledge of how to navigate a pathway through it, and a spatial description of its layout and landmark features. Both kinds of description can result in very substantial mental representations which might be quite close in content to those formed on the basis of visual maps, and can be as valuable in functional terms as a visual representation.

How maps do the job that they do is not a simple matter, as MacEachren (1995) has demonstrated. A point emphasised by Wood and Fels (1986, 1993) who analyse the meaning which can be found in maps in terms of no less than five different codes (tectonic, temporal, iconic, linguistic and presentational) with each of these codes having an effect in a different way. Whatever the complications in

---

responsibility for the mistakes. Subsequent work with Emma Huckett of the Department of Architecture at the University of Cambridge also made a contribution to what is discussed here, as did many valuable discussions with Mark Prowse of the Royal National Institute for the Blind in Great Britain.

[2] This observation should not be taken to imply, though, that the practical is divorced so simply from the social and the psychological. Any impediment to one's capacity to take part in everday life makes it much harder for the individual to create and understand him or herself in the way that others do for themselves. While this paper is very concerned with the practical, the broader benefits of increased mobility and independence that this would give should not be forgotten.

how maps do their job, and we will return to some of these below, it is clear that maps are valuable. Unsurprisingly, therefore, those who have worked on mobility aids for the blind have tried to develop versions, of the maps and verbal route descriptions used by sighted people which can be used by blind people.

A common strategy in creating maps for the blind is to take a graphically based map, and render the features in a way which can be discerned through touching. These tactile maps have also been linked to verbal descriptions, most interestingly in the NOMAD system (Parkes, 1988). In this a touch sensitive pad not only provides raised features to indicate spatial arrays as an analogue to the visual lines on an ordinary map, but also a spoken account of the what and where of the locations a user is touching at any particular point in time.

The success of these different systems has, according to the reports, been mixed. Some recent work by Ungar, Blades and Spencer (1997) has reported more positive and encouraging results. Using simplified tactile maps, some of their subjects showed clear benefits from the familiarisation with a novel place which these maps permitted when those subjects had subsequently to make a journey through it.

Contemporaneous aids

There is long history of various aids which provide the blind person with additional information about the environment as he or she moves through it. Interestingly, their characteristics seem also to have often been driven by the sighted persons engagement with and experience of the world. Sometimes this has been with a remarkable degree of success. The best known example of this is the long cane technique. In this, a blind person uses a white stick not as a support aid for when difficulties are encountered, and stumbles occur, but as a sensing device. The essence of the long cane technique is for the blind person to explore the ground ahead by sweeping the tip of the cane across it in the same way that a sighted person who was being very careful might inspect the same patch of ground with his or her eyes. This scanning provides not only advance warning of any changes in the terrain directly by the positional changes it offers and the feeling transmitted through it, but also the tapping provides a sound source which can be reflected off other aspects of the locale thereby providing useful auditory cues to the spatial layout.

Exploiting auditory cues has been at the heart of a number of devices which began with the Sonic Torch invented by Leslie Kay. This was the first of many devices including amongst others, the ***Sonicguide***, the ***Sonic Pathfinder***, the ***Mowat Sensor***, and the ***Polaron***, all of which exploited the idea of sweeping the environment with some kind of ultrasound scan. The reflections received back from objects at various distances from the transmitter were then transformed by the device into either some audible signal or vibration which by its very nature could be structured so as to provide size, distance and location information about those objects. In a similar vein, the **Laser Cane** provides a scrutiny of the environment beyond the range of the usual long cane to which it is attached by sweeping three specific areas beyond the end of the cane with an infra-red laser beam. Again transformed feedback is provided to the user. See Dodds (1993) for details of these and other devices.

While the ultrasound devices do exploit the acoustic properties of the environment, and provide acoustic signals to the user, it would be wrong to see them as trading on the kind of capacity which blind people ordinarily exploit to make sense of the acoustic cues to space which are available in the world. This point is amply demonstrated by the **Laser Cane** which achieves the same effect by making use of light, and is, according to Dodds more successful, and indeed cheaper. Furthermore, a common report is that these devices tend to overwhelm the user with information, and those who have found success in using them have needed extensive training and a long time to adapt to the equipment.

The final kinds of device in this category are those which seek to guide the user by providing direct descriptions as to the user's location. This has been done in a technologically simple way by using beacons of one sort or another placed on, for example various bits of street furniture which emit space and locale descriptions. It has also been done in a more technologically sophisticated way by systems which exploit the information available from Global Positioning Satellites which can provide a fairly precise fix on where someone is. The success of these systems has been somewhat mixed. One problem which they face is that they necessarily interfere with the blind person's other ways of handling the environment, and in so much as they contribute new information they also hinder the use of other sources.

A summary judgement?

It is not my intention in this paper to review in any depth the full strengths and weaknesses of these devices. However, apart from one of them, a very noticeable feature of all of them is that they are driven by a sighted person's conception of what is needed to understand space in the world, often at the cost of either ignoring or even interfering with the information which is ordinarily available to the blind person. The one device which does not do this, and seems more in accord with human design of CT principles is the Long Cane. Ironically this is the technologically simplest of these devices, but it is successful because of the way in which it meshes with and extends the blind person's capacities.

Recognising this weakness, we[3] embarked on an exercise which sought to exploit the acoustic cues available in the environment, and which are typically used by many blind people to help them navigate their way through the world. The

---

[3] John Barrable, Richard Bennett and the current author. Sadly, John Barrable died following a heart transplant eighteen months after this work began.

stimulus for this work was the desire of the London Underground Disability Unit to provide assistance to their blind passengers. In helping them to satisfy this desire, our aim became to record and map the acoustic character of a place in a way which would enable a blind person listening to that recording to build an understanding of that place. So having done so we hoped to enable them to navigate it more successfully when they first went there than they might otherwise be able to do. This was the beginning of our developing what eventually became known as the 'Sound Maps' project. As we were to discover, what constitutes a map, how it should be created, and how its use can be developed are far from simple matters.

SOUND MAPS[4]

The acoustic cues which blind people use are many and various. They include not only those which are due to the simple physical nature of the world[5], but also those which derive from the meaning of the objects which are identified. The net result of using them has been in some cases the production of a capacity which can seem quite miraculous.[6] As John Hull observed in his autobiographical account of becoming blind, this can indeed be a very rich sensory world about which the sighted have little idea:

> "As trains came in and out, currents of air are pushed along the platforms - these are full of the fragrance of newspapers, metals and oils, food and peoples clothing. Between the stations there is nothing to see through the windows so I did not feel frustrated about missing the view. I found I could easily distinguish the metallic click of the wheels on the rails, the electric hum of the engines as the train gathered power, the swish of the automatic doors opening and closing, and the rushing noise of the air in the tunnel itself. The sound of the wind when you are approaching a platform is quite different from when you are leaving it. As well as all this, there are the human noises, the conversation in the compartment, the rustle of clothes and footsteps as people get in and out, and the whole background noise of the station which comes flooding into the

---

[4] This section draws heavily on a project reports which we submitted to London Underground in November 1993 and April 1994.

[5] The exact machinery by which sound can provide information about space has been the subject of much psychoacoustic work. Those who are interested in this subject and would like to know more should consult Blauert (1983), Moore (1997) and McAdams and Bigand (1994).

[6] The extent of these skills and the degree to which the power of a blind person's capacities in one domain reflect a compensation for the losses elsewhere has long been a subject of academic interest dating back, at least, to the work of Diderot.

compartment each time the doors are opened - the sounds entirely envelop me. I am in the middle of them."   (Hull, 1990)

Obviously, the way in which this collection of sounds is recorded will make a tremendous difference to how a recording of a place sounds. Clearly a single microphone located in a fixed position would be useless, and so we looked for alternatives. The obvious choice was binaural sound recording technique. As Dodds independently observed:

"Given that there is an auditory representation in the blind traveller's head it is surprising that no-one has thought of devising a binaural recording of a route to see if that helps the individual navigate it better after listening to it."

(Dodds, 1993,: 123)

Binaural recording

Binaural sound recording, first used in Germany during the twenties and thirties, enjoyed a resurgence of interest in the late seventies as the result of a well publicised transmission of a Radio 4 documentary entitled 'Oil Rig", which had been recorded using the technique.

This technique involves a two channel stereo process which makes use of a cephloid or 'dummy head' with microphones mounted in the ears. The technique produces amplitude, phase, and diffraction effects in close simulation of the human hearing process with unparalleled realistic and natural results. Trials of several binaural systems and subsequent testing of the recordings produced, enabled the identification of features in the recordings which supported the diverse audience response obtained by the BBC's Engineering Information Department after the 'Oil Rig' broadcast. However the short-comings identified in the technique, which preclude it from more widespread use in the broadcasting and recording industries, would seem, in many ways, to be of positive benefit to the sound maps project. Such short-comings are identified in the following extract from a BBC report issued soon after the broadcast.

The binaural recordings were made on a Nagra machine using Sony ECM 50 microphones. Two of these were mounted either on a light headband and worn in the operator's ears, or mounted 6" apart and separated by a 10" disc of Perspex. Owing to the very high background noises, ordinary interviewing techniques could not be used in many instances and so the commentary recorded by crewmembers was recorded with the speaker himself wearing the microphone headband. This gave good separation from the background, but placed the speaker's voice inside the listener's head.

The location of sounds was at the heart of the project, and high background noise, regarded in conventional recording terms as a nuisance factor, is to be the vital central component of the sound map. Also, placing the navigational commentary in the listeners head with good separation from the out of head sounds has real advantages with regard to the clarity of the brief descriptions we had decided to record on the sound maps.

Initial trials carried out in the lecture theatre of the Department of Design at Portsmouth University using a mock-up dummy head were initially very encouraging. A 360° sound field with good pantophonic and periphonic sound spacing and separation was apparently achieved. However, further assessment trials using individuals not present at the time of the recording, or familiar with the lecture theatre's acoustics as had been the case in the previous trials, proved disappointing, with the majority attributing sounds to the sides or back. This tendency had been observed by John Collis reporting in 'The Listener' at the time of the 'Oil Rig' preview:

> "The purpose of binaural is to get stereo outside the head, so that, ideally, one can locate sounds, pinpointing their relative distances and positions within 360 degrees. In the case of this programme, one should appear to be standing on the rig, with noise and activity all round. Interestingly, the only people for whom this happened at the preview were those directly concerned with making the documentary."

Figures based on comments received after the 'Oil Rig' transmission indicated that over half the listeners experience sounds only to the sides and back. At the time this caused much bewilderment, but it is a quite intelligible phenomena. Simply put, seeing is believing, our eyes are invariably the blind spot in the sound field of the earphones, at least for the sighted, but as another journalist observed at the time of the broadcast, 'the most valuable response to this invention would be that of a blind person - and its most rigorous test'.

It had been noted at the initial trial stage that once specific information concerning location and orientation relating to the test recording was given to individuals who had experienced a sound field restricted to the rear hemisphere, a second hearing invariably produced a delighted recognition and appreciation of a much extended sound vista. Suggestibility would appear to have a remarkable healing effect on the impaired acoustic, a fact long appreciated by enthusiasts of radio drama. Further confirmation of this was obtained while we were testing the suitability of two pairs of microphones at an exterior location.

It was now clear, however, that the dummy head used for the earlier trials was too fragile to withstand the rigours of location work. For this reason, a headset was adapted to secure a pair of miniature microphones in the ears of the sound recordist. We were not to realise it at the time, but the fragility of the dummy head

To test the new arrangement, a number of different coloured traffic cones were placed in a circle around a sound recordist who maintained a fixed position. A child was asked to run from cone to cone, stopping at each cone to face the sound recordist and shout out the colour of the chosen cone before moving on to the next at random. Note was made of the coloured cone's position in relation to the sound which lead to this change effectively pointed us in the right direction for the development of the mapping technique.[7]

Recordist, and those asked to take part in the trials were informed of the cone configuration, but not the individual colour positions. The end result, produced in all cases a full appreciation of a 360 degree sound field, indicating that if specific limited descriptive information is made available prior to a hearing, in psychoacoustic terms, the gap can be filled in the sound field. Colour placing was generally accurate with the occasional complete transposition of the extreme forward and backward acoustic, sometimes referred to as 'flip-over'. There would appear to be several possible explanations for this transposition and the confusion generally in locating recorded sound sources in what is known as the 'Mohican Plane'.

Warren Street

Having established a form for the recording apparatus, arrangements were then made to record routes both in and out of a London Underground station. For this purpose, Warren Street which is on the Victoria and Northern Lines was chosen. It is a fairly, but not excessively busy station, and similarly its layout is neither overly straightforward nor too complicated. It is also the most convenient stop for the RNIB headquarters in Great Portland Street.[8]

It was decided that five transits through the station from entrance hall to platform and back again should be done. The variants were due to our decision to make recordings both with commentary and without which were made by both

---

[7]The two microphones tested were the Maplin Lavaliere and the Knowles, 1759. Power supply and leads were custom made and adapted for use with the Sony TCD-D3 portable DAT recorder. Ultimately, we chose the Maplin microphones.

[8] The recordings were made on December 10th, 1993. Those present were John Barrable, Director of the New Media Centre, Portsmouth University; Richard Bennett, Research Associate Portsmouth University; Colin Denahay, Sound Engineer, Portsmouth University; Mark Prowse, Technology Resources Officer, The Royal National Institute for the Blind; Joanna Simpkins, Mobility Trainer, The Guide Dogs for the Blind Association; and Tim Young, Special Projects Officer, London Underground.

sighted and blind sound recordists, and to the recognition that the fixed head position would be both difficult and unnatural for the blind recordist. Table 1 following table gives the details of the full set.

Before the recording began, it was not clear how useful the recordings which did not use the fixed-head technique would be. On the one hand it allowed the blind recordist to act naturally, but the fear was that this natural recording would produce an idiosyncratic and uninterpretable acoustic record. We quickly discovered, however, that the technique in general, and the scheme used in Transit 5 to create the sound maps was very effective.

Transit	Recordist	Fixed Head ?	Route commentary
1	Sighted mobility trainer	Yes	By recordist
2	Blind and familiar with the route.	No	By recordist
3	Blind and familiar with the route.	No	By accompanying sighted mobility trainer
4	Sighted	Yes	By accompanying sighted mobility trainer
5	Blind and familiar with the route.	No	No

Table 1: Warren Street recording data form

The first indication of the success of the recording technique became apparent when the tapes were checked by the Research Team while still on location at Warren Street. Mark Prowse, who has been totally blind since childhood, recorded transits 2 and 5. On listening to the tape of transit 5, he observed with what can only be described as a fair degree of amazement that he had heard corners many times before, but that he had never expected to hear a recording of one. In other words, his acoustic experience of moving through a place had been captured on tape because the recording had also captured the way in which he moved his head to maximise the salience of the acoustic cues. Indeed, with regard to the overall experience of binaural sound reproduction, he described them as "home movies for the blind".

To gain further insight into the value of the recordings, they were presented to blind and partially sighted judges at Dorton College of Further Education in Sevenoaks, Kent which is a Royal London Institute for the Blind establishment.

Twenty-nine students were asked to listen to tapes from transits 1 and 2. The age range was 16-45, with a mean age of 27. 17 could be described as having moderate visual impairment, and 12 were severely impaired. Of the latter group, 5 had no sight at all.[9]

Several things emerged from this testing, and from the commentary of other blind subjects, and two in particular stand out. One is that all the judges felt that the tapes were very evocative and informative about the places in ways which related to their everyday experience.[10] However, as a second point they nevertheless felt that they could be better, and that the weaknesses in them did not seem to be tied to the general quality of the recording.

Our consideration of how this technique might be developed has lead us to the development of what we have called the "Sound Camera", and to the application of what is effectively a CT approach. In doing this, it becomes clear that technological concerns, narrowly considered, are only one part of the story.

TECHNOLOGY, COGNITIVE TECHNOLOGY AND MAP-MAKING

While the results of this work to date, including a further study by Huckett (1996), have provided clear support for the idea that binaural recordings can produce useful images of an environment there are many ways in which the technology and its application need refinement. To consider what these refinements might be, it is useful to consider how common every day maps, as used by the sighted, work as communicative device, and then to consider how the functional rather than the structural aspects of that communicative system might be made available to the blind.

Spatial maps for the sighted

The maps which sighted people use depend on many features both conventional and natural for their success. Clearly one needs the key on a British Ordnance Survey Map to know that a filled in black square with a cross coming out of the top is a church with a tower, and that a filled circle with a cross coming out of the top is a church with a spire. Equally, it is clear that there is a physical correspondence between the structure of the map in terms of features such as coastlines and roads, and the structure of the real world of roads and coastlines. Although even here, the

---

[9] By Richard Bennett on 28th February 1994

[10] It should be noted here that the potency of the tapes was greatly affected by the extent of a persons visual loss, and the time since the loss happened. Those who had been totally blind from birth found them to be most effective.

isomorphism it proposes depends on a convention as to which physical characteristics are important, and thus should be represented, and which are not. The means of representation do, in turn, depend on conventions, but equally they depend on a conventional notion of perspective or point of view, and a shared sensory domain between map-maker and map user which also links the world and the map. In other words, the visual map depends on both a degree of intersubjectivity between maker and user on the medium of representation and the world to which it relates, as well as a set of shared conventions.

Spatial maps for the blind

As noted above, one failure of many aids for the blind is that they seek to take a sighted understanding of space and provide a substitute for the blind person. Thus, tactile maps take a sighted persons representational system which depends on not only convention, but also a shared sensory world, and seeks to make the contours and features available through another medium. The promise of the sound maps we have created in this project resides not only in the technology of binaural recording, but also in the fact that it enables a map-making process for the blind user wherein there is again a shared sensory domain similar that shared by the maker and the user of visual maps.

We have yet to build on this promise in any substantial way, but a pathway ahead which links the technology to a series of human considerations now seems clear. Part of it depends on a number of technological developments, but part also depends on recognising how that technology will be configured, and be meaningful in its use by a community. To see what this might mean, the following four points should be taken into consideration.

1) To develop the mapping technique and assist the blind map-maker we are developing what we have termed the "Sound Camera". This is, perhaps, a rather overblown description of a binaural recording device which (a) allows the user to adjust the pickup of the headset microphones in a way which is analogous to the photographer's use of, for example, aperture and exposure settings; and (b) allows that user to playback and thus edit recordings which have just been made in a way which is akin to the video-camera's playback view and edit facility. However, the Sound Camera itself is in many ways less interesting than what it permits as the following points propose.

2) When we were initially concerned about allowing binaural recordings to be made by any arrangement other than a fixed head one, we were failing to pay attention to the fact that the blind person's head movements provide crucial variation which increases the value of acoustic cues, and that these movements are neither arbitrary nor idiosyncratic. They are tied to the physical events in question. Thus by having intelligent head movements the information value of the recording is increased.

To make this point clear, consider what recording one might get if a video camera were to be given to a blind person with the instruction to provide a helpful record of a place to a sighted person who might visit it. If that blind person decided that the best way of doing this was a fixed camera position, then we might get something useful for the sighted, but equally we might get some less than helpful shots of the ground. Our blind person would do much better if he or she recruited a sighted person to point the camera at scenes which would be helpful to the sighted visitor who wanted to find their way around. This leads to the third point.

3) If a user of the sound map knows that it has been created for their use by another blind person, then the recording takes on a different quality because the user knows that the acoustic material has been intentionally attended to by the map-maker who did the recording. In an important sense, allowing for this kind of choice to enter into the creation means that the map is elevated to a different plane. It is no longer simply informative with respect to the environment, but it is also a communicative device in the sense which Lyons (1972) proposed.

4) It is also the case that not only is the sensory environment of the acoustic map shared, but it, and its very features are now known to be shared by the blind who might use this system. This is a potentially very exciting feature of this technology. As Mark Prowse observed, he had never had chance before to listen to a corner. Previously, he had only had chance to hear one as he was in the process of negotiating his way through the world. Thus, with this system not only could he reflect on what he was hearing when listening to the tape, but he could also provide his particular version of it to someone else, and it could become an object of scrutiny allowing each to refine their judgements, and, one might presume their recording techniques if both were using the system.

Cognitive Technology

The last part of the previous section is, at the moment, based more on speculation than actual discovery. Nevertheless, it is not implausible, nor is it without its underpinnings. If one thinks of it in CT terms, then interestingly the emphasis is shifted from the technological to the cognitive, communicative and social. The design in contrast to pre-existing mobility aids for the blind, has been driven by a focus on the actual skills of the user community, and how the technology effectively creates a communicative link between them. Too often when using new technologies, and indeed when designing them, we forget that they constitute a communication between designer and user. In focusing on that communication, it is very easy to become focused on the physical details of some system to the detriment of our understanding of the functional characteristics which are needed, and the structure of the task domain. In this case we have tried to focus on the functional aspects and the characteristics of the users, and this has produced a quite technologically simple answer. Equally though, it might be said that the technology has taken on a complex character because of the ways in which it could become embedded in a social and communicative structure of map-making by blind people for blind people.

If that prospect of a group of blind map-makers is realised, then they would effectively be the creators and *designers* of the maps, and from the CT point of view it is interesting to note the importance of *design* and the *designer*. It is tempting to suggest that one part of the CT project could be usefully accomplished by understanding the role that designers have played in the production of other goods and services in modern industrial societies. It is an essential part of the acceptability and commercial success of those products that properly trained designers who are able to intimately understand the position of the consuming public are involved in their creation. This rarely happens with ICTs, and the classic elements of design education which involve understanding how to take a brief and exploit materials and technologies to create a desirable and useful product do not form part of the education of those who create products of this type.

In general, I would argue that anyone who takes the CT agenda seriously might well find this happens frequently. While it is given its special emphasis by the technological changes we have seen in computing and communication in recent years, its emphasis must be on technologically appropriate solutions, and these might not be technologically advanced ones.

CONCLUSION

In this chapter I have reported on a novel device which addresses the problems faced by blind people in negotiating novel spaces. Various technologically sophisticated schemes have been proposed to help the blind in such circumstances. These range from the use of GPS satellites combined with hand-held microcomputers so that the blind user can get an accurate fix on his or her location, to the use of fixed local radio beacons in an "intelligent environment" which can guide a blind person in a locally sensitive fashion. While there has been some limited success with these systems, they have yet to solve many difficult operational problems. Working from a perspective that is in accord with CT principles, I and my colleagues developed a radically different system through which the existing competence of blind people in interpreting acoustic spatial cues can be enhanced and exploited by enabling them to communicate with one another about their auditory experience of the environment.

This system was based on an important reconceptualisation of the problem. Traditionally, technology has been applied to helping the blind find their way around by assuming that the character of, and the facility provided by, a sighted person's conception of space was the ultimate target of any new device or aid. This assumption leads one to ignore the fact that blind people are often much more adept at navigating a space they know, than one they do not because they are able to use various acoustic cues to guide themselves. Consequently, it appeared appropriate to focus our energies on finding technologies which would allow that acoustic knowledge and experience to be communicated by one blind person to another.

The solution we have proposed relies on the technique of binaural recording with the addition of certain important additional elements. It enables one blind person who knows a place to effectively "draw an acoustic map" of it in line with their auditory experience. This map is of use to another blind person before he or she encounters that place for the first time. The idea of a map is being exploited in this work by reference to its functional rather than physical characteristics, a move which nevertheless acknowledges that the importance of a map lies in its physical characteristics in relation to shared sensory experiences.

The emphasis, therefore, became one of using the technology to facilitate communication between those who share a particular sensory world, thereby, avoiding the biases which the sighted usually bring to the solution of this problem. Initially, this solution was remarkably simple in the technology it required. However, in turn it can be capitalised on in novel ways by the exploitation of various other new technologies. In this exploitation, it is likely that the kinds of acoustic map which can be used in systems for sighted people to enhance their experiences of virtual spaces.

This example provides many important lessons for how a CT agenda should be pursued in the development of new technologies that are sensitive to human needs and abilities, and can yet extend those abilities by fostering novel means of communication

REFERENCES

Blauert, J., 1983. *Spatial Hearing: The psychophysics of human sound localisation.* Cambridge, Massachusetts: MIT Press.

Dodds, A., 1993. *Rehabilitating Blind and Visually Impaired People.* London: Chapman and Hall.

Huckett, E., 1996. *Architecture Revealed through Sound: A Study of Space through Acoustic Spatial Maps.* Diploma Dissertation, Department of Architecture, University of Cambridge.

Hull, J., 1990. *Touching the Rock.* London: Arrow Books.

Lyons, J., 1972. Human Language. In Robert Hinde, ed., *Non-Verbal Communication.* Cambrdige: Cambridge University Press.

McAdams, S. and E. Bigand, 1994. *Thinking in Sound: The Cognitive Psychology of Human Audition.* Oxford: Clarendon Press

MacEachren, A., 1995. *How Maps Work: Representation, Visualization and Design.* New York: The Guilford Press.

Moore, B. C. J., 1997. *An Introduction to the Psychology of Hearing.* London: Academic Press.

Ungar, S., M. Blades, and C. Spencer, 1997. The Use of Tactile Maps to Aid Navigation by Blind and Visually Impaired People in Unfamiliar Urban Environments. *Proceedings of the Royal Institute of Navigation, Orientation and Navigation Conference* 1997, Oxford; Royal Institute of Navigation. Available at http://fhis.gcal.ac.uk/PSY/sun/INTACT/Papers/Ungar2.html

Wood, D., and John Fels, 1986. Designs on signs: Myth and meaning in maps. *Cartographica* 23(3), pp. 54-103

Wood, D., and John Fels, 1993. *The Power Of Maps* London: Routledge, c1993.

Humane Interfaces: Questions of method and
practice in Cognitive Technology
J.P. Marsh, B. Gorayska and J.L. Mey (Editors)

Chapter 14

BETWEEN THE IDEA AND THE REALITY... THE CASE FOR QUALITATIVE RESEARCH IN EDUCATION[1]

Ian Hart

The University of Hong Kong

Between the idea
And the reality
Between the motion
And the act
Falls the shadow
T.S.Eliot "The Hollow Men"

Do you think it is drawing too long a semiotic bow to suggest that "the shadow" might signify the outer darkness into which academic "hollow men" are cast by the gatekeepers of university life if they do not produce "the right kind of research"? You do? Read on...

DATA: RESEARCH BIAS

There is little doubt that quantification rules the roost in the hen house of educational research. Qualitative data, if it is considered at all, is viewed as a decorative addition to "flesh out" the impersonal figures, but not something on which we can base conclusions. Ph.D. supervisors warn students away from qualitative research methods fearing that the approach might lead to a lack of rigour. And words like "soft" (qualitative) as opposed to "hard" (quantitative) carry loaded meanings. Reeves (1995) has demonstrated the bias towards empirical/theoretical goals and quantitative methods in articles accepted by the leading reviewed Educational Technology journals. For example,
Table 1 analyses the 104 papers published in the influential journal *Educational Technology Research and Development* over a five year period in terms of research goals and methods.

---

[1] A draft version of this chapter first appeared on the Internet discussion group ITForum, March 1997.

Research goals		Research methods	
Empirical	48	Quantitative	39
Theoretical	31	Qualitative	7
Interpretivist	1	Critical Theory	0
Postmodern	0	Literature Review	38
Developmental	6	Mixed Methods	11
Evaluation	9		
Other	9	Other	9

Table 1. Analysis of articles in ETR&D 1989-94 (Reeves, 1995)

DATA: LETTER FROM GRANDMOTHER

My grandmother sent me a newspaper clipping in which it is reported that a gentleman from California taught half his class using lectures and tutorials and the other half using the Internet: on the final test the students on the Internet course did better than the classroom group. I think there was a number somewhere, which proved this. "You must be so pleased, dear," wrote grandma, "to know that you have finally been proved right." okay, I confess, I've been delivering course material via the Internet since 1994 but until now it has been a guilty secret between me and the students, and because they said they liked it I kept going in spite of the conflicting research evidence (see below). (By the way, granny asked me to thank the nice California man for his Christmas present of a laser-driven virtual egg-sucker, "The piano doesn't wobble now," she says.)

DATA: Educational technology research

For the past 50 years research into the effectiveness of media in teaching as been driven by quantitative, positivist paradigms in which learning from mediated instruction was compared to "conventional" classroom methods. The results of this research can be summed up in three words: *No significant difference*. Russell (1995) quotes 248 research reports from 1928 to 1995, which reached the ubiquitous "NSD" conclusion. Russell is by no means the first to have pointed out this phenomenon:

- Mielke (1968) in *Educational Broadcasting Review* predicted that research on the learning benefits of various media would yield no significant difference between them.
- Lumsdaine (1963) and Levie & Dickie (1973) took the same positions in the first two editions of the *Handbook of Research on Teaching*.

- Schramm (1977) in a comprehensive meta-analysis of research in educational technology concluded that learning is influenced more by the content and instructional strategy than by the qualities of the medium.
- Clark (1983: 445) writing in the *Review of Educational Research* claimed that on the evidence from 30 years of research, the media are "mere vehicles that deliver instruction but do not influence student achievement any more than the truck that delivers our groceries changes our nutrition".

Why, given all this counter-evidence, is research on media so persistent? Reeves (1996) believes that: (1) it is easy to do, conducted as it is under controlled circumstances far removed from the rough and tumble world of actual education and training; (2) it is easily published, and the need to "publish or perish" is what drives the research agendas of far too many academics; (3) on the surface, it appears to have utility to practitioners anxious for answers to questions such as should we invest in televisions or computers for our schools or training centres? But ultimately, research on media has proven to be an infinitely branching path. Even if we could find reliable relationships between different media and different outcomes, no less an authority than Lee J. Cronbach (1982) has illustrated that we will never pile up generalisations from these studies fast enough to have a meaningful influence on the actual practice of teaching and learning. "As socially responsible researchers, we need to pay far more attention to the complexity of learning rather than trying to oversimplify it for the sake of our analytic research methodologies" (Reeves, 1996).

Jonassen, Campbell & Davidson (1994) propose that we should cease to be concerned about the question of learning *from* media; a more productive field of enquiry is learning *with* media.

> "We believe that excessive effort has been expended for the past decade... arguing the wrong issue. We recommend restructuring the debate to focus not on the role of media as conveyors and deliverers of the designer's message to a stationary learner at the end of instruction, but rather on how media, however defined, can be used to facilitate knowledge-construction and meaning-making on the part of the learner. Questions about the role of media should focus on the effects of learners' cognitions with technology as opposed to the effects of technology."   (Jonassen, Campbell and Davidson, 1994: 35)

If we accept Jonassen's argument, we need to consider a style of research, which explores and describes what is going on in the complex interactions between student characteristics, media forms, content, context and cognition. Single-variable media comparison studies are simply not adequate to the task, they are in Kozma's (1994: 10) view, rather like examining the effects of a tornado by taking photographs before and after the event: "the photographs enable us to assess the extent of the damage but not the process by which the damage was wrought."

MEMO: THE SUBSTANCE

This essay is not a polemic in praise of humanistic, ethnographic, holistic, phenomenographic, artistic, warm and fuzzy, trendy, "soft" or postmodern research methods: my purpose here is to make a case for widening the field of view and considering non-quantitative methods as an indispensable monkey-wrench in the research toolbox; and to demonstrate that the outcomes of qualitative investigation can be equally productive, though often differently valid, to the selective, positivist, analytico-deductive, scientific, statistical research methods sanctioned by the gatekeepers of our discipline.

DATA: DEFINITIONS

Let us agree, first of all, that the terms "quantitative" and "qualitative" are ambiguous: they are commonly used for both the contrasting paradigms and the methods associated with them. However the contrasting paradigms could equally well employ either or both quantitative and qualitative methods. Although adherents of the quantitative paradigm are more likely to use experimental and quasi-experimental tools, while qualitative researchers are more likely to employ more descriptive techniques. (Fetterman, 1988)

Salomon (1993) contrasts "analytic" and "systemic" approaches to research design. The goal of analytic research is to manipulate and control situations so as to increase internal validity and isolate specific causal mechanisms and processes; whereas systemic research is based on the assumption that "each event, component, or action in the classroom has the potential of affecting the classroom as a whole." He proposed that ethnographic or naturalistic methods, such as long-term observation, interviews and artefact analysis provide a richness of detail about the social processes within which cognition is embedded.

The two approaches are by no means exclusive: they can co-exist perfectly well and the methodologies can complement one-another.

CASE STUDY 1: RACE, MEMORY AND CULTURE

An article in the *Australian Journal of Psychology* by Kearins (1986) reports an investigation of Lockard's (1971) hypothesis that human populations are shaped by natural selection to fit a particular ecological niche. Why is it, asked Lockard, that Aboriginal people do so poorly on IQ tests, yet possess such remarkable survival skills? Perhaps there are different, genetically determined patterns of intelligence.

Kearins first conducted a series of carefully controlled experiments to establish whether the IQ hypothesis was valid. She used a standardised "visual memory test" in which groups of suburban European and Western Desert Aboriginal children were given 30 seconds to memorise a set of objects presented on a tray, then to recall them: the Aboriginal children scored significantly worse at this test than the Europeans. She then administered a set of "spatial relocation tests" in which objects which could not always be differentiated by name (rocks, leaves, twigs) were arranged on a grid and presented for 30 seconds; they were then disarrayed and the children were asked to replace them in the original positions. The Aboriginal children scored significantly better than the Europeans at these tasks. Her studies confirmed Lockhard's hypothesis that the Aboriginal children had differently developed visual memory skills, but the statistically significant results provided no clues to the underlying causes of the difference.

Kearins notes Rowe's (1985: 10) observation that, "Intelligence does not operate in a vacuum... if our assessment of intelligence is to increase in validity... we shall have to observe the individual's functioning in real life, rather than in a laboratory or in a standardised testing situation".

Kearins recognised that there are serious methodological problems in trying to conduct experimental studies in a cross-cultural situation. Her follow-up research used a more ethnographic methodology, consisting of long-term observation, interviews with teachers, and artefact collection. The outcomes of these studies were even more fascinating: e.g. she observed that Aboriginal babies' heads are not supported when they are carried, forcing them to develop their neck muscles, and consequently their visual acuity, much earlier than European children; additionally, Aboriginal value systems have little or no sense of "ownership" and the memorisation of objects by name is of far less importance to Aboriginal than to European children, whereas the need to observe and memorise spatial relationships in a desert landscape is an essential navigation skill.

Most fascinating of all is her observation that "White children who performed well on the visual spatial memory test were... derogated by teachers, who considered them lazy, inattentive underachievers - views *not supported by school records*. It is possible that their cognitive strategies did not fit teacher expectations..." (Kearins, 1985: 212) (my emphasis). A totally unpredicted outcome, and a dramatic insight into the ecological nature of schooling, which requires further research.

Kearins' work is an example of the complexity, which arises once you begin to delve into what Schon (1987) described as the "slimy swamp... of real-life problems of the classroom eco-system". And such complexity does not sit comfortably with those who search for simple, definitive answers within what Biggs (1995: 50) termed "the whistle-clean, four-square symmetry of the psycho-lab".

DATA: LAB VS. LIFE

The "laboratory vs. life" debate is controversial in the social sciences, particularly psychology, a discipline which has long craved scientific respectability. Neisser (1978) writing in *Practical Aspects of Memory* (a precursor to the educational technology debate provoked by Clark's 1983 article) attacked the laboratory approach that emphasises internal validity over external validity, charging that nothing interesting or important had resulted from roughly 100 years of effort in the laboratory. Ten years later, Banaji & Crowder (1989: 1192) were still arguing that "the more complex a phenomenon, the greater need to study it under controlled conditions, and the less it ought to be studied in its natural complexity".

MEMO: OBJECTIVISM VS. REALISM

The fundamental difference between quantitative and qualitative positions is based on philosophical and epistemological, not methodological, grounds. The paradigms are derived from the philosophical positions of positivism/objectivism on the one hand and phenomenology on the other. Typically, positivists search for social facts apart from the subjective perceptions of individuals; by contrast phenomenologically oriented researchers seek to understand human behaviour from the "insider's" perspective. A qualitative researcher argues that what people believe to be true is more important than any objective reality (Fetterman, 1988).

Lakoff (1987) makes the following distinction:

"Scientific objectivism claims that there is only one fully correct way in which reality can correctly be divided up into objects, properties, and relations. Accordingly, the correct choice of objects is not a matter of a choice of conceptual schemes: there is only one correct way to understand reality in terms of objects and categories of objects. Scientific realism on the other hand, assumes that "the world is the way it is," while acknowledging that there can be more than one scientifically correct way of understanding reality in terms of conceptual schemes with different objects and categories of objects."

(Lakoff, 1987:265)

CASE STUDY 2: DRIED FISH

My colleague Dr. Daniel Lam Tai-pong, of the University of Hong Kong's General Practice Unit, is researching the health and lifestyle beliefs of the Hong Kong fishing community, who share a strong ethnic identity. They call themselves *séui seuhng yàhn* in Cantonese, meaning "people who live on the water" and are thought to be the original inhabitants of these islands.

Epidemiological studies have clearly demonstrated a link between the consumption of dried fish and naso-pharyngeal cancer and Hong Kong has abnormally high levels of this form of cancer due to the popularity of the food in the southern, coastal diet. This link could only have been established by using large statistical samples and sophisticated quantitative methods. Since the link became widely known, dried fish consumption and naso-pharyngeal cancer has begun to fall – everywhere but in the tightly knit fishing community.

In his harbour-side clinic Dr. Lam is conducting open-ended interviews with fishing families to see how lifestyle factors contribute to health problems. He has found that the *séui seuhng yàhn* are quite aware of the link between their traditional food and cancer, but they attribute it to the commercial drying process "which uses chemicals"; in contrast to their own "natural" product, which they continue to consume with confidence. (Unfortunately this is not true as the carcinogen is related to the drying process.) But they justify their "traditional" lifestyle choice by quoting the slogans of the health food lobby. People act on what they believe.

MEMO: PERSONAL REMINISCENCES

My approach to research could also be described as a "lifestyle choice" based on my own background and beliefs. I have worked for over 20 years as a documentary film maker: the highly subjective and most unscientific art of recording, structuring and interpreting other people's lives on film and videotape. My heroes were Dziga-Vertov, Robert Flaherty, Jean Rouche, Fred Wiseman, the Maysles bros., Claude Levy-Strauss...

When I gave up full-time film-making in the late 1970s to work in a university, which required me to do research into educational technology, I stood aghast before the body of media comparison studies which uniformly regard the central participant in the learning process, the learner, as no more than a "black box." I wrote a rather bitter polemic about it (Hart, 1982) in the *Journal of Educational Television* (still quoted back to me at conferences as a source of embarrassment.) But at the time, I recall seeing Richard Clark's (1983) notorious trucks and nutrition metaphor as a personal vindication of my position.

DATA: DEALING WITH DATA

For qualitative researchers, data is the fundamental matter from which everything is derived: the ideas and the theories emerge from the data – in contrast to positivist research, where the data is a means of testing the hypothesis. Quantitative researchers work within a structured environment and refine their data down to a representative abstraction such as a number or a graph; by contrast a qualitative researcher seeks to remain as close to his data as possible all the way through the research process. The original data should still be recognisable in the final report.

The most manageable form of qualitative data is text. e.g., transcripts of interviews, records of discussions, historical or literary documents, field notes, newspaper clippings, reports, etc. But data can also be non-textual, e.g., photographs, videotapes, musical recordings or scores, artefacts, etc. It is subjective and unstructured and requires the researcher using or developing indexing systems in order to manage it.

Qualitative research involves the development of ideas about the data and exploration of these ideas. This involves developing a system of categorisation and linking these categories in ways, which describe the data. Theories are constructed and tested by exploring their links with data.

MEMO: VALIDITY & INTERPRETATION

According to Richards (1992), the test of the ultimate conclusion is to see how elegantly and methodically the evidence was shaped into the conclusion, how the conclusion was coaxed (never forced) to "emerge" from the data, "how evidence and grand account form a well-connected, seamless web of belief that illuminates and enriches our perceptions and understanding of phenomena we see every day. To be credible, the report must show these processes in action, and demonstrate how the conclusions were reached."

So, in the best Postmodern tradition (if that is not an oxymoron), this essay is presented as a set of "unstructured" blocks which you, the reader, are invited to make sense of in your own subjective and qualitative fashion.

DATA: CONSTRUCTIVISM – A QUALITATIVE VIEW OF COGNITION

Cole (1990) distinguished what she called the quantitative and qualitative traditions in our educational thinking. Those with a quantitative outlook see learning as the aggregation of content: to be a good learner is to know more. The contents of learning are treated as discrete quanta or destructured units of declarative or procedural knowledge, any one unit being functionally independent of any other. This is the common lay view of learning, where intelligence is equated with memory for facts. And unfortunately, as Shepherd (1991) points out, it is also a view espoused by many professional educators, particularly by educational evaluators responsible for central curricula and external examinations.

Those with a qualitative outlook see meaning as the focus of a learning episode. Learning the meaning of an event, topic or phenomenon is a holistic activity. It is not achieved by learning piecemeal, however accurately, the units constituting the object of learning. Further, the learner acquires a progressively more complex knowledge base, and as the knowledge base is used to construct meaning, meanings change with experience. The learner's comprehension of taught content is therefore "more like climbing a spiral staircase than dropping marbles into a bag, with qualitative changes taking place in the nature both of what is learned and how it is structured at each level in the spiral." (Biggs, 1995)

The family of teaching and learning theories based on qualitative assumptions is known as *constructivism* which is a perspective on learning emphasising that: (1) knowledge is actively constructed by people for themselves, not absorbed from outside like a sponge absorbs water, and (2) the frameworks used to construct and interpret knowledge come from social interaction, rather than direct instruction.

Constructivism has enjoyed a recent surge of popularity, but it is by no means a new theory. Bruner (1986) postulated that constructivism began with Kant, who in his *Critique of Pure Reason* (1952) argued for *a priori* knowledge that preceded all reasoning. It is what we know, and we map onto it *a posteriori* knowledge, which is gained from our perceptual interactions with the environment. What we know as individuals is what the mind produces. Kant believed in the external, physical world but says that it is known only through our sensations — how the world appears to us.

From the viewpoint of constructivism, thinking is grounded in the perception of physical and social experiences, which can only be comprehended by the mind. What the mind produces are mental models that explain to the knower what he or she has perceived. According to Kant, rather than being driven by external structures, these mental models are *a priori*.

The influence of thinkers such as John Dewey, Jean Piaget, Lev Vygotsky and Jerome Bruner has been profound in reshaping our view of education as active engagement rather than passive reception of given knowledge. According to Laurillard (1993: 15) although active engagement with learning is increasingly evident in K-12 curricula, the idea of knowledge as an abstract Platonic form still lives on in many universities and has been given encouragement by information processing models of cognition "which use the metaphor of knowledge structures or conceptual structures in order to describe mentalistic entities that can be changed through instruction or even represented in a computer program.".

By contrast, the now accepted view of cognition as situated stems from the Vygotskyan view of the social character of learning (Vygotsky, 1978). The learner is seen as located in a certain situation and what is known from that experience is known in relation only to that context:

> "We should abandon once and for all any notion that a concept is some sort of abstract, self-contained substance. Instead, it may be more useful to consider conceptual knowledge as in some ways similar to a set of tools."
>
> (Brown, Collins, & Duguid, 1989:5)

We can view learning then, as a process of acquiring what Piaget termed "cognitive complexity" whereby the learner develops a mental structure made up of links between different types of knowledge (declarative, procedural, contextual, structural) as a prerequisite to cognitive construction, or the creation of new knowledge (Piaget, 1987).

This constructivist view of learning is neatly summed up in two of Minsky's (1986) pithy *Principles*:

> ***Papert's Principle:*** Some of the most crucial steps in mental growth are based not simply on acquiring new skills, but on acquiring new administrative ways to use what one already knows.   (Minsky 1986: 102)

This principle is particularly relevant to the development of knowledge structures as a child, but as one grows one develops a considerable baggage of acquired knowledge and structure which needs to be overcome:

> ***The Investment Principle:*** Our oldest ideas have unfair advantages over those that come later. The earlier we learn a skill, the more methods we can acquire

for using it. Each new idea must then compete against the larger mass of skills the old ideas have accumulated.   (Minsky, 1986: 146)

We can observe the Investment Principle at work in the following case study as students struggle to reconcile their acquired knowledge and skills in design with the novel demands of a computing environment.

CASE STUDY 3: LEARNERS AS DESIGNERS

In 1993 I was invited to collaborate on a research project to establish whether a constructivist, problem-based approach to the teaching of Architecture was as valid as the conventional lecture-assignment method. Validation of teaching methods is important for professional accreditation and a controlled study was required to establish this.

It was first proposed by the accrediting body that we divide the class into two: one half would take the lectures, the other half would work collaboratively in the computer lab... (sounds familiar?). Thankfully, the Architecture Department accepted my argument that this neo-scientific paradigm had been discredited for over 10 years and there were other, equally sound, methods of validating the new curriculum. Why not use Action Research, I suggested, which is widely accepted in other disciplines? So, for my pains, I was given the direction of the project.

The course we chose was 'Building Systems', which covers issues of construction materials, maintenance and management. Students worked collaboratively on real-life problems that required them to build three-dimensional computer models of buildings. They had to master very complex modelling software on SGI workstations and to apply it to existing structures in Hong Kong. Their final presentation was to be a multimedia report explaining these issues to others.[2]

We began with the methodology of the documentary film maker: record everything with as few preconceptions as possible, then try to make sense of the data through reflection at the "editing" stage. To accomplish this we rigged up a video splitting device which enabled us to record both the student at work and the computer screen they were working (Figure 1); we conducted regular interviews with the students, individually and in groups; we gave them standardised tests; we asked them to draw concept maps; we generated multidimensional scales in the form of Pathfinder Nets; and we systematically collected their sketches and

---

[2] The resulting student projects from this and following years can be viewed on the WWW at: http://arch.hku.hk/projects/bsys1/buildingServices/servicemenu/mainmenu.html

storyboards. We also provided feedback – both to the teaching staff and to the students themselves – according to the action research "spiral" model (act → observe → reflect → act... etc.).

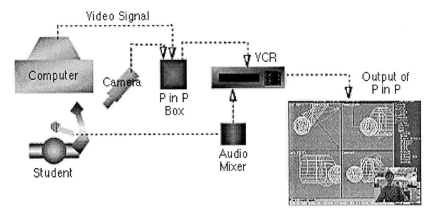

Figure 1. Connection diagram for video observation system

DATA: MENTAL MODELS

At an early stage in the project it became evident that many students were having problems with visualising the relationship between their files, the workstation and the server. We asked them to draw a picture of this relationship and indicate where their files resided in relationship to their terminal, other people's terminals, the LAN (Architecture Laboratory network) and the SGI server, which resided in the technician's office.

Figure 2 shows four of these mental models. Figure 2a is a reasonably accurate hierarchical model of the file structure produced by one of the group leaders, indicating that she had a clear picture of how files were organised on the server; Figure 2b is an architectural style of drawing showing five workstations and the links between them, the hidden computer network is described as being "like bamboo structure underground"; Figure 2c is a picture of the SGI screen when the student first turns on the computer; and Figure 2d is a whimsical attempt to anthropomorphize the computer into a representation of a human brain, complete with eyes (the files are located in the left frontal lobe!)

DATA: PATHFINDER NETS

A more or less iterative method of testing theories arising from qualitative data is to feed them back to the learners using instruments such as multidimensional scales. Figure 3 illustrates four contrasting Pathfinder networks (PFNets) derived from semantic association tests in which subjects were asked to rank the "relatedness" of pairs of concepts which had been identified as significant. The result is a graphic representation of the subject's concept map of the eleven terms. Multidimensional Scaling and PFNets are techniques more commonly used in

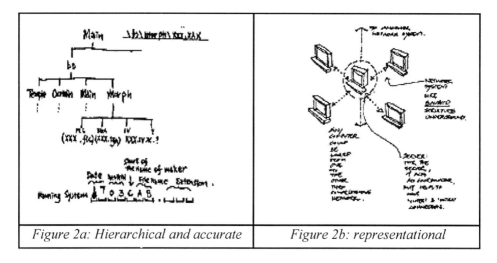

| *Figure 2a: Hierarchical and accurate* | *Figure 2b: representational* |

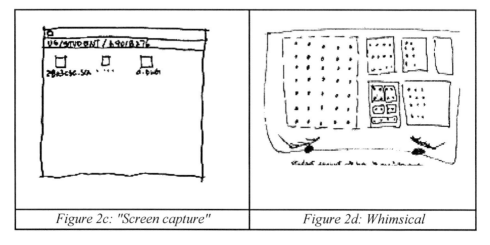

| *Figure 2c: "Screen capture"* | *Figure 2d: Whimsical* |

Figure 2. Mental models of network structure

market research than learning research, but it proved to be a valuable tool, particularly when followed up by an interview in which the student was asked to interpret the resulting "network". (For a more detailed explanation of PFNets, see Schvaneveldt (1990)).

The 11 concepts compared were: **me, my group, computer, software, presentation, calculation, modelling, creative, research, learning**, and **memory**. Students ranked each pair of words (11 words produce 55 pairs) in terms of their relatedness. The software used to produce the nets was KNOT[3].

The four patterns show a progression of relatedness of concepts. In 3a all concepts are related equally, indicating either an excessively deep approach or the student's inability to make up her mind; in 3b everything is related to one central concept, in this case *computing*; 3c shows a well-structured branching pattern in which "personal" concepts (*me, learning, creativity*, etc.) are linked to computing concepts through the *presentation*; 3d is from a student who displayed a predominantly surface approach to learning: the single linking concept here is *memory* , and note that *research* is at the maximum distance from *learning*. (Hart, 1996)

MEMO: AFFORDANCES OF COMPUTERS

Ellul (1964) divided technologies into two classes in terms of their afforded use: machines that work for us and tools with which we work. "The lever, the watch, and the automatic pilot work for us; the pencil, the hoe, the microscope, the camera, the slide rule require that we work with them; they do little without our active participation." (p.16) To this latter category, developed in the 60s, we could add the word processor, the CAD package and the database. "Machines with which we work" are relevant to the learning environment in this study, for these machines (unlike the ones that work for us) afford an "intellectual partnership in which results greatly depend on joint effort." (Salomon, Perkins, & Globerson, 1991) In this study computers are cognitive tools for both the students (building 3D interactive models) and the researchers (analysing data; testing theories).

DATA: ANALYSIS

The rich but unstructured data from this study was indexed and analysed using NUD*IST[4], a sophisticated and flexible qualitative research tool developed by Lynn and Tom Richards at LaTrobe University in Melbourne. This too was a

---

[3] KNOT is available from Interlink Inc. P.O. Box 4086 UPB, Las Cruces, NM, 88003-4086.

[4] NUD*IST (Non-numeric, Unstructured Data - Indexing, Searching & Theorizing), is a flexible computer tool for Mac and Windows published by Qualitative Solutions & Research Pty. Ltd., 2 Research Avenue, La Trobe University, Vic. Australia 3083. Version 4.0 was released in 1997.

cyclic process: the indexing classifications were first developed using a grounded theory approach and were then fed back into our research methodology and further refined by an iterative process. This was managed with the assistance of NUD*IST's flexibility and memo facility.

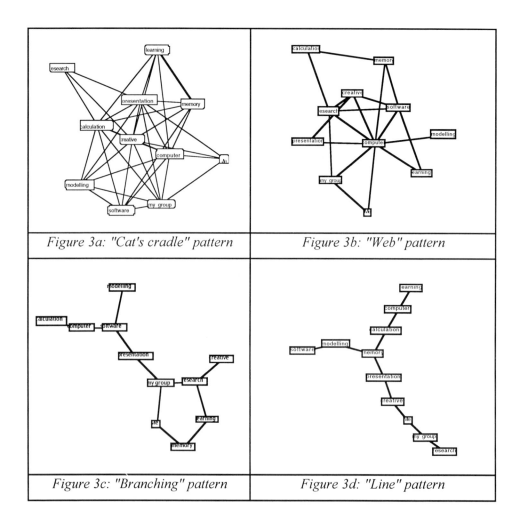

Figure 3a: "Cat's cradle" pattern

Figure 3b: "Web" pattern

Figure 3c: "Branching" pattern

Figure 3d: "Line" pattern

Figure 3. Sample PFNets

The project ran for 18 months. Not surprisingly, we did not feel able to conclude there was "no significant difference" between the old lecture method and the project method – although this was what the accreditation body may have wanted to hear. We concluded that the course was a substantial improvement on the lecture method and were able to demonstrate that:

- the problem-based, computer-intensive curriculum promoted a "deep" approach to learning,
- students valued the situated nature of the task,
- for the more successful students, the computer system was a cognitive tool, which they manipulated consciously, and
- the outcomes (the projects) demonstrated the development of complex cognitive constructions

We were also able to point to aspects of learning which needed to be more strongly reinforced, such as:

- metacognition,
- distributed cognition, and
- contextual (in contrast to declarative and procedural) knowledge. (Hart, 1996)

MEMO: SCIENCE AND ART

Isaac Asimov, in his great "Foundation" series of novels (1951-1953) describes the ultimate quantitative science of "psychohistory" which employs statistical methods to predict the future of the galaxy for a thousand years and build a "Foundation" on a distant planet which would eventually be ready to step in and save humanity from itself. Throughout the first two novels it appears to work remarkably smoothly, but in the final episode it is revealed that a secret "Second Foundation" of powerful thinkers, poets and philosophers has been in the background all the time to nudge things back on track when the mathematics of psychohistory went astray.

THEORY: TO BE TESTED USING THE DATA

If it is the purpose of Science to *explain* the world, it is the job of poets and philosophers (and qualitative researchers) to help us to see it more clearly for ourselves – the better to appreciate its ecological complexity.

And the end of all our exploring
Will be to arrive where we started
And know the place for the first time
         - T.S.Eliot "Four Quartets" Little Gidding

REFERENCES

Asimov, I., 1951-1953. *The Foundation Trilogy* (Foundation, Foundation and Empire, Second Foundation). London: Panther Books.

Banaji, M. R., & R. G. Crowder, 1989. The bankruptcy of everyday memory. *American Psychologist*, 44, pp. 1185-1193.

Biggs, J., 1995. Quality in education: A perspective from learning research and theory. In P.-k. Siu & T.-k. P. Tam. eds, *Quality in education: Insights from different perspectives*, Hong Kong: Hong Kong Educational Research Association, pp. 50-69

Brown, J. S., A. Collins, & P. Duguid, 1989. Situated cognition and the culture of learning. *Educational Researcher*, 18(1), pp. 32-41.

Bruner, J., 1986. *Actual minds, possible worlds*. Cambridge, MA: Harvard University Press.

Clark, R. E., 1983. Reconsidering research on learning from media. *Review of Educational Research*, 53(4), pp. 445-459.

Cole, N. S., 1990. Conceptions of educational achievement. *Educational Researcher*, 19(3), pp. 2-7.

Cronbach, L. J., 1982. *Designing evaluations of educational and social programs*. San Francisco, CA: Jossey-Bass.

Ellul, J., 1964. *The technological society*. New York: Alfred A. Knopf.

Fetterman, D. M., 1988. A qualitative shift of allegiance. In D. M. Fetterman, ed., *Qualitative approaches to evaluation in education* . New York: Praeger.

Hart, I., 1982. Educational television: The gulf between researchers and producers. *Journal of Educational Television*, 8(2), pp. 91-98.

Hart, I., 1996. *Learners as designers: computers as cognitive tools in architectire education*. Unpublished Ph.D., University of Wollongong, Wollongong, NSW.

Jonassen, D. H., J. P. Campbell, & M. E. Davidson, 1994. Learning with media: Restructuring the debate. *Educational Technology Research & Development*, 422, pp. 31-39.

Kant, I., 1952. *Critique of pure reason*, translated by Norman Kemp Smith, London, Macmillan

Kearins, J., 1986. Visual spatial memory in Aboriginal and white Australian children. *Australian Journal of Psychology*, 38(3), pp. 203-214.

Kozma, R. B., 1994. Will media influence learning? Reframing the debate. *Educational Technology Research & Development*, 42(2), pp. 7-19.

Lakoff, G., 1987. *Women, fire and dangerous things: What categories reveal about the mind*. Chicago: University of Chicago Press.

Laurillard, D., 1993. *Rethinking university teaching: A framework for the effective use of educational technology*. London: Routledge.

Levie, W. H., & Dickie, K. E., 1973. The analysis and application of media. In R. M. W. Travers, ed., *Second handbook of research on teaching*. Chicago, IL: Rand McNally.

Lockhard, R. B., 1971. Reflections on the fall of comparative psychology - is there a message for us all? *American Psychologist*, 26, pp. 168-179.

Lumsdaine, A. A., 1963. Instruments and media of instruction. In N. Gage. ed., *Handbook of research on teaching* . Chicago, IL: Rand McNally.

Mielke, K. W., 1968. Questioning the questions of ETV research. *Educational Broadcasting Review*, 2, pp. 6-15.

Minsky, M., 1986. *The society of mind.* New York, NY: Simon & Schuster.

Neisser, U., 1978. Memory: what are the important questions? In M. M. Gruneberg, P. E. Morris, & R. N. Sykes, eds, *Practical aspects of memory.* San Diego, CA: Academic Press, pp. 3-24.

Piaget, J., 1987. *Possibility and necessity. Vol 1: The role of possibility in cognitive development.* Minneapolis, MN: University of Minnesota Press.

Reeves, T. C., 1995. Questioning the questions of instructional technology research. *Paper presented at the Annual Conference of the Association for Educational Communications and Technology,* Anaheim, CA.

Reeves, T. C., 1996. The "Research on Media" monster lives again! Internet mailing list: *ITForum.* Address: ITFORUM@uga.cc.uga.edu. University of Georgia

Richards, T., & L. Richards, 1992. Qualitative computing: making data work. *Paper presented at the International Conference of the Australian Evaluation Society,* Melbourne.

Rowe, H., 1985. 17-18 October. So intelligence tests don't work. *Paper presented at the First Australian Conference on Testing and Assessment of Ethnic Minority Groups,* Darwin.

Russell, T. L., 1995. *The "No Significant Difference" Phenomenon (4th Ed.).* WWW Site: http://tenb.mta.ca/phenom/phenom.html. USA. Office of Instructional Telecommunications, North Carolina State University.

Salomon, G., ed., 1993. *Distributed cognitions: Psychological and educational considerations.* New York: Cambridge University Press.

Salomon, G., D. N. Perkins, & T. Globerson, 1991. Partners in cognition: Extending human intelligence with intelligent technologies. *Educational Researcher,* 20(3), pp. 2-9.

Schon, D. A., 1987. *Educating the reflective practitioner: Towards a new design for teaching and learning in the professions.* San Francisco, CA: Jossey-Bass.

Schramm, W., 1977. *Big media, little media.* Beverley Hills: Sage.

Schvaneveldt, R., ed., 1990. *Pathfinder associative networks: Studies in knowledge organization.* Norwood, NJ: Ablex.

Shepherd, L. A., 1991. Psychometricians' beliefs about learning. *Educational Researcher,* 20(6), pp. 2-16.

Vygotsky, L. S., 1978. *Mind in society: the development of higher psychological processes.* Cambridge, MA: Harvard University Press.

Humane Interfaces: Questions of method and
practice in Cognitive Technology
J.P. Marsh, B. Gorayska and J.L. Mey (Editors)
© 1999 Elsevier Science B.V. All rights reserved.

Chapter 15

COMPUTER ENVIRONMENTS DESIGNED TO PROMOTE COGNITIVE CHANGE THROUGH THE DEVELOPMENT OF WELL REASONED RECOMMENDATIONS

Alex Kass and Joe Herman

Institute for the Learning Sciences
Northwestern University

INTRODUCTION: WHEN THE COGNITIVE "SIDE-EFFECTS" ARE REALLY THE MAIN EVENT

The emerging field of Cognitive Technology highlights the cognitive effects that interactive systems have on those who use them. An interactive system can help users perform better than they could unaided, but it can also, often unintentionally, pressure users to think about the task differently, and often in ways that are less natural and less desirable. If insufficient attention is given to the cognitive ergonomics of an interactive system it can cause cognitive strain, stunting, or maladaption in the same way that improper use of a keyboard can lead to carpal tunnel syndrome. It is, therefore, important for cognitive technologists to discover techniques and principles to allow designers to predict and control the cognitive influence that interactive systems will have on their users.

While much of the focus of human factors research is about the unintended cognitive side effects, there is another side to this issue of cognitive influence which should not be overlooked. Cognitive influence is not always an unintended side effect of some other activity: What about the times when we *want* the use of computer programs to change the way people think? For example, modification of cognition is the primary *desired* effect of an educational activity. In computer-based learning-by-doing environments the role of the main effects and side effects are exactly the reverse of most interactive software: The user (the student) works to accomplish a task in a computer-based environment which is *designed* to cause cognitive change. The principles that are employed to minimise undesirable cognitive effects and those developed to maximise desirable ones should bear a strong relationship to each other. Thus, in this chapter we hope to shed some light on these issues by what we have learned about how to design desirable cognitive effects into a particular class of computer-based learning environments in which the student's task is to produce a well-reasoned recommendation.

THE COGNITIVE TECHNOLOGY OF COMPUTER-BASED LEARNING-BY-DOING ENVIRONMENTS

Our long-standing interest is in developing a particular approach to computer-based environments in which students learn by doing in the context of a simulation. The environments we build, which we call Goal-Based Scenarios, or GBSs (Schank, 1992; Schank, Fano, Bell, and Jona, 1994) are essentially simulations in the spirit of the flight simulators used to train airline pilots, with the equivalent of experienced pilots available for tutoring built in. The learner is invited to pursue an interesting goal and engage in realistic, motivating tasks in the safety of a simulated environment, with the benefit of mentoring from experts, who have been captured on video, and who can be used by the system to coach, critique, and provide help – often in the form of first-person stories – as the student needs it.

The GBS approach to computer-based learning environments follows in the constructivist school of educational theory (Piaget, 1954), and is allied with approaches such as anchored instruction (Bransford, 1990), cognitive apprenticeship (Collins, 1989) and constructionism (Papert, 1986). The designs are also strongly influenced by certain cognitive theories, particularly those which outline mechanisms of case-based reasoning (Schank and Riesbeck, 1989, Kolodner, 1993), situated cognition (Lave and Wenger, 1991) and learning from failure (Schank, 1982).

Over the past several years, we have developed a fairly large number of such systems, for a broad range of students and subject areas, including K-12, university, and various levels of professional and military training. Some examples include simulations for teaching social skills, e.g. selling yellow pages ads (Kass, Burke, and Fitzgerald, 1996), scenarios for teaching about scientific principles like genetics (Bell, 1996; Dobson, 1998; Riesbeck and Dobson, 1998), simulations of physical systems, e.g. a house fire (Towle, forthcoming), scenarios to teach procedural tasks such as filling orders in a restaurant (Guralnick, 1996), and scenarios in which the student plays a reporter, interpreting several newsworthy events (Kass, Dooley, Luksa, and Conroy, 1994) .

In order to improve the educational effectiveness of the systems we build, we are constantly seeking answers to three crucial questions, which seem to relate to issues that lie at the heart of cognitive technology.

The three questions are as follows:

1. What, specifically, are the sorts of cognitive effects that we want such learning-by-doing environments to achieve?
2. What interface elements of a computer-based learning environment contribute to facilitating desirable cognitive effects? And,
3. What sorts of problems can arise which can prevent the desirable cognitive effects from occurring?

Attempting to explore these questions at too abstract a level is unlikely to yield useful insights. We believe that the set of all computer-based learning environments, or even all educational simulations or all GBSs is too varied in structure and objective to allow for many useful generalisations. On the other hand, looking at individual systems in isolation is also rather unsatisfying since doing so makes it difficult to generalise the resulting insights to a level that can guide the design of future systems.

There is a level of analysis, which we call the *educational architecture* level, which can cut across a broad range of subject areas, yet we believe shares enough similarities in structure and objective to yield useful principles. A GBS architecture is a reusable specification for learning environments which can be applied across a broad range of subject areas (Schank, 1992). Unlike a GBS *design,* an *architecture* specifies a great deal about the structure of a learning environment – including the structure of the student's task, the ways that help and advice will be available – but remains neutral with repect to the content.

Identifying and refining reusable architectures of this sort is a key part of our research and development paradigm, since it allows us to develop highly structured, theory-rich, reusable *authoring tools* which are architecture specific, but subject-matter independent. We have developed several sets of these architecture-specific authoring tools (Riesbeck and Dobson, 1998; Schank and Korcuska, 1996; Bell, 1996; Towle, forthcoming). These authoring tools, in turn, enable authors who are not programmers to create complex GBSs relatively quickly by reusing many of the structural elements inherent in the architecture.

In theory at least, the tools should also facilitate the *study* of these GBSs by encouraging the creation of a large, varied set of GBSs which share enough common elements to allow an observer to make useful observations about the set as a whole. This chapter is intended to begin turning that theory into reality by examining the cognitive technology of the *Advise* architecture. In the sections that follow we'll describe the Advise architecture in some detail, and will discuss what we've learned about what features contribute to the effectiveness of this cognitive technology, and what cognitive design challenges remain.

THE ADVISE ARCHITECTURE

Overview of the Advise Architecture

Advise is a computer-based learning architecture which places a student in the role of advisor to an important decision-maker, such as the President of the United States, the CEO of a big company, or the mayor of a city. The architecture, which is constantly evolving in our laboratory, has been used to build several systems, so that we can begin to see what works and what doesn't at the *architectural* level, and to distinguish that from the particulars that are peculiar to any single application of the architecture.

The design of the first version was led by Michael Korcuska (Korcuska, forthcoming). Further discussion can be found in (Korcuska, Herman, and Jona, 1996; and Korcuska, Kass, and Jona, 1996).

A good example of an Advise system is *Crisis in Krasnovia*, a scenario in which high-school students are asked to construct arguments about foreign policy options using evidence drawn from previous international crises. Another example is *Emerging Economies: Feeding Frenzy*, a scenario in which business school students are asked to evaluate alternate plans for taking a baby-food company into a new Eastern European market, relying on the expert testimony of business people who have already tried to expand companies into new markets.

To help the student complete the task, the environment contains a template specifying the structure of the recommendation, a panel of simulated advisors who represent conflicting perspectives about the issue, and a large hypermedia reference library of information and expert stories pertaining to the issue. As the students stake out a position, they receive critiques focusing on the quality of the evidence they used to support his conclusions. Students can revise their thinking in light of criticism, or search for evidence to rebut the criticism.

Elements of Advise Systems: Tools, Characters, and Props

Understanding the simulated world that comprises an Advise GBS means first understanding characters, props, and tools that are found in that world, and then understanding the events and activities that the learner participates in within that simulated world. These are the topics of the next two subsections.

The Advise architecture has the following elements:

4. **A complex problem, prompting a need to take some form of action:** All of the student's activity in Advise systems revolves around determining which course of action to recommend for addressing a complex problem. The problem must be one which suggests multiple possible solutions, with no single plan which is clearly the best approach to solving the problem. In *Crisis in Krasnovia*, for example the problem is a civil war in the fictional country of Krasnovia.

5. **A set of plans:** Rather than forcing students to invent their own solution in an unfamiliar domain, the problem is posed to the student as a set of 'prefabricated' alternatives, each with their own features. In *Crisis in Krasnovia*, the plans include a "Full Court Press" plan involving unilateral military action, a plan involving covert action and a boycott to create

instability in the aggressive country, a "Land for Peace" plan involving a negotiation, and a Wait and See (do nothing) option.

6. **A set of goals**: An important feature of most complex decisions is that they involve multiple goals, which may even be in conflict. In *Krasnovia*, these goals are to Solve the Immediate Problem, Prevent Future Conflicts, Ensure US Domestic Welfare, and Preserve the United States' role as a world leader.

7. **A decision maker**: The decision maker is the "customer" of the student's recommendation. The decision maker is responsible for determining the goals which are to guide the decision-making process, for outlining the plans under consideration, and for offering feedback on the student's overall recommendation. Including a 'customer' for the recommendation as part of the framework, as opposed to putting the student in the role of the actual decision-maker, has two important effects: First, it emphasises analysis, rather than execution; the student doesn't need to worry about exactly *how* to execute the plan they've selected, but instead can focus on the choice itself. Secondly, a decision maker can give particular, well specified reasons why he/she needs the recommendation, helping the student keep in mind the importance of the information they'll be learning, and better understand the role of the specific goals affecting the decision.

8. **A panel of advisors:** Presented to the student as a set of assistants who can help with the recommendation task, advisors represent extreme versions of typical approaches to similar situations. Advisors typically differ in their area of expertise or in which of the decision-makers goals they value most, and help expose the student to a broad range of plausible opinions. The *Krasnovia* scenario includes as advisors a Diplomat, a Hawk, an Isolationist, and a Humanitarian.

9. **Domain Experts:** These real-life subject-matter experts do not directly address the scenario at hand, but present stories from their own knowledge and experiences which students can apply to the situation they're analysing. Experts in the *Crisis in Krasnovia* GBS included several former ambassadors as well as professors of history and political science.

10. **The recommendation itself:** The student's analysis is presented as a notebook, with sections for each plan, plus a 'conclusion' section where the student summarises his/her analysis and makes a final choice of a plan to recommend. Each 'plan' section contains several index cards, one for each goal. On a card, students can rate the goal as to how well it will be satisfied by the selected plan, and can support their rating with "points" - sentence-long summaries which are presented along with expert stories or other information from the reference library. These elements are then put to use to create the following sort of environment to exercise a student's analytical and argumentation skills:

11. **Crisis Presentation:** The student first learns of the crisis, in the context of the fictional role they'll be playing in the scenario. In *Krasnovia*, this comes in the

form of an emergency phone call from the White House, asking the student to come over immediately to help with an emerging crisis.

12. **Background Presentation:** Before plunging into an analysis of the situation, the student learns about what the crisis entails, and why it's an important problem that needs to be solved. In *Krasnovia*, this background information is delivered via a news report, which the student watches "on the way" to the White House. The newscast gives a brief background on the conflict, and explains that the fighting in the Krasnovian capital has intensified and there is new pressure on the US to respond.

13. **Request for Recommendation:** Separately from the introduction of the crisis, the student learns of the need for a decision, probably from the decision-maker him/herself. This request stresses that the important, difficult task in this situation is not the execution of a plan, but the decision of which plan to execute. In *Krasnovia*, the President tells the student that he needs help because his knowledgeable advisors are providing mutually contradictory advice. He asks the student to evaluate the possible options and recommend one.

14. **The Plan/Goal Evaluation Process:** This is the meat of the scenario; here, the student must evaluate each of the options and decide how well each one meets the goals the president described earlier. For each plan/goal combination, the student can rate the effectiveness of the plan with respect to that goal, to create claims like (for example): "The *Land-for-Peace* plan will have a *positive* effect on our goal of *Preventing Future Conflicts*." Having made such a claim, however, students also need to justify it with evidence, provided via expert stories, and to answer critiques of their claims brought up by the advisors.

15. **Submitting the Final Recommendation:** When the student decides on an option and recommends it to the President, the President will be satisfied only if the student has provided enough evidence for his position, and has responded to all of the counter-arguments raised by the advisors.

It is important to note that more than one of the options for solving the problem can be defended using the evidence in the hypermedia reference library. The advisors play a crucial role in this part of Advise applications. A student can ask them specific questions about their opinions of particular plans, and each advisor can critique the student's arguments and offer advice about how to improve them. This means that a student can't write a successful recommendation simply by finding a set of opinions that no one disagrees with. Instead, he must concentrate on ensuring that good support is provided for the opinions that are included in his analysis. Another important feature of Advise applications is that, since they deal solely with proposal formation and analysis, they avoid the complications associated with intricate simulation.

WHAT AN INTERACTION WITH AN ADVISE SYSTEM IS LIKE

To give a sense of what a typical Advise GBS interaction looks like, we'll describe the beginning of a hypothetical student's interaction with *Crisis in Krasnovia*.

As described above, the scenario begins with the student receiving a phone call at home and being summoned to the White House to help the President with an urgent overseas crisis involving a civil war in the fictional country of Krasnovia. On the way there, the student watches a newscast which gives a brief overview of the crisis. At the White House, the President briefs the student on the need for a quick, well-supported recommendation, and introduces the guide, who delivers task and interface help throughout the student's analysis (see fig. 1).

Figure 1. Introduction to *Crisis in Krasnovia*: The President introduces the task in the Oval Office scene.

The scene then shifts to the student's 'office', which the guide briefly explains to the student. The office includes a "Resource Folder" which contains background information on the crisis, introductory stories on the experts, and stories about other world conflicts, which the student may read in order to learn more before starting his analysis. It also contains a 'memo' from the president, giving a quick overview of the alternatives under consideration and the goals that affect the decision. In this interaction, our hypothetical student decides to ignore the extra resources and start his analysis by looking at the plan that looks the most interesting to him; in this case, the *Full Court Press* (military action) plan.

The student might then open up the recommendation to the section on the Full Court Press plan, and click the button marked "Plan Detail" to learn more about it. In response to this, the "story browser" presents a brief video explaining the actions and objectives of the plan. Follow-up questions are offered that allow the student to ask the advisors how well they think the plan will perform on each of the president's goals (see fig. 2). Consequently the student would discover that the Full Court Press plan involves a unilateral military action against Krasnovia's aggressive neighbour, Voles, who is providing aid to the Krasnovian rebels.

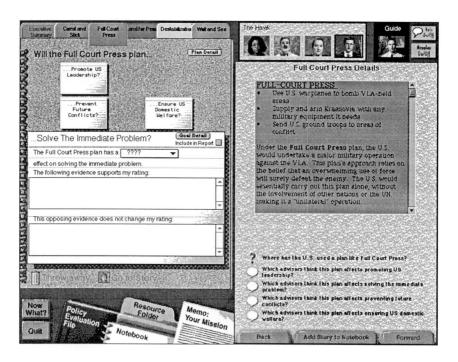

Figure 2. The Advise Desktop – Displaying an 'empty' student claim.

The student might decide to begin investigating how effective the plans are, starting with the goal of Preventing Future Conflicts. By opening the "Prevent Future Conflicts" card in the report, and he or she can ask, "Which advisors think the Full Court Press plan will prevent future conflicts?"

The Humanitarian, the Hawk, and the Diplomat all respond, with the Hawk suggesting it will do well, and the Humanitarian and Diplomat both disagreeing, claiming instead that it will actually lead to *more* conflicts in the future. The student decides to listen first to the Diplomat, who says:

"I believe the Full Court Press plan would make it harder to prevent future conflicts. It would undermine the United Nations. A unilateral use of force by the United States without the UN's approval is a clear violation of the UN Charter. It would be a slap in the face which could eventually lead to the entire collapse of the UN. Remember, the demise of the League of Nations helped pave the way to World War Two."

The student could then ask to see what actual information supports the Diplomat's opinion; this information is available via several follow-up questions, one of which points to the relevant section of the United Nations charter, and another to a story in which a history professor stresses the importance of the UN. One of the follow-up stories the student might watch is told by Thomas Boyatt, a former ambassador who worked in the Middle East in the 1970s, and who explains how without US support, the League of Nations failed to be effective. One point of his story is that *"Without support from the US, international bodies have no power."* Our student thinks this point is relevant to the claim, so he drags it over to act as support for the claim about the effectiveness of the Full Court Press plan on future conflicts, and he gives the plan a highly negative rating. (see fig. 3)

This support might seem pretty straightforward to the student, so he may indicate that he had done working on the claim by clicking on the 'include in report' button. This acts as a signal to the other advisors to look at the claim and offer critiques. Two of them *do* have critiques to offer, which they indicate to the student by saying:

Hawk: "I strongly disagree with that opinion"
Humanitarian: "I agree, but for a different reason"

A typical student might then click on the Hawk's picture, who would suggest that military action against Voles will make future conflicts less likely by punishing Volusian aggression. As support, he draws an analogy to Britain's failure to stop Nazi aggression in the months before W.W.II. Searching for an expert story to support this evidence, the student finds a story describing the Munich conference, from which Neville Chamberlain returned announcing he had achieved "Peace in our time", shortly after which Germany invaded Czechoslovakia.

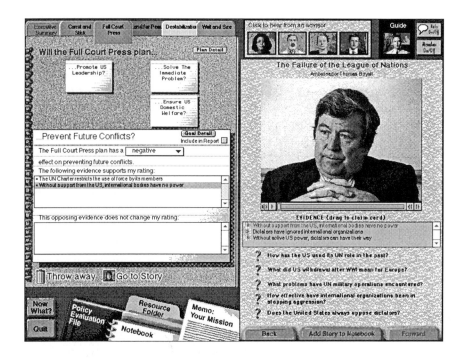

Figure 3. The Advise Desktop – Displaying an expert story and a student's claim about the effectiveness of a plan on one of the goals.

At this point, the student would likely be confused by these conflicting opinions, both of which seem to be supported by reasonable historical precedent. However, as one of the follow-up questions from the Hawk's opinion, the student notices a link titled "The Diplomat disagrees." The student could follow this link, and hear the Diplomat explain that the situation in Krasnovia is quite unlike pre-W.W.II Europe, as Voles is a small, relatively weak island nation with local, not global, aims. Thus, she argues, punishing Volusian aggression isn't necessary here.

With this new information in mind, the student decides to drag the evidence about the Munich conference, "A weak response to aggression encourages more aggression" into the section of the claim entitled "This opposing evidence does not change my rating", and to leave the rest of the claim the way it was. Now, if the student again checks the "Include in Report" button, the Hawk will no longer disagree, because the student had at least considered the evidence relevant to his claim.

Our detailed description ends here, but normally students would continue to work on the analysis until they're satisfied that they had made a strong case for one of the plans over the others. It's through this process of making evaluations, getting critiqued and hearing what different advisors have to say that students will learn about foreign policy issues, in a context similar to that in which they are usually discussed. When the student feels he's done, he turns to the conclusion section of the recommendation, and selects his favourite plan from a pull-down menu. At this point, he also needs to give a reason for preferring that plan (see fig. 4). To do this the student does not have to evaluate all the plans with respect to all the goals, but there is a reasonable minimum standard for completeness, e.g. he cannot recommend a plan without evaluating it against all the goals. The guide checks the student's work and lets him/her know if the analysis is incomplete, or inconsistent. If the guide has no problems, the report goes on to the President, who thanks the student and says "come back tomorrow and I'll tell you how that press conference went." Finally, the student sees a screen announcing "The Next Day" and is handed a newspaper article giving the details of the President's successful (if the student's analysis was thorough enough) press conference. The President thanks the student again and the program ends.

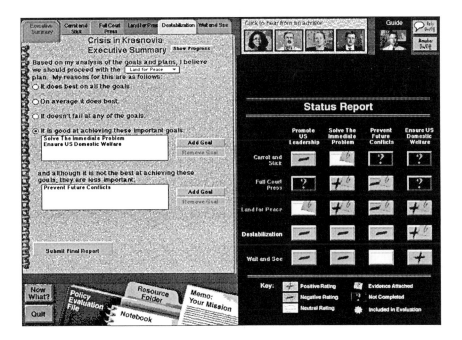

Figure 4. The Advise Desktop – Displaying the student's progress and final recommendation.

Other Advise Applications

In order to give a clearer sense of the breadth of subject areas that can be attacked using the Advise architecture, we offer the following brief descriptions of the main Advise systems that have been developed or prototyped in our lab during the past 24 months:

- **Crisis in Krasnovia:** Described above. *Krasnovia* is aimed at early high-school students.
- **Emerging Economies**: In this GBS, the student is asked to evaluate alternate plans for taking a baby-food company into a new Eastern European market, relying on the expert testimony of business people who have already tried to take companies into new markets. This GBS was built for a Northwestern University graduate business school course on emerging markets in formerly communist eastern Europe.

The below four scenarios were built using the Advise tool by teams of three graduate students over four-month periods:

- **Outsourcing Strategist:** Student plays the vice-president of a camping-equipment manufacturer, advising the CEO on how best to outsource overseas manufacturing of a new backpack. This scenario targeted strategic consultants.
- **What's the Game Plan?:** Student advises the mayor of the fictional city of Seaport on how to respond to a pro football team's threat to move out of town unless they get a new stadium. This GBS is aimed at teaching early high-school students about issues in economics, civics, and city planning.
- **Beyond the Bomb:** The student is sent back in time to help President Truman decide whether to use nuclear weapons to end World War II.
- **Help the Homeless:** Student advises a philanthropist on how to most effectively aid the homeless population of a large city. Aimed at junior-high school students.

The below four projects are prototypes were created by graduate students over a six week period as part of a course in educational software design.

- **Wheeler Dealer:** Student assists a startup bicycle company in choosing a marketing plan for a new type of frame. Designed to teach 11th and 12th graders about basic marketing techniques.
- **Killer Controversy:** Student advises a record company CEO on how to respond to a particularly violent album by one of its hot artists.

- **1491:** Student advises the Queen of Spain on best trade route to the Indies, during the time of Columbus. This less-typical "historical" approach to Advise teaches about the historical context of Columbus' voyage, by having the student make a decision with the information that was known *at the time*, rather than on what we know now.
- **Cyberspeech:** In this prototype student project, the student advises a senator on what position to take regarding censorship on the internet. Aimed at high-school students.

COGNITIVE EFFECTS

How advise systems are intended to work

The key aspects of an Advise system that are intended to lead to effecting desirable changes in students' thinking include the following:

1. Students are required to argue using evidence from past events, and are therefore motivated to analyse a wide range of historical cases;
2. Students are challenged on the relevance of cited evidence to the current situation;
3. Students are critiqued on the coherence of their arguments.

The net effect is to expose students to an interesting range of information, in a context where they will analyse and synthesise that information to draw important conclusions. We'll analyse which design factors contribute to such systems' ability to deepen understanding of the material covered and to help model and develop habits of mind that are generally useful.

Like most learning environments, Advise GBSs are built with specific content in mind, which the designer wants the student to learn about. But as learning environment designers, we want to change not only what students think about, but how they think about it. In controversial domains, where even the experts may disagree on the best approach to a situation, we believe the following habits are particularly valuable, and have designed the Advise interface and framework to encourage them.

- **Supporting opinions with evidence:** Students often form opinions based on what they know, but aren't good at articulating the reasons for them. We want students to concentrate more on articulating the reasons for their opinions as they form them. In order to do this, they need to think explicitly about what factors influence their decisions, and how.

- **Anticipating counter-arguments:** Moreover, teachers report that high school students with opinions are frequently unable to suggest reasons why someone might disagree with them, or to explain how they might respond to that disagreement. An important set of cognitive habits we wish to develop is the habit of anticipating, interpreting, and responding convincingly to arguments that conflict with the student's own opinions.

- **Goal prioritisation:** Differences in opinion surrounding a decision often arise not because one party has the facts wrong, but because frequently the alternatives each satisfy (fail to satisfy) different goals. Controversy often arises due to different beliefs regarding which underlying goals are most important. We want students to regard controversial decisions not in terms of determining the best alternative from some objective, neutral standpoint, but rather in terms of which plan is best given their own prioritisation of the multiple goals under consideration. This involves 'sub-habits' of recognising what the goals are, recognising how differences in opinion are influenced by different beliefs about which goals are important, and deciding upon which goals actually *are* most important.

- **Reasoning from cases:** When considering a situation, students should look to other cases that they're aware of, searching for similarities and drawing conclusions about the current situation based on past cases. This use of old cases to understand new ones is an important reason for learning history, economics, government, and a variety of other domains, but is typically left out of traditional instruction in those areas.

- **Focus on domain-specific issues:** While the cognitive habits above are useful in all domains, it's not safe to expect that cultivating them in one domain will lead to their use in all domains. What's more, understanding and participating in debates involves the correct use of a great deal of domain-specific knowledge, not about the specific facts of particular cases, but about general issues that require particular attention in the domain. For example, consider a business' decision of whether to outsource certain supplies overseas. In such a decision an important concern, often ignored, is that of hidden costs: hidden labour costs, transportation costs, communication costs, etc. Understanding how such costs can affect a decision is an issue which pervades most decision making in this domain. We want students to focus on such pervasive issues, bringing them to the forefront when reasoning about the domain.

How Advise Attempts to Achieve the Desired Cognitive Effects

The initial design of the Advise interface, and the conceptual framework underlying it, was driven by a desire to achieve the cognitive effects described above. It should be clear how the high-level structure of Advise, like the analysis-and-recommendation task and the placing of the student in role of an advisor to a decision-maker, are designed to facilitate these goals. Many smaller details of the interface were designed to achieve these effects as well. Below are listed several features of the Advise interface, and the interactions they allow. We believe these contribute to the cognitive effects desired by Advise GBS designers. We can group these interface features into two groups; first, interface features which don't directly respond to the students' actions, but which suggest the appropriateness of certain kinds of reasoning, and second, more dynamic behaviours of the environment which react to students' actions, changing the way they are thinking about the task, and the domain, in a more targeted manner.

Passive Interface Features

- **Highly structured Recommendation template:** To keep the student's analysis focused on the goals their decision is meant to serve, we made the 'recommendation' highly structured, dividing it into sections for each plan, inside which there are cards for each goal, representing the student's opinion about that plan's effect on the given goal. This structure keeps consideration of the goals in the forefront, and highlights the differences between the plans in terms of which goals they do and don't satisfy.

- **Claims implicitly require support:** In the student's recommendation, every 'claim card', in which the student rates a plan with respect to a goal, includes a place to attach supporting evidence. This implicitly suggests that an integral part of making a claim is providing support for it.

- **Advisors support their own claims:** The advisors further stress the importance of supporting evidence by providing evidence for their own opinions, in the form of follow-up questions; that is, when advisors offer their own opinion regarding a plan and goal, the student can ask follow-up questions of any advisor regarding what factual evidence supports that claim.

- **Claims implicitly require consideration of opposing evidence:** Claim cards also contain a place to put "considered but rejected" evidence, a feature which emphasises the fact that not all relevant evidence is supporting evidence, and which requires students to make judgements both about whether a given piece of information is relevant, and whether it supports their opinion.

- **Students can explicitly prioritise goals:** In the section of the recommendation structure in which students make their final choice of a best plan, the student can prioritise individual goals as more or less important than the others. The ability to prioritise goals is important, as the structure of the rest of the recommendation template does not afford it.

Active Interface Behaviours

- **Advisors actively disagree with student on claims:** Advisors don't only offer their opinion on the issues when asked by the student; whenever a student claims to be done working on a particular plan/goal claim, any advisors with a different rating will 'wake up' and voice their disagreement with the student. Such constant disagreement could get frustrating, if there was no way to avoid it. If the student indicates he/she has considered an advisors claim by finding the evidence it's based on, and adding it to the "Opposing Evidence" portion of their claim card, then the advisor will no longer disagree. Thus, by listening to all the advisors' opinions, and considering the evidence that supports them, students can pre-emptively avoid disagreement from advisors with different opinions.

- **Student's evidence is subject to domain-specific critique:** Advisors can also respond to a student's claims by disagreeing with specific evidence. These more specific disagreements prevent the student from viewing the analysis as a simple process of collecting all the evidence from all the advisors, without also considering whether it's valid. Advisors can also raise specific critiques of a student's claim to encourage him or her to consider other issues that might also affect their claim. For example, in the *Outsourcing Strategist* GBS, a student's claim about the cost of a given plan, which takes into account labour cost, will be critiqued by an advisor who points out other potential costs, like transportation and tariffs.

- **Recommendation is critiqued on completeness, consistency:** When a student believes they are finished with the complete report, and submits it to the president, it is first checked for completeness and consistency. If the student hasn't analysed the plans completely enough, or if their choice of plan isn't consistent with their individual plan/goal claims, then the guide responds with a description of why the analysis isn't yet up to snuff, and sends the student back to fix the problem. This focus on the overall consistency of the recommendation reminds students at the end of this complex analysis task that although their task is broken into discrete parts, it's still part of a single decision.

Evidence is embedded in cases: In most Advise systems, much of the evidence necessary for a complete recommendation is only available in stories about previous cases, rather than in the form of facts about their own situation, or general rules about the domain. Of course, a student could also misapply many of the stories to the situation in the GBS, using them to make claims which aren't appropriate, and which may cause the advisors to disagree with the student. Thus, the student needs to consider the applicability of past cases carefully when using them for evidence.

COGNITIVE DESIGN CHALLENGES, AND IMPROVEMENTS TO THE *ADVISE* PROGRAMME.

The initial design of Advise and the first few projects built with the framework have been successful in engaging student interest. They also seem, based on informal observation (no formal studies have yet been conducted), to be achieving some of the cognitive effects we desired. However, we have also uncovered important areas for improvement, which we think shed some interesting light on the general issues of designing interfaces to achieve cognitive effects.

We are currently implementing a second version of the Advise framework and interface, which we believe will solve many of the problems uncovered by our experience with the initial version. We've made changes in three major aspects of the interface: the recommendation-writing interface itself, the interface to the panel of advisors, and the behaviour of the advisors in response to students' actions. Below, we look at several of the weaknesses we've uncovered, and describe how we've changed one or more of these three aspects to deal with those weaknesses.

Structured framework for output, but not for task

The student's recommendation is highly structured in a way that breaks the analysis task into approachable chunks. However it is not structured in such a way as to indicate where students should begin their analysis. That is to say it does not indicate what issues they should look at first, what the important questions are, nor what domain-specific issues are most likely to effect the decision as to which plan is preferable. What's more, students often have no sense of how an advisor's many plan/goal opinions fit together to form a coherent attitude about the situation under consideration. As a result, students often tend to take a 'brute force' approach to the analysis task. They work through all the plans and goals one by one, using the recommendation structure to drive their analysis, rather than focusing first on the most important features of the plans, as would make sense in a real-world analysis and recommendation task.

In the newest version of the Advise interface, we've used two means to discourage the student from letting the plan/goal grid drive their analysis. First, we've made the recommendation template more flexible. Rather than being filled with 'empty' claims about each of the plans and goals, implying that all plans need to be considered with respect to all goals, students now start their task with an empty report, to which they can add individual claims as they see appropriate. Secondly, we've made it easier to ask the advisors high-level questions which lead the students more directly to important issues. For example, in the original Advise interface, a student could only ask a question like "Which advisors think the *Land for Peace* Plan will affect the *Preserve Domestic Welfare* goal?" What's more, they could only ask it at a certain point in the interaction, immediately after seeing a story providing a summary of the Land for Peace plan. In the new interface, a student can still ask these specific questions, but can ask them anytime. They can also ask one (or all) of the advisors questions like: "Which plan do you think is best?" or "Which goal do you think is the most important?" (See fig. 5) Advisors will answer these questions with stories explaining their overall attitude, focusing on the key aspects of particular plans or goals, thus affording student a place to begin their analysis.

The two mechanisms above may *allow* a more flexible interaction, but they don't necessarily *support* or *encourage* it. We're currently working on a version of Advise which will explicitly present the student with several high-level approaches to choosing a plan, and provide guidance specific to each of those approaches. For example, a student may already believe they know which plan is the best, and want to structure their research around finding evidence for their plan and against others; or a student might feel that one goal is particularly important, and so would want to start out by eliminating all the plans which fail on that goal.

Advisors don't act enough like advisors

In the initial implementation, the panel of advisors was essentially a simple set of buttons; when an advisor had an opinion or a critique to offer, the advisor's picture would light up and a very short video would play (something like "I disagree with that opinion"). A student could then click on the advisor's picture to hear more about their opinion; this caused a story to appear in a 'browser', where expert stories and other information about the scenario normally are shown. This seemingly reasonable interface convention caused an unfortunate side-effect; it didn't sufficiently distinguish the advisors from the other "characters", particularly experts, in the system. This was dangerous for two reasons; first, it made it easy for students to confuse "opinions" from biased advisors with "experience" from experts. Secondly, it discouraged students from treating the advisors as information resources; because the range of possible questions to advisors was so narrow, it was easy to regard advisors simply as pointers to expert stories.

The advisor panel interface in the newest version of Advise behaves differently in several ways which we believe minimise the two above effects. Rather than appearing in an story browser along with the stories from experts, the advisors now always appear in the advisor panel itself, which is enlarged to emphasise its importance. To ask an advisor a question, a student can click on an advisor at any time, and choose what to ask from a series of context-specific, nested menus. This friendlier interface to question-asking, as well as a behaviour which is distinct from "experts", makes the advisor panel a resource which students are both more likely to use, and more likely to understand for what it is; a set of consistent, if caricatured, opinions. (see fig. 5)

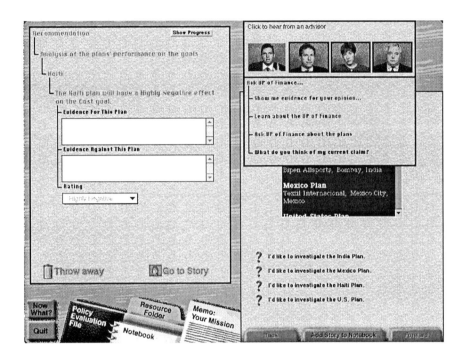

Figure 5. The Advise Interface – Displaying an outline based recommendation and a pop-up menu of questions for advisors.

A planned future enhancement of Advise will attempt to further expand the role of advisors. We hope to allow students to ask even more specific questions, and to use their advisors' opinions in claims, providing they support them with evidence. A continuing design challenge we face is how to allow designers this increased flexibility, without overburdening them with additional authoring requirements.

Importance of goal prioritisation under-emphasised

The first Advise recommendation structure let the student choose a set of "Most Important Goals" while making their final plan recommendation. Because this ranking of the relative importance of the goals was post-hoc, students didn't really consider the importance of the goals until the end of their analysis, if at all. This is especially important, because only if students really come to *care* about one or more of the goals will they develop a strong interest in analysing the plans.

In the newer version of the recommendation, students can consider the relative importance of the goals in a separate section, *before* analysing the plans. This new section may also (according to individual designers' discretion) require a student to provide evidence for claims that a particular goal is particularly important or unimportant. By focusing their attention early on the goals, students will lay the groundwork that will guide the rest of their analysis.

Simple critiquing allows only simple arguments

One of the most obvious problems with the initial version of Advise was that students frequently took a 'more is better' approach to each of their claims, they often drag evidence into their claims without considering its relevance, in an attempt to 'satisfy' the advisors so they could move on to another claim. In fact, this often worked; most of the critiques written by designers were designed to catch specific mistakes, and the many of the more general responses only prompted students to add more evidence without specifying where.

In later versions of Advise, a greater emphasis is being placed on critiques regarding relevance of evidence, to encourage students to use evidence a little more judiciously. A planned future version even allows students to create more structured claims, allowing them to explain why they've supported their opinion in the way they did. By increasing the amount a student can say when making a claim, we can also increase the accuracy of the feedback we give the student.

Simplistic depiction of plans, goals

In Advise, students don't need to discover the relevant goals, or appropriate plans; they're just handed them. This feature was in some sense deliberate; leaving the task too open-ended by providing too many possibilities could overwhelm designers as well as students, especially students who are unfamiliar with the domain. However, real-world decisions rarely involve a small, fixed set of plans and an agreed upon set of goals. One of the first tasks of a decision-maker must often be to distil the most obvious alternatives, and agreed-upon goals, out of a morass of suggestions and objections.

One potential solution to this problem, which we haven't yet implemented, is to add a 'preliminary analysis' task, before the recommendation task, in which the student is assisted in discovering which goals, and which potential plans, merit inclusion in the more detailed analysis. Thus, in a sense the students would 'invent' the recommendation template structure before starting their analysis, albeit with a very limited number of possible 'approved' structures.

Students led too directly to evidence

In an effort to emphasise the importance of supporting evidence, the original Advise always provided links from advisors' "opinion stories" to the expert stories that provide evidence to support those opinions. While this helped students quickly find relevant stories, it also led to a fairly obvious pattern: Students could ask advisors for their opinion, follow links to stories, and drag the points from those stories into their own corresponding claim. In this pattern, students never needed to search for support. They could just keep asking for opinions, and the support would be handed to them. This meant that students weren't likely to gain any experience in analysing the potential relevance of a story to a given plan or goal. All the relevant stories they need will always appear to be right at their fingertips.

The most obvious way to solve this problem is to stop leading the students so directly to the evidence. Rather than always providing links to the most appropriate story, we could simply point them to a well-organised, easily searchable database of stories and make them find the evidence to support an opinion they agree with. While this approach is reasonable, it puts a much greater burden both on the argument critiquer, who must be able to respond better to inappropriately used evidence, and on the student, who now needs to remember the argument they have just heard while off searching for evidence to support or refute it. One of the current major research goals for the Advise project is to lighten both of the above burdens; first, by improving the tool so that GBS developers can more easily create GBSs that respond helpfully to inappropriately used evidence, and also by helping the student to more easily keep track of the argument they're researching, (possibly through the use of a notebook or through a more expressive recommendation template that allows for the expression of high-level arguments as well as more detailed support.).

CONCLUSION

In the beginning of this chapter we outlined three crucial cognitive technology-related questions that we think ought to guide the thinking of designers of computer-based learning environments: What cognitive effects do we want the learning environment to have, what interface elements and behaviours contribute to causing those effects, and what problems can arise when attempting to achieve those effects?

We have attempted, in the rest of the paper, to examine a particular class of environments - *Advise systems*- in terms of these questions. In addition to shedding some light on this particular class of interactive systems, and the ways in which it's components can contribute to learning, we hope that we have encouraged other researchers to pose a similar set of questions about other learning environments. By doing so we can, as a field, build up a large repertoire of well-understood tools and techniques we can draw upon when whenever we need to design a new type of learning environment to achieve a new set of cognitive effects.

REFERENCES

Bell, B., 1996. *A special purpose architecture for building educational software.* PhD. Diss, Northwestern University.

Bransford, J. D., et al, 1990. Anchored instruction: why we need it and how technology can help. In R. Spiro & D. Nix, eds, *Cognition, Education, and Multimedia: Exploring Ideas in High Technology.* Hillsdale, NJ: Lawrence Erlbaum.

Collins, A., J. S. Brown, S. E. Newman, 1989. *Cognitive Apprenticeship: Teaching the Crafts of Reading, Writing, and Mathematics. In Knowing, Learning, and Instruction: Essays in honor of Robert Glaser.* Hillsdale, NJ: Lawrence Erlbaum Associates. 453-494.

Dobson, D., 1998. *Authoring Tools for Investigate-and-Decide Learning Environments.* Ph.D. Diss. Northwestern University

Guralnick, D. A., 1996. *An Authoring Tool for Procedural Task Training.* Ph.D. Diss. Northwestern University

Kass, A., S. Dooley, F. Luksa, and C. Conroy, 1994, Using Broadcast Journalism to Motivate Hypermedia Exploration. In *Educational Multimedia and Hypermedia Annual.* Charlottesville, VA: Association for the Advancement of Computing in Education.

Kass, A., R. Burke, E. Blevis, M. Williamson, 1994. Constructing Learning Environments for Complex Social Skills. *Journal of the Learning Sciences.* 3(4).

Kass, A., R. Burke, and W. Fitzgerald, 1996. How to Support Learning from Interaction with Simulated Characters. In B. Gorayska & J. Mey, eds, *Cognitive Technology: In Search of a Humane Interface.* New York: Elsevier/North-Holland

Kolodner, J. L., 1993. *Case-based Reasoning.* San Mateo, CA: Morgan Kaufman

Korcuska, Michael., forthcoming. *Knowledge-based Authoring Tools for Educational Software,* Ph.D. Diss. Northwestern University.

Korcuska, M., A. Kass and J. Menachem, 1996. Design Choices for Learning-by-Doing Software: When to Choose Advise. *The International Conference on the Learning Sciences: Proceedings of ICLS '96.,* edited by Daniel C. Edelson and Eric A. Domeshek, Charlottesville, VA: Association for the Advancement of Computing in Education, pp. 196-203

Korcuska, M., Joe Herman and Menachem Jona, 1996. Evidence-based reporting. *Proceedings of ED-MEDIA/ED-TELECOM 1996.* Boston, MA

Lave, J. and E. Wenger, 1991. *Situated Learning: Legitimate Peripheral Participation*. Cambridge University Press

Papert, S., 1986. *Constructionism: a new opportunity for elementary science education*. MIT Media Laboratory, Proposal to the National Science Foundation. Quoted in Mitchell Resnick. Beyond the Centralized Mindset. The International Conference on the Learning Sciences: Proceedings of the 1991 Conference in Evanston, IL., edited by L. Birnbaum,. Charlottesville, VA: Association for the Advancement of Computing in Education, 1991, pp. 389-396

Piaget, J., 1954. *The construction of reality in the child*. New York: Basic Books

Riesbeck, C. K. and Wolff D. Dobson, Authorable Critiquing for Intelligent Educational Systems. *Proceedings of International Conference on Intelligent User Interfaces '98* Los Angeles: Association for Computing Machinery, pp. 384-391

Schank, R. C., 1982. *Dynamic Memory*. New York: Cambridge University Press.

Schank, R. C., 1992. *Goal-Based Scenarios*. Technical Report #36. Institute for the Learning Sciences, Northwestern University.

Schank, R. C., and C. Riesbeck 1989. *Inside Case-Based Reasoning*. Hillsdale, NJ: L. Erlbaum.

Schank, R. C. and M. Korcuska, 1996. *Eight Goal-Based Scenario Tools*. Technical Report #67. Institute for the Learning Sciences, Northwestern University.

Schank, R. C., A. Fano, B. Bell, and Menachem Jona, 1994. The Design of Goal-Based Scenarios. *The Journal of the Learning Sciences*, 3(4), pp. 305-345.

Towle, Brendon. forthcoming. *A learning architecture for teaching students how to manage complex situations*. PhD. Diss, Northwestern University.

Humane Interfaces: Questions of method and practice in Cognitive Technology
J.P. Marsh, B. Gorayska and J.L. Mey (Editors)
© 1999 Elsevier Science B.V. All rights reserved.

Chapter 16

EVOLUTION OF MAN'S NEEDS AND TECHNOLOGICAL PROGRESSION
Pragmatic foundations for a relational coupling

Colin T. Schmidt

Sorbonne University

Patrick Ruch

University of Geneva

INTRODUCTION: CONSENSUS AND THE STRUGGLE OF KNOWLEDGE

Humankind is in transformation and as such so is the technology it commands. The field of Human-Computer Interaction provides examples concerning the pivotal point of this ever-changing relationship. Matching up technology with people (and vice versa) seems to take on an ethical dimension as the race to harness the power of the information explosion picks up speed. The subjective realm of technology assessors—that contains non-publicly debated recommendations—is seen as playing an increasingly important role as it acts as the moderator of communication between peoples' needs and technological responses to them. At this point in time, synoptically considering questions on both Cognitive Technology (CT) and Technological Cognition (TC) (Gorayska & Marsh, 1996), along with those concerned with *conceptual* Technology Assessment, rather than its *institutionalised* counterpart (Smits, 1990), leads one to wonder whether perspectives on HCI problems are not likely to provide the analogical framework for renewing the more traditional field of Technology Assessment (TA). On a par, fields like graphic design, industrial design, architecture and urban planning, and the list goes on (fields originally separated by boundaries because of their distinct concerns), have generated general design thinking open-eyed to the point of proactively getting involved in the more common problems of Planet Earth's sustainability (Margolin, 1996)[1]. The goal we have in mind for tackling TA

---

[1](Margolin pegs the trend in which designers are increasingly being encouraged to take over corporate responsabilities.

problems with a model meant for HCI would be to nurture objectivity through consensual validation.

The current methods of some technology assessment groups fail the purpose of technology insofar as a separation of focus, between the technologically possible and/or the humanly acceptable causes pessimism. In institutions part of this problem remains hidden beneath a consensual validation in which "peer pressure" may be used in the first instance to achieve union, followed by the use of media to augment the acceptability of a proposition to public opinion. In the decision-making process that deals with technological matters by establishing a TA attitude among politicians, the desire to take into account social perspectives does not by any stretch of the imagination entail forgetting the specificity of technico-scientific knowledge. Increasing the robustness of methods and obtaining more operative and precise tools for investigating micro-structures (information tools, consequences of computerisation...) is what conceptualised assessment is all about. There seems to be a need for this for there is already a tendency towards investigating more pragmatically-sound views with regards to our technological landscape; for example, the field of HCI has made room for CSCW (Computer-Supported Co-operative Work) in going beyond its traditional one-on-one relationship. Also, the consequences of bringing TA and any technological field together can only benefit the technology in question. Ethically, HCI and TA stand to gain in a reciprocal manner, seeing that the field of investigation of the former is widening its socio-political scope, as seen in the interests of Cognitive Technology Theory, and the latter is striving to understand questions concerning *particular* technologies in order to affirm sound decisions.

We must re-emphasise that this chapter aims to treat questions as raised by technological objects in a conceptual manner, rather than grapple directly with the thorniness of institutional debate. And it is in starting our investigation from technological tools and methods and moving towards the larger socio-political machinery that we develop an explanatory mobility opposed in direction to that traditionally adopted by TA researchers. Due to this fact we run the risk of being too attached to the artificial, but will endeavour of course to push forward and accommodate a common referent, a matter seemingly a little superficial (if at all present) in institutional TA. Mey & Talbot (1988) noticed the specious character of the social dimension in mainstream cognitivism[2]. Progressively, we aim to integrate the discursive Cognitive Technology approach in the march towards our newer autotelic being. At the same time, by example, we will be further specifying some of this 'Otherhood', as implied by the progress of cognitive and related (individualistic) theories. We feel that such examples are forward-looking and of additional value for today's TA theorists.

---

[2]According to them, the social was being neglected through the prevalence of mentalism. With metaphor we go beyond physical reality to empasise what is at stake, increasing the force of language use, as well as its dangers, in order to get a (stronger) message across. It is important to keep in mind that we are actually importing a word with all its habitual links into a context which is foreign; the phenomena in question are thus of distinct orders, and we should never lose sight of this fact. For a critique of metaphor overuse in Sperber & Wilson's *Relevance: Communication and Cognition, cf.* Mey, J. & Talbot, M., (1988).

First of all we shall review the different postures that can be taken in regards to a problem, then look at how communication and the conditions necessary for it to take place can help us with TA, and finally, sketch out a dialogical model for "rating" political manoeuvres as actions that are decisive for the future of Humankind.

PERSPECTIVES OF ENQUIRY & TECHNOLOGY ASSESSMENT

This departure from mainstream TA, HCI (and maybe even CT) could be a result of the instruments used, those developed with extreme care for long-term research programmes. In fact, acting in this manner preserves the *more ideal* tenets of the institutional cause in the end. Would this not be desirable? Along our journey we will cover some TA components and focus on dialogical systemic models, specifically the one developed by French philosopher Francis Jacques for human interaction (Jaques, 1985)[3], which Schmidt subsequently " applied " to an HCI conceptualisation in order to compare human communication and human-machine interaction as a means to advancing the latter by properly differentiating it from the former. It strongly seems to be the case that people designing machine instructions who choose to filter technical 'how-to-do-it' questions through the sieve of a *dialogical stance* become further concerned with pragmatic issues, indeed both those of HCI and the Cognitive Sciences in general. This broader investigative scope better enables them to express just how their goals come about (schmidt, 1997b), not unlike the breadth of enquiry dear to Gorayska & Marsh (1996)[4]. An example of this would be a designer having an acquired understanding with respect to the origins of pressure brought to bear in a hierarchical way upon his daily professional activities, (such as from the social, psychological and economic nature of a particular client for whom his superiors are contracting). The intention here is to aid the evolution of these models in order to be able to integrate a further enhanced social perspective required for TA problems. Obviously we are working on surpassing the technical issues of TA., which are also 'how-to-do-it' questions though they involve a different subject matter than those of concern to the HCI field (i.e. selection criteria concerning projects and entrepreneurial activities), with an aim to looking into fundamental questions.... the *'why?'* questions. While the *'how?'* questions of HCI seem to pervade the community (and it is easy to see why this would also be the case in TA), the *'why?' questions really are quite personal* in nature and verge on entering (or even blatantly enter) the realm of ethics and morality with respect to one's choices regarding technology. Just as the pragmatic understanding of the HCI designer could over-extend its usual hierarchical limits, the technological assessor could perform evaluation based on informed views on world improvement rather than abide by the priorities of Congress: the question becomes a version of "should I

---

[3]*Cf.* pp. 209-215.
[4]*Cf.* particularly p. 34.

actually act taking this information into account, or ignore it and just follow orders?"

Increasing the pragmatic dimension of one's understanding of a situation evidently allows one to take a step back from one's work and, in a way, critique the field in which one works using positive suspicion. In the HCI field, the critical eye of the observer has brought about a greater acknowledgement of the role of this Self in design activities (Schmidt, 1997b) by integrating the designer himself into a model of the interaction between man and machine. Thus stressing the fact that the relationship between the two can be at best pseudo-referential (Schmidt, forthcoming). The technological conclusions that may immediately be drawn for that field are, in short, that because of the designer's *necessary* personal interference, the autonomy of the machine is dependant on Man. This dependency destroys communication in the full human sense of the word. (Fortunately, for if communicative autonomy in machines were possible, the relative horrors of science fiction would become reality!) Furthermore, users will be lead astray if encouraged to personify machines as long as the function of true reference is not available to their relationship. Limiting the creation of the appearance of human intelligence should be a major principle of HCI theory to be respected by practicians.

So be it for HCI. This brings us to the question of what the *pragmatic approach of dialogism* can do for Technology Assessment. Using analogical reasoning, the integration of assessors into the TA process itself could prove to be just as beneficial as such action was in the HCI field, but one has to beware of the temptation to generalise afore-gained knowledge without thorough verification. The destination field usually will have different constraints. When undergoing transportation from HCI to conceptual Technology Assessment, the "What do we wish to achieve?" agenda of investigation—complete with the whys and wherefores of those goals—tends to be reset again; this time its expression carries the philosophically interrogative tone similar to that of "Who are we and who do we want to be?" questions. This is especially true when one considers the fact that technology pinpoints the intentional limits of policy (i.e. the unpredictable consequences of technological choice, our ignorance of natural events, etc.), which has implications for the future of our social well being. Therefore, HCI models—those rooted in dialogism—revealing an undesirable prevalence of domain intra-theoretical design principles can henceforth be transposed onto TA, for the benefit of TA. Through the *a priori* nature of the questions involved—in relation to the genesis of a technical object—, the aim is to achieve a constructive TA that will play a dynamic role in the decision process.

Let us take a look at some TA details to get a feel for the domain. The Office for Technology Assessment (OTA), the very first parliamentary TA entity, came into being in the US Congress during the early seventies. Its goal was originally to give the people's representatives (legislative power) proper means to assess the administration's (executive power) technological decisions, through the creation of an independent mixed committee composed of scientists and representatives. Since then, numerous TA offices of various forms have come to life in Western Europe, and lately in East European countries (Ruch, 1995)[5]. They however are not all faring well. For instance, though the American OTA still exists legally, since 1995 its money flow has been severely cut back.

We have defined three levels of TA activity (Ruch, 1995): 1) the economical/ecological level redefines a new value, no longer the classical economic added value, but a "life" value; 2) the epistemological level confronts the independence of experts and theories with the social background; and 3) the political level asks "who does what in the decision-making process?" We note that, although the economical/ecological and epistemological levels sit nicely at home with both TA and CT/TC, the political level is TA specific. This level of enquiry constitutes a shift from authentic intersubjective dialogism to "subject-only supported dialogism" (the subject being Congress), that lends itself to support discourses like, "which words are to be used in order to make our decisions acceptable?" In our opinion this is *a*dialogical. The *constructive turn* in European TA has made a fundamental improvement in what concerns this level, allowing TA to perform its true work of critiquing technology[6]. The general idea behind TA should be more cogitable now.

Any decision-making process entails a cognitive system. The notion of "cognitive system", quite vast indeed, tends to be understood in a variety of ways. The *term* "cognitive system" is often used to refer to a self-sufficient psychological unit, but sometimes it refers to a functionally partial one, as some open unit capable of supporting social cogitative processes or 'swarm intelligence' and so forth for group decisions. These all being homonymous, "cognitive system" has different referential functionalities in the machine fabrication fields stretching across traditional HCI (one machine, one user) to the newer CSCW field (one Machine for many users), and something beyond this in future (?). Let us integrate the notion of cognitive system into our study with a view to recovering the implications of working in technological fields; such analytical practices instigated the beginnings of Cognitive Technology, a field of study that has been largely overlooked because of the implicitness involved in epistemological shifts in a field where the tangibility of the final product seems to fill up too much of the picture. Users' needs may represent a question, technological endeavours at the interface may represent the response. *And the other way around, simultaneously.* Genuine communication is thus established in a conceptual model. Analogical thinking in coordination with erotetics (the logic of questions and answers) will produce the verification required of the resulting relationships in order to establish whether or not communication may hold in other situations. If a concept can be both a question vis-à-vis another concept, and the response to the question it triggers in that same concept (and vice versa), a genuine contract of communication is "signed" between the two.

---

[5] Amongst many of the European elements there is the OPECST in France, the BMFT in Germany, the OMFB as the Hungarian National Commitee for Technological Development and STOA, the Scientific and Technological Options Assessment at the European Parliament.
[6] The reader should consult in particular Dr R.E.H.M. Smits' work (1990), and also, Pettrella, R. (1992).

COMMUNICATION AND THE EXTENSION OF DIALOGISM

Our approach in the past has been aimed at the absence of genuine communication in man-machine situations in an attempt to shed light on practices that deficiently lay claim to communication. The reasons for that unmasking activity were 1) to point out the necessarily subjective nature of design, and consequently 2) to stress the fact that the communicative process between the Self and the Other must involve an authentic referent. Reworking such an approach is done with a view to drawing parallels in other domains. While endeavouring to accomplish this through dialogism, we aim to provide an improved conceptual vantage-point for scientists concerning their own role and the communicable interplay between the concepts they master.

Reasonably, the concept of dialogism forces us to abandon the code model used to simulate interpersonal communication because human communication is therein described as a process in which information is conveyed to and fro *between two* systems; we favour using a singular systemic model that shelters information as being communicated *within one* system (only the referents would be outside). This would be a major step to correctly describing the conditions for genuine communication. This brings us to the next question: "what is dialogism exactly?" Actually, dialogism is a vast concept. The strange word seemingly enough is only found in specialised linguistic and philosophical dictionaries. It was Bakhtine who wrote significantly on this topic, but our conception of dialogism is not polyphonical in nature (voices in parallel) as his seems to be (if taking Bakhtine's stance, an inference that could possibly be drawn is that a "fusible alloy" of the type text-upon-text-upon-text... can solder together a relationship in the heat of scholarly debate); our conception is one that seeks to explore the immediacy of the plurivocity missing in literary structure, so we mean to distinguish the co-speakers from one another in the same system. *Dialogism denotes the quality of two entities that, before action, already form one within a system* (in this case, the structure text-upon-text-upon... is seen as the *result* of the relationship). In this capacity, we feel dialogism can be used as a method of explanation—like one might use metaphor, to get an idea across, although one must avoid overdoing it. Quite obviously this approach has greater affinity with analogy than analysis. However, if dialogism can provide for a sort of empty model to be filled in, it may then simulate situations other than human communicative processes thereby having explanatory value for a variety of other fields of research. We shall call this its *power of notional communicability.* Here we extend the notion of dialogism possibly at our own peril[7] as we are not familiar with many of the technological programmes for which we have a hunch may be implicated here. According to Von Schomberg, "... individual disciplines, as they advance, are generating more and more knowledge on a small number of details, or microfields. However, they

---

[7]As Jacques would say, "A model attains its extreme limit of relevance when it is abusively extrapolated...". He goes on to use *communication* as an example: "How is one to take realities as different from one another as the physical transfer of information and the genesis of verbal messages and label both as communication?" *Cf.* Jacques, F., (1985), p. 190, (translation courtesy of the authors).

would appear to have to leave certain crucial questions unanswered, because discussing ecological questions scientifically means attempting to understand open systems. As a result, certain epistemological viewpoints can be considered true only if we assume the existence of more or less plausible presuppositions, which we nevertheless cannot assume are exhaustive" (Von Schomberg, 1995). Our main premise is that there exists a process of genuine communication concerning the exchange of information that shapes Man's needs and technological progression, each in respect of the other, *within a single (open) system*. Admittedly, the presuppositions of our conceptual work can only be subject to the verdict of tomorrow's practicians (not to mention historians) in a retrospective way.

It is time to take a look at the original model of dialogism as put forth by Francis Jacques with a view to schematising interpersonal communication:

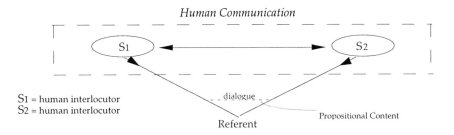

Figure 1: Human Communication

Cognitivist notions like input and output are of no explanatory value for interpersonal communication as information is physically grounded outside the system *a priori* to interaction. Explicit recording of much data relevant to the exchange does not occur within the system—as lexical entries in a data base; in fact, in order to accommodate true reference, the piece of information in question is neither in reach nor is it physically transferred—out of reach, it *can* be referred to. So, in figure 1, the line linking S_1 and S_2 is abstract in nature, like a contract. Adjacently to work in HCI, the ideal machine for a task still stumps designers according to dialogical modelling for society's needs with technology's productions[8]. For instance, when I (S_1) speak of "freedom", none of my neuro-physiological being actually has ownership of that notion, nor does my interlocutor's being (S_2). The propositional content, the semantic level of our dialogue, is 'hung' between us, and constitutes the thread by which the relational coupling in the system is sustained. My access to the exact notion is thus restricted by a pragmatic filter inherent to the workings of reference and that leaves me with a notional residue just as radically indeterminate from the one accessed by my interlocuter through his filter as his is to mine. It is also true that the other is always present and conscious of his version of that object with me, whether that

---

[8] *Cf. infra* footnote n° 10.

other be real or putative. Can one say that both interlocutors are focalised on the same thing?

By now the reader is wary that there is the risk of exchanges remaining purely informational. Seeing that machines cannot speak *of* something (which by the way is reason enough for them being given a lesser isolated psychological presence, and such is the case, given the advent of CSCW-type applications, thanks to the *social turn* of cognitive systems), it would seem reasonable to say that all reference *is* co-reference (Jacques, 1979). Thus "split referentiality" prevails when a machine simply *denotes* the "same referent" as a user as co-reference is severed. Unless both (referent-oriented) poles are involved in the production of an exchange, as in the case of human speakers consciously converging upon the same referent together, there is nothing but denotative information flow. Even though dialogical modelling was not of direct use in HCI because of this 'minor' difficulty, it has been useful for modelling processes that embed problems of monologism. Working on dialogism spurs long-term fundamental research insofar as it is only by escaping the Denigration of Denotation that the pace of interaction between culture and technology will quicken, a toilsome hill indeed. The unreachability of the referent provides the rationale for the existence of motivation, intention, cooperation and investigation in the probing of referential vectors towards the referent. This will be of major importance enabling the transportation of our model to the wider socio-political landscape. The very nature of the ultimate referent implied by conceptual TA "matches" that of the ideal machine.

DEGREES OF CONVERGENCE IN TA DECISION-MAKING

We mean to circumscribe the possible conditions under which technology assessors may construct interaction, whatever the quality of that interaction may turn out to be. This is aimed not only at re-creating the discursive structure found in Cognitive Technology Theory, but the beginnings of a scalar function for measuring the dynamic interlocutivity of political strategies on the TA agenda. With regards to everyday assessment activities, the idea was not incubated to thwart Speech Act Theory as a scientific method but to try and embed its pragmatic aspect in a genuine account of *communicability,* commonly missing from this political assessment of matters technological (often "directives") which can encumber *scientific* assessment. In this respect, the pre-assessment measures taken and the decisive acts of the technology assessor are like Speech Acts in that they have to meet certain conditions in order to transpire (Searle, 1969). Constructive Technology Assessment takes a look back at the relationship from whence the technology comes (figure 2).

In order for assessors to perform decision-making whereby the various technological options are sifted through, they must have a (more or less good) grasp on what public research and development preferences currently are on one hand, and on the other, the nature, needs and plans of the people, the satisfaction of whom remains in the balance.

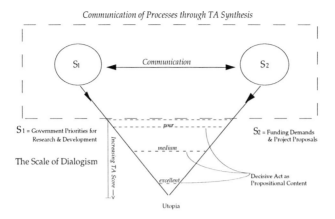

Figure 2: Communication of Processes through TA Synthesis

The vision of the future for the group concerned is subject to the magnet of the referent: the elaboration of the priorities in S_1, (fig.1) along with the lobbying efforts in S_2, are represented in a *referential convergence upon Utopia*. But not quite. The selected projects and encouraged enterprises, *as a result of technology assessors' decisive acts,* have their *raison d'être* in the fact that the world has not already attained this State. How close a politico-social strategy comes to achieving this goal is reflected in the *personal* criteria of the technology assessor. Each strategy—however efficient for the two poles—is portrayed by a fine line along which one finds "re-election" and the "electorate's satisfaction" criteria. All strategies sustain the communication contract between S_1 and S_2, each with its own rating on a scale of dialogical connivance. Subsidised make-work funding or tax cuts for entrepreneurial undertakings will help produce technology to be evaluated in this realm of notional communication; the higher the factor of dialogism present, the higher its TA appreciation will be.

The approach rejoins the more familiar Political Science horizons inasmuch as the notion of co-reference designates a non-reducing (transdisciplinary) area "outside" the dialogical system. Though referring to the ultimate referent in this area is clearly the main generator of progress, the area neither belongs to the system nor is independent of it but represents something commonly known as *non lieu* or Utopia (an inescapable project, but unachieved). We sought to explore this imaginary land in a logical manner, that is without going into the details of TA manoeuvres. The remark that would have to be made is that Utopia is the referential anchor for Technology Assessment, a stronghold to which the destiny of TA theories are consequential, as on the one hand Utopianism intuitively has always been the driving force behind how policy-makers imagine the seat of humanity tomorrow[9], and secondly, technology more than any object is related to our future. Gaining further knowledge of this region will help preserve sound intersubjective premises to the pursuit of the objectives, including methods of

---

[9]Habermas defines technology as "Intentionality with a view to an end", *cf.* Habermas, J., (1973).

scoring and ethical decision-making for Genetic Engineering, or technical risk and other endeavours as in fields like HCI. For example, one might transpose notions from HCI into the dialogical model if one were a political advisor or observer concerned with that particular field of work[10].

CONCLUSIONS: TOWARDS EMPATHETIC GUIDANCE IN TA

The background for the current article consists partly in giving up the "narrow" laboratories of HCI research for wider social horizons as the notion of *communication* is inappropriate there[11]. As a consequence, we tried to unify ideas in two neighbouring fields, Human-Computer Interaction and Technology Assessment, both working towards a greater "humaneness" of technologies—to be understood not in the sense of "making human" but "humane" or "benevolent" and thus inflicting the minimum of 'pain'. The line of thought is parallel to the *Cognitive Technology/Technological Cognition* opposition/attraction that Gorayska and Marsh use to investigate the relationship between cause and effect. Comparison between HCI and TA are possible through analogy. Both have their own specific genesis and evolution: HCI studies carried out by researchers in cognition for the CT/TC paradigm, American Congress and Political Science

---

[10]*Cf.* Schmidt, C., (forthcoming), a Special Topic Issue on 'Cognitive Technology' of *AI & Society,* in which the diagram below is proposed. The strategic planning in this field may include choosing from the various technical methods used at the interface—such as Natural Language Processing or Graphic User Interface. The advisor or observer may rate these techniques according to how close they come to the ultimate touchstone of artefactual purpose. The desire for immortality mentioned by Gorayska & Mey (1996, p. 5) may well be a part of their vision of a Utopian State which would include computational artefacts, and which we introduce in a very general formula in the present article.

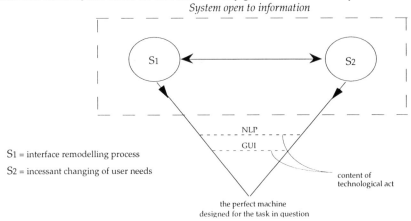

System open to information

S1 = interface remodelling process
S2 = incessant changing of user needs

the perfect machine
designed for the task in question

[11]An in depth treatment of this problem started with (Schmidt, 1996). It would equally be true to say that models based on *communication* are not suitable for portraying the relationship between equilibrists and expansionists given their current discourses. They just do not speak the same language. Respectively, the two groups put forth ideas for radically reducing consumption and minimising the precarious ecological state of our home planet. There is a "massive denial of the need to bring into relation the conflicting values of these two models" according to Victor Margolin.

researchers for Technology Assessment. Dialogism (Jacques, 1985; Schmidt, 1997b) is proposed above as an instrument of conceptual guidance for modelling progress in constructive TA. The recognition of a point of reference for TA helps sketch out the conditions for communicability between peoples' needs and responses to meet these needs with a view to inaugurating a genuinely neutral scale for assessing technology.

Although the TA cause was our principle concern here, the specialised design activity of Human-Computer Interaction (one which conceives of objects of interaction from a utilitarian perspective) was the spawning place for our thoughts. The two are not of the same order. Intuitively, we feel the *pragmatic approach of dialogism* could have further general uses. We are confident of the *exportability* of dialogism and that it can successfully be used to describe/explain phenomena in other domains having an important technological factor, or even domains having a stake in the Arts, Sciences or Culture. An important point to develop in future would be to weigh technological innovation against the social and human innovation of organisations like the UN and to elaborate on techniques for monitoring their (reciprocal?) impacts. Can we not find solid grounds for co-reference between ecology and enterprise too? The concept of dialogical modelling, as it has frequently been understood within the context of design for Human-Computer scenarios, has in this study undergone heavy modification and mass expansion to accommodate the contentious politics surrounding the various purposes of technological development. Therefore, it is amenable to being developed as a useful means of measurement with respect to other like mandates of human kind.

REFERENCES

Austin, J., 1962. *How to do Things with Words*, Oxford University Press.
Bimber, B. & D. Guston, 1995. Politics by the Same Means: Government and Science in the United States. in Jasanoff, S., et al, eds, *Handbook of Science and Technology Studies*, London: Sage.
Bourdieu, P., 1982. *Ce que parler veut dire: L'économie des échanges inguistiques*, Fayard.
Card, S., T. Moran, & A, Newell, 1983. *The Psychology of Human-Computer Interaction*, Hillsdale, NJ: Lawrence Erbaum Associates.
Dennett, D., 1987. *The Intentional Stance*, MIT Press.
Dupuy, J.- P. & P. Dumouchel, 1983. *L'Auto-organisation : de la physique à la politique*, Paris: Seuil.
Engel, P., 1992. *États d'esprit : questions de philosophie de l'esprit*. Aix-en-Provence: Alinéa.
Gorayska, B. & J. Marsh, 1996. "Epistemic Technology and Relevance Analysis: Rethinking Cognitive Technology", in Gorayska, B. & J. L. Mey, eds, *Cognitive Technology: In Search of a Humane Interface*. Amsterda: Elsevier/North Holland, pp. 27-39
Gorayska, B. & J. L. Mey, 1996. *Cognitive Technology: In Search of a Humane Interface*. Amsterdam: Elsevier/North Holland.

Gorayska, B. & J. L. Mey, 1996. Cognitive Technology. In K. S. Gill, ed., *Information Technology and the Culture of the Post-Industrial Society. Human Machine Symbiosis*, Berlin: Springer Verlag, pp. 287-294.

Grice, P., 1975. Logic and Conversation. In Cole, P. & J. Morgan, eds, *Syntax and Semantics : Speech Acts, Vol. 3*, New York/London: Academic Press, pp. 41-58.

Habermas, J., 1973. *La technique et la science comme ideologie*, Gallimard. [Techniks und Wissenschaft als Ideologie].

Habermas, J., 1990. *The Philosophical Discourse of Modernity: Twelve Conferences*, Oxford: Polity/Blackwell; also at 1987 Cambridge Mass.: MIT. [Der philosophische Diskurs der Moderne].

Hronszky, I & Låszlô, T. (eds.), 1995. *Introduction into Technology Assessment*, Budapest: OMFB.

Jacques, F., 1991. "Argumentation et stratégies discursives". In Lempereur, A., ed., *L'Argumentation*, Liège: Mardaga, pp. 153-171.

Jacques, F., 1990. *De "On Denoting" de B. Russell à "On Referring" de P. F. Strawson, l'avenir d'un paradigme, Hermès VII : Bertrand Russell, de la logique à la politique*, Paris: Éditions du CNRS, pp. 91-100.

Jacques, F., 1985. *L'Espace logique de l'interlocution*, Paris: Presses Universitaires de France.

Jacques, F., 1982. *Différence et subjectivité : Anthropologie d'un point de vue relationnel*, Paris: Aubier Montaigne.

Jacques, F., 1979. *Dialogiques : recherches logiques sur le dialogue*, Paris: Presses Universitaires de France.

Laurel, B., ED., 1990. *The Art of Human-Computer Interface Design*, New York: Menlo Park, Apple Computer/Addison-Wesley.

Lobet-Maris, C. & B. Kuster, 1994. Savoir et politique: mutations de valeurs dans le cadre de la cooperation scientifique et technique europeenne, *Revue Politique et Management Public*, 11(2), June.

Lobet-Maris, C., & B. Kuster, 1992. Technology Assessment: un concept et des pratiques en evolution, *Technologies de l'information et Société*, 4(4), pp. 435-457.

Margolin, V., 1996. Global Expansion or Global Equilibrium? Design and the World Situation, *Design Issues*, 12 (2), Cambridge, MA: The MIT Press.

Maturana, H. & Valera, F., 1980. Autopoiesis and Cognition: The Realization of the Living, *Boston Studies in the Philosophy of Science*, 42, Dordrecht: Reidel.

Mey, J. & M. Talbot, 1988. Computation and the Soul, *Journal of Pragmatics*, 12, pp. 743-789.

Norman, D., 1988. *The Psychology of Everyday Things*, New York: Basic books.

Pettrella, R., 1992. Le printemps du Technology Assessment en Europe, *Technologies de l'information et Société*, 4(4), pp. 425-435.

Putnam, H., 1981. *Reason, Truth and History*, Cambridge: Cambridge University Press.

Quine, W. V. O., 1960. *Word and Object*, Cambridge, MA: The MIT Press.

Ruch, P., 1995. Eastern Europe and Technological Assessment: The Genesis, in, *Proceedings of the IEUG conference on "Relations between EU and Countries of Eastern and Central Europe"*, Geneva, 7-9 June: Institut Europeen de l'Universite de Geneve.

Ryle, G., 1973. *The Concept of Mind*. London: Penguin Books; (Preface for French tr. by F. Jacques).

Schmidt, C., forthcoming. The Person-machine Confrontation: Investigations into the Pragmatics of Dialogism, Special Topic Issue on 'Cognitive Technology' of *AI & Society*, Springer International.

Schmidt, C., 1997a. Pragmatically Pristine, the Dialogical Cause, 'Open Peer Community Invited Commentary' on MELE, A., "Real Self-deception" in *Behavioral and Brain Sciences*, 20(1), Cambridge University Press.

Schmidt, C., 1997b. The Systemics of Dialogism: On the Prevalence of the Self in HCI Design, Special Topic Issue on 'Human-Computer Interface' of the *Journal of the American Society for Information Science*, 48(11), pp. 1073-1081.

Schmidt, C., 1996. La rencontre homme-machine: pour une approche systémique du dialogisme. *Technologies de l'information et sociéte*, 8(1), pp. 7-25.

Schmidt, C., 1995. Information Processing, Context Creation, Setting Minds in Public Arenas: Investigative Techniques for Client/automaton Dialogue, The IJCAI-'95 Workshop on Modelling Context in Knowledge Representation and Reasoning, *Proceedings of the 14th International Joint Conference on Artificial Intelligence*, (Montréal), Paris: Institute Blaise Pascal, pp. 121-131.

Searle, J., 1969. *Speech Acts*. Cambridge University Press.

Shannon, C. & W. Weaver, 1949. *The Mathematical Theory of Communication*, Urbana: Univ. of Illinois Press.

Smits, R.E.H.M., 1990. State of the Art of Technology Assessment in Europe, (STB-TNO), a report to the 2nd European Congress on Technology Assessment, *People and Technology, Ways and Practice of Technology Assessment*, Milan 14-16 Nov.

Sperber, D. & D. Wilson, 1986. *Relevance: Communication and Cognition*, Oxford: Blackwell.

Suchman, L., 1987. *Plans and Situated Actions: The Problem of Human-Machine Communication*, Cambridge, MA: Cambridge University Press.

Vernant, D., 1996. *Le Dialogique, sur les formes philosophiques, littéraires, linguistiques et cognitives du dialogue*, Berne: Peter Lang.

Vernant, D., 1996. L'intelligence de la machine et sa capacité dialogique. In Rialle, V. & D. *Fisette, eds, Penser l'esprit : des sciences de la cognition à une philosophie cognitive*, Grenoble: Presses Universitaires Grenoble, pp. 85-101.

Von Schomberg, R., 1995. *The Erosion of the Valuespheres. The Ways in which Society Copes with Scientific, Moral and Ethical Uncertainty, Contested Technology: Ethics, Risk and Public Debate*, Tilburg: International Centre for Human and Public Affairs.

Vygotsky, L., 1979. The Genesis of Higher Mental Functions, in Wertsch, J., *The Concept of Activity in Soviet Psychology*, Sharpe.

Wittgenstein, L., 1989. *Investigations philosophiques*, Gallimard. [Philosophical Investigations].

Humane Interfaces: Questions of method and
practice in Cognitive Technology
J.P. Marsh, B. Gorayska and J.L. Mey (Editors)

Chapter 17

SUCCESSFUL TECHNOLOGY MUST ENABLE PEOPLE TO UTILIZE EXISTING COGNITIVE SKILLS

Muneo Kitajima

National Institute of Bioscience and Human-Technology

INTRODUCTION

Many of our activities are purposeful because we interact with our environment to achieve specific goals. What we actually do at a given moment, however, is determined not only by goals and the environment but also by the knowledge utilised to comprehend the situation. To select what to do, we integrate these sources of information: goals, information from the environment, and knowledge relevant to the current situation. This is especially true when we must discover the actions necessary to accomplish goals in unfamiliar situations.

In this chapter, text comprehension is regarded as one of the fundamental cognitive skills that could be applied to deal with these situations. Text comprehension is a highly automated collection of cognitive processes that make use of massive amounts of knowledge stored in long-term memory. Readers activate knowledge from long-term memory relevant to the current reading goal and integrate this knowledge with the current goal and representation of text. Conflict among activated knowledge elements may exist which necessitates an integration process to arbitrate this conflict within an appropriate time frame.

The goals of reading are diverse—from collecting information from technical documentation and solving word problems to guessing who a criminal might be in a detective story but people still apply a universal, and fundamental primary text comprehension skill to each comprehension activity. This chapter suggests yet another goal-directed activity where the text comprehension skill is employed—interacting with graphical user interfaces (GUI). In this activity, people read task descriptions and interact with computer applications to achieve their tasks. Objects on the screen replace the text of ordinary reading. This chapter presents a comprehension-based model for these processes, called the **LI**nked model of

<u>C</u>omprehension-based <u>A</u>ction planning and <u>I</u>nstruction taking (**LICAI**).[1] This model is based on the construction integration theory, a well-established cognitive model of text comprehension, developed by Kintsch (1988).

Text comprehension is probably one of the most fundamental skills people employ when they interact with their environment in goal-directed activities. However, when this skill is applied to different domains such as human computer interaction, it might not work properly if the environment is not designed to facilitate its use. Therefore, I suggest that the LICAI model be used to identify cognitive problems that might occur when people engage in activities where they take instructions to perform tasks. A LICAI simulation is presented to demonstrate this point.

This chapter begins by describing an example situation identifying two fundamental cognitive processes indispensable to generating comprehension-based, goal-directed interactive activities. One is the goal formation process, and the other is the goal–action mapping process. Experimental results supporting the goal formation process are then described. The next section describes the LICAI model, which assumes that these activities are controlled by specific comprehension processes; it is followed by a simple simulation which involves taking realistic instructions to perform tasks. Results are summarised in light of the factors to be considered in designing instructions and interface displays that conform to these comprehension processes.

ACCOMPLISHING GOALS ON UNFAMILIAR INTERACTIVE DEVICES

Coordinating Goals and Actions

Imagine a situation where one is faced with an unfamiliar interactive device to accomplish a certain goal. He or she may or may not successfully discover appropriate actions. What would determine the results? What kinds of cognitive processes would work? How would they work? This section addresses these issues by introducing one of my experiences in Germany. The episode was as follows:

I arrived at the airport in Stuttgart, Germany, at about 9 p.m. I decided to go to my hotel by train. I had no trouble finding the train station by following well-designed signage. Then I had to buy a ticket from Stuttgart airport station to the station where my hotel was located: Neckartor. I stood facing a ticketing

---

[1] When LICAI is pronounced [li kai], the pronunciation represents a two-kanji Japanese word,

理解 , meaning 'comprehension.'

machine. As this was my first visit to Germany, I had never used this machine. Even worse, I could not read German. I could not find anyone to ask how to operate it. For a few minutes, I observed the machine and the board next to it. I thought I understood what was expected. I read a three-digit code off the board representing the destination and entered the code from a ten number key pad on the panel. The machine then showed the fare. I inserted the necessary coins in the slot. The machine issued the ticket. I took it.

I discovered a successful sequence of actions by myself. However, the sequence of actions was completely different from the one I normally use in my home country, Japan. The question is: How did I perform this task successfully without knowledge of the sequence of correct operations?

What follows describes a rather informal analysis of the above episode to show the basic ingredients that support goal-directed activities in novel situations. The analysis is based on Norman's (1986) action theory framework, which consists of goals, the stage of evaluation, the stage of execution, and the environment. In addition, the analysis assumes that I transferred the knowledge I normally employ in Japan to the situation I encountered in Germany. Thus the analysis maps terms used to explain my ticket-buying activity in Japan to similar activity in Germany. Table 1 summarises the results of the analysis.

Goals

In the analysis, two common subgoals were identified that are decompositions of the top level goal, "Obtain a ticket to the destination (G0)":
Subgoals:

G1. Communicate the fare.
G2. Communicate the destination.

In Japan, I obtain the information about fare first, then insert necessary coins and communicate the destination by pressing an appropriate button. Thus, G1 applied first, followed by G2 and G0. By contrast, in Germany, the order of the subgoals was reversed. What I had to do first was to obtain the code for the destination. Then I had to enter the 3-digit code, say '345,' into the ticket machine, then the machine displayed the fare, and I inserted coins in the slot on the machine. What has to be emphasised here, however, is that the subgoals I know from experiences in Japan were successful in the completely novel situation, even if the order of application was changed.

Actions

Similarly, four common actions were identified:

A1.   Read X from Y.
A2.   Insert coins.
A3.   Press buttons.
A4.   Take the ticket and change.

In Japan, the sequence of action–goal pairs were A1 followed by A2 for G1, then A3 for G2. In Germany, A1 followed by A3 for G2, then A2 for G1. In both countries, A4 was performed for accomplishing the top level goal, G0. The first actions A1 in both countries were apparently the same, but the purposes were different; in Japan, "Read the *fare* from the *table* (A1) in order to communicate the fare (G1)", whereas in Germany, "Read the *code* for the destination from the *board* (A1) in order to communicate the destination (G2)." A2 and A3 were performed to accomplish the goals G1 and G2, respectively. Because the order of the goals were reversed, the order of these actions were reversed.

Necessary Processes for Mapping a Top Level Goal on Actions

The analysis shows the pieces — the sub-goals and the actions — that were successfully reorganised to achieve the top level goal in an unfamiliar situation. There are three important processes:

The first process is to generate correct subgoals for a top level goal and to make these available during the task. In the example, G0 was decomposed into G1 and G2, and they were maintained during the interaction [*the goal formation process*].

The second is to select a correct subgoal from the available subgoals. The selection was done by integrating information from the environment with the available subgoals. In Japan, the presence of the fare table was critical when the subgoal "communicate the fare (G1)" was selected, whereas in Germany, the presence of the table of destination was critical when the subgoal "communicate the destination (G2)" was selected [*the goal selection process*].

The third is to map the selected subgoal onto a correct sequence of actions. Again, the selection of an action is done by integrating pieces of information such as information from the environment (e.g., the appearance of the ticket machine, the fare table, highlighting of buttons, etc.), its elaboration by using knowledge from long-term memory (e.g., a button can be pressed for communication), and the current subgoal [*the goal–action mapping process*].

In Japan			In Germany		
State of the environment	*Goal*	*Action*	*State of the environment*	*Goal*	*Action*
Railway map, Fare table			Railway map, Table of destination		
	Communicate fare (G1)			Communicate destination (G2)	
		Read fare from table (A1)			Read code from board (A1)
Ticket machine, Slots for coins			Ticket machine, Numeric keypad		
		Insert coins (A2)			Press buttons (A3)
Ticket machine, Buttons			Ticket machine, Slots for coins		
	Communicate destination (G2)			Communicate fare (G1)	
		Press button (A3)			Insert coins (A2)
Ticket Machine, Change, Ticket			Ticket machine, Change, Ticket		
	Obtain ticket (G0)			Obtain ticket (G0)	
		Take ticket and change (A4)			Take ticket and change (A4)

Table 1. A comparison of the sequences of actions involved in the ticket buying activity.

GENERATION OF GOALS FROM INSTRUCTIONS

In this episode, the correct actions would have never been discovered unless the correct set of workable subgoals had been generated. Having the knowledge to transform the top level goal into the subgoals was crucial. Such transformation is a well-known process that has been studied in detail in the context of word problem solving (Kintsch, 1988; Kintsch and Greeno, 1985). The original problem statement, for example, "Joe had 8 marbles. Then he gave 5 marbles to Tom. How many marbles does Joe have now?" must be transformed into an abstract form that is useful for arithmetic calculation before actual calculation is performed. Even if one has excellent calculation skills, they are useless if a correct transformation has not been achieved.

This section introduces a laboratory experiment conducted by Terwilliger and Polson (1996) that shows how people really transform their original goal given as task instructions into workable subgoals in the context of human computer interaction. Terwilliger and Polson measured the time it took experienced Macintosh users, who had never used a graphing application, to interact with two forms of the variable selection dialog box. They found clear evidence that people make such transformations.

In the experiment, the user first read a single sentence of instructions, then created a graph from pre-existing data by pulling down a menu, releasing on a menu item, and then assigning variables to axes in a dialog box. The variables in the data to be graphed were "absences" and "month."

Two versions of instructions were considered:

Instructions:
- XY instructions
    "Create a graph with month on the X-axis and absences on the Y-axis."
- FN instructions
    "Create a graph of absences as a function of month."

Similarly, two versions of dialog box for the assignment of axes were devised:

Dialog boxes:
- XY dialog box
    The left selection list was labelled "X Axis:" and the right selection list was labelled "Y Axis:".
- FN dialog box
    The left list was labelled "Plot:" and the right list was labelled "As a Function of:".

Different subjects were exposed to all combinations of instructions and dialog box type. Sixteen subjects were drawn from the introductory psychology subject pool at the University of Colorado and received course credit for their participation in the experiment. Four versions of the system were created, one for each combination of "XY" or "FN" instructions with an "XY" or "FN" dialog box. Subjects read the instructions on one sheet of a workbook, then switched to a different sheet to perform the necessary actions. The total time to create the graph was recorded automatically for each subject. The average times for each condition are shown in Table 2. An ANOVA with two between-subjects variables revealed that, on average, the task took significantly longer when the dialog box had the "FN" labels than when it had the "XY" labels. There were no other significant effects or interactions. A set of planned comparisons revealed that the average times for the two versions of dialog box were significantly different for each version of the instructions, but that the times for the two versions of the instructions were not significantly different for either version of the dialog box.

| Dialog Box Type | Instructions Type | | |
	XY	FN	Average
XY	M = 80.31 SE = 10.52	M = 78.59 SE = 6.43	M = 79.45 SE = 5.71
FN	M = 117.58 SE = 11.89	M = 113.55 SE = 8.45	M = 115.57 SE = 6.80
Average	M = 98.95 SE = 10.18	M = 96.07 SE = 8.23	M = 97.51 SE = 6.34

Table 2: Average time in seconds to create graph by instructions and dialog box type. (adapted from Terwilliger and Polson, 1996)

In this experiment, the subjects would have transformed "FN" instructions into the form comparable with the representations for "XY" instructions when they finished reading it. In my episode in Germany, the internally generated top level goal, G0, would have been transformed into the subgoals, G1 and G2. In both cases, the representations of goals were different from the original ones. People would use goals represented in very specialised forms suitable for selecting actions on the interfaces. These goals would have been generated by decomposing and/or transforming their original goals, which can be either internal, like 'obtain ticket,' or external, like 'XY' or 'FN' instructions.

A COMPREHENSION-BASED MODEL OF GOAL FORMATION AND GOAL–ACTION MAPPING: LICAI

Above, I outlined the three processes indispensable for discovering correct actions when interacting with novel interfaces: the goal formation, goal selection, and goal action mapping processes. Goal formation through transformation has been evidenced by the laboratory experiment described in the previous section. Goal action mapping has been studied extensively in the field of human computer interaction (e.g., Hutchins, Hollan, and Norman, 1986; Payne, Squibb, and Howes, 1990).

This section describes a model that integrates these three processes. The basic idea is that each of these processes can be modelled as a comprehension process, characterised as highly automated cognitive processes that use massive amounts of knowledge stored in long-term memory. The model is called **LI**nked model of **C**omprehension-based **A**ction planning and **I**nstruction taking (**LICAI**), developed by Kitajima and Polson (1996, 1997), which deals with situations where people take instructions and map their understanding onto actions on interfaces. It is currently being applied to model people's interaction within office automation and flight automation environments.

The cognitive processes specified in LICAI are implemented using the construction integration architecture developed by Kintsch (1988). Thus, I start by describing this architecture and then explain the LICAI model.

Construction–Integration Architecture for Comprehension Process

The construction integration architecture is symbolic-connectionist and has been applied successfully to model cognitive processes such as text comprehension (Kintsch, 1988), word problem solving (Kintsch, 1988), and action planning (Mannes and Kintsch, 1991; Kitajima and Polson, 1995). The construction integration architecture assumes that parsers map surface representations into propositional semantic network representations (text in Kintsch, 1988, and visual displays in Kitajima and Polson, 1995), and a bottom-up, weakly constrained, rule-based process generates alternatives from the semantic representations. The rules are not context sensitive; therefore, the alternatives represented in the network may not be consistent with the current context.

The construction phase generates a network of propositions that contain a representation of the input (text or visual display), alternative meanings and interpretations of the input, and possible alternative actions. This network also incorporates the knowledge necessary to select among the alternatives. This knowledge includes goals, information retrieved from long-term memory, and information carried over from previous construction integration cycles. A fundamental linking mechanism assumed by the construction integration theory is the argument overlap mechanism: when two nodes share symbols, they are connected.

The integration phase selects an alternative by integrating information represented in the network generated during the construction phase. Integration can be thought of as a constraint satisfaction process. The network of interconnected propositions defines a collection of constraints that are satisfied by the selected alternative. Integration is performed in a spreading activation process. The nodes in the network can be further divided into sources of activation, targets of activation, and links between sources and targets. Goals and the representation of the current context (i.e., text or visual display) are typical sources, and the targets are alternatives. The linking information comes from long-term memory and other sources, and the spreading activation process is controlled by the pattern of links in the network. When the integration phase terminates, the most highly activated alternative represents the result of the construction integration cycle that satisfies the constraints. Because propositions in the network are linked by shared arguments, the pattern of argument overlap plays a key role in the results of the integration phase.

The LICAI Model

Overview

Figure 1 schematically describes the LICAI model. The three main processes are expressed by various construction integration cycles along with the kinds of information that constitute networks at various moments.

The *goal formation process* is modelled as a problem-model construction cycle, which is a strategic form of the basic text-comprehension process that generates representations specialised for interacting with devices; that is, the goals that control the solution of a task described in instructions.

If the text contains descriptions of multiple goals, LICAI assumes that they are stored in episodic memory during the goal formation process. When the user finishes reading the instructions and attempts to perform one or more steps of the task, LICAI uses information from the current application display as retrieval cues to select a single goal from the episodic memory. This *goal selection process* is modelled as a memory retrieval cycle, a variation of the basic construction integration cycle developed by Kintsch and Welsch (1991) as a model of cued recall.

The *goal action mapping process* takes the goal retrieved from the episodic memory and attempts to generate one or more actions to satisfy the goal on the interface display. This process is a generalisation of the model of skilled performance using a computer with a graphical user interface developed by Kitajima and Polson (1995), modelled as the pairing of an attention cycle and an action planning cycle.

When reading instructions, a user attempts to extract goals that should be accomplished on an interface. LICAI assumes that this process is analogous to solving word problems. Instructions are processed by executing a single construction integration cycle for each sentence. In the construction phase, LICAI generates a network that includes semantic representations of a sentence as well as elaborations that translate the semantic representation into goals. In the integration phase, LICAI selects a single meaning for the sentence and links this representation with the memory representation of earlier parts of the text. Thus, after reading the entire text, the memory contents represent the result of instruction comprehension. LICAI incorporates three kinds of schema that work during the construction phase. A schema is a knowledge structure that takes a semantic representation of the instructions as input and generates one or more specialised propositions defined by a predicate and slots it with strong constraints on the admissible arguments. The *Global instruction reading schemata* represent the top-level strategy used by a reader to process text that describes a given task. All verbs with the implicit subject YOU are mapped into a text base proposition of the form DO [YOU, verb, object].

Task-domain schemata elaborate DO propositions and generate a more complete description of a task. For example, the original "FN" instructions,

DO [YOU, PLOT, AS-A-FUNCTION-OF [ABSENCE, MONTH]]

will be converted into two propositions:

DO [YOU, PLOT, ON [MONTH, X-AXIS]],
and
DO [YOU, PLOT, ON [ABSENCE, Y-AXIS]].

Task-goal formation schemata transform DO propositions into propositions that represent goals that control the goal action mapping processes. For example, the transformed instructions will be converted into the following forms:

PERFORM [PLOT, MONTH, X-AXIS],
and
PERFORM [PLOT, ABSENCE, Y-AXIS].

Goal Selection Process (See Figure 1)

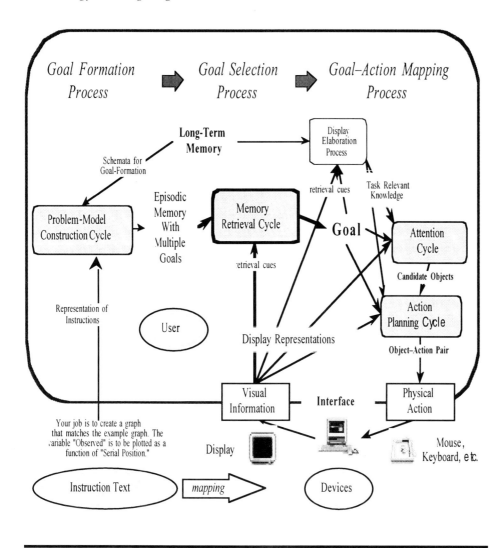

Figure 1. The LICAI model (Kitajima and Polson, 1997).

After reading the instructions, the user tries to select a goal from memory to perform in the current situation. LICAI assumes that a goal is selected from memory by a single construction–integration cycle. In the construction phase, the memory and the current interface display constitute a network. In the integration phase, a goal consistent with the current interface display is selected; that is, the most highly activated goal is selected. Since the sources of activation are the nodes representing the display, and the pattern of links in the network is largely determined by the argument overlap mechanism, a goal that overlaps the currently visible screen objects is likely to be selected. For example, if the representation of the goal includes matching labels on any screen objects, it will be selected.

Goal Action Mapping Process (See thick lines in Figure 1)

After selecting a goal, the user tries to generate a sequence of one or more actions that will accomplish the selected goal. This process is a generalisation of the model of skilled, display-based action planning developed by Kitajima and Polson (1995), which involves two construction integration cycles: the attention cycle and the action planning cycle.

Just as semantic knowledge of words is required to comprehend texts, knowledge about objects on the screen is also indispensable for successful interaction with display-based interfaces. The initial display representations contain only limited information about the identity of each object and its appearance, including visual attributes (e.g. colour, highlighting). The poor display representations are augmented by retrieving relevant knowledge from long-term memory. This display elaboration process is simulated by a random memory sampling process: the retrieval cues are the selected goal and the propositions representing the current display. The elaboration process is stochastic and is taken from Kintsch (1988) where Raaijmakers and Shiffrin's (1981) model was used to describe the retrieval process. The probability that each cue retrieves particular information in a single memory retrieval process is proportional to the strength of the link between them. The model carries out multiple memory retrieval in a single elaboration process. A parameter, *the elaboration parameter*, controls the number of times each argument in the display and goal representations is used as retrieval cue. Kitajima and Polson (1995) discussed in detail the predictions and implications that follow from this stochastic elaboration process.

The retrieved information elaborates the display representation, providing information about interrelationships between display objects, relationships between the goal and display objects, and other attributes of display objects. For example, if Object23 is the screen object in the X-Axis selection list labelled by Month, then the following items are stored in long-term memory about Object23 and can be retrieved by the display elaboration process:

- Object23 has-label Month
- Object23 is-a-member-of Line-Graph-Dialog-Box
- Object23 can-be-pointed-at
- Object23 can-be-selected

The elaborated display representation is the model's evaluation of the current display in the context defined by the goal. This corresponds to the stage of evaluation of Norman's (1986) action theory framework.

In the goal action mapping process, the model first limits its attention to three screen objects (out of ~100 objects displayed on the screen) by applying an attention cycle. These screen objects are candidates for the next action to be operated upon. During the construction phase, a network is generated that consists of nodes representing the goals, the screen objects and their elaborations, and candidate object nodes of the form 'Screen-Object-X is-attended.' Any screen objects are potential candidates. During the integration phase, the conflict is to be resolved. The sources of activation are the goals and the screen objects. The targets are the candidate object nodes. When the spreading activation process terminates, the model selects the three most highly activated candidate object nodes. These nodes represent screen objects to be attended to during the action planning cycle.

The result of the integration process is dominated by two factors: the strengths of links from the representation of the goals, which is defined as *the attention parameter*, and the number of propositions that are necessary to bridge the goals and the candidate objects.

The second construction integration cycle is an action planning cycle. As preparation for constructing a network, the candidate objects carried over from the preceding cycle are combined with any possible actions to form object action pairs of alternatives. The model considers all possible actions on each candidate object. The Kitajima and Polson (1995) model incorporates 18 possible actions.[2] Examples would include 'single-click Object23,' 'move Object23,' and the like.

During the construction phase, the model generates a network that includes the goals, the screen objects and their elaborations, and representations of all possible actions on each candidate object. During the integration phase, the sources are the goals and the screen objects, and the targets are the nodes representing the combinations of object actions. The pattern of activation is determined by the same factors for the attention cycle. At the end of the integration phase, the model selects the most highly activated object action pair whose preconditions are satisfied as the next action to be executed. The action representations include conditions to be satisfied for their execution. The conditions are matched against the elaborated display representations. Some conditions are satisfied by the current screen, others by information that was retrieved from long-term memory in the elaboration process. For example, the model cannot select an action to double click a document icon for editing unless the icon is currently pointed at by the mouse cursor and the information is available that the icon can be double clicked. Observe that if information about a necessary condition is missing from an elaborated display representation, the model cannot perform that action on the *incorrectly* described object.

---

[2]Representations of actions define different functions of single physical actions in many different contexts. For simulating a graph drawing task, the model defines eighteen cognitive actions on six physical actions; Move-Mouse-Cursor, Single-Click, Double-Click, Hold-Mouse-Button-Down, Release-Mouse-Button, and Type.

Failure in Goal–Action Mappings

In a set of simulation experiments reported in Kitajima and Polson (1995), it was found that the goal action mapping can fail due to the following three reasons.

The first is that the attention cycle can fail to include the correct object on the list of candidate objects. The second is that the action planning cycle can fail in which the correct object action pair cannot become the highest activated among the set of executable ones. In the model's terms, these kinds of errors are ascribed to both or either of two reasons: low values of the attention parameter, and /or missing bridging knowledge that had to be retrieved from long-term memory.

The third reason for failure is that the elaboration process fails to incorporate all of the conditions for the correct action in the elaborated display representation. Low values of the elaboration parameter cause this error. Parameter values in the range of 12 to 20 caused the model to simulate error rates in the range of 10% to 20% (Kitajima and Polson, 1995).

The first and the third reasons are internal to the model, whereas the second reason, missing bridging knowledge, would be controlled externally; for example, we can reduce the possibility of failure by carefully designing instructions and interfaces. However, note that this insight comes only from the nature of the goal action mapping process where the goal has already been selected. The goal action mapping process does not know whether the selected goal is the correct one or the wrong one.

The next section focuses on LICAI's simulation of the whole processe to show the second reason can also result in failure to select correct goals. Thus, possibility of failure increases dramatically if the whole process is considered. The final section provides a summary of these analyses.

SIMULATION OF TAKING AND CARRYING OUT LONG INSTRUCTIONS

This section applies the LICAI model to the experimental situation studied by Franzke (1994, 1995). In her experiment, the participants were given instructions as a HyperCard stack. Tasks that participants were given were to create a graph specified in the instructions and make several edits on the default graph. This section reports the results of LICAI's simulation and identifies potential cognitive problems that the participants would have faced. A comparison of Franzke's results with LICAI's simulation can be found in Kitajima and Polson (1997).

Simulation of Performance

Following Franzke's (1994, 1995) experiments, let's assume that the participants have read the following instructions and memorised them. Then they tried to map the results of comprehension onto actions.

Instructions:

In this experiment you are going to learn a new Macintosh application, Cricket Graph, by exploration. The task you are going to perform will be presented to you as a series of exercises. The data you are going to plot is contained in a Cricket Graph document, "Example Data." Your overall goal is to create a new graph that matches the example graph shown in the instructions. Your first exercise is to plot the variable "Number of Accidents" as a function of the variable "Month." After you have created a new graph, you will modify it so that it more closely matches the example given in your instructions.

Goal Formation

The LICAI model reads the above sentences and extracts any potentially useful goals by transforming the textual representation with the help of comprehension schemata for goal formation. For example, by reading the first sentence, LICAI elaborates it to generate a goal 'perform "Learn Cricket-Graph."' Before reading the second sentence, the goal is stored in episodic memory with a memory strength that reflected the degree of the consistency with the other elements in the current working memory. After reading the entire instruction set, the following nine subgoals are generated:

- perform "Learn Cricket-Graph"
- perform "Perform Task"
- perform "Plot Data"
- perform "Create Graph"
- perform "Plot Number-of-Accidents As-a-Function-of Month"
- perform "Put Month on X-Axis"
- perform "Put Number-of-Accidents on Y-Axis"
- perform "undefined-action on a document labelled Example-Data"
- perform "Modify Graph"

Goal Selection

After generating, these nine subgoals are stored in episodic memory. In the course of task performance, when the display shown in Figure 2 is provided, LICAI retrieves a subgoal that is consistent with the current display. Note that the overlapping arguments in the representation of subgoals and screen objects are critical determinants of this selection. The labels on screen objects are part of their representations, and they can be linked to the subgoals. In this case, three goals shown below are likely to be selected:

- perform "Plot Number-of-Accidents As-a-Function-of Month"
- perform "Put Month on X-Axis"
- perform "Put Number-of-Accidents on Y-Axis"

Depending on how these goals were encoded when they were originally generated during the goal formation process, the result of goal selection might differ. Let's assume that 'perform "Put Month on X-Axis"' be selected.

Action Planning

Given the selected goal, 'perform "Put Month on X-Axis"', the LICAI model elaborates the display shown by Figure 2 by using knowledge stored in long-term memory. For example, part of the following knowledge would be incorporated: knowledge about scrolling lists, titles of the list, items of the list, such as, 'the scrolling list items are selectable,' 'the scrolling list titles are not selectable,' etc., and others concerned with the GUI basics. A network elaborated by these pieces of knowledge is linked and integrated. The correct screen object, 'Month,' in the scrolling list labelled by 'Horizontal (X) Axis' would be selected as the object to be

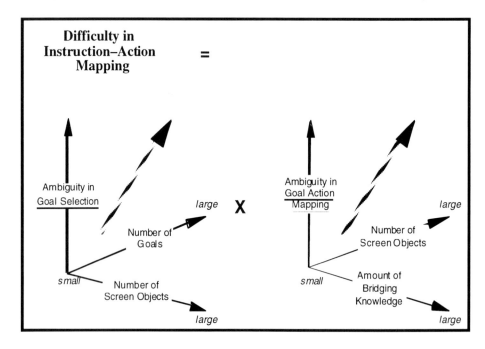

Figure 2. LICAI's predictions on difficulties in mapping instructions onto actions.

acted on, and the sequence of actions, first point at Month, then single-click, would be selected. All these selections are done by comprehension of display on the basis of the given sub-goal and the use of lots of knowledge retrieved from long- term memory.

POTENTIAL DIFFICULTIES IN MAPPING INSTRUCTIONS ON ACTIONS

The LICAI model describes the underlying mechanism that controls users' instruction mapping onto interface actions. A series of construction integration cycles depicts the various component processes executed. Mapping from instructions to an action is successful if the goal formation process generates the correct goal, if the goal selection process selects that goal, and if the goal action mapping process generates the correct action sequence. We predict that this process will be more difficult with longer instructions, more screen objects, and/or an increase in possible actions.

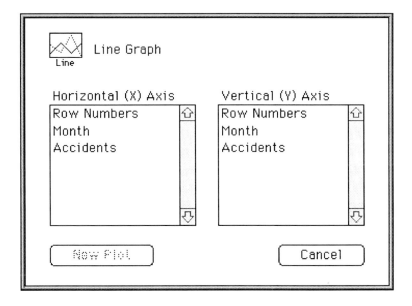

Figure 3. Dialog box that is presented after comprehending the instructions.

Figure 3 schematically illustrates potential difficulties in mapping instructions on actions that the LICAI model predicts. In the simulation described in the previous section, nine subgoals were extracted from the original instructions.

When reading the instructions, the model does not know which subgoals will be relevant or irrelevant, nor the order of their accomplishment. This ambiguity must be resolved by an interface display to be provided. The comprehension process for disambiguating the multiple subgoal problem tends to get difficult as the number of subgoals increases and the number of screen objects that have to arbitrate the problem increases (see the left part of the figure). Likewise, in the goal action mapping process, the attention cycle tends to fail as the amount of knowledge that is necessary to bridge the goal and the correct object gets larger. This would become worse as the number of screen objects increases (see the right part of the figure).

Understanding how people comprehend instructions and how they map their understandings onto interface displays helps us to identify locations where potential problems might occur, and subsequently design strategies to eliminate, or reduce, such problems. I conclude this chapter by suggesting ways to avoid introducing unnecessary difficulties by controlling external sources (i.e., instructions, interface displays):

- Design instruction materials so that the correct goal is generated.
- Design interface displays so that the correct goal is retrieved from the episodic memory generated during the instruction taking process.
- Design interface display so that the correct screen object overlaps with the correct goal.
- Design interface display so that the condition for the correct action is retrieved from long-term memory during the display elaboration process.

REFERENCES

Franzke, M., 1994. *Exploration, acquisition, and retention of skill with display-based systems.* Unpublished doctoral dissertation, Department of Psychology, University of Colorado, Boulder.

Franzke, M., 1995. *Turning research into practice: Characteristics of display-based interaction.* Proceedings of human factors in computing systems CHI '95,. New York: ACM, pp. 421-428

Kintsch, W., 1988. The role of knowledge in discourse comprehension: A construction–integration model. *Psychological Review*, 95, pp. 163-182.

Kintsch, W., and Welsch, D. M., 1991. The construction–integartion model: A framework for studying memory for text. In: W. E. Hockley and S. Lewandowsky, eds., *Relating theory and data: Essays on human memory,.* Hillsdale, NJ: Erlbaum, pp. 367-385.

Kintsch, W., and J. D. Greeno, 1985. Understanding and solving word arithmetic problems. *Psychological Review*, 92, pp. 109-120.

Kitajima, M., and P. G. Polson, 1995. A comprehension-based model of correct performance and errors in skilled, display-based human–computer interaction. *International Journal of Human–Computer Systems*, 43, pp. 65-99.

Kitajima, M., and P. G. Polson, 1996. *A comprehension-based model of exploration.* Proceedings of human factors in computing systems CHI '96,. New York: ACM, pp. 324-331

Kitajima, M., and P. G. Polson, 1997. A comprehension-based model of exploration. *Human–Computer Interaction: Special Issue on Cognitive Architectures in HCI*, 12(4), pp. 345-389.

Hutchins, E. L., J. D. Hollan, and D. A. Norman, 1986. Direct manipulation interfaces. In D. A. Norman and S. W. Draper, eds, *User centered system design*. Hillsdale, NJ: Erlbaum, pp. 87-124.

Mannes, S. M., and W. Kintsch, 1991. Routine computing tasks: Planning as understanding. *Cognitive Science*, 15, pp. 305-342.

Norman, D. A., 1986. Cognitive engineering. In D. A. Norman and S. W. Draper eds, *User centered system design.*. Hillsdale, NJ: Erlbaum, pp. 31-61.

Payne, S. J., H. R. Squibb, and A. Howes, 1990. The nature of device models: The yoked state hypothesis and some experiments with text editors. *Human–Computer Interaction*, 5, pp 415-444.

Raaijmakers, J. G., and R. M. Shiffrin, 1981. Search of associative memory. *Psychological Review*, 88, pp. 93-134.

Terwilliger, R. B., and P. G. Polson, 1996. *Task elaboration or label following: an empirical study of representation in human-computer interaction.* Conference companion of human factors in computing systems CHI '96, New York:ACM, pp. 201–202.

Humane Interfaces: Questions of method and practice in Cognitive Technology
J.P. Marsh, B. Gorayska and J.L. Mey (Editors)
© 1999 Elsevier Science B.V. All rights reserved.

Chapter 18

PALMTOP REMINDING DEVICES
Capabilities and limitations

*Douglas Herrmann, Carol Yoder, Virgil Sheets,
Justine Wells, and Brad Brubraker*

Indiana State University

INTRODUCTION

Failure to remember appointments and chores leads to uncompleted personal and professional obligations. In the past decade, palmtop reminding devices have been developed that allow people to record their scheduled events and subsequently remind them to carry out the intended activity at a certain time by presenting a signal (such as an audible beep) and a message that describes what is to be done (called here a directive). As compared to unaided memory, both the signal and the directive often improve remembering because physical stimuli elicit more attention than ideas that might lead to performing an intended act. The purpose of this chapter is to explore the psychological effects of these reminding devices. The chapter reviews recent findings about how these devices remind people of their intentions and then presents a theoretical examination of the fundamental cognitive processes involved in the use of these devices. Finally, consideration is given to the variety of features of reminding devices that influence their effectiveness.

PALMTOP REMINDING DEVICES: CAPABILITIES AND LIMITATIONS

Intentions must be performed by a deadline or within a certain interval. For example, most prescriptions must be followed at certain times of the day (Leirer, Morrow, Tanke, and Pariante, 1991; Park and Kidder, 1996), and, appointments are supposed to be met approximately on time. Chores do not require the same precision but they still must be completed sometime during an interval. Remembering appointments is often an onerous task, particularly for people with many responsibilities. Likewise, remembering chores can be difficult too.

In the past decade, palmtop computing devices have been developed that actively remind people of their scheduled intentions (Shelly, Cashman, Waggoner, and Waggoner, 1997). The purpose of this article is to examine how these devices may improve remembering. Do these devices remind people any better than when people remember without an aid or when people are reminded by written notes on a calendar or diary?

We begin by reviewing how people schedule events and remind themselves of these events without the benefit of the palmtop reminding devices. Subsequently, the potential for these reminding devices to affect psychological processes will be discussed, along with the psychological advantages that these devices bring to mental processes. Finally this article will address a variety of the characteristics of such technological reminders and recommend some features of their design which may be particularly useful.

THEORY OF REMINDING

There are two kinds of reminding processes: spontaneous and pre-arranged. For a person to spontaneously recall an intended act, a memory of the intention must emerge from unconsciousness to consciousness. The emergence of the prospective memory is presumably triggered either by an unconscious awareness of the passage of the appropriate amount of time (spontaneous reminding) or the presence of environmental cues that are associated with the intended act (arranged reminding) or both (McDaniel and Einstein, 1992).

If a person does not trust in his or her ability to remember an intention spontaneously, a cue is arranged to be available (e.g., audible, visible) prior to the time that the act is to be executed (Doerner, 1987). For a cue to be successful, it must be capable of capturing the person's attention. Across recorded history, a wide variety of objects (e.g., pads of paper, calendars, arrangements of stones, and notches in wood) have been used to provide cues regarding intentions (Harris, 1980a, b; Hunter, 1957).

Components of a Scheduled Intention.

The scheduled intention is comprised of certain components: the action that is to be performed, the deadline that is to be met, and a pre-selected cue that the individual associates with the intention that is expected to elicit awareness of the intended act in time for it to be performed. The expectation for performing an intention on a deadline varies in precision; sometimes the response must be carried out precisely on time and other times the response need only fall somewhere within an interval that contains the deadline (Ellis, 1988).

Intention Signals.

One way to alert someone to an intention is to arrange for an audible signal to occur shortly before the intended act is scheduled to occur. Signals provide a highly salient sensory cue (such as a sound or light) to illicit awareness of the intention. Although sensory signals indicate that an appointment is impending, they do not convey explicitly the intention. Because people can forget what action a signal is intended to cue, a signal must be supplemented by a *directive*: a written cue that describes the intended act. The signal "externalises" the fact that there is an intention to be executed (Gorayska and Mey, 1996) and the directive informs the individual what intended act is be executed just as the user has been made aware by the signal that there is an intention to execute.

Personal Reminding Systems

Paper calendars, memo pads, and even physical objects (Hunter, 1957) work well for reminding people (Harris, 1980a,b; Herrmann and Petro, 1990). However, people are renown for failing to remember the designated time that events occur, both retrospectively and prospectively (Brewer, 1994; Herrmann, 1994; Wagennar, 1986). Calendars and memo pads require people to periodically check a clock and the written reminder (Ceci and Bronfenbrenner, 1985; Ceci, Baker, and Bronfenbrenner, 1988) in order to perform intentions on time. If clock checking could be eliminated, the remembering of intentions might be more accurate. Thus, personal reminder systems have been developed to provide a clear advantage over paper calendars by making clock-checking unnecessary. The device presents a signal on or near the time of the scheduled intention which alerts a person to remember to perform some action at a time that this person may not otherwise think to check his or her schedule.

Most current reminding devices are one component of more complex electronic devices called personal data systems. These devices are usually not much larger than a scientific calculator, and are sometimes referred to as "palmtops." Personal data systems carry out a variety of functions: a telephone and address directory with search mechanisms; a calculator; a clock; a memo directory with search mechanisms; a daily alarm function; schedule planning and reminders (Herrmann, Yoder, Wells, and Raybeck, 1996).

Differences in Reminding Systems.

Access Functions: A striking feature of the reminding devices is that they differ considerably in how they display information about the scheduled events to be accessed. For example, people often like to review their schedule well ahead of time in order to prepare for scheduled events. However, visual review of scheduled intentions is accomplished differently by different devices. Some show only the events of a given day at a time where others allow more global viewing of scheduled intentions (such as an entire week or a month).

Most reminding devices cue the onset of an opportunity to perform an intended act by an audible signal (such as high pitched tone, sometimes called a "beep"). The signal is supplemented by a presentation of a verbal reminder, keyed into the device when the user registers the time of the intention. Some devices provide a beep for every appointment; other devices allow the setting of a beep to be optional (Herrmann et al., 1996).

Human Factors: Keyboard variables, such as size, hardness, and texture of button, are critical to the ease with which a reminding device can be used. Additionally, the legibility of visual display and other factors greatly influence the effectiveness of a reminder. Personal data systems also differ in their durability in that some can withstand being stepped on or dropped whereas others are more fragile. As would be expected, smaller personal data systems are more portable but easier to lose than larger devices.

A THEORETICAL ACCOUNT OF A SIGNAL'S EFFECTS ON PROSPECTIVE MEMORY.

Prospective memory performance has been conceptualised as involving different information processing stages (Ellis, 1996). These stages include encoding the intention, specifying the retention interval, deploying a response to occur within the response interval (which may be at a precise time or within an interval), observing the outcome of the act, and finally evaluating the effect of the intended ·act. In focusing on the effects of a signal, the present article addresses the stages of retention and execution of the intended act. This chapter focuses on the final stage of this process, i.e., deploying a response to occur, as triggered by a signal.

For an intention to be executed in a timely manner, the individual must become aware of the task just prior to the appointed time and remain aware until he or she executes the act. Becoming aware at the appropriate time and remaining aware is probably the most difficult part of prospective memory tasks. Nearly everyone has had the experience of remembering some intention shortly before the act, only to become distracted and later discover that one failed to do something one was supposed to do. A critical part of remembering an intention is to arrange for a reminder to signal with sufficient lead time to prepare for executing the intention. However, the signal must not be set so early as to allow distraction to occur.

Monitoring Intentions in Memory

Theoretically, responding properly to a signal rests on two kinds of monitoring processes that may alert us to perform an intended act. The first kind of monitoring is *active monitoring.* Here, the person attempts to continually monitor the clock and then to execute the intended act as scheduled. The second kind of monitoring is *passive monitoring.* In this circumstance, the person is aware that a task coming up in the near future but the person is not preoccupied with thinking about the task because he or she is aware that a signal will occur to indicate when the task is to be done.

In active monitoring, the individual executes the intended act when a clock or time perception suggests that the appropriate time is at hand. Thus, the individual must remain consciously aware of the passage of time. In passive monitoring, the individual executes the intended act when the memory of the intention emerges into conscious awareness and active monitoring takes over. Signals serve to *trigger* the emergence of an intention into conscious awareness, alerting a person to an upcoming intention and eliciting active monitoring which leads to the execution of the intended task.

Previously only one process, "cueing," has been suggested to account for why signals elicit active monitoring. According to the theory of cueing, people perform the intended act when a *cue* (in the environment or in the individual's body), that has been previously associated with the act, elicits the intention which the individual then executes (cf. Tulving, 1983). Cues that arrive too late are useless and cues that arrive too early may be forgotten prior to task execution.

Cues may be classified as two types. Cues that are written down are regarded as inactive (Harris, 1984a, b) because a person may fail to look at the cues or process them properly while looking at them. Cues that consist of an inescapable sensory experience (light, touch, odour) are said to actively cue the remembering of an intention (Harris, 1984a, b).

The Shift Between Active and Passive Monitoring Processes

A signal provides a highly efficient means for eliciting the memory of an intention as compared to spontaneous recall of the intention. The effectiveness of the signal appears to lie in the signal's ability to shift passive monitoring to active monitoring. Thus, successful recall of intentions rests on factors that lead people to shift back and forth between active and passive monitoring.

The assumption that two different processes underlie the remembering of intentions has been raised from the outset by research involving remembering intentions (Meacham and Leiman, 1982). For example, Wilkins and Baddelely (1978) required subjects to press a button on a device at specified times throughout the day, simulating such tasks as taking medicine at certain times. The device recorded when a button was pressed. The results showed that people generally pressed the button somewhat before the specified time. Because several hours passed between designated times, it was assumed that people did not perform this task by remaining continually conscious of the time. Some subjects would forget altogether to press at a designated time but they, nevertheless, usually remember to press at the next designate time.

In a subsequent study, Harris and Wilkins (1982) required subjects to perform a task of recording specified time intervals while they viewed a movie. These subjects had the task of shifting attention from watching a movie to performing a record keeping task. Ceci and Bronfenbrenner (1985; see also Ceci, Baker, and Bronfenbrenner, 1988) adapted the Wilkins and Baddeley (1978) task for adolescents. Their adolescent subjects performed two intention tasks: baking some cookies and recharging a battery. Both of these tasks require a precise time of task performance. The adolescents were allowed to do other things in the waiting period, e.g., watch a movie. Apparently, those subjects who avoided making an error shifted from passive monitoring to active monitoring immediately before the time of task execution.

The results of these experiments showed that there were few errors of lateness. Instead, the bulk of responding occurred prior to the scheduled time of performance while the subjects did other activities. Thus, subjects were shifting between current activity and monitoring. We propose here that a passive form of monitoring occurs when a person is not consciously thinking about the impending task. This form of monitoring keeps track of the passage of time unconsciously and makes a person aware as the time of an intended act approaches. A well known example of passive monitoring occurs when people awaken prior to their alarm going off or without having set an alarm. Also common is the sudden feeling of knowing that one should be doing something that, with checking, has been scheduled.

Active monitoring occurs when a person is in a heightened state of consciousness, as is typical of vigilance and other attention tasks and involves checking a clock or watch and keeping oneself mindful of the impending task. As a result, active monitoring makes it hard to perform other cognitive tasks concurrently. Perhaps because passive monitoring does not involve clock checking, it is less accurate than active monitoring; however, being unconscious, passive monitoring requires less energy and allows an individual to engage in other tasks. When passive monitoring works effectively, it initiates active monitoring sufficiently ahead of the time that the intended act is to be carried out, whereupon active monitoring takes over and ensures the task is executed.

A Model of Monitoring in Prospective Memory Performance

Figure 1 presents a model of prospective memory based on active and passive monitoring processes. As the figure shows, the model assumes that a person can chose to monitor intentions actively or passively. A person in the active mode can choose to respond whenever it seems appropriate. A person in the passive mode must switch to the active mode before responding. Thus, when a person is in the active mode, he or she will be more accurate than when a person is in the passive mode. However, as the figure shows, a person can switch from the active mode back to the passive mode. Such a shift is always a risk in vigilance tasks that require an individual to actively monitor longer than their attentional capabilities permit. A warning signal, such as is provided by a reminding device, can be expected to elicit active monitoring.

As has been discussed earlier, responding to a warning signal will be dependent on various temporal variables. For example, the time of day that an intention must be carried out can be expected to affect responding. Presumably, as the day goes on, passive monitoring occurs more often relative to active processing. Thus, a signal may be less likely to elicit active monitoring later in the day than earlier in the day. Also, active monitoring elicited by a signal may be more likely to revert

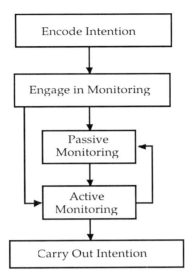

Figure 1. A model of prospective remembering based on active and passive monitoring.

to passive monitoring later in the day than earlier in the day. In addition, since all responses must be executed within an interval of time, signals that anticipate responding too close to the response or, conversely, at too great of an interval, might be expected to result in less accurate responses than when the signal permits just enough time to respond

RESEARCH ON RESPONDING TO WARNING SIGNALS

Subjects in four studies (Herrmann, Sheets, Wells, and Yoder, 1997) carried a My Private Diary (MPD) personal data system, manufactured by Casio Computer Company and Tandy Corporation in 1993. The MPD screen presents the time of an appointment and a brief directive that has been programmed in when the time of the appointment was set. Appointments can be viewed chronologically (by scrolling through one appointment at a time or by searching by date).

The subjects were undergraduate and graduate students in psychology courses at Indiana State University. Each of the four studies involved different groups of students.

The pre-arranged times were programmed into the MPD so that it would signal subjects to call a designated telephone number at the Psychology Department at Indiana State University when the alarm sounded. The pre-arranged times differed according to the time of day of the alarm (morning and evening in Experiments 1 and 4; or morning, afternoon, or evening in Experiments 2 and 3) and the amount of time by which the alarm preceded the call-in time (0 minutes in Experiment 1, 2 and 10 minutes in Experiment 2, and 2, 10, and 20 minutes in Experiments 3 and 4). After the call-in procedure was finished, the subjects were asked to complete a questionnaire that called for ratings about the effectiveness of the MPD and their own performance. Each subject's calls were scored as accurate if within plus or minus one minute. Thus, the results consisted of answers to the questionnaires and the timeliness of call ins. The analyses of the questionnaire data is discussed first and then the analyses of the punctuality of call-ins subsequent to the sounding of the MPD alarm are discussed.

Questionnaire Results

Study 1: Using a seven point scale (ranging from "not at all" to "a lot"), the questionnaire used in the first study asked students to report on (1) how much the MPD helped them remember intentions, (2) the ease with which they learned to use the MPD, (3) whether learning how to use the device was worthwhile, and (4) whether they would continue to use MPD or a similar device.

Eighteen subjects completed the questionnaire. These students reported that it was easy to learn how to use the device (a rating of 4.8 on the seven point scale), and that the MPD helped them remember to perform some intentions (a mean of 3.9 on the seven point scale where 7 was the highest rating) that they might have missed otherwise. These subjects reported that their performance was lower in the evening than in the morning because they were more tired in the evening and because they were involved in activities that led them to ignore the MPD's signal. Fifteen subjects indicated that they would not use such devices in the future but would use a written planner instead. The majority of the subjects complained that entering in scheduling information on the reminder's keyboard was more time-consuming than handwriting the information in a planner.

Study 2: The students in the second study filled out a questionnaire that instructed them to state the specific reason for each appointment they missed. The subjects reported that because of the differences in their state of mind at different times of day, their performance was lower in the evening than in the morning. For instance, in the morning, the subjects were oriented to the responsibilities of the day ahead, including having to call when the reminder sounded but in the evening, the subjects were following their own schedule of study and relaxation, so they were not inclined to think about the call-in task.

Study 3: As in the previous study, Study 3 used a questionnaire that asked subjects to indicate the specific reason for each appointment they missed. The subjects also reported that the cueing effectiveness of reminding devices was not as straightforward as some might assume. With continual signalling indicating multiple intentions, the subjects reported that they began to ignore the signal. This suggests that to maximise the effectiveness of signals, the signal should be set for only the most important intentions rather than all intentions (Andrzejewski, Moore, Corvette, and Herrmann, 1991). In addition, some users said that they felt anxious when they heard the signal.

Study 4: Upon completion of the experiment, the students in the final study completed a questionnaire that instructed them to choose the specific reason that they missed an appointment out of six possible reasons. Subsequently, they participated in a focus group procedure and volunteered reasons why they did not respond to a signal, or responded to it more slowly, in the evening than in the morning. The subjects noted that in the morning, school obligations were on their minds. In the evening however, the subjects were at home studying and usually not thinking about school. Their orientation to school in the morning was held by the subjects to enhance their attention to the signal because responding to the signal was a school task. Alternatively, a lack of orientation to school in the evening resulted in paying less attention to school tasks, including the signal.

The subjects also reported that the different anticipatory lags affected their performance. They concluded that a two minute lag did not give them enough time to get to a phone, but that a twenty minute lag provided enough time to access a phone. A 10-minute lag, though, was reported as "ideal" because it gave enough time to get to a phone, but produced less chance to forget than did the twenty-minute lag. However, as will be shown below, not all of these perceptions were supported by their data. Notably, in all of the studies, the subjects reported being late or missing appointments less often than they actually did.

EXPERIMENT	Time of Day		
Proportion Late	**AM**	**Midday**	**Evening**
1	.21	.58	.58
2	.35	–	.23
3	.06	–	.08
4	.14	.34	.24
Proportion Missed	**AM**	**Midday**	**Evening**
1	.11	.05	.05
2	.05	–	.25
3	.31	–	.46
4	.14	.28	.29
Proportion Late or Missed	**AM**	**Midday**	**Evening**
1	.32	.63	.63
2	.40	–	.48
3	.37	–	.54
4	.28	.62	.53

Table 1: Represents the mean proportion of late responses/ missed response

As mentioned above, the four experiments investigated the effectiveness of a warning signal as a function of the time of day an intention was to be executed and as a function of the amount of time the warning signal anticipated the intended act. The subjects carried the reminding device from a few days to a month before using it in the experiment.

The likelihood of noticing a signal was expected to affect appropriate responding because previous research has shown memory performance to depend on the time of day in which the cue occurs (Eysenck and Folkard, 1980; Folkard, 1979; Folkard and Monk, 1980; Harma, Illmarinen, Knauth, and Rutenfranz, J. et al., 1988; Humphreys and Revelle, 1984; Revelle, Humphreys, Simon, and Gilliland, 1980). The present research demonstrated that an audible warning signal was most effective early in the day. The interval between the signal and time to carry out the act, i.e., the anticipatory lag, did not significantly influence the timeliness of responses and remembering. Table 1 presents the mean proportion of late responses and missed response as a function of time of day.

The results of all four experiments provide some insights into how people are affected by warning signals that are intended to alert people to an impending appointment. It has been proposed that computerised devices externalise the mind (Gorayska and Mey, 1996) in that the screen of a MPD presents information that previously was retained by an individual. The research reported above reveals that the externalisation of the mind varies in effectiveness, depending on when in a day the external signal is presented and on the temporal relationship between the external signal and the intended act.

The likelihood of performing an action upon hearing a signal.

Because proper responding depends on the time of day the signal occurs, our results and subjects' reports suggest that the school-related weekend appointments may be more problematic than similar weekday appointments. The importance of the intended action to the ongoing events of a day has been shown to affect performance (Meacham and Singer, 1977). People will forget an appointment after remembering spontaneously or after being reminded, especially if the intention is unpleasant (Andrzejewski et al, 1991). Not surprisingly, performance also fails if the user misplaces the device (such as leaving it in one's coat; leaving it on one's desk).

GENERAL DISCUSSION

Implications for Basic Research

The analysis presented here has implications for basic cognitive theory. Although the process of remembering intentions is difficult to study, reminding appears to be a fundamental cognitive process (Shank, 1982). Because reminding is a part of everyday life, the cognitive requirements for planning and executing intentions merits investigation.

The effectiveness of reminding devices may vary according to how these devices influence the processing characteristics of active and passive monitoring. The processing of these two kinds of monitoring probably differ in several ways. They probably involve different amounts of cognitive effort. Also, active and passive monitoring may make different demands on attentional capacity and on working memory. Additionally, the conceptualisations of automatic and effortful processes might be useful in understanding reminding.

Reminding most likely is affected by metacognitive planning since it is generally an important part of intelligent behaviour (Sternberg, 1986). A more detailed analysis of the stages involved in scheduling and reminding could be helpful in organising and accommodating today's schedules of busy people. Multimodal influences on memory also play an important role in remembering to execute intentions (Herrmann, 1996). Although reminding devices provide an important function for users, there are clearly a number of other factors that affect successful use.

Personal Characteristics of Successful Users

Regardless of the nature of the reminding device, a profile emerges from the research reported here and from previous research (Herrmann et al., 1996, in press) which indicates potential users must have certain characteristics to successfully use these devices. The eventually successful user must (1) find it acceptable to have one's mind "externalised" (Gorayska and Mey, 1996) and aided by a device, and (2) feel comfortable using these devices.

Although anyone can make good use of a reminding device, these devices work better for certain tastes and lifestyles. Obviously, potential users must enjoy learning about devices; if the user is technophobic, he or she will not adopt use of a reminding device. Also these devices are not very useful for people who only have a couple of appointments a day to remember. When the number of appointments is few, people tend to remember their appointments, at least better than when they have many appointments (Andrzejewski et al., 1991). Thus, a reminding device is most useful when the number of scheduled nonrecurring events are burdensome to remember. Our subjects reported tuning out recurring appointments because they were already aware of them and then, because they were not attended to, these appointments were sometimes forgotten.

The potential user must develop insight into one's own idiosyncratic habits for committing intentions to memory (Rosenberg, 1990). Specifically, the user must learn what type of scheduled event is critical enough to be signalled. The potential user must also learn the optimum number of events that can be signalled without causing habituation to the beep. In addition, the user must learn to carefully phrase directives because of spatial limitations of the screen. In contrast, written planners involve none of these considerations but they also provide no active signal.

Personality differences dispose people to differ in how they approach prospective memory. For example, highly organised individuals remember intended acts in time more than less organised individuals (Searleman and Gaydusek, 1996). In addition, lifestyle is relevant to using reminding devices (Reason, 1988). For instance, people who cram too much into a day planner often discover they miss appointments because they do not look at their planner soon enough or carefully enough to anticipate them. Memory failures may also occur because people habituate to the signal or they fail to notice frequent signalling. Lastly, increased age is sometimes associated with decreases in remembering intentions (Dyck and Smither, 1984; Mantyla, 1994; McDaniel and Einstein, 1992; Petro et al., 1991).

Considerable learning and adapting is required to make successful use of a scheduler. If a potential user does not appreciate the complexity of a reminding device, he or she will likely be discouraged and quit before the necessary time is invested in learning. Like VCRs and many other electronic appliances, reminding devices come with intricate instruction booklets that require considerable time investment to master.

Profile of Successful Reminding Devices

The research reported here and elsewhere indicates that a reminding device must have certain properties to attract and maintain users. First, effective devices allow for rapid data entry. Second, effective devices provide for simple periodic review. Appointment by appointment review is not adequate for most people; most people prefer a day view and also a week view, e.g., as is provided in the screen of the Sharp Wizard, the Newton, and the BOSS (Herrmann et al., 1996). Third, effective reminding devices employ a signal that elicits attention, but is a rapid, unambiguous, and socially sensitive signal.

Fourth, devices with voice cueing provide the most effective cue and directive; however, an audible directive has the liability of informing everyone present of the intentions a user might prefer to keep secret. Signals appear to have inherent properties that make them more or less effective in eliciting intentions. For example, a vibration seems to be more effective than an auditory beep. Additionally, signals may vary in effectiveness because of other properties, such as cue pleasantness, perceptual salience, and personal relevance.

Fifth, reminding devices vary in effectiveness also because of the way in which different devices structure time. That is, different devices present time in different ways. Linear presentation of time places all appointments or chores on a single time line. Hierarchical presentation of time puts appointments within days which are grouped within weeks; weeks in turn are grouped within months. Alternatively, some reminders group days within months and bypass weeks. Generally, a hierarchical arrangement works best for most people, but users must feel comfortable with the time organisation employed by a reminding device to make best use of it.

Sixth, a reminding device should not require a substantial amount of learning in order to be used successfully. The operation of the device should be intuitively obvious and not require much consultation with the documentation.

The reminding devices that are available now are far superior to the digital watch and to some of the first such devices on the market. Future reminding devices will most likely employ designs that compensate for some of the problems raised here and elsewhere (Petroski, 1994).

Training

Currently no one has developed an effective way to train healthy, normal adults to remind themselves spontaneously (Herrmann, 1996). However, there is evidence that people spontaneously learn on their own to use external aids to facilitate remembering chores, obligations, and appointments (Baddelely, 1984; Herrmann and Petro, 1990; Hunter, 1957; Petro, Herrmann, Moore, Burrows, 1991; Intons-Peterson and Fournier, 1986; Intons-Peterson, 1993). Moreover, there is clear evidence that people with neurological impairments can be taught to use external aids, including reminding devices (Baddeley, 1984; Bourgeois, 1990, 1993; Camp, Foss, Stevens, and O'Hanlon, 1996; Cockburn, 1996; Fowler,Hart, and Sheehan, 1972; Jones and Adam, 1979; Kurlychek, 1983; Naugle, Prevy, and Naugle, and Delaney, 1988; Sandler and Harris, 1991; Skilbeck, 1984). In such uses, the reminding device is said to be a mental "prosthetic" (Searleman and Herrmann, 1995). For a review of trained use of external aids by individuals with head injuries, see Wilson (1987) and Parente and Herrmann (1996).

CONCLUSIONS

Making appointments and doing chores is an important part of our private and professional lives. Failure to effectively schedule and remember intentions can delay or even prevent the implementation of certain actions. Also, failing to remember intentions leads others to infer personal negative attributes about the person who has forgotten an appointment or a chore. In some cases, forgetting an appointment or a chore can lead to the loss of a job or the breaking off of a relationship (Searleman and Herrmann, 1994).

Nevertheless, research into these important everyday tasks has occurred only recently (Brandimonte, Einstein, and McDaniel, 1996), and research has been done on the use of external reminding devices only recently. The present chapter has reviewed the available research on the effectiveness of these devices. It is clear that these devices can remind people in a timely manner of things that they have to do. Although the present research makes it clear that reminding devices can help avoid forgetting intentions, the research also shows that these devices do not guarantee that users will stop forgetting their appointments or chores. Even after having been signalled by these devices, people sometimes forget to carry out the intended act. Skillful use of these devices requires self knowledge about when one is likely to pay attention to the signal they provide (Andrzejewski et al, 1991; Hayes-Roth and Walker, 1979). Thus, a well-used reminding device can decrease forgetting but mental strategies are still needed to supplement a person's use of a reminding device. Undoubtedly, reminding devices are among the things that can "make us smart" (Norman, 1993) but they can only do so if through research we can become smarter in our use of them.

REFERENCES

Andrzejewski, S. J., C. M. Moore, M. Corvette, and D. Herrmann, 1991. Prospective memory skills. *Bulletin of the Psychonomic Society*, 29, pp. 304-306.

Brewer, W., 1994. The validity of autobiographical recall. In: N. Schwarz and S. Sudman, eds.,. *Autobiographical Memory and the Validity of Retrospective Reports*. New York: Springer Verlag.

Baddeley, A. D., 1984. Memory theory and memory therapy. In: B. A. Wilson and N. Moffat, eds, *Clinical Management of Memory Problems*, Rockville, Maryland: Aspen Systems.

Bourgeois, M., 1990. Enhancing conversation skills in patients with Alzheimer's disease using a prosthetic memory aid. *Journal of Applied Behaviour Analysis*, 23, pp. 29-42.

Bourgeois, M., 1993. Effects of memory aids on the dyadic conversations of individuals with dementia. *Journal of Applied Behaviour Analysis*, 26, pp. 77-87.

Brandimonte, M., G. Einstein, and M. McDaniel, eds, 1996. *Prospective memory:Theory and applications*. Hillsdale, N. J.: Erlbaum.

Brewer, W., 1994. The validity of autobiographical recall. In: N. Schwarz and S. Sudman, eds, *Autobiographical Memory and the Validity of Retrospective Reports*. New York: Springer Verlag.

Camp, C. J., J. W. Foss, A. B. Stevens, and A. M. O'Hanlon, 1996. Improving prospective memory task performance in persons with Alzheimer's disease. In: M. Brandimonte, G. Einstein, and McDaniel, eds, *Prospective memory: Theory and applications*. Hillsdale, N. J.: Erlbaum.

Ceci, S. J. and U. Bronfenbrenner, 1985. "Don't forget to take the cupcakes out of the oven": Prospective memory, strategic time-monitoring, and context. *Child Development*, 56, pp. 152-164.

Ceci, S. J., J. G. Baker, and U. Bronfenbrenner, 1988. Prospective remembering, temporal calibration, and context. In: M. Gruneberg, P. Morris, and R. Sykes, eds, *Practical Aspects of Memory, Current Research and Issues, Vol. 2*. Chichester: Wiley.

Cockburn, J., 1996. Assessment and treatment of prospective memory deficits. In: M. Brandimonte, G. Einstein, and McDaniel, eds., *Prospective memory: Theory and applications*. Hillsdale, N. J.: Erlbaum.

Dyck, J. L., and J. A. Smither, 1984. Age differences in computer anxiety: The role of computer experience, gender, and education. *Journal of Educational Computing Research*, 10, pp. 239-248.

Doerner, D., 1987. Memory systems and the regulation of behaviour. In: E. van der Meer and J. Hoffmann, eds, *Knowledge Aided Information Processing*, Amsterdam: North Holland.

Ellis, J., 1996. Prospective memory or the realisation of delayed intentions. In; M. Brandimonte, G. Einstein, and McDaniel, eds, *Prospective memory: Theory and applications*. Hillsdale, N. J.: Erlbaum.

Ellis, J. A., 1988. Memory for future intentions: Investigating pulses and steps. In; M. M. Gruneberg, P. E. Morris, and R. N. Sykes, eds., *Practical Aspects of Memory: Current research and issues*. Chichester, England: Wiley, pp. 371-376.

Eysenck, M. W. and S. Folkard, 1980. Personality, time of day, and caffeine: Some theoretical and conceptual problems in Revelle et al. *Journal of Experimental Psychology: General*, 109, pp. 32-41.

Folkard, S. and T. H. Monk, 1980. Circadian rhythms in human memory. British Journal of Psychology, 71: 295-307.

Folkard, S., 1979. Time of day and level of processing. *Memory and Cognition*, 7, pp. 247-252.

Fowler, R., J. Hart, and M. Sheehan, 1972. A prosthetic memory: An application of the prosthetic environment concept. *Rehabilitation Counselling Bulletin*, 15, pp. 80-85.

Gorayska, B. and J. L. Mey, 1996. Of minds and men. In B. Gorayska and J. L. Mey, eds, *Cognitive Technology: In search of a Humane Interface*. Amsterdam: Elservier.

Harma, M. I., J. Illmarinen, P. Knauth, and J. Rutenfranz, et al., 1988. Physical training intervention in female shift workers: II. The effects of intervention on the circadian rhythms of alertness, short-term memory, and body temperature. *Ergonomics*, 31, pp. 51-63.

Harris, J. E., 1980a. Memory aids people use: Two interview studies, *Memory and Cognition*, 8, pp. 31-38.

Harris, J. E., 1980b. We have ways of helping you to remember. *Journal of the British Association for Service to the Elderly*, 17, pp. 21-27.

Harris, J. E., 1984a. Remembering to do things: A forgotten topic. In: J. E.Harris and P. E. Morris, eds, *Everyday memory, actions, and Absentmindedness*. Academic Press: London.

Harris, J. E., 1984b. Methods of improving memory. In: B. A. Wilson and N. Moffatt, eds., *Clinical Management of Memory Problem*, Croon Helm: Beckenham.

Harris, J. E. and Wilkins, A. J., 1982. Remembering to do things: A theoretical framework and an illustrative experiment. *Human Learning*, 1, pp. 123-136.

Hayes-Roth, B. and Walker, C., 1979. Configural effects in human memory: The superiority of memory over external information sources as a basis for inference verification. *Cognitive Science*, 2, pp. 119-140.

Herrmann, D., 1996. Improving Prospective Memory. In: M. Brandimonte, G. Einstein, and McDaniel, eds., *Prospective memory: Theory and applications*. Hillsdale, N. J.: Erlbaum.

Herrmann, D., 1994. The validity of retrospective reports as a function of the directness of retrieval processes. In N. Schwarz and S. Sudman, eds., *Autobiographical Memory and the Validity of Retrospective Reports*. New York: Springer Verlag.

Herrmann, D., 1996. Improving Prospective Memory. In: M. Brandimonte, G. Einstein, and McDaniel, eds., *Prospective memory: Theory and applications*. Hillsdale, N. J.: Erlbaum.

Herrmann, D. J. and Petro, S., 1990. Commercial memory aids. *Applied Cognitive Psychology*, 4, pp. 439-450.

Herrmann, D., Sheets, Wells, J., and Yoder, C. (in press). Palmtop Computerised Reminding Devices: The Effectiveness of the Temporal Properties of Warning Signals. *AI and Society*.

Herrmann, D., Yoder, C., Wells, J., and Raybeck, D., 1996. Portable electronic scheduling and reminding devices. *Cognitive Technology*, 1, pp. 36-44.

Humphreys, M. S., and Revelle, W., 1984. Personality, motivation, and performance: A theory of the relationship between individual differences and information processing. *Psychological Review*, 91, pp. 153-184.

Hunter, I. M. L., 1957. *Memory*. Penguin: Harmondsworth.

Intons-Peterson, M. J. and Fournier, J., 1986. External and internal memory aids: When and how often do we use them? *Journal of Experimental Psychology: General*, 115, pp. 267-280.

Intons-Peterson, M. J., 1993. External and internal memory aids: When and how often do we use them? In: C. Izawa, ed., *Applied Cognitive Psychology*, Hillsdale, N. J.: Erlbaum.

Jones, G. and Adam, J., 1979. Towards a prosthetic memory. *Bulletin of the British Psychological Society*, 32, pp. 165-167.

Kurlychek, R. T., 1983. Use of a digital alarm chronograph as a memory aid in early dementia. *Clinical Gerontologist*, 1, pp. 93-94.

Leirer, V. O., Morrow, D. G., Tanke, E., and Pariante, G. M., 1991. Elder's nonadherence: Its assessment and medication reminding by voice mail. *Gerontology*, 31, pp. 514-520.

Mantyla, T., 1994. Remembering to rememberg: Adult age differences in prospective memory. *Journal of Gerontology*, 49, pp. 276-282.

McDaniel, M. A. and Einstein, G. O., 1992. Ageing and prospective memory: Basic findings and applications. In: T. E. Scruggs and M. A. Mastropieri, eds., *Advances in Learning and Behavioural Disabilities. Vol. 7*, Greenwich, CT: JAI Press, pp. 87-105.

Meacham, J. A. and Leiman, B., 1982. Remembering to perform future actions. In: U. Neisser, ed., *Memory Observed: Remembering in Natural Contexts*. San Francisco: Freeman, pp. 327-336.

Meacham, J. A. and Singer, J., 1977. Incentive effects in prospective remembering. *Journal of Psychology*, 97, pp. 191-197.

Naugle, R. , Prevey, M., Naugle, C., and Delaney, R., 1988. New digital watch as a compensatory device for memory dysfunction. *Cognitive Rehabilitation*, 6, pp. 22-23.

Norman, D. A., 1993. *Things that make us smart: Defending human attributes in the age of the machine*. Reading, Massachusetts: Addison-Wesley Publishing Company.

Parente, R. and Herrmann, D., 1996. *Retraining Cognition*. Gaithersburg: Aspen.

Park, D. C., and Kidder, D. P., 1996. Prospective memory and medication adherence. In: M. Brandimonte, G. Einstein, and McDaniel, eds., *Prospective memory: Theory and applications*. Hillsdale, N. J.: Erlbaum.

Petro, S., Herrmann, D., Burrows, D., and Moore, C., 1991. Usefulness of commercial memory aids as a function of age. *International Journal of Ageing and Human Development*, 33, pp. 295-309.

Petroski, H., 1994. *The evolution of useful things*. New York: Vintage Books.

Reason, J. T., 1988. Stress and cognitive failure. In: S. Fisher and J. T. Reason, eds., *Handbook of Life Stress, Cognition and Health*. New York: Wiley.

Revelle, W., Humphreys, M. S., Simon, L. and Gilliland, K., 1980. The interactive effect of personality, time of day, and caffeine: A test of the arousal model. *Journal of Experimental Psychology: General*, 109, pp. 1-31.

Rosenberg, M., 1990. Control of environment and control of self. In J. Rodin, C. Schooler, and K. Schaie, eds., *Self-directedness: Causes and effects throughout the life course*. Hillsdale, New Jersey: Erlbaum.

Sandler, A. B. and Harris, J. L., 1991. Use of external aids with a head injured patient. *The American Journal of Occupational Therapy*, 46, pp. 163-166.

Schank, R. C., 1982. *Dynamic memory*. New York: Cambridge University Press.

Searleman, A. and Gaydusek, K. A., 1996. Relationship between prospective memory ability and selective personality variables. In: D. Herrmann, C. McEvoy, C. Herzog, P. Hertel, and M. Johnson, eds., *Basic and Applied Memory. Vol. 2*. Mawah: Erlbaum.

Searleman, A. , and Herrmann, D., 1994. *Memory from a broader perspective*. New York: McGraw Hill.

Shelly, G. B., Cashman, T. J., Waggoner, G. A., and Waggoner, W. C., 1997. *Discovering Computers: A link to the Future*. Cambridge, Mass.: Course Technology.

Skilbeck, C., 1984. Computer assistance in the management of memory and cognitive impairment. In: B. A. Wilson and N. Moffat, eds., *Clinical Management of Memory Problems*. Rockville, Maryland: Aspen Systems.

Sternberg, R. J., 1986. *Intelligence applied: Understanding and increasing your intellectual skills*. San Diego: Harcourt Brace Jovanovich.

Tulving, E., 1983. *Elements of Episodic Memory*. Oxford: Oxford University Press.

Wagenaar, W. A., 1986. My memory: A study of autobiographical memory over six years. *Cognitive Psychology*, 18, pp. 225-252.

Wilkins, A. J. and Baddeley, A. D., 1978. Remembering to recall in everyday life: An approach to absent-mindedness. In M. M. Gruneberg, P. E. Morris, and R. N. Sykes, eds., *Practical Aspects of Memory*. London: Academic Press.

Wilson, B. A., 1987. *Rehabilitation of Memory*. New York: Guilford.

Humane Interfaces: Questions of method and practice in Cognitive Technology
J.P. Marsh, B. Gorayska and J.L. Mey (Editors)
© *1999 Elsevier Science B.V. All rights reserved.*

Chapter 19

A USER-DESIGNED CONTEXTUALISATION METHOD FOR AN ARGUMENTATION SUPPORT TOOL

John A.A.Sillince

Management School, Royal Holloway, University of London

INTRODUCTION

Argumentation support systems enable the user to create, manipulate, and exchange issues positions, questions, options, criteria, assumptions, decisions, problems, and design objects. Such systems are becoming widely available both as research prototypes (Conklin and Begeman, 1988; Conklin and Burgess Yakemovic,1991; Lee, 1990; Balasubramaniam and Dhar, 1992) and as commercial systems (e.g. CMSI, 1992),

The problem considered in this paper is how to introduce contextualisation into an argumentation support tool. In the support tool, each participant makes a statement in turn. Each statement may contain the argumentation elements of premises, claims and warrants (rules mapping from premises to claims). At any moment there is an agreed intention (or focus goal - Daniels, 1986) to concentrate attention on one particular set of argumentation elements (Litman and Allen, 1987; Pollack, 1986; Sidner, 1985; Sidner and Israel, 1981, Shin and Wallfesh, 1990; Farley and Freeman, 1994). The whole debate has an agreed topic (Grosz, 1978) or scope goal (Sillince, 1994). For a review of the literature see Sillince (1997).

Although commercial systems exist which utilise argumentation ideas they tend to emphasise the rationality gains, pointing to the reduction in 'hand waving', the ability to remember previous argumentation, and the ability to externalise debate in the form of argument diagrams. However, when individuals argue, they often do not make their intentions or even their warrants explicit. For example, when arguing for the organisational advantages of a new project we do not say that it will benefit our department the most. Moreover, individuals may wish to add contextual information - such as assumptions, expectations, intentions, or off the record opinions. Individuals may wish to hedge on their degree of confidence in their own claims - whether it is high or just guesswork, or their degree of commitment to a set of rules or norms. Also, individuals often ambiguate rather than clarify. All these modifications - implicitness, hedging and ambiguation provide a context for the hearer to understand what the argumentation is really intended to mean (Sillince, 1996). This paper considers the problem of how contextual information can be elicited within an ongoing electronic argumentation interaction, and how users can be enabled to design such contextualisation for themselves.

EXAMPLE

Table 1 shows a fragment from a debate text (a much fuller analysis of a much larger text is in Sillince, 1995b). Table 2 shows the main changes in argumentation elements. Each turn is identified by a new primary number. A turn may contain several changes in argumentation elements - for example, turn [1] contains a choice of both emphasis and explanation goals.

Turn	Original text	Short comments
0	T. Women have responsibility for childcare and housework (unstated)	Topic [0] introduced by tutor T.
1	T.....But it's difficult to know why it's the *woman* who is seen to have the responsibility in terms of being the key significant parent rather than the father.	Scope goal is to explain [0]
2	A. Maybe it's because it's seen as natural......Women have the babies......and should look after them .	Weak argument [2] explains [0]

Table 1. Debate text fragment (Moyse and Elsom-Cook, 1992).

Table 2 investigates how much of the argumentation changes can be automated and how much requires the intervention of the human user. Human interventions are underlined. The Claim column would be the most salient text for the user to see on a screen as the dialogue proceeds. In turn [0.1] the user chooses the warrant A = X has Y and then instantiates these variables X = women and Y = responsibility for housework and childcare, and also chooses the focus goal of evaluating A. Therefore in turn [0.1] the user has made four choices. Turn [0.2] is completely automated, because a pre-coded warrant (identified by a matching routine) exists to generate a new claim B = X should have Y and to shift focus to B. In turn [1.1] the

Turn	Claim	Warrant	Premise	Focus	Focus/ scope goal
[0.1]	Women have responsibility for housework and childcare	A = X has Y	X = women, Y= responsibility for housework and childcare	A	Evaluate A
[0.2]	Women should have responsibility for housework and childcare	If Focus goal = Evaluate A then claim B = X should have Y and move focus to B.		B	Claim B
[1.1]	Women (rather than the father should have responsibility for housework and childcare			A,B,C	Emphasise X
[1.2]	Only one parent is key and significant	If B = X should have Y and Focus goals = Emphasise X and Select X then C = not-X should have Y and D = B stronger than C and move focus to A,B,C.		A,B,C	Select X
[1.3]	We should explain why women should have responsibility for housework and childcare.	If Scope goal = Explain D and D = B stronger than C then Focus goal = Support B and move focus to B.		A,B,C	Explain D
[2.1]				B	Support B
[2.2]		If two warrants exist then use weaker one first.			Ambiguate B
[2.3]	It is natural that women should look after babies	W1=If X has Y and b part of Y and b R X then X R^{-1} b W2=If D benefits men then D is strong	X have babies, babies part of Y, R = need looking after by, need Z is inverse of Z should do W1 weaker than W2	B	Use W1

Table 2. Changes in argumentation elements in text fragment.

user identifies the father (by means of making X = the father in C = X should have Y) as distinct to women, and emphasises women. Turn [1.2] claims that only one parent is significant and involves a user selection of women rather than the father. In turn [1.3] the user chooses the scope goal of explaining D = B stronger than C

Two warrants are identified by the matching routine at this point, a naturalnesness warrant (it is natural for women to look after babies) and an interest warrant (it is in men's interest to ensure that women look after babies). The user resolves this selection problem by choosing the weaker warrant in turn [2]. So Table 2 shows that the user makes 11 decisions in order to represent 3 turns.

USER DESIGNED CONTEXTUALISATION

Although an argumentation support system can be initially provided with contextualisation, it is much more likely that the changing situation will determine what contextualisation is needed. It is therefore necessary to provide a means for relatively easy user design of contextualisation. The design process involves recording instances of pragmatic clues in text and using these to generate options which can be implemented at the user interface level as menu selections (Belkin and Windel, 1984).

Turn	Pragmatic clue	Contextualisation by means of focus goals and warrants
[0.1]		Evaluate
[1.1]	"....the *woman*.....rather than the father"	Emphasise
[1.2]	".......in terms of being the key significant parent"	Select
[1.3]	"But it's still difficult to know why..."	Explain
[2.1]	"...it's because"	Support
[2.2]	"Maybe"	Weak first strategy
[2.3]	"....it's seen as natural"	Naturalness warrant

Table 3. Pragmatic context markers.

Table 3 gives a very limited example of this process. Tables 2 and 3 show that the process involves very little effort for users wishing to contextualise their own argumentation elements using new functions. These functions could merely be in terms of function definition (e.g. Evaluate, Command, Request, Give priority to, Resolve conflict, Answer question, Test hypothesis) or in terms of warrant definition such as some of the if-then rules (which then make use of the function definitions) shown in Table 2. The process of collecting data is therefore the same as the user's task of constructing functions or warrants which better enable the expression and situating of subtle arguments.

Sillince (1998) gives another example of how task variables can be observed to deduce rules about which context is best suited to a particular warrant. He uses the following list of task variables: Claim, Premise, Solution, Goal, Means, Problem, Description, Argument, Role, Expectation, Resolution, Conflict, Priority, Attribute, Resource, and Task. An example of such a rule is "If Description is X is Means to Y and if Description is Y is powerful and if Goal is contact with powerful then Elicitor should Claim Warrant is X is Means (to Y) and Solution is give Priority to X".

Such a process may involve some disagreement between argumentation participants. Examples of rules of thumb to use for umpiring such a process of negotiation about such contextualisations are:

1. If a focus goal or warrant do not exist for a particular context, then the presumption is that the proposed addition to the set of warrants or focus goals should be accepted.
2. Focus goals and warrants have implications for the group or organisation. For example, the warrant "If a project is late, project team members are expected to work overtime on it" addresses a particular problem from the organisation's point of view.

PHILOSOPHICAL POSITION

These remarks bear on the philosophical position taken here. Some of the assumptions which have guided this approach are:

1. The avoidance of over-explicitness. A user may wish that some reasoning is kept private. For example, it is not necessary that the reason for choosing warrant W1 (made explicit in turn [2.1]) be made known to other users (with whom there is disagreement).
2. The avoidance of too much dialogue interruption. This design goal can be achieved by a careful balance of user-defined and automated changes to the argumentation state. Too much user definition creates a slow dialogue with too many interruptions (Buckingham Shum and Hammond, 1994). Too little user definition leaves little scope for the user to add contextual and other nuances to the dialogue. For example Table 2 shows that the focus goal to evaluate a claim in turn [0.1] drives the change from a descriptive to a prescriptive warrant

form (from "has" to "should have"). If that particular change required user intervention, the dialogue would be more longwinded.

3. Collect data as part of a normal dialogue by enabling ongoing addition of focus goal or warrant definitions. In the approach described, users can introduce their own definitions of focus goals and warrants, and thus are able to provide their own interpretation of organisational context and its meanings. For example, in Table 2, the user in turn [0.1] chooses the focus goal to evaluate claim A. If such a focus goal does not exist (and the warrant in turn [0.2] which refers to it) then the user should be able to add these to the system.

4. Users are able to see the effects of their interventions immediately. This requirement is answered by providing the user with information about argumentation changes which have been triggered by their past interventions. For example, in turn [0.1] the user chooses to intervene and choose to evaluate claim A. The warrant which is triggered by this and which the user needs to see immediately is "If scope goal = evaluate A then claim B = X should have Y and move focus to B".

5. Provide a choice between slow and subtle or fast and sketchy interaction. The user who slows down the dialogue by introducing new warrants and focus goals may not be challenged by other users interested in speeding things up. If a common problem becomes slowness then some kind of agreement could be reached and coded as an if-then rule about the acceptable balance between user-defined and automated warrants and focus goals. This balance is quantifiable. In Table 2, it is 11 (user-defined interventions) out of a total of 21 actions - so human and machine actions were about evenly balanced.

DESIGN METHOD

The example can be generalised into a step by step method of design.

1. Observe a naturalistic communication. This may be in the form of verbal dialogue as in the current example (see Table 1), or in the form of video recordings, or a transcription and interpretation of any other communication genre.

2. Simulate the communication via a communication tool such as an argumentation support tool. This will involve a formal model of what is involved in the communication. The current paper has focussed on argumentation, the elements of which are claims, premises, warrants, focus definitions, and focus and scope goals (see Table 2).

3. See how many contextualisations can be expressed by the tool. In the case of natural language, one way of judging the trueness of the simulation is to look for pragmatic clues (as in Table 3) about nuances of meaning affected by contextualisations (Sillince, 1996). For example, focus shifts are marked by

"frame words" (Sinclair and Coultard, 1975) and are justified by special warrants (Sillince and Minors, 1992).

4. Investigate the degree of freedom to vary automated and user-defined dialogue control. The more heavily programmed the knowledge domain and premise and warrant database, the easier it will be to increase automation. However, there will still be a base number of functions enabling the user to add nuances, and so an important constraint on any tool's effectiveness and usability is how easy, quick and non-disturbing of dialogue flow they are.

5. Investigate how much the users can observe or refine their own understanding of what they are trying to say. This will depend upon how much the system enables the users to spot distortion of communication, and how much they are enabled to do something about it in order to emancipate themselves from such a communication distortion.

EMANCIPATION FROM COMMUNICATION DISTORTION

When individuals argue they often attempt to fool their opponent into believing that they intend one thing (e.g. the achieving of organisational goals) when they actually intend something different (e.g. achieving their own department's goals). Therefore, it becomes difficult to define exactly what is meant by distortion of communication during argumentation. However, taking the debate as a whole, one assumes that at the end of the debate, all participants are able to understand the positions and intentions of their opponents.

Yet there is a more limited and more relevant definition of communication distortion within argumentation. Distortion occurs when the tool changes the content and meaning of what it is that the user wants to say, and when the tool does not enable users to say what they want to say. One reason this occurs is when the tool is not flexible enough to enable contextualisation to occur.

For example, in Table 2, if the tool had not enabled the emphasising of "women (rather than the father)" in turn [1.1], then the next participant in turn [2.2] may not have picked up on warrant W2 - which was about men ensuring social practices that benefit themselves versus women.

REFERENCES

Conklin J., and M. L. Begeman, 1988. IBIS: a hypertext tool for exploratory policy discussion. *ACM Transactions of Office Information Systems*, 6(4), pp. 303-331.

Conklin J., and K. C. Burgess Yakemovic, 1991. A process-oriented approach to design rationale. *Human Computer Interaction*, 6 (3/4). pp. 357-391.

CMS, 1992, *Product description*. Austin, TX: Corporate Memory Systems.

Balasubramaniam R., and V. Dhar, 1992. Supporting systems development by capturing deliberations during requirements engineering. *IEEE Transactions on Software Engineering*, 18 (6), pp. 498-510.

Belkin N. J., and W. Windel, 1984. Using MONSTRAT for the analysis of information interaction. In: Deitschmann H.J., ed., *Representation and exchange of knowledge as a basis of information processing.* Amsterdam: Elsevier Science.

Buckingham Shum S., and N. Hammond, 1994. Argumentation based design rationale: What use at what costs? *International Journal of Human Computer Studies*, 40, pp. 603-652.

Daniels P.J., 1986. The user modelling function of an intelligent user interface for document retrieval systems. In Brookes B.C., ed., *IRFIS-6: Intelligent Information Systems for the Information Society.* Frascati, Italy, September, 1985. Amsterdam: North Holland, pp. 162-176.

Farley A.M., and K. Freeman, 1994. Burden of proof in a computational model of argumentation. *Proceedings of the 3rd International Conference on Argumentation*, Amsterdam, June 21-24.

Grosz B. J., 1978, Discourse knowledge. In: Walker D.E, ed., *Understanding spoken language.* Amsterdam: Elsevier, North Holland, pp. 229-346.

Lee J., 1990. SIBYL: a tool for managing group decision rationale. *Proceedings of the Conference on Computer Supported Cooperative Work, (CSCW 90).* New York: ACM.

Litman D. J., and J. F. Allen, 1987. A plan recognition model for subdialogues in conversation. *Cognitive Science*, 11, pp. 163-200.

Moyse R., and M. Elsom-Cook, 1992. *Knowledge negotiation.* London: Academic Press.

Pollack M. E., 1986. A model of plan inference that distinguishes between the beliefs of actors and observers. *Proceedings of the Meeting of the Association for Computational Linguistics.* New York.

Shin D. G., and S. K. Wallfesh, 1990. An expectation-driven approach to Q-A processing. *Proceedings of the First International Conference on Systems Integration.* New York: IEEE, pp. 520-527

Sidner C. L., 1985. Plan parsing for intended response recognition in discourse. *Computational Intelligence*, 1, pp. 1-10.

Sidner C. L., and D. J. Israel, 1981. Recognising intended meaning and speakers' plans. *Proceedings of 7th AJCAI.* Vancouver, Canada.

Sillince J. A. A., and R. H. Minors, 1992. Argumentation, self-consistency, and multidimensional argument strength. *Communication and Cognition*, 25(4), pp. 325-338.

Sillince J. A. A., 1994. Multi-agent conflict resolution: a computational framework for an intelligent argumentation system. *Knowledge-Based Systems*, 7(2), pp. 75-90.

Sillince J. A .A. 1995. Argumentation dynamics: justifying shifts in focus and scope. *Journal of Pragmatics*, 24, pp. 413-431.

Sillince J. A. A., 1996. Would electronic argumentation improve your ability to express yourself? In Gorayska B. and Mey J., eds, *Cognitive technology: In search of a humane interface.* (Advances in Psychology Series, Vol. 113) Amsterdam: Elsevier-North Holland, pp. 375-388

Sillince J. A. A., 1997. Intelligent argumentation. In Kent A., and Hall C.M., eds, *Encyclopedia of Library and Information Science.* Martin Dekker Inc., New York, Vol. 59, Supplement 22, pp. 176-217

Sillince J. A. A., 1998. Warrant selection for an intelligent argumentation tool. *Applied Artificial Intelligence*, 12, pp. 49-69.

Sinclair J., and R. M. Coultard, 1975. *Towards an analysis of discourse: the English used by teachers and students.* Oxford: Oxford University Press.

*Humane Interfaces: Questions of method and
practice in Cognitive Technology
J.P. Marsh, B. Gorayska and J.L. Mey (Editors)*

Chapter 20

COGNITION ORIENTED SOFTWARE VERIFICATION

Wolfgang A. Halang

Chair for Computer Engineering and Real Time Systems
Faculty of Electrical Engineering
FernUniversität
58084 Hagen
Germany

INTRODUCTION

For many years computerised automation systems have been gaining significance in almost all application fields. Among other factors, this is due to the rapid progress in microelectronics enabling cheap and flexible implementations. Economical considerations impose stringent boundary conditions on the development and utilisation of technical systems. This holds for safety related systems as well. Since manpower is becoming increasingly expensive, safety related systems need to be highly flexible in order to be able to adjust them to changing requirements at minimal cost. In other words, safety related systems must be program controlled. Thus, it is expected that the use of hardwired safety systems will diminish in favour of computerised ones.

In society, growing concern for safety and environmental hazards is producing an increased demand for dependable technical systems which help to prevent environmental disasters and loss of human life. To enable the flexible adaptation of system functions to new needs and to enhance the productivity of system development processes, computer based systems are increasingly being applied to both control and automation functions under real time constraints. These systems have the special property that hardware and software are closely coupled to complex mixed-technology systems such as manufacturing systems and process or traffic control systems.

When assessing their dependability, hardware and software have completely different qualities. Hardware is subject to wear. Faults occur at random and may be of a transient nature. To a very large extent, these sources of non-dependability can successfully be coped with by applying a wide spectrum of redundancy and fault tolerance methods. Software failures, on the other hand, are neither caused by wear nor by environmental events such as radiation or electric impulses. Instead, all errors are requirement analysis, design, or programming errors, i.e., they are of a systematic nature, and their causes are always (latently) present. Dependability of software cannot be achieved by reducing the number of errors contained close to zero by testing, reviews, or other heuristic methods, but only by rigorously proving that it is error free. According to the present state of the art, however, the widely advocated formal methods can only meet this requirement when applied to the verification of rather short and simply structured code segments.

There are already a number of established methods and guidelines, such as IEC 880 (1986), which has proven its usefulness for the development of high integrity software employed for the control of safety critical technical processes. Prior to its utilisation, such software is further subjected to appropriate measures for its verification and validation. However, according to the current state of the art, these measures cannot guarantee the correctness of larger programs with mathematical rigour. The problems encountered are exacerbated by the need to verify real time behaviour. Therefore, rigorous software verification is, in general, still an unsolved problem due to the complexity of the software involved. Moreover, for purposes of safety licensing object code (i.e., the only version of a program actually visible to and executed by a machine) must be considered, because the transformation of a program's representation from source to object code by a compiler or assembler may introduce errors into the object code. As a result, depending on national legislation and practice, the licensing authorities are still very reluctant or even refuse to approve safety related systems whose behaviour is exclusively program controlled. In general, safety licensing is denied for highly safety critical systems relying on software with non-trivial complexity.

Indeed, software based solutions are still considered to be less trustworthy than conventional hardwired implementations, which is justified, for instance, by the longer tradition of hardware engineering and therefore many decades of experience in the development of strategies to cope with corresponding failures. Assessing software with respect to dependability or safety aspects is a task which was neglected for a long time. Only substantial improvements which aim at supporting the process of program verification promise a step in the right direction, because verifiability is the main prerequisite to enable the certification of larger software based application systems. The importance of this statement becomes evident when considering the fact that, for practicability reasons, the workload involved in verifying safety related software has to be restricted to an economically feasible amount.

Until now approaches to achieve improvements in the field of software safety have not yielded results which serve to enhance confidence in software based solutions. The certification authorities are, therefore, hesitant to license exclusively software based safety related systems. As a consequence, nowadays system designers often still prefer to employ conventional hardwired approaches, despite their manifest disadvantages with respect to the economic aspects mentioned above.

To obtain a remedy for this unsatisfying situation, i.e., to enhance the dependability and, hence, the trustworthiness of software based safety related systems, this paper presents some designated concepts for suitable software verification. To this end, some fundamental concepts and inherent characteristics of software, are discussed with particular regard to the differing nature of software and hardware failures. Then, we identify simplicity as the leading principle assumed to be decisive for verification concepts to be used in safety related software engineering. An assessment of the available software verification methods reveals that they are all inappropriate, either due to lack of rigour, or because they are too difficult to understand and apply.

Whereas in general cases one has to yield to the complexity problem, in this paper we shall show workable ways of safety licensing by exploiting the intrinsic properties of a special, but not untypical (and from the viewpoint of safety engineering very important) case, that was identified in industrial control problems. Here complexity turns out to be manageable because the application domain demands software of limited variability only. Moreover, here software may be implemented in a well structured way, simply by graphically interconnecting carefully designed and rigorously verified building blocks or by filling decision tables. Such software can then easily be verified by common sense methods.

A computing architecture directly supporting diverse back translation is presented. Diverse back translation is a software verification method whose utilisation in the traditional context turns out to be extremely tedious and time consuming. However, when based on a graphical programming paradigm and the re-use of verified standard building blocks for software, diverse back translation becomes very easy, economical, and time efficient. The presented approach is unique in providing support for software verification already in the architecture. The leading idea followed throughout this design was to combine mature software engineering and verification methods with architectural support. In this way, the semantic gap between software requirements and the capabilities of the execution environment could be closed, thus eliminating the need for compilers and operating systems which are not safety licensable.

FUNDAMENTAL CONCEPTS

Safety

In the German industry standard DIN 31000 (1987), *safety* is defined as a status in which the risk does not exceed the *limit risk*, with the latter being the highest acceptable and still justifiable level of specific risk in a technical process or state. Given a process, the risk potential can usually be calculated and compared to a limit risk selected to determine whether or not the process is safe. The limit risk itself is not an absolute quantity. In industrial environments it mainly depends on the current standards in engineering. The following examples, however, clearly show that in many areas of life the limit risk is chosen according to cultural and social values.

First, we consider two countries, Germany and the U.S.A., and the use of motor cars and hand guns in each. In contrast to the U.S.A., there is no speed limit on German motorways. On the other hand, it is the constitutional right of U.S. citizens to carry weapons, while the issue of corresponding licences in Germany is very restricted. It comes as no surprise that (relatively) more people are killed on roads in Germany while more people are shot in the U.S.A.

Secondly, let us assume that things happen regularly which have never happened before and which precipitate disproportionally strong responses. For example, if full B- 747 flights crashed regularly over Germany, it would cause air traffic to be discontinued, even though "only" around 100,000 persons would be killed per year — the same death toll as caused by smoking.

Real Time Control

Real time systems are found in process control and automation, where they are increasingly involved in safety related applications. The real time operating mode is defined in the German industry standard DIN 44300 (1985) as the operating mode of a computer system, in which programs for the processing of data arriving from the outside are permanently ready, such that their results will be available within predetermined periods of time; the arrival times of the data can be randomly distributed or determined a priori depending on different applications. Hence, real time computer control systems are always embedded in larger environments with whose dynamics they must keep pace. Therefore they are often referred to synonymously as embedded systems.

Real time operation is characterised by the explicit involvement of the dimension *time*, manifesting itself in the fundamental *timeliness* requirement, which real time systems must fulfil even under extreme load conditions. Upon request from external processes, data acquisition, evaluation, and appropriate reactions must be performed on time. Processing speed is not decisive for this, but rather *timely* reaction within predefined and *predictable* time bounds even though the state of the art is still far away from allowing us to guarantee such bounds. Hence, it is characteristic of real time systems that their functional correctness does not only depend upon the processing results, but also upon the instants, when these results become available. Particularly for error situations the user expects predictable system behaviour, such as a graceful performance degradation. Only fully *deterministic system behaviour* will ultimately enable an effective safety licensing of computers for safety critical applications. Predictability of system behaviour is, therefore, of central importance to real time operating mode. It supplements the timeliness demand, for the latter can be met only if the system behaviour is precisely predictable, with respect to both time and external event reactions.

Problems Inherent to Software

When analysing malfunctions of computerised systems it can be noticed that often the reasons are not found in random hardware failures. That is to say, the kind of failures which occur at random times and result from a variety of physical effects and mechanisms which have a degrading influence on hardware. Such failures emanate from certain states which the system assumes during operation, having not been considered or encountered in the specification or implementation phases.

By its immaterial nature, software has a totally different quality than hardware. Consequently, unlike hardware it is immune to outside physical effects and does not degrade over time through use, i.e., it does not wear out. On the other hand, it is inherently error-prone and contains systematic errors. That is, *design errors* which are due to mistakes or omissions in one or more of the software development phases, and which are always present. Furthermore, software is *not continuous* (in the sense of mathematical analysis), i.e., the effect of small errors is not necessarily small, and may not even be bounded.

Software must be valid and correct. This necessitates two verification steps, which constitute serious problems:

1. Demonstrating that software fulfils its problem specification (i.e., that it does not contain systematic errors committed during program design or while coding, or caused by the use of software tools) establishes its *correctness*. Such proofs need to be rigorous since only testing can show up the presence of errors.
2. Showing that some specifications really meet the specifier's requests (which can be vaguely formulated), or even his thoughts, is the task of proving *validity*.

As a matter of fact, correctness alone is not sufficient. Indeed correct software may meet its specification but still not behave as expected. In such cases an often the specification itself is incorrect, incomplete, or inconsistent. Thus, the specification and consequently the resulting software is not valid. Unfortunately, although a program may be proven to verify its correctness against its specification, there exists no supervising mechanism which serves to assess whether a specification itself is valid. Consequently, to produce proper software based application systems it is essential to invest a lot of effort first in the specification phase.

Although there is still no satisfactory solution to the first of the two verification steps mentioned above, it appears to be solvable by scientific and technical means. However, the second problem may never be completely solved, because of the human factors involved.

Simplicity as Guiding Principle

In order to enable the proof of software correctness with maximum trustworthiness and minimum effort, it appears essential to employ, as much as possible, programming concepts and architectural features which support the process of verification. As already emphasised, the verification and subsequent assertion that a program is apparently free of software errors is indeed the major prerequisite for the granting of a safety licence by the authorised certification institutions.

As discussed above, the requirements and objectives to be met by safety related computerised systems can only be achieved by employing straight forward approaches which centre around *simplicity* as the appropriate fundamental design principle, thus following Dijkstra's (1989) advice pronouncing the necessity to fight against complexity:

> "It is time to unmask the computing community as a Secret Society for the Creation and Preservation of Artificial Complexity."   (Djikstra, 1989)

It is by no means easy to obtain simple designs, on the contrary, as Biedenkopf (1994) pointed out,

> "Simple solutions are the most difficult ones: they require high innovation and complete intellectual penetration of issues."   (Biedenkopf, 1994)

Given the present state of the art in program verification, simplicity is a fundamental characteristic and pre-condition to increasing confidence in computer based systems and to enabling the licensing authorities to formally approve the utilisation of computers for purposes of safety critical control. This becomes evident considering its position in the following causal relations:

> *Simplicity → (intellectually easy and economically feasible)*
> *Predictability → Dependability*
> *Simplicity → Easy Understandability → Feasibility of Verification*

At first, it is surprising to encounter the notion of predictability in connection with computers since, in principle, all digital computers work fully deterministically and are, therefore, predictable in their behaviour. To precisely express the special meaning of predictability, which is appropriate as a fundamental concept of computer control, the adjective "easy" was used in the first implication. It qualifies the notion of predictability by paying tribute to the economical and intellectual effort which needs to be invested in order to establish this property for a given system. If this is simple, it can be easily understood, which is a main step towards the verification of its correct behaviour in the sense of Descartes (1641): "verum est quod valde clare et distincte percipio".[1]

Software Verification as a Cognitive Process

Descartes' notion of clear and distinct comprehension is also the key to understanding the nature of verification, which is neither a scientific nor a technical, but a *cognitive process*. This holds for mathematical proofs as well, whose correctness is based on a consensus of opinion among members of the mathematical community that certain chains of reasoning lead to given conclusions, thus adding a *social component* to the cognitive nature of the process. Applied not only to

---

[1] "Truth is verified by clear and distinct ideas"

safety related computerised systems, and considering their importance to human lives and health, but also to those which are environmentally and economically added, it becomes important that this consensus ought to be as wide as possible. Hence, systems must be simple and appropriate software verification methods must be easily understandable for non-experts without compromising the rigour they afford.

ASSESSMENT OF SOFTWARE VERIFICATION METHODS

Software verification involves a review process at each phase of the software development and implementation cycle to determine whether all requirements of one phase are correctly implemented in the next. The complete verification process shows whether a program behaves in accordance with its detailed specifications. To be more precise, verification is the process of evaluating a software component to determine whether or not it satisfies the conditions imposed on it at the beginning of the implementation stage. This means that software correctness is checked with respect to the description resulting from the previous (i.e., design) stage. In other words, verification attempts to answer the question whether or not software components have been built correctly. Verification has to be clearly distinguished from validation, which is the process of evaluating a software item to determine whether or not it fulfils the user requirements. This means that software correctness is checked with respect to a set of requirement specifications, which are usually part of the legal contracts between customers, who order software development, and development teams. In other words, validation attempts to answer the question whether the correct software items have been built.

Software perfection, i.e., unambiguous specifications and correct programs, represents an especially difficult problem. Theoretically, software errors may be removed by complete tests. Owing to software complexity, complete tests can usually not be carried out within a limited number of program runs. Therefore, quality assurance measures are of special importance in the software development phase as are, subsequently, the verification and validation processes. This means careful specification of requirements, good modularisation of programs, application of structured programming methods, use of pre-fabricated and already verified program modules, comprehensive documentation, and above all keeping software complexity low as it is the major cause of system design faults. All measures to prevent safety critical faults have only limited scope and effectiveness. Therefore, no measure is so powerful that one can rely on it alone. The efficiency of measures can be increased by using them in combinations.

In the literature a large number of software verification and validation methods is reported. The survey article by Hausen et al., (1987) gives a good overview of the well known software examination methods. Another source of information is the fundamental work done by EWICS TC7 (1985). However, there is, in principle, no technique that can detect all software errors on its own. Therefore, techniques must always be applied in combination. One must distinguish between static and dynamic software analysis methods.

Testing in all its varieties is by far the most widely used dynamic analysis method for software verification and validation, since in only very few cases can correctness proofs of software modules be carried out with mathematical rigour. Testing consists of executing software components under specified conditions, recording the results, and evaluating the results against the corresponding expectations. For a systematic compilation of the major software testing procedures we refer to Trauboth, (1993). Although being quite an effective means of detecting errors in software modules and components, correctness can not generally be certified based on testing. Because of the large numbers of cases to be covered, it is usually not exhaustive enough. Thus, testing cannot confirm the absence of all errors.

Two different approaches to software testing, viz., black box and white box tests, are distinguished by whether the test data are derived from the program specifications alone, or from inspection of the internal program structures as well. As a rule, test data should cover all cases and involve all actions that a program is to perform. To select them accordingly, the program's specification is explored, describing the normal execution conditions and defining special cases and invalid input situations; such as values out of scope, or conditions leading to end of file processing. There are three general types of systematic design for white box testing: 1) statement testing, in which each statement of the software component under test is executed at least once, 2) branch testing, in which each outcome of each decision point in the software component is executed at least once, and 3) path testing, in which each path through the software component is executed at least once. It should be noted that statement testing requires the least effort, while path testing requires the greatest.

- The group of static software analysis methods comprises
- reviews and audits,
- inspections,
- walkthroughs,
- formal correctness proofs,
- symbolic execution, and
- diverse back translation.

A review is a process of presenting a product to other interested people, for comments or approval. An audit is a formal and independent examination of a product to assess its compliance with specifications or contractual agreements. The goals of conducting reviews and audits in the course of a software development project are twofold. The technical goal is to evaluate the adequacy of a portion of the work, and the degree to which it conforms to the prescribed requirements and expectations. The managerial goal is to determine the extent of progress and to assess the current status of the project. A review is usually organised as a formal meeting at which a product, in this case a requirements specification, a design description, or a program, is examined. The purpose of a meeting is to identify and record any problems with the product under review. If no critical errors are found, the product can be formally accepted. It should be emphasised, however, that neither the discovery of problems nor attempts to solve them are addressed during a review meeting. The potential problems should be identified by the reviewers at an earlier time, while preparing for a meeting. Subsequently the analyst or the designer rectifies the errors after the meeting. A functional audit is a final examination, held prior to software delivery, to decide whether or not a software product satisfies all its requirements. A physical audit is a formal consistency check between software code and the corresponding design and code documentation.

The reviews and audits described above involve formal meetings, conducted by the project management to assess the status of projects. Two other techniques, which bear a superficial similarity to reviews, are called structured walkthroughs and design and code inspections. They can be employed for verifying both documents and code. As a matter of fact, inspections and walkthroughs are the most widespread methods for code verification. For large scale software systems they represent the only feasible quality assurance methods for software development.

Design and code inspections lie somewhere between formal reviews and informal walkthroughs. They are formal meetings which take place at two points in the software development cycle: after detailed design, and after implementation. The goals of inspections are to detect as many errors as possible in reviewed products, and to assess the productivity of designers and programmers. The membership to a meeting is usually limited to four people:

1. The chairperson, who controls the activities,
2. The designer, who developed the software component being inspected,
3. The programmer, who has programmed, or who will program the component,
4. The tester, who will be responsible for testing the component.

The results of an inspection, i.e., the errors discovered, are classified and recorded. Management representatives usually do not attend inspection meetings; however, they are informed of the results.

Structured walkthroughs are similar to reviews in that a group of people meets to review a portion of work. However, a walkthrough meeting is informal, and its primary goal is not to assess the work, but rather to help the designer, or the programmer, in finding as many errors as possible in his or her work. Management representatives usually do not participate in such a meeting, as their presence may make the person presenting his or her work feel threatened and prevent free discussion. A walkthrough meeting can be organised to review a software specification, a program design, code, a test plan or test results, or software documentation. Unlike a formal review, however, a walkthrough meeting does not deal with a complete product, but with a small fraction of it. A number of meetings can be organised to correspond to each step of the software development cycle. Major issues addressed by the reviewers are similar to those defined for review meetings. The word "structured" used in naming the technique is equivalent to "well organised", and suggests that appropriate preparations must take place before a meeting to ensure its success. The participants should be provided with copies of the material for review well before the meeting date. Experience has shown that the amount of material to review should not exceed the equivalent of one hundred lines of program code, or five to ten pages of written specification or description. To prevent long and chaotic discussions, the membership of a walkthrough meeting should be limited to at most six persons, and the duration to half an hour (or at most three quarters). It is essential that participants at a meeting concentrate on the product and not on the designer or programmer. This contributes to a better working atmosphere and a more friendly team spirit.

The advantages of structured walkthroughs are numerous. The companies using this technique over several years report improvements in software quality, designer and programmer expertise and productivity, and in meeting deadlines and budget. The improvement in software quality results from a dramatic reduction in the number of errors in requirements specifications, software design, and final program code. What is also important is that errors are revealed relatively early, so that the correction process does not ruin nearly ready and optimised software structures. This facilitates systematic program testing and increases overall software reliability. Furthermore, the collective construction of test plans and test data can make the testing process more effective.

Specifications standing at the beginning of the software development process, namely, requirements specifications and detailed requirements specifications, can, according to the present state of the art, only be verified with non-mathematical and non-automatic methods such as inspections and walkthroughs performed by teams of human inspectors under guidance of moderators. Experience shows that about 80% of the errors can be detected in each inspection round. Particularly, the verification of specifications requires the greatest effort, since errors are frequently due to complexity and the employment of natural languages, and can easily spread over complete projects. Specifications should, if possible, be formulated in a semi-formal way to improve their degree of correctness. Decision tables are good tools for this as they show all properties of a formal notation without sacrificing their general understandability. They allow a description of the logical control flow of subprocesses by means of their internal states. Thus, they facilitate a complete check.

Formal verification can be defined as showing that a software implementation has the properties described in its specification by mathematically rigorous proofs. Here the proof is a sequence of reasoning steps designed to convince the reader about the truth of some formula. To be able to apply formal verification specifications need to be formalised. For this purpose a wide range of formal methods have been devised. These are becoming more and more advocated for as an approach to achieving dependable software, particularly in safety and security critical application domains. In certain circles there is even a euphoria about formal methods, seeing them as a panacea for all problems in system trustworthiness.

In general, however, and in the field of safety related automation systems in particular, there is a large gap between academic research, user needs, and industrial practice. With respect to formal methods it was concluded in the 1992 NATO Advanced Study Institute on Real-Time Computing that:

"... While formal descriptions are valuable, the state of the art has not evolved to a point, yet, where they can be widely applied. In particular, the number of people who could be trusted to make formal descriptions of non-trivial systems is extremely limited." (Let alone the number of people that can manipulate these descriptions to prove correctness.)   (Halang and Stoyenko, 1994)

The formal approach has several weaknesses and drawbacks, being the reasons why it is still not utilised in practice:

- Formal methods may efficiently be applied only to those problems which have natural and well established mathematical (arithmetic or algebraic) models. In applications with no such models defined, significant effort is required to build a mathematical theory of a domain prior to starting a development process.
- Formal specifications are not readable to users, so that the early validation of requirements specifications is difficult.
- The application of formal verification techniques requires special mathematical expertise.
- When done by hand, the usually rather lengthy program correctness proofs inevitably lead to human errors, which may remain undetected by peer review and may persist for long times.
- There is a lack of adequate tool support. The tools that do exist are difficult to use, even for experts, because they were designed with a strong focus on method demonstration, and less on supporting particular work processes and making methods transparent and easy to use.

As a result of this, formal correctness proofs are presently applicable to relatively small software modules, only. Although this is insufficient in the general case, it already allows us to cope with many safety related functions. Fortunately, in this area it is frequently possible to apply symbolic program execution, a formal method only requiring standard algebraic transformation.

The development of techniques for the safety licensing of computer programs is still in a very early stage. Our considerations so far have shown, that the informal (in the mathematical sense) static analysis methods (reviews, audits, inspections and walkthroughs) inherently lack the rigour necessary to be able to detect all errors contained in some specified software. On the other hand, formal methods turn out to be inappropriate as well because they do not take into account the human element.

Currently, to prove that a large program fulfils the requirements of a safety related automation system, namely, functional correctness and timeliness of results with regard to the time demands of the environment, only the technique of diverse back translation is available as a means to software verification (Krebs and Haspel, 1984). It was jointly developed by Technischer Überwachungsverein (TÜV) Rheinland, Cologne, Gesellschaft für Reaktorsicherheit, Garching (both in Germany) and Institut for Energitechnikk, Halden, Norway, in the course of the OECD Halden experimental nuclear power plant project. The method fulfils, to a certain extent, ergonomic criteria, and is assumed to be not only the most powerful, but also the only generally applicable and officially recognised (by the licensing authorities) method for software verification.

Safety licensing of programs written in high level languages is still not possible, since there is not yet a compiler, for which correct operation has been verified. For the same reason, one must also renounce the use of assemblers, linkers, and operating systems in the development and application of safety related software. Thus, to circumvent the problem of non-safety-licensed compilers, correctness proofs must be based on considering object code, i.e., the only form of programs available to machines executing them. Meeting these restrictions, diverse back translation consists of reading machine programs out of computer memory and delivering them to a number of different review teams working without any mutual contact. These teams manually disassemble and decompile the code, from which they finally try to reconstruct original specifications. A safety license is granted to a software system if its original specification agrees with all inversely obtained re-specifications.

However, as reported by Dahll et al. (1988) and Pofahl (1994), for non-trivial programs running on Von Neumann machines this method is generally extremely cumbersome, time consuming, and expensive. This is due to the semantic gap between specifications, formulated in terms of user functions and safety requirements, and the conventional machine code implementation of them in terms of memory, register accesses, and other low level operations. On the other hand, diverse back translation does not require expert knowledge. This is especially important when considering the legal aspects of safety licensing. During litigation judges and juries do not need to rely solely on expert advice but can draw their own conclusions.

The experiences mentioned show that trying to verify classical "spaghetti code" is an inappropriate approach. A better approach, based on the demand that computing ought to serve people, is to use programming paradigms which facilitate verification. Two examples of such paradigms will be presented in the following sections. Utilising them, the effort involved is economically justifiable, since one easy step leads back from machine code directly to the problem specification level. The principles of simplicity and clarity serve as basic guidelines when selecting a verification method for the implementation of software supported safety related systems. This is because the simplicity of a software verification process directly correlates to the trustworthiness of the computer based control systems thus engineered. It is evident that diverse back translation fulfils the simplicity requirement. It remains to be shown that it becomes very useful when combined with appropriate programming paradigms and supported architecturally.

The most creative process in a software project is requirements analysis and specification. Once a complete and unambiguous specification is constructed, it describes in detail the behaviour of the system to be developed. The semantics of such a description must not be changed at the design and implementation stage. This observation leads to the concept of the direct execution of requirements specifications (or implementations which can be obtained by carrying out only slight transformations on requirements specifications) which can easily be proven correct. This approach will be taken in the following sections. Its advantages are obvious. The labour intensive steps of design, implementation and still not trustworthy verification disappear. Instead, the development process is viewed as consisting mainly of requirements analysis, specification and validation. The primary system documentation comprises the (executable) requirements specification. Maintenance is no longer performed on code. It is the specification which is being modified transformed and re-implemented, just like during the original development phase.

CAUSE EFFECT TABLES

A programming paradigm that appears to be appropriate in the presence of the highest safety requirements is constituted by cause effect tables. This concept is well established in engineering mainly as a means to constructing protection systems (e.g., emergency shut-down systems, that are responsible for reacting to the occurrence of application dependent dangerous situations) so as to preserve a system and its environment from serious damage. Basing software on cause effect tables is characterised by the utmost simplicity and clarity; to such an extent, that its verification by direct inspection and widespread social consensus is enabled for both validity and correct implementation.

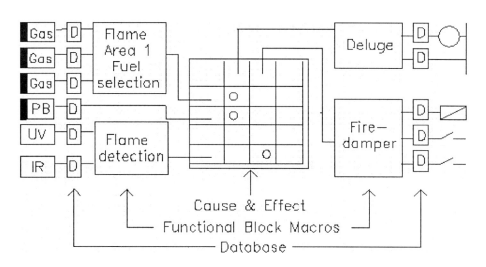

Figure 1. A typical cause/effect table

As illustrated by the example in Figure 1, software for protection systems is represented in the form of filled-in decision tables, the so-called cause effect tables. Their rows are associated with events, whose occurrences give rise to Boolean pre-conditions. Just by marking fields that belong to certain columns of a table and which are respectively associated with specific actions, the user selects preconditions and specifies which corresponding actions shall be performed when all these pre-conditions (in the sense of a logical conjunction) become true.

The contents of the cause effect tables become the only application "software" implemented in the protection system. Here, software does not mean executable programs fetched from writable memory as in the classical Von Neumann computer architecture. Instead, it is better characterised as a parameterisation by which a multipurpose controller is configured to perform specific functions. Since cause effect tables must be kept in read only memories due to safety requirements, this kind of software generally takes on the form of firmware.

For the following reasons we consider cause effect tables to be ideal for the implementation of computer based control systems with high safety requirements.

- Specifications are formulated in a commonly understandable, but nevertheless formal manner, namely, as decision tables.
- Hence, it is easy to verify specifications by social consensus.
- Specified operations can be directly interpreted and executed by a machine (Halang et al., 1996) without requiring complicated transformations and, therefore, correct implementation verification.

Since this paradigm allows the need for generally difficult software verification to simply disappear, automation technology ought to employ cause effect tables as widely as possible.

FUNCTION BLOCK DIAGRAMS

A second programming paradigm which allows for software to be easily grasped and verified with respect to both source and object code is available in form of the language Function Block Diagram (FBD). It was defined in the international standard IEC 1131-3 (1992) as one of two graphical languages for the coding of programmable logic controllers. Based on a long tradition in control engineering, this type of graphical programming is already well established in automation technology. Function block diagrams were derived from blueprints of digital circuits, in which each chip represents a certain module of an overall functionality. The straightforward programming procedure thus closely resembles the traditional assembling of control systems from hardware elements and devices (i.e., wiring analogue regulators, operational amplifiers, electromagnetic relays, TTL elements etc. cp., e.g., Hunter, 1978) or any other text on classical control equipment. Here, however, the function blocks are software equivalents of conventional control elements and devices.

The basic language elements in FBDs are instances of functions and function blocks which, for the purpose of program composition, are interconnected with connection lines between their inputs and outputs, respectively. Functions and function blocks represent high level application oriented and re-usable language elements. They differ from each other in so far as functions are to be interpreted in the mathematical sense, hence, they include no internal states, whereas function blocks may exist in the form of distinguishable instances. The function oriented graphs, resulting from this method of program development, provide direct impressions of the application dependent underlying dataflows. Figure 2 depicts an example of a program segment composed according to the procedure outlined above. Programs represented in FBD have a modular structure and are able to facilitate both software development and verification by reason of their inherent documentation value, (i.e., their capacity to reflect the underlying problem structure.).

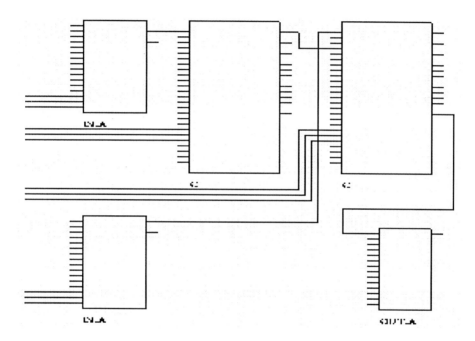

Figure 2. Example of a function block diagram

Function blocks are essentially subroutines and yield one or more values upon execution. Multiple named instances (i.e., copies) of a function block can be created. All values of the output variables and the internal variables carry over from one execution of a function block instance to the next. Therefore invocation of a function block with the same arguments does not necessarily yield the same output values. This is necessary to be able to express internal feedback and storage behaviour. Only the input and output variables are accessible outside of a function block instance (i.e., the function block's internal variables are hidden from the outside).

For the formulation of automation applications, the user just invokes, places, and interconnects function block instances from given libraries, which results in diagrams that look like the dataflow diagrams used for functional or activity modelling. The boxes in the function block diagram depicted in Figure 2 represent program activities, while lines model unidirectional flow (from left to right) of the type of information necessary for the function blocks to carry out these activities. Individual function blocks are invoked according to the partial ordering given by the "wiring" and, in the course of this, they pass data along their connecting lines. Lines may branch to represent fan-out, wherein multiple identical copies of data can be delivered coincidentally to other function blocks acting as consumers of those data. But lines may not join in the sense of fan-in or merging of incoming data.

Besides the provision of constants as parameters, (such as "bar" connected to external input XUNIT of function block B1 in figure 7) the function blocks' instances and the data flows between them are the only language elements used in this programming paradigm. Software development is carried out in graphical form using appropriate CAD tools. Once a diagram is satisfactory, a compiler transforms the graphically represented program logic into object code. Because this logic is only able to assume a simple structure, the generated programs contain no features other than sequences of procedure calls and some internal moves of data.

As an essential characteristic of the programming paradigm, FBD bases its ability to facilitate the handling of even very large systems on comprising, as shown in Figure 3, connected function blocks into new units. The latter constitute function blocks at higher abstraction levels and may, henceforth, occur in other diagrams as more abstract and functionally more complex components which are application oriented on a higher level. Thus strict rules control the correct hierarchical (de-) composition of diagrams (Halang and Krämer, 1992) consequently the interconnection complexity of single diagrams can always be kept low. Furthermore, the employed principle of re-use oriented software engineering reduces the number of possibilities to solve a given problem in different ways.

A function block library consists of standard components, which are a) universally applicable to automation purposes, b) usually provided by system vendors, and c) of user defined project specific elements. There are two extremes in the range of approaches taken to define such libraries, viz., either small numbers of highly sophisticated function blocks allowing the selection of specific algorithms with various parameters, sometimes numbering more than 50, or large numbers of quite simple function blocks with at most a few inputs each and in the order of 10 parameters. As we shall see in the sequel, the re-usability of libraries is crucial to the software-licensing problem. The libraries offered by leading manufacturers are "locally complete" in the sense that practically all individual problems which occur in a particular application area can be solved with them. The "practically all" statement is a matter of experience developed over the years from numerous applications. Essentially, for any application area, there is a specific set of function blocks, although certain modules like analogue and digital input and output have more general relevance. Some blocks may be tied to machine resources such as sensors, actuators, communication channels, or man-machine interfaces. They are represented by I/O blocks in function block diagrams. Usually, rather small numbers of library elements suffice to formulate all programs within certain areas of process automation. For instance, as the guideline VDI/VDE 3696 (1995) shows,

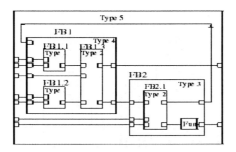

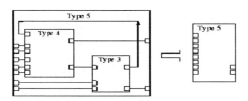

Figure 3. Function blocks with 2 or 3 levels of detail

for chemical engineering the number is 67. The following list of function blocks defined in the guideline gives an impression of typical functionalities:

1. Monadic mathematical functions: Absolute value, Cosine, Sine, Exponential function, Natural and Base 10 logarithms, Square root, Limiter, Non-linear static function, Linear scaling
2. *Polyadic mathematical functions*: Addition, Subtraction, Multiplication, Division, Modulo, Exponentiation
3. *Comparisons*: Equal, Greater or equal, Greater, Less or equal, Less, Not equal
4. *Monadic Boolean function*: Negation
5. *Polyadic Boolean functions*: Conjunction, Disjunction, Antivalence
6. *Edge detectors*: Falling and Rising edge detection
7. *Selection functions*: Maximum and Minimum selections, Selection by 1 out of N bits, Demultiplexers for Booleans and numbers, Multiplexers for Booleans and numbers, Binary selections of a Boolean or a number
8. *Counters, monostables, bistables, timers*: Up/down counter, Flow counter, Bistable elements with set/reset dominance, Pulse duration modulator, On/ Off delays, Non-re-triggerable monostable element
9. *Process input/output*: Analogue input/output, Binary input/output, Digital word input/output, Impulse input

1. Monadic mathematical functions: Absolute value, Cosine, Sine, Exponential function, Natural and Base 10 logarithms, Square root, Limiter, Non-linear static function, Linear scaling
2. *Polyadic mathematical functions*: Addition, Subtraction, Multiplication, Division, Modulo, Exponentiation
3. *Comparisons*: Equal, Greater or equal, Greater, Less or equal, Less, Not equal
4. *Monadic Boolean function*: Negation
5. *Polyadic Boolean functions*: Conjunction, Disjunction, Antivalence
6. *Edge detectors*: Falling and Rising edge detection
7. *Selection functions*: Maximum and Minimum selections, Selection by 1 out of N bits, Demultiplexers for Booleans and numbers, Multiplexers for Booleans and numbers, Binary selections of a Boolean or a number
8. *Counters, monostables, bistables, timers*: Up/down counter, Flow counter, Bistable elements with set/reset dominance, Pulse duration modulator, On/ Off delays, Non-re-triggerable monostable element
9. *Process input/output*: Analogue input/output, Binary input/output, Digital word input/output, Impulse input
10. *Network communication input/output*: Communication input/output for a Boolean or numerical value
11. *Dynamic elements and regulators*: Universal and Standard controllers (PID-T1), Running time average, Dead time, Differentiation with lag (D-T1), Integrator (I), Lead lag (PD-T1), 2nd order
12. *Conditioning for display and operation*: Limit switch with alarm or message storing, Alarm or message storing, Trend registration, Manual value entry with switch and limitation

The complexity of library elements is usually quite manageable, because the software typical to specific application areas is of limited variability. Written in a Pascal-like textual high level language, the above mentioned software modules are quite short: their source code does not exceed two pages. Unbounded iteration and recursion do not occur in these modules. Therefore, their correctness can be formally proven with bearable effort, (e.g., using predicate calculus, but also symbolic execution or, in some cases such as with Boolean functions, even complete test.).

In another typical example, the programming of emergency shut-down systems, which is usually represented graphically in the form of functional logic diagrams which describe the mapping from Boolean inputs to Boolean outputs as functions of time such as,

if a pressure is too high
then a valve should be opened
and an indicator should light up
after 5 seconds

it requires as few as four function blocks, viz., three Boolean operators and a timer. For a more in-depth treatment of the function block concept we refer to (Zöller, 1991).

Using FBD programming for software verification, with respect to the verification of software expressed in the FDB programming language it is essential, that the two step development procedure

1. Building a library of function blocks — only once for a certain application area, and
2. Application specific interconnection of function block instances

also propagates into the verification phase. Accordingly, the latter proceeds in the following two steps:

1. Formal verification of all elements within a given function block library employing appropriate formal methods before being released, and
2. For any given application program, verification by diverse back translation of the proper implementation of the particular interconnection pattern of invoked function block instances (i.e. a certain data flow), only.

Employing diverse back translation for software verification is facilitated by the problem oriented architecture introduced in the next section.

A SAFETY ORIENTED ARCHITECTURE

As an architecture for a safety oriented computer control system we select a standard microcomputer endowed with a firmware interpreter implementing a set of basic function blocks. For the envisioned purpose of executing software represented in the form of function block diagrams the interpreter is required to perform just two instructions on the user programming level:

GET <operand-address>
PUT <operand-address>

A function block invocation gives rise to an object program segment, which consists of a number of parameter fetches from RAM or ROM locations carried out with GET instructions, and a number of result storage operations with the help of PUT instructions. First, the interpreter fetches the identification of a function block to be invoked. From this the appropriate number of input parameters and, if need be, of the block's internal state variables is derived, which are then fetched. Subsequently, the object program implementing the function block is executed. In the course of this, the interpreter performs all necessary data manipulations and communications with the environment. The elaboration of the function block ends with storing into RAM the results and new internal states generated.

In order to prevent any modifications by malfunctions, in this architecture all programs must be provided in read only memories. For practical reasons, there will generally be two types of these memories. However, there is no program RAM at all. Instead, the code of the basic function blocks resides in mask programmed firmware ROMs, which are produced under supervision of and released by the licensing authorities, only after the latter have rigorously established the correctness of the blocks and their object code. On the other hand, the sequences of block invocations, together with the corresponding parameter passing which represent application programs at the architectural level, are written into (E)PROMs by the user. This part of the software is subject to project specific verification again to be performed by the licensing authorities which, finally, still need to install and seal the (E)PROMs in the target process control computers. This program memory configuration is chosen to physically separate two software parts from one another: one with general scope which only needs to be verified once, and the other one being application specific.

The architecture outlined above can also be implemented in hardware. This approach has been pursued toward developing a programmable logic controller for safety critical applications. I have provided elsewhere (1993) a detailed description of the architecture and the hardware implementation.

SOFTWARE SAFETY LICENSING

All elements of an employed function block set contained in a library are first verified with appropriate (formal) methods. Note that this rather costly safety licensing needs to be carried out only once, after a certain function block set has been identified and standardised for a given application area. The licensing costs can, thus, be spread over many implementations leading to relatively low costs for each single automation project. Actually, the function blocks occurring in practice are of relatively low complexity and, for that reason, their formal verification is indeed feasible. As the implementation details of the function blocks used are part of the firmware, they remain invisible from the application programming point of view and no longer require safety licensing in this context.

Hence, for any new application program, only the proper implementation of a particular interconnection pattern of invoked function block instances needs to be verified. For this purpose the object code processed by the interpreter is subjected to diverse back translation, fortunately eliminating the need for an - apparently still impossible and, therefore, presently unavailable - safety licensed compiler which transforms graphical software representation into object codes as a necessary pre-condition to employing the function block diagram paradigm. Although it may be considered as a rather non-elegant brute force method, diverse back translation is especially suitable for the verification of the correct implementation of graphically specified programs on the architecture introduced above. This is due to the following reasons:

The method is essentially informal, easily comprehensible, and immediately applicable without any training. Thus, it is extremely well suited for use on the application programming level by people with the most heterogeneous educational backgrounds. The ease of understanding and use inherently fosters error free application of the method.

By programming in the form of function block diagrams, specifications are directly mapped onto object code consisting of procedure calls and parameter passing only while a single conventional machine instruction taken out of a program context does not reveal its purpose, the occurrence of a certain function block instance usually gives a clue about the problem, its solution, and the block's role in it. Since graphical programming based on application oriented function blocks has the quality of specification level problem description, and because, by design, there is no semantic gap in our architecture between level of interfacing (provided by the interpreter) machine and human, diverse back translation leads back in one easy step from machine code to problem re-specification in graphical form. Consequently equivalence with the original specification can be easily checked.

Owing to the use in our architecture of basic function blocks with application specific semantics as the smallest units of software development, the effort required for the utilisation of diverse back translation is several orders of magnitude less than for the regular Von Neumann architecture (Dahll et al., 1988) not enhanced with an interpreter for application specific firmware. Tools for the graphical back translation of memory resident programs are already part of the standard support software of distributed process control systems, thus facilitating the application of diverse back translation for verification purposes.

As its name already implies, diverse back translation is a verification method to be carried out with diverse redundancy. Originally, this called for different teams of human inspectors. Since, in the case considered here, there is only one rather simple reverse translation step, we are optimistic that the licensing authorities will eventually accept the following procedure. Verification by back translation is carried out by a number of different programs, which should be proven in practice, but do not need to be formally verified. Such programs yield graphical outputs. An official - human - licensor performs the back translation and, compares results with those of the verification programs on one hand, and the original graphical application program under inspection on the other, then, upon coincidence, issues a safety license. Such a procedure is in line with the dependability requirements for diversely redundant programs demanded by the licensing authorities, and necessitates only a minimum of highly expensive human involvement, viz., one licensor, who remains indispensable as legal responsibility must be taken the for issuing a safety license.

TEMPORAL BEHAVIOUR

Many automation programs including safety related ones take the form of sequence controls composed of steps and transitions interconnected by directed links. To give an example, we consider the following very simple, but also quite typical automation task (VDI/VDE 3696, 1995). If a start button is pressed and the temperature is less than 40°C, then - in phase or step 1 - the filling valve of a reaction container is opened until its filling state has reached 90%. Afterwards - in the second step - the container casing is heated with steam by opening a heating valve until the temperature of the container content has risen to 90°C. Then - in the third step - the emptying valve of the container is opened until its filling state has dropped by more than 5%. Then the control returns to its initial state - the first step. Figure 4 shows a corresponding step control program in the form of a Sequential Function Chart, a unique graphical programming language, which was also defined in the international standard IEC 1131-3 (1992).

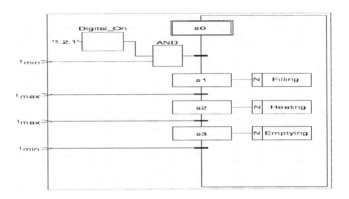

Figure 4. Sequence control of a container automation

Upon initiation of a program structured with a sequential function chart, its initial step is activated. When a step becomes active, an associated program organisation unit expressed in form of a function block diagram is executed. As final part of this, the transition condition associated with the transition between the step and its successor in the sequential function chart is evaluated. If the transition condition is not fulfilled, the step remains active and the function block diagram is executed again. When the transition condition is found to be fulfilled after one of these repetitions, the step is deactivated and the one immediately following the transition along a directed link is activated.

Many features of contemporary computing systems such as pipeling, caches, direct memory access, and asynchronous multitasking render it hopelessly difficult to predict, and hence safety license, the temporal behaviour of computerised automation systems. The only acceptable way out of this situation for safety related systems is simplicity: all potentially harmful features must be relinquished, and a strict regime must be observed which provides and guarantees clear and simple temporal behaviour which is consistent under any circumstances. We base the definition of such a regime on the concept of sequential function charts and the execution mode implied by them. Only linear sequences of steps and alternative branches of such sequences are permitted (see Figure 5).

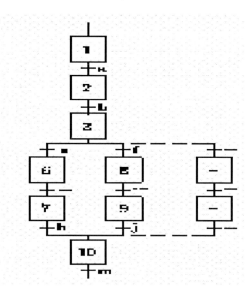

Figure 5. A sequential function chart

For safety reasons, parallel branches, as also introduced in IEC 1131-3 (1992), must either be implemented by hardware parallelism, or already resolved at design time by explicit serialisation. The regime chosen is depicted in Figure 6. Although rather restrictive, it is widely applicable, because most controllers and real time systems work in a cyclic fashion. Moreover, it reduces the verification of computerised systems' time behaviour to a common sense exercise.

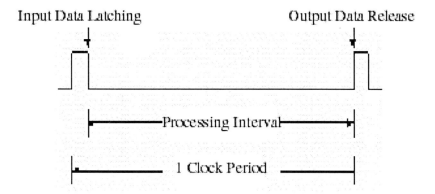

Figure 6. Strictly periodic control operation

The regime is based on a hardware clock marking processing periods. The length of the cycle is selected to accommodate the execution of the most time consuming step occurring in an application. Furthermore, the instruction set of the interpreter implementing the safety oriented architecture introduced above is extended by the operandless STEP instruction. Since being expressed as sequential function charts, the programs executed by the interpreter consist of sequences of steps. A STEP instruction is inserted behind the program segment of each step, which checks whether or not the segment was executed within a step cycle frame. If the execution of a segment does not terminate within a step cycle, the program is terminated and the controlled process is safely shut down. Normally, segment execution finishes before the instant of the next step cycle signal. Then, the occurrence of the clock signal, which marks the beginning of the next cycle, is awaited. When the clock signal finally arrives, depending upon the current value of the transition condition, a decision is made whether the same step segment is to be executed once again, or the execution of the logically subsequent step is to commence. Since program branching is only possible in this restricted form, erroneous access to the code of other (inactive) steps as well as to program locations other than the beginnings of step segments, is effectively prevented.

Although the a priori introduction of the step cycle determines exactly the periodic execution of single steps, the processing instants of various operations within a cycle, may still vary and, thus, remain undetermined. Since a precisely predictable timing behaviour is important only to the outside, (i.e. for input and output operations) exact temporal determinism is achieved as follows. Input and output operations are performed by independently working devices synchronised with the clock. The input devices always provide current input data, which are all latched at the beginning of the processing periods, regardless of whether or not they will be needed in a particular period, to form so-called process images. Calculated output data are first buffered, then released by the next clock pulse, which also resumes program execution.

A WORKED EXAMPLE

The application of back translation is to be illustrated by working out a relatively simple, but realistic example. The different representation levels of a program, viz., function block diagram, net list, and object code for the interpreter in our architecture, are shown in full detail. It will become evident that it is straightforward and very easy to draw a function block diagram from a given object program establishing the feasibility of back translation as a software verification method.

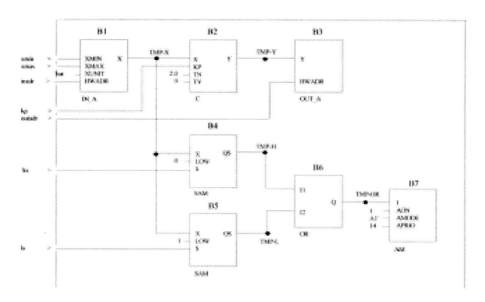

Figure 7. A pressure regulation and supervision program

Figure 7 shows a typical industrial automation program in graphical form. It performs the supervision and regulation of a pressure. The program is expressed in terms of standard function blocks as defined in the guideline VDI/VDE 3696 (1995). An analogue measuring value, the controlled variable, is acquired by a function block of type IN_A from the input channel with address INADR, and scaled within the range from XMIN to XMAX to a physical quantity with unit XUNIT. The controlled variable is fed into a function block of type C performing proportional-integral-differential (PID) regulation subject to the control parameters KP, TN, and TV. The resulting regulating variable is converted to an analogue value by a type OUT_A output function block, and switched onto the channel addressed by OUTADR. In addition, the controlled variable is also supervised, with the help of two instances of the SAM limit switch standard function block type, to be within the limits given by the parameters LS and HS. If the controlled variable is outside of this range, one of the QS outputs of the two SAM instances becomes logically true and, hence, the output of the type OR function block as well. This, in turn, causes the type AM alarm and message storing function block to create a timed alarm record. The inputs of the standard function blocks comprised by the program which are neither fed by externally visible inputs of the program itself nor internally by outputs of other standard function blocks, are given constant values.

The net list representation of the above example program as generated by a utility program of the OrCAD schematic capture tool is shown in Figure 8. Net lists constitute textual representations which are fully equivalent - except for geometrical aspects - to the original drawings.

<<< **Component List** >>>

IN A	B1
C	B2
OUT A	B3
SAM	B4
SAM	B5
OR	B6
AM	B7

<<< **Wire List** >>>

NODE	REF	PIN #	PIN NAME	PIN TYPE	PART TYPE
[00001] N00001	B1	5	X	Output	IN_A
	B2	1	X	Input	C
	B4	1	X	Input	SAM
	B5	1	X	Input	SAM
[00002] N00002	B2	5	Y	Output	C
	B3	1	Y	Input	OUT A
[00003] N00003	B4	4	QS	Output	SAM
	B6	1	I1	Input	OR
[00004] N00004	B6	3	Q	Output	OR
	B7	1	I	Input	AM
[00005] N00005	B5	4	QS	Output	SAM
	B6	2	I2	Input	OR
[00006] XMIN	B1	1	XMIN	Input	IN_A

Figure 8. Net list representation of the example program

The object code for the interpreter finally obtained by automatic translation of the sample program's net list representation is listed in Figure 9. It shows a (readable) assembly language version. Of the different function block types instantiated in the example, C, SAM, and AM have internal state variables, (viz., C has 3 and the other two types have 1 each).

GET ROM-loc-ID-IN_A	GET ROM-loc-ID-OUT_a	GET ROM-loc-ID-OR
GET RAM-loc-XMIN	GET RAM-loc-TMP-Y	GET RAM-loc-TMP-H
GET RAM-loc-XMAX	GET RAM-loc-OUTADR	GET RAM-loc-TMP-L
GET ROM-loc-BAR	PUT RAM-loc-TMP-OR	
GET RAM-loc-INADR	GET ROM-loc-ID-SAM	
PUT RAM-loc-TMP-X	GET RAM-loc-TMP-X	GET ROM-loc-ID-AM
GET ROM-loc-0	GET RAM-loc-TMP-OR	
GET ROM-loc-ID-C	GET RAM-loc-HS	GET ROM-loc-1
GET RAM-loc-TMP-X	GET RAM-loc-B4-isv	GET ROM-loc-A1
GET RAM-loc-KP	PUT RAM-loc-TMP-H	GET ROM-loc-14
GET ROM-loc-2.0	PUT RAM-loc-B4-isv	GET RAM-loc-B7-isv
GET ROM-loc-0.0	PUT RAM-loc-B7-isv	
GET RAM-loc-B2-isv1	GET ROM-loc-ID-SAM	
GET RAM-loc-B2-isv2	GET RAM-loc-TMP-X	STEP
GET RAM-loc-B2-isv3	GET ROM-loc-1	
PUT RAM-loc-TMP-Y	GET RAM-loc-LS	
PUT RAM-loc-B2-isv1	GET RAM-loc-B5-isv	
PUT RAM-loc-B2-isv2	PUT RAM-loc-TMP-L	
PUT RAM-loc-B2-isv3	PUT RAM-loc-B5-isv	

Figure 9: Object code representation of the example program

The object code listed in Figure 9 illustrates that all function block instance invocations occurring in a program are directly mapped onto procedure calls. Each of them commences with a GET instruction, which transfers the identification (e.g., ID-C) of the corresponding block out of an appropriate ROM location to the interpreter. Then, the input parameters are supplied by reading appropriate ROM (for constants) or RAM (for program parameters and intermediate values) cells. Finally, if there are any, the values of the procedure's internal state variables are read from appropriate RAM locations. There is a set of correspondingly labelled (e.g., RAM-loc-B2-isv i) locations for each instance of a function block with internal states. When the interpreter has received all these data, it executes the procedure and returns, if there are any, values of output parameters and/or internal state variables, which are then stored into corresponding RAM locations. A connection between an output of one function block and an input of another one is implemented by a PUT and a GET instruction: the former storing the output value in a RAM location for a temporary value (e.g., TMP-X), and the latter loading it from there. In other words, each node in a net list gives rise to exactly one transfer from the interpreter to a RAM cell, and to one or more transfers from there to the interpreter. The implementation details of the various procedures are part of the architecture's firmware and, thus, remain invisible.

According to the above described structure of the interpreter's object programs, the process of back translation - disassemble and decompile object code - turns out to be very easy. To perform back translation, first the STEP instructions are searched, which clearly separate the different (sequential) steps contained in a program from each other. The code between two STEP instructions corresponds to one function block diagram. Then, the first GET instruction is interpreted. It identifies a function block to be drawn into the function block diagram to be set up. By comparing the subsequent GETs with the function block's description contained in the library used, the correct parameter passing can be easily verified. Moreover, for each such GET which corresponds to a proper parameter (and not to an internal state variable) a link is drawn into the diagram. There are two kinds of links. First there are connections from program inputs or constants to inputs of function blocks or from function block outputs to program outputs. Second there are, half connections, namely, from function block outputs to named connection points in the diagram, i.e., net list nodes, or from such points to function block inputs. When the diagram is completely drawn, the names of these points can be removed. With respect to the internal state variables, it needs to be verified that the corresponding RAM locations are correctly initialised, and that the new values resulting from a function block execution are written to exactly the same locations from where the internal states were read in the course of the block's invocation. The process of function block identification and parameter passing verification, as well as the drawing of the symbol for the block and the corresponding connections is repeated until a STEP instruction is reached which terminates the step and, thus, the corresponding function block diagram.

EXPERIENCES AND RESULTS

We have built a prototype of a computerised controller according to the architecture outlined above and implemented a function block interpreter performing Boolean negation, conjunction, and disjunction as well as time delays. Whereas the first three of these functions are trivial, the delay timer required a formal correctness proof, which was carried out employing HOL and which turned out to be rather laborious and lengthy (Halang et al., 1995). The controller's utilisation in practice showed that implementing the functionality of a hard-wired emergency shut-down system with a programmable electronic system is feasible, and that the programming paradigm based on formally verified function modules and on application programs verified by diverse back translation can render error free software. The latter together with a fault tolerant hardware platform allows the implementation of programmable safeguarding systems sharing the fail safe feature with well established hard-wired solutions.

For ergonomic reasons, complex software should be hierarchically structured in such a way that the formulations of its modules in form of function block diagrams always fit on one page of a terminal screen. As outlined before, these modules occur as function blocks on the next higher level of a hierarchical software structure, whose interna are abstracted away and which are executed by the interpreter described. Hence, the complexity of a function block diagram will never be greater than approximately ten times that of the example given in Section 8, which results in a verification effort of at most a few hours' work (for any particular function block diagram).

CONCLUSION

In society there is a growing concern for safety (which comes hand in hand with increasing awareness of the environmental concerns). This has important consequences for the assessment of computer controlled technical systems. We have begun to realise the inherent safety problems associated with software. Since it appears unrealistic to abandon the use of computers for safety related automation purposes (on the contrary, for the reasons mentioned above, there is no doubt that their utilisation in such applications is going to increase considerably) the problem of software dependability will exacerbate severely.

Given this situation, this paper addresses a pressing problem. It does not present solutions to all open questions in software safety licensing, but a beginning is made which is practically feasible and applicable to a wide class of safety related control problems. Hence, it is expected that the concepts presented here will ultimately lead to the replacement of discrete or relay logic by programmable electronic systems executing safety licensed software in charge of safety critical functions in process automation. While meeting the need of society for more trustworthy computerised systems under the prevailing economical restrictions, the concepts presented can immediately be transferred into workable industrial implementations.

Our approach particularly observes ergonomic criteria. It is a step towards a software engineering paradigm which features simple, inherently safe programming which results in better and more immediate specification. It is characterised by design integrated verification which not only has the quality of mathematical rigour, but is also oriented at the *comprehension capabilities of non-experts*. It could replace empirical a posteriori validation (testing) in facilitating safety licensing. Software verification, when regarded as a social process of reaching a consensus is facilitated by features such as graphical programming, re-use of prefabricated and certified components, specification level programming by filling in decision tables and, generally, striving for utmost simplicity in all aspects.

Software based control systems are still considered to be less trustworthy than those built out of conventional hardwired components, which is justified, in part, by the longer tradition of hardware engineering and, therefore, many years of experience in the development of strategies to cope with corresponding failures. To overcome this situation, we have proposed dedicated programming methods following the guiding principle, that the more *safety critical* a system is, the more *simple* the related control software should be. Accordingly, at the highest level of safety requirements, one should be in a position to verify the safety of a "software" system just by looking at a cause effect table and reaching consensus, i.e., without employing formal proofs. For slightly reduced requirements one is able to graphically construct control software on the basis of already proven function blocks, easing the process of software development as compared to textual languages, and still keeping the task of safety proofs still rigorous yet relatively easy and, informal.

REFERENCES

Biedenkopf, K., 1994. Komplexität und Kompliziertheit. *Informatik-Spektrum*, 17, pp. 82 - 86.

Dahll, G., U. Mainka and J. Märtz, 1988. Tools for the standardised software safety assessment (The SOSAT Project). In W.D. Ehrenberger, ed., *Safety of Computer Control Systems*. IFAC Proceedings Series, No. 16, Oxford: Pergamon Press, pp. 1 – 6.

Descartes, R., 1641. *Medidationes de prima philosophia, in quibus Dei existentia et animae humanae a corpore distinctio demonstrantur*. Paris.

Dijkstra, E.W., 1989. *The next forty years*. Personal note EWD 1051,.

DIN 31000 Teil 2, 1987. *Allgemeine Leitsätze für das sicherheitsgerechte Gestalten technischer Erzeugnisse. Begriffe der Sicherheitstechnik. Grundbegriffe*. Berlin-Cologne: Beuth Verlag.

DIN 44300, 1985. *Informationsverarbeitung*. No. 9.2.11. Berlin-Cologne: Beuth Verlag.

EWICS TC7 Software Sub-group, 1985. Techniques for the verification and validation of safety-related software. *Computer and Standards*, 4, pp. 101 - 112,.

Halang, W. A. and B. J. Krämer, 1992. Achieving High Integrity of Process Control Software by Graphical Design and Formal Verification. *IEE/BCS Software Engineering Journal* , 7(1), pp. 53 - 64.

Halang, W. A., S. -K. Jung, B. J. Krämer and J. J. Scheepstra, 1993. *A Safety Licensable Computing Architecture*. Singapore-New Jersey-London-Hong Kong: World Scientific.

Halang, W. A. and A. D. Stoyenko, eds, 1994. *Real Time Computing*. NATO Advanced Science Institutes Series, Series F, Vol. 127. Berlin-Heidelberg-New York: Springer-Verlag.

Halang, W.A., B. J. Krämer and N. Völker, 1995. Formally Verified Building Blocks in Functional Logic Diagrams for Emergency Shutdown System Design. *High Integrity Systems*, 1(3), pp. 277 - 286,.

Halang, W. A., G.-H. Schildt and M. Colnaric, 1996. A Fuzzy-Logic-Based Programmable Electronic System for the Control of Safety-Critical Processes. In R. Karba and J. Kocijan, eds., *Artificial Intelligence in Real-Time Control*. Oxford: Elsevier Science, pp. 236 – 242.

Hatton, L., 1995. *Safer C: Developing for High-Integrity and Safety-Critical Systems*. McGraw-Hill,.

Hausen, H .L., M. Müllerburg and M. Schmidt, 1987. Über das Prüfen, Messen und Bewerten Von Software. *Informatik-Spektrum* , 10, pp. 123 - 144,.

Hunter, R P., 1978. *Automated Process Control Systems: Concepts and Hardware Englewood Cliffs*. Prentice Hall.

IEC International Standard 880, 1986. *Software for Computers in the Safety Systems of Nuclear Power Stations.* Geneva: International Electrotechnical Commission.

IEC International Standard 1131-3, 1992. *Programmable Controllers, Part 3: Programming Languages.* Geneva: International Electrotechnical Commission

Krebs H. and U. Haspel, 1984. Ein Verfahren zur Software-Verifikation. Regelungstechnische *Praxis rtp*, 26, pp. 73 – 78.

Pofahl, E., 1994. *TÜV Rheinland*, Private communication,

Trauboth, H. 1993. *Software-Qualitätssicherung: Konstruktive und analytische Maßnahmen. Handbuch der Informatik, Band 5.2.* München-Wien: R. Oldenbourg Verlag.

VDI/VDE-Richtlinie 3696, 1995. *Vendor independent configuration of distributed process control systems.* Berlin-Cologne: Beuth Verlag.

Zöller, H., 1991. *Wiederverwendbare Software-Bausteine in der Automatisierung.* Düsseldorf: VDI-Verlag.

INDEX